PERFECT WORLD

3

Rie Aruga

Research Help:
Kazuo Abe (Abe Kensetsu Inc.)

contents

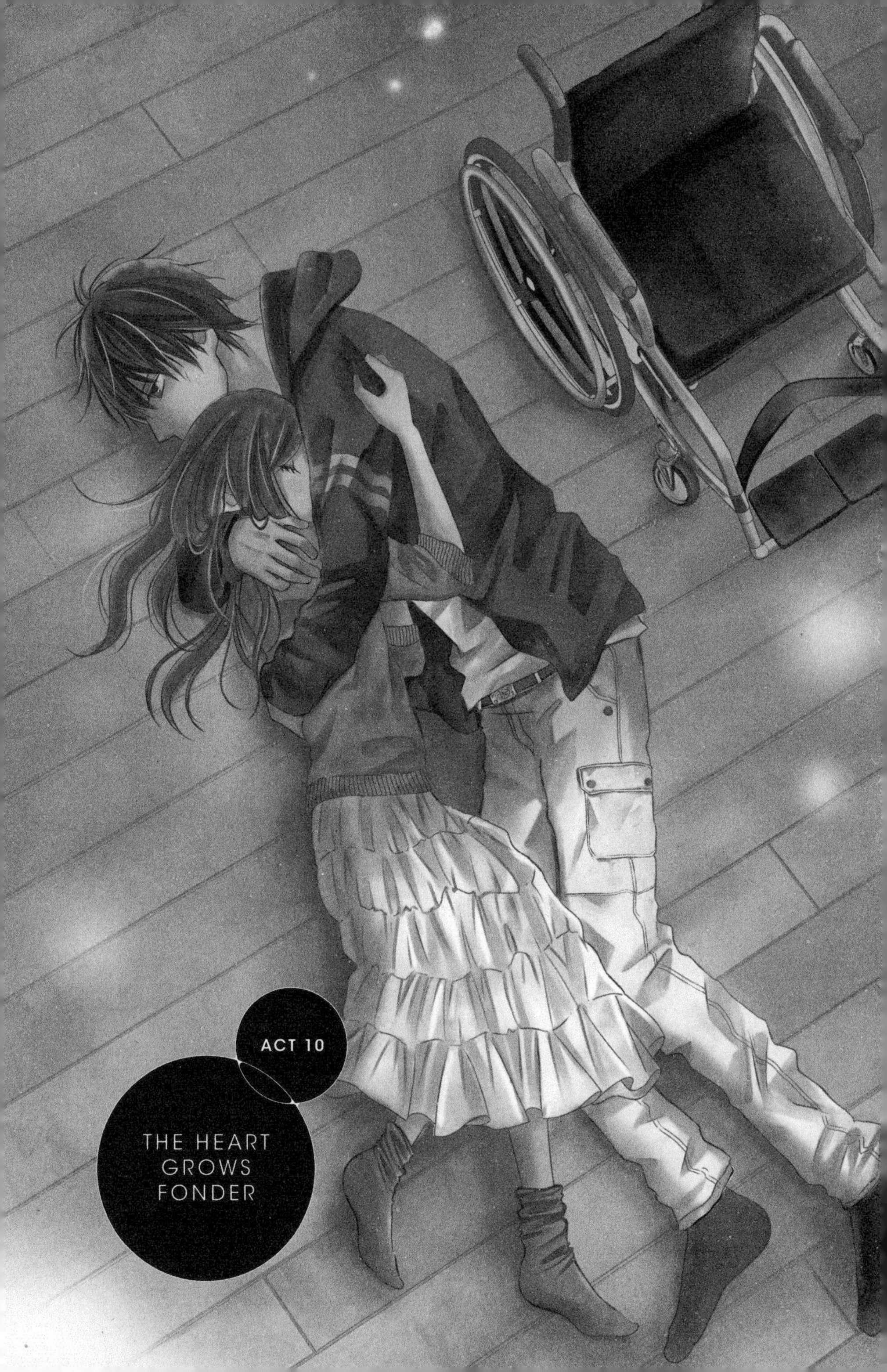
ACT 10
THE HEART GROWS FONDER

PERFECT WORLD

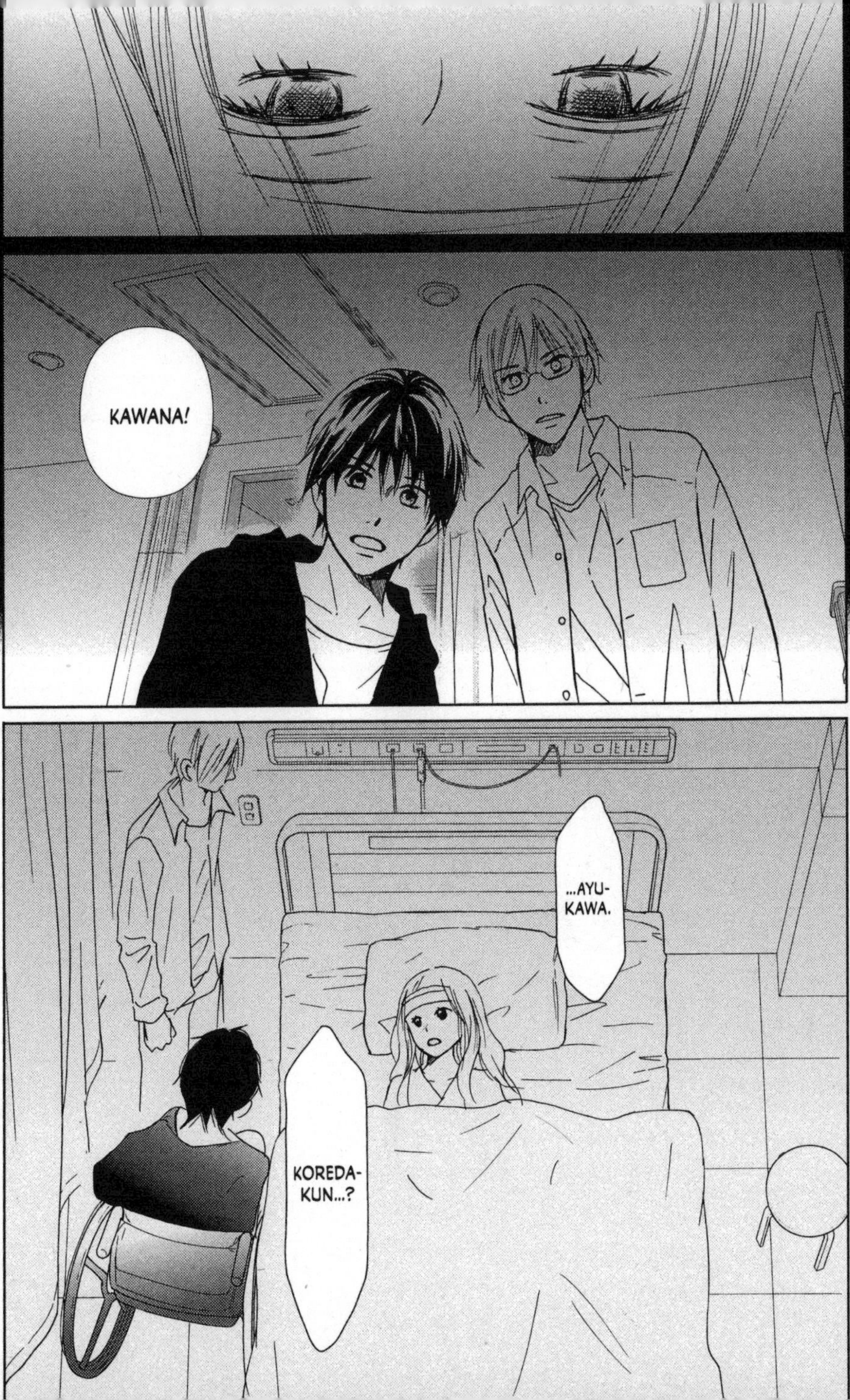
KAWANA!
...AYU-KAWA.
KOREDA-KUN...?

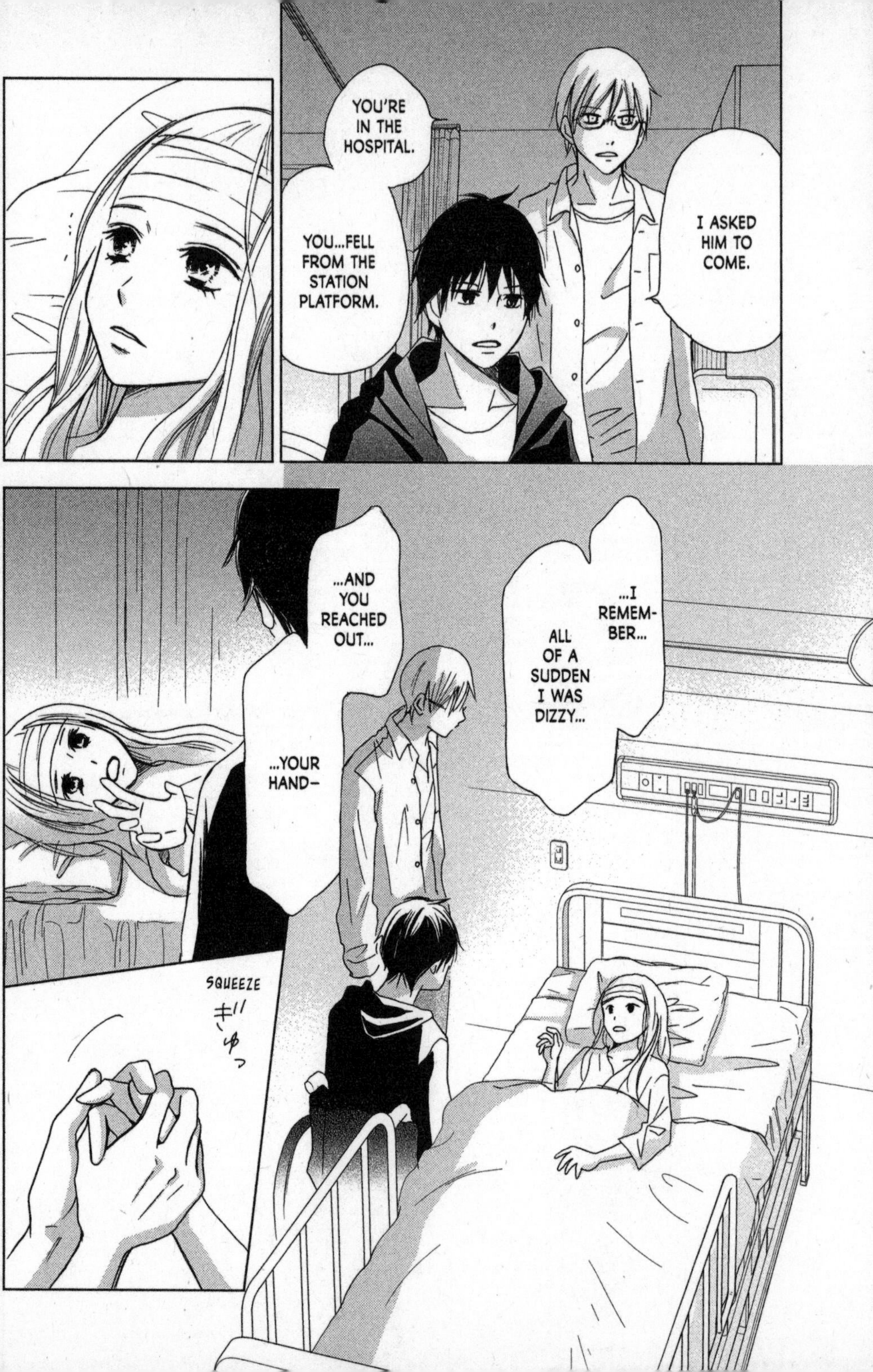
YOU'RE IN THE HOSPITAL.
YOU...FELL FROM THE STATION PLATFORM.
I ASKED HIM TO COME.
...I REMEMBER...
ALL OF A SUDDEN I WAS DIZZY...
...AND YOU REACHED OUT...
...YOUR HAND—
SQUEEZE

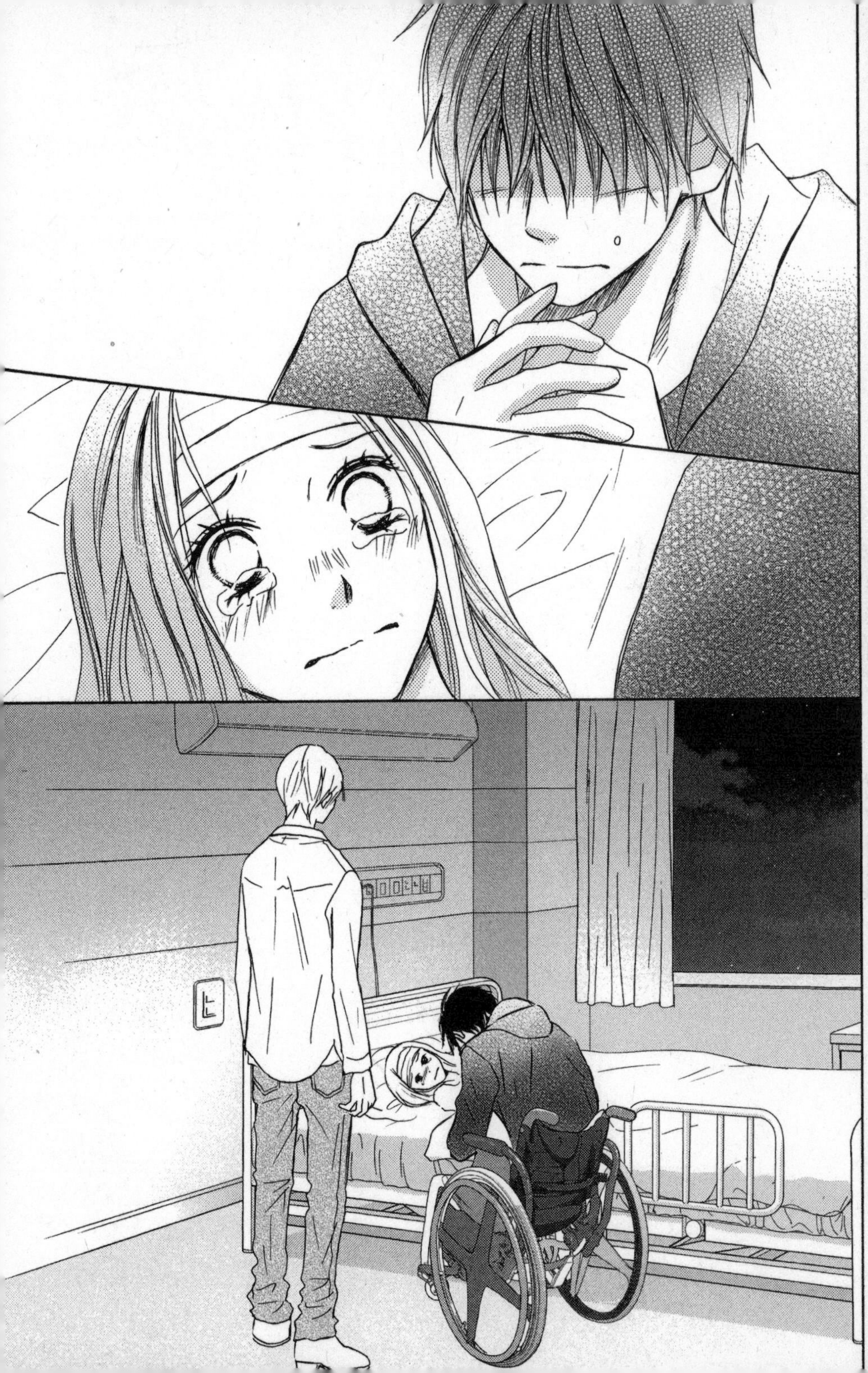

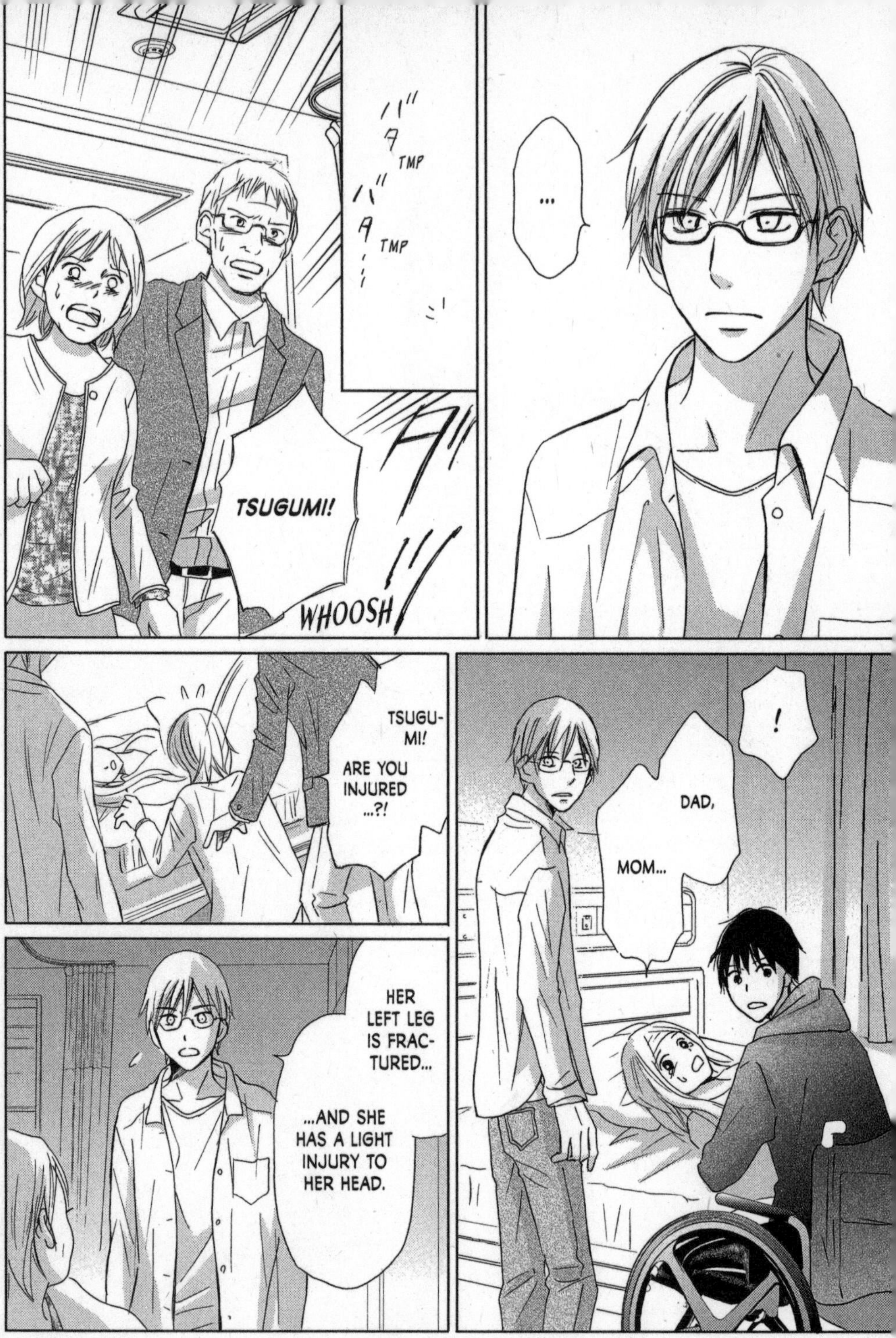
...
TMP
TMP
TSUGUMI!
WHOOSH
!
DAD,
MOM...
TSUGU-MI!
ARE YOU INJURED ...?!
HER LEFT LEG IS FRAC-TURED...
...AND SHE HAS A LIGHT INJURY TO HER HEAD.

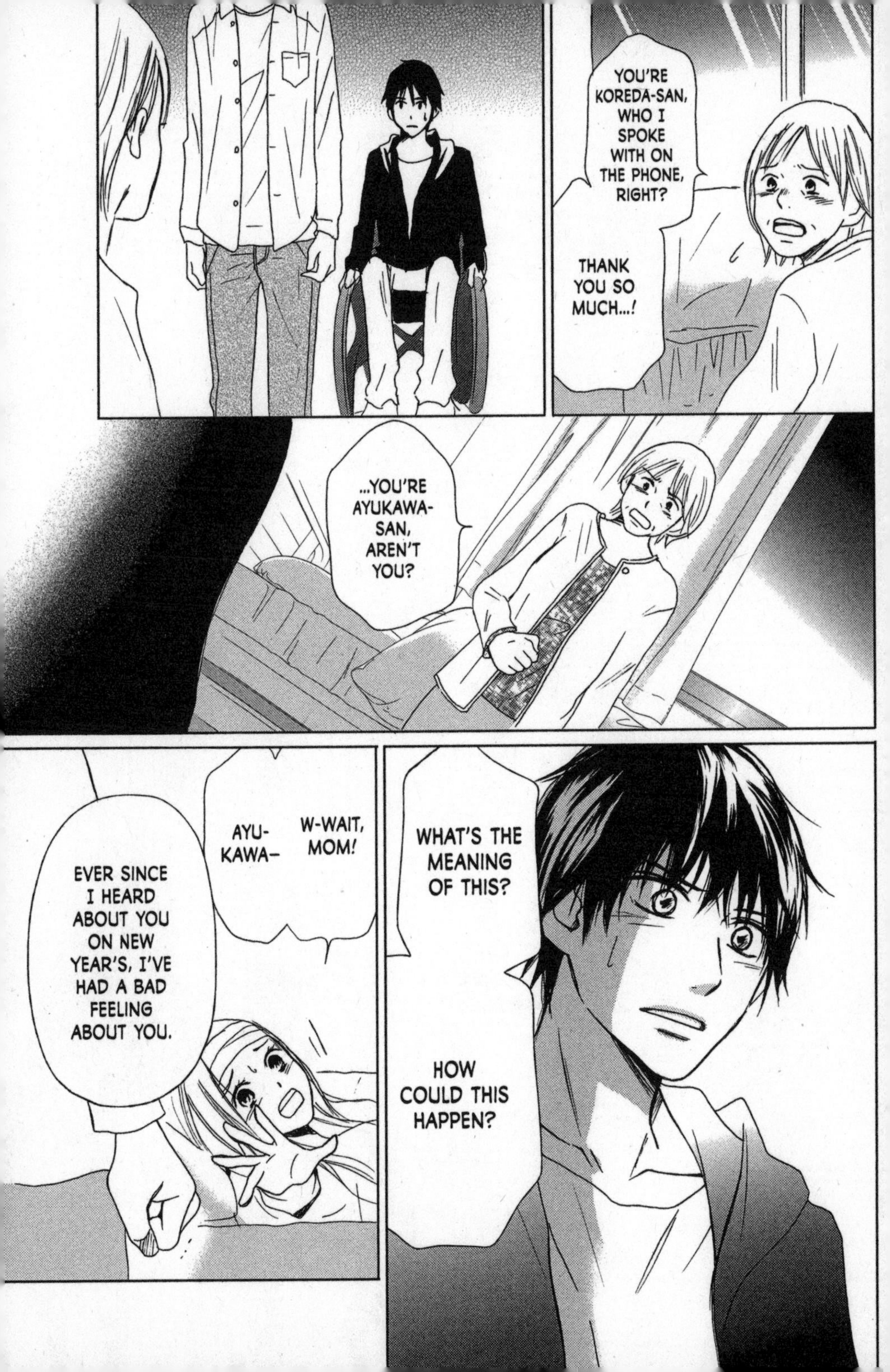
YOU'RE KOREDA-SAN, WHO I SPOKE WITH ON THE PHONE, RIGHT?
THANK YOU SO MUCH...!
...YOU'RE AYUKAWA-SAN, AREN'T YOU?
WHAT'S THE MEANING OF THIS?
HOW COULD THIS HAPPEN?
W-WAIT, MOM!
AYU-KAWA–
EVER SINCE I HEARD ABOUT YOU ON NEW YEAR'S, I'VE HAD A BAD FEELING ABOUT YOU.

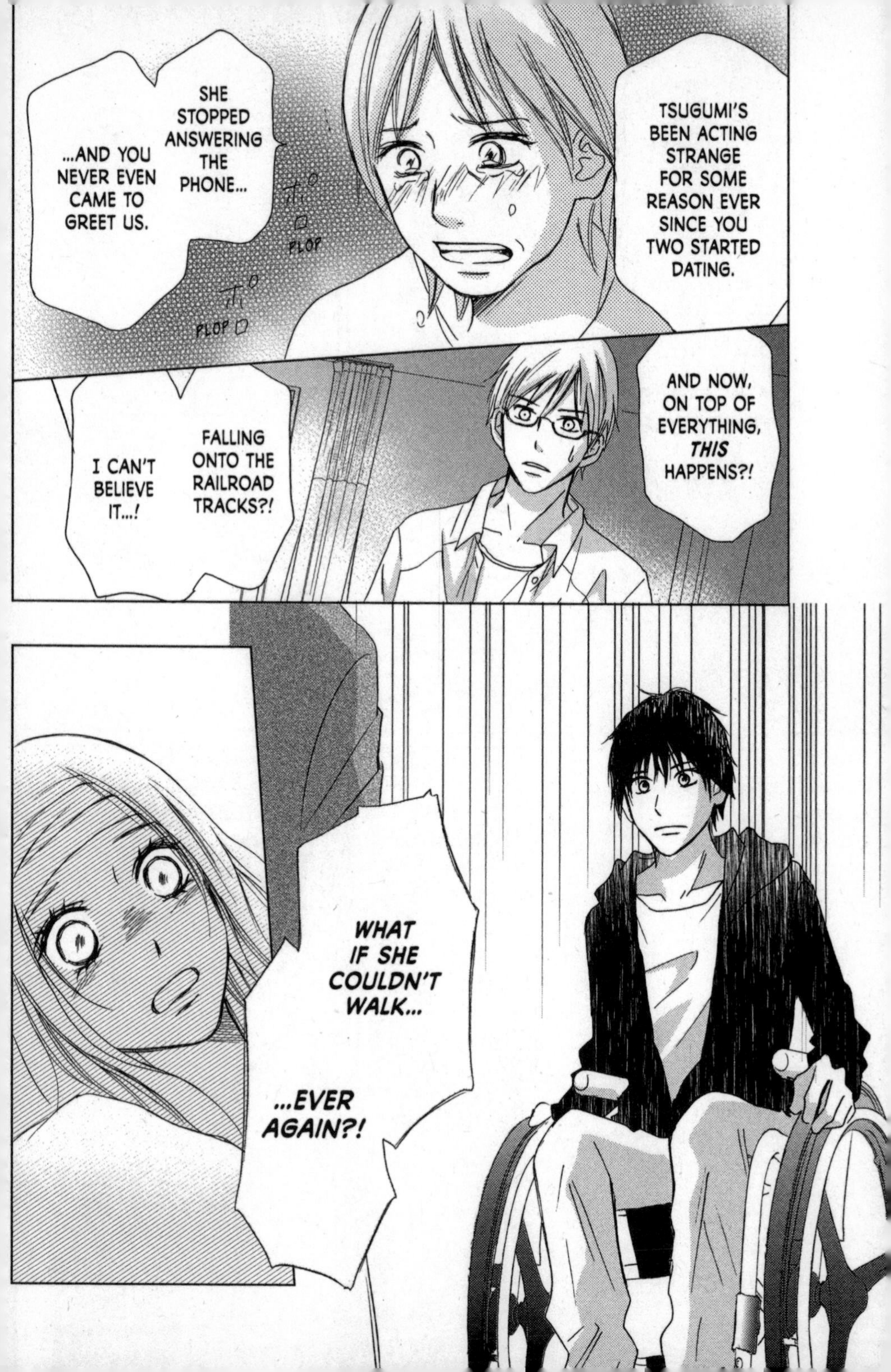
TSUGUMI'S BEEN ACTING STRANGE FOR SOME REASON EVER SINCE YOU TWO STARTED DATING.
SHE STOPPED ANSWERING THE PHONE...
...AND YOU NEVER EVEN CAME TO GREET US.
PLOP
PLOP
AND NOW, ON TOP OF EVERYTHING, *THIS* HAPPENS?!
FALLING ONTO THE RAILROAD TRACKS?!
I CAN'T BELIEVE IT...!
WHAT IF SHE COULDN'T WALK...
...EVER AGAIN?!

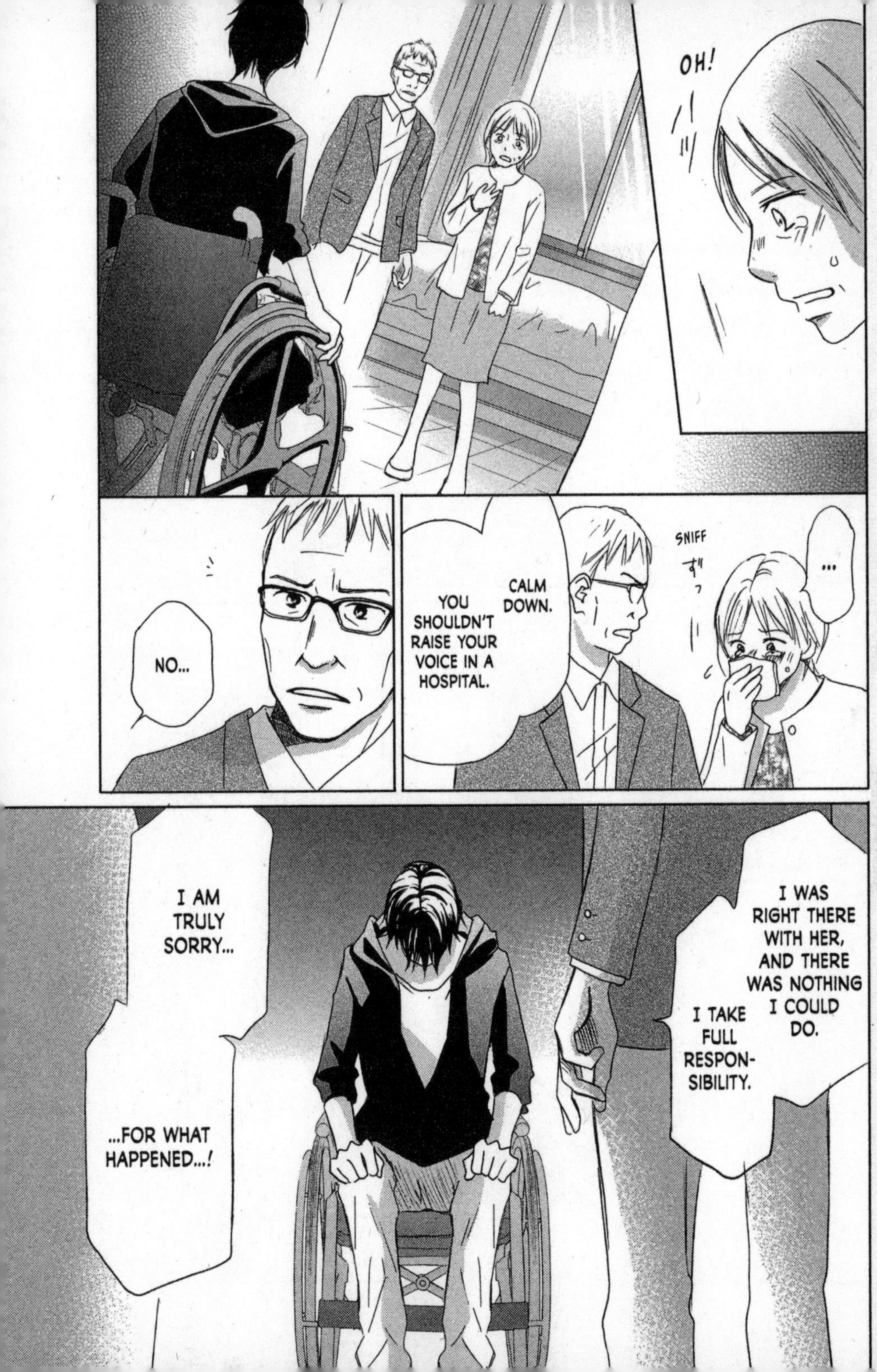
OH!
...
SNIFF
ずっ
CALM DOWN. YOU SHOULDN'T RAISE YOUR VOICE IN A HOSPITAL.
NO...
I WAS RIGHT THERE WITH HER, AND THERE WAS NOTHING I COULD DO.
I TAKE FULL RESPONSIBILITY.
I AM TRULY SORRY...
...FOR WHAT HAPPENED...!

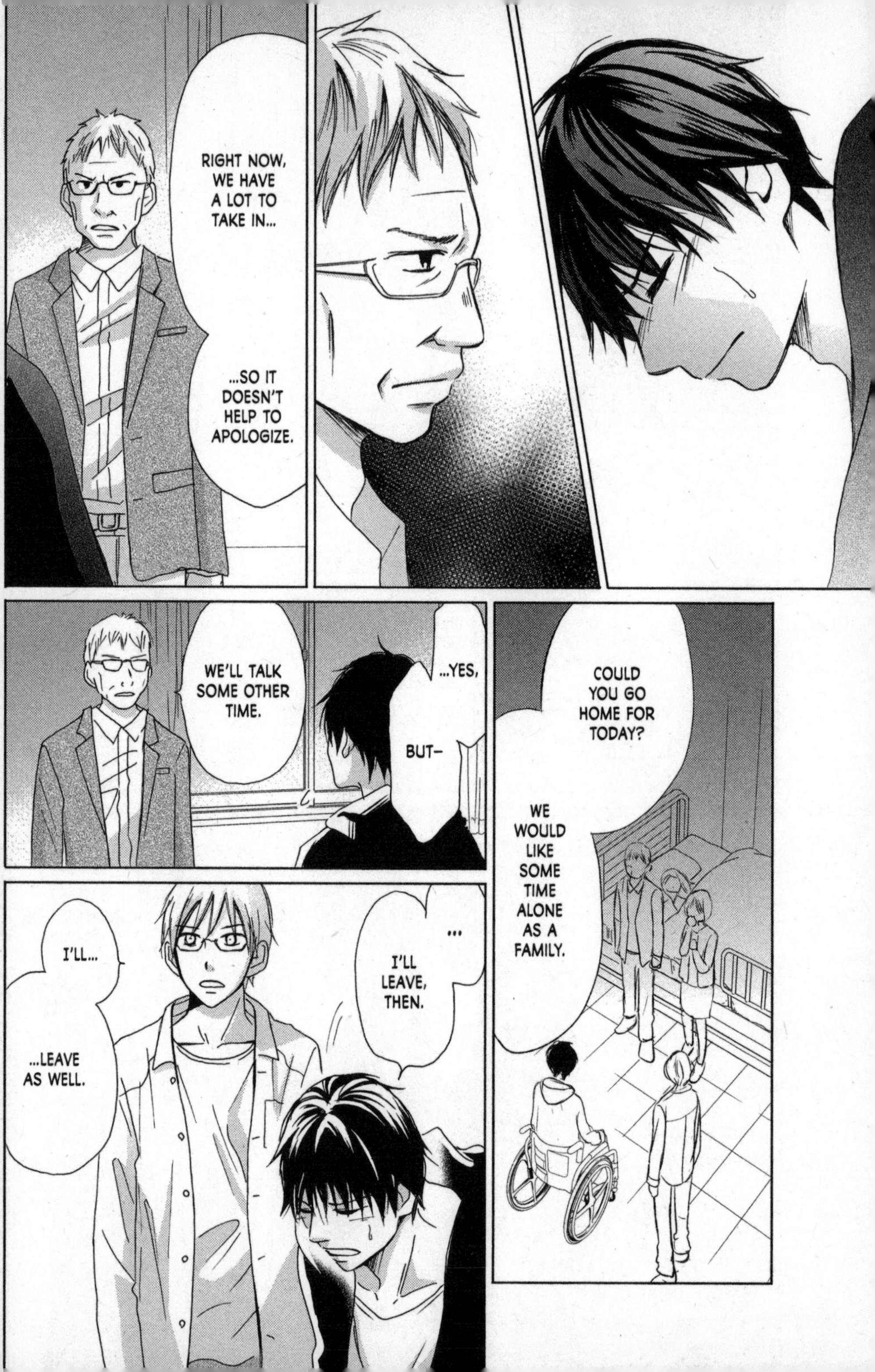
RIGHT NOW, WE HAVE A LOT TO TAKE IN...
...SO IT DOESN'T HELP TO APOLOGIZE.
COULD YOU GO HOME FOR TODAY?
WE WOULD LIKE SOME TIME ALONE AS A FAMILY.
...YES,
BUT–
WE'LL TALK SOME OTHER TIME.
...
I'LL LEAVE, THEN.
I'LL...
...LEAVE AS WELL.

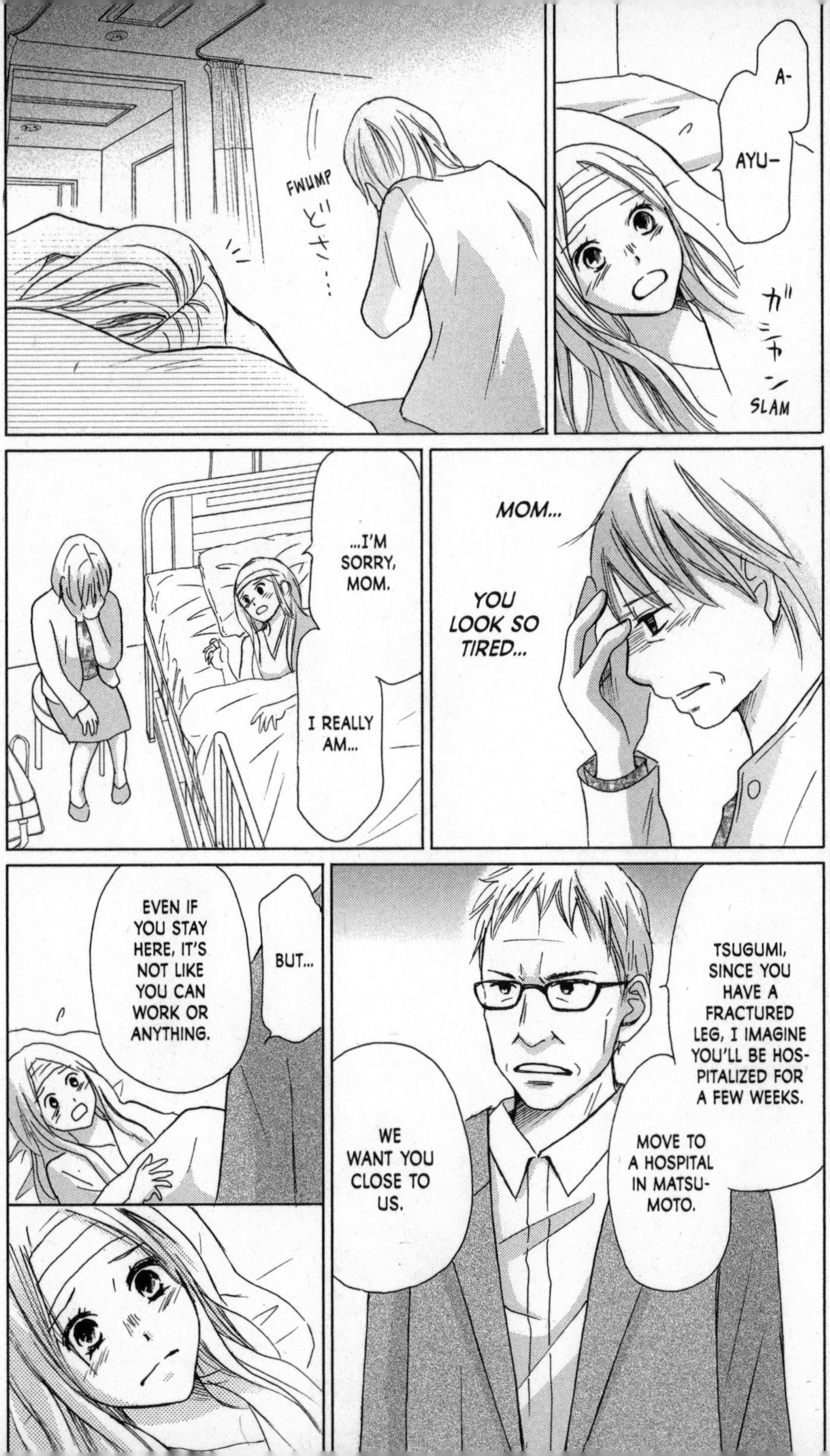
A-
AYU–
ガシャン
SLAM
FWUMP
どさ…
MOM...
YOU LOOK SO TIRED...
...I'M SORRY, MOM.
I REALLY AM...
TSUGUMI, SINCE YOU HAVE A FRACTURED LEG, I IMAGINE YOU'LL BE HOS-PITALIZED FOR A FEW WEEKS.
MOVE TO A HOSPITAL IN MATSU-MOTO.
WE WANT YOU CLOSE TO US.
BUT...
EVEN IF YOU STAY HERE, IT'S NOT LIKE YOU CAN WORK OR ANYTHING.

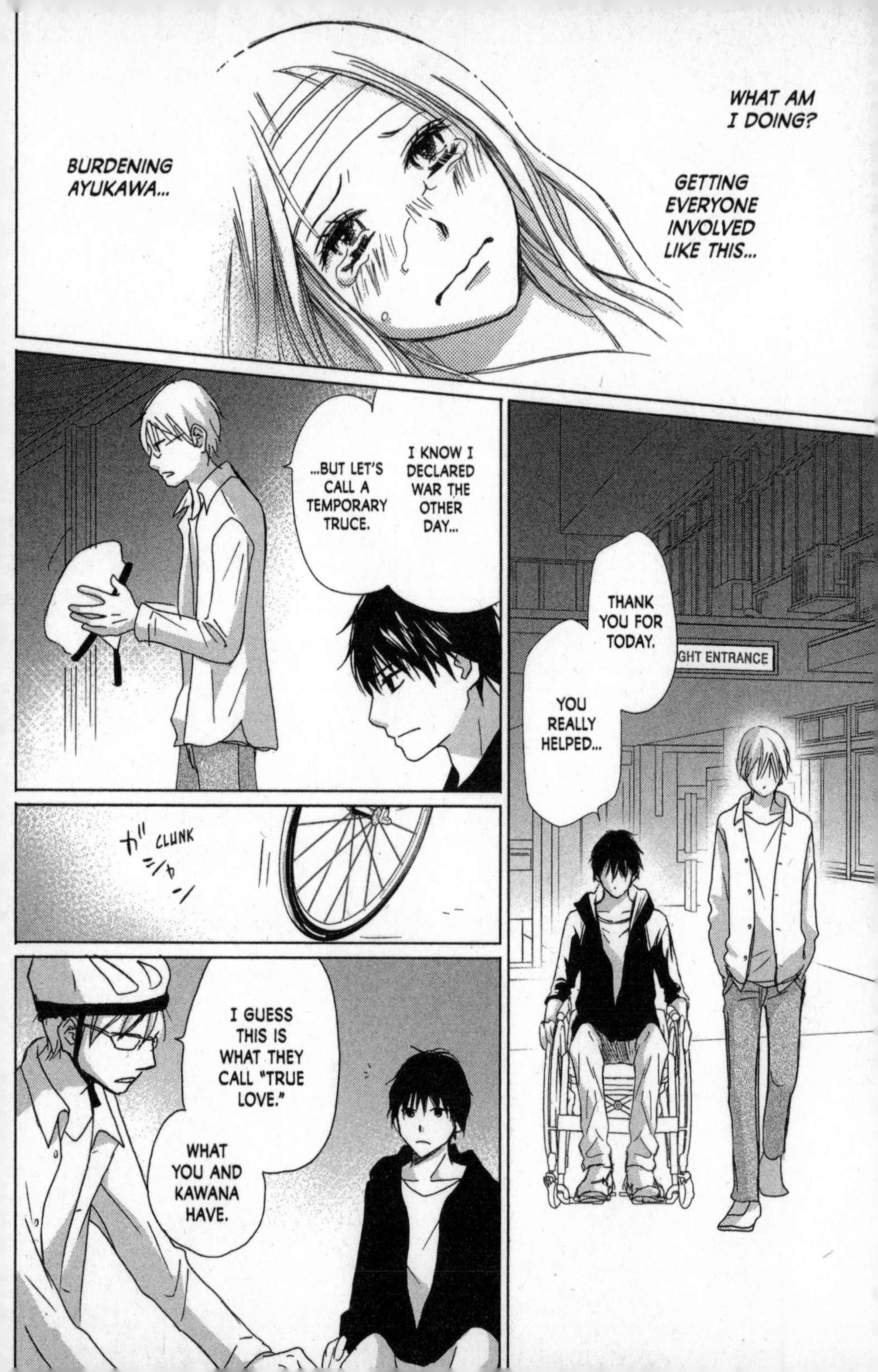
WHAT AM I DOING?
GETTING EVERYONE INVOLVED LIKE THIS...
BURDENING AYUKAWA...
THANK YOU FOR TODAY.
YOU REALLY HELPED...
GHT ENTRANCE
I KNOW I DECLARED WAR THE OTHER DAY...
...BUT LET'S CALL A TEMPORARY TRUCE.
CLUNK
I GUESS THIS IS WHAT THEY CALL "TRUE LOVE."
WHAT YOU AND KAWANA HAVE.

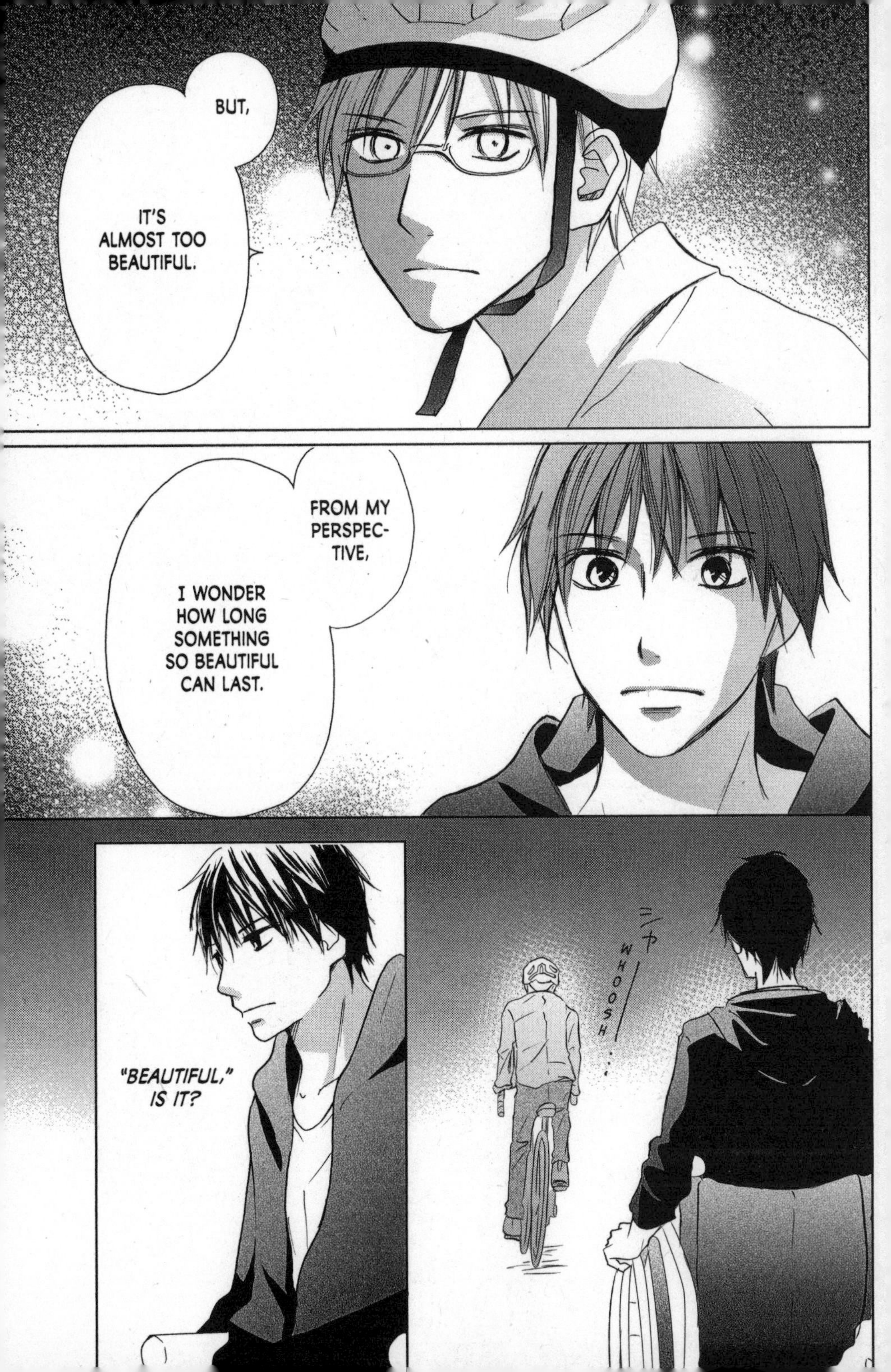
BUT,
IT'S ALMOST TOO BEAUTIFUL.
FROM MY PERSPECTIVE,
I WONDER HOW LONG SOMETHING SO BEAUTIFUL CAN LAST.
WHOOSH...
"BEAUTIFUL," IS IT?

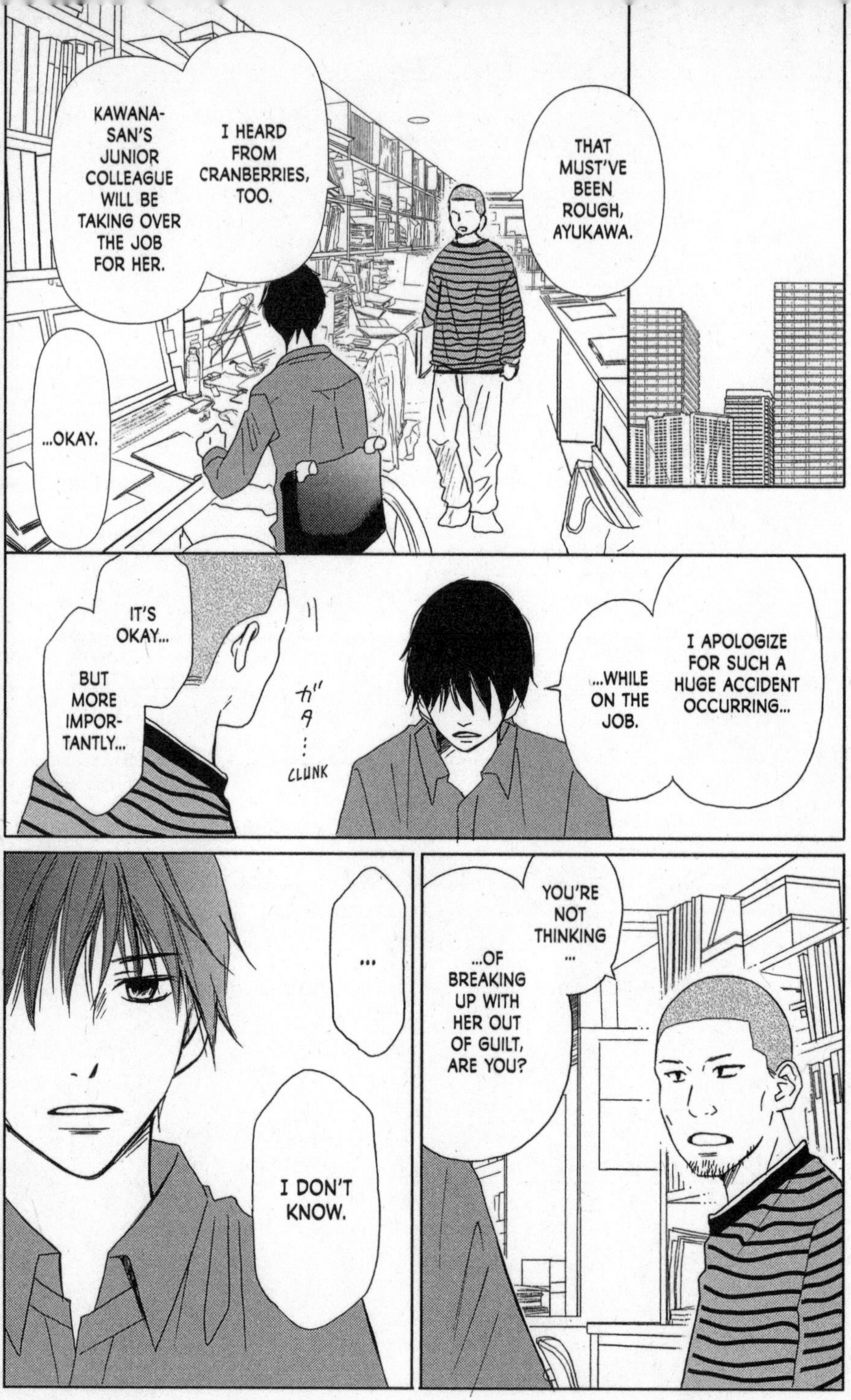
THAT MUST'VE BEEN ROUGH, AYUKAWA.
I HEARD FROM CRANBERRIES, TOO.
KAWANA-SAN'S JUNIOR COLLEAGUE WILL BE TAKING OVER THE JOB FOR HER.
...OKAY.
I APOLOGIZE FOR SUCH A HUGE ACCIDENT OCCURRING...
...WHILE ON THE JOB.
ガタ…
CLUNK
IT'S OKAY...
BUT MORE IMPORTANTLY...
YOU'RE NOT THINKING ...
...OF BREAKING UP WITH HER OUT OF GUILT, ARE YOU?
...
I DON'T KNOW.

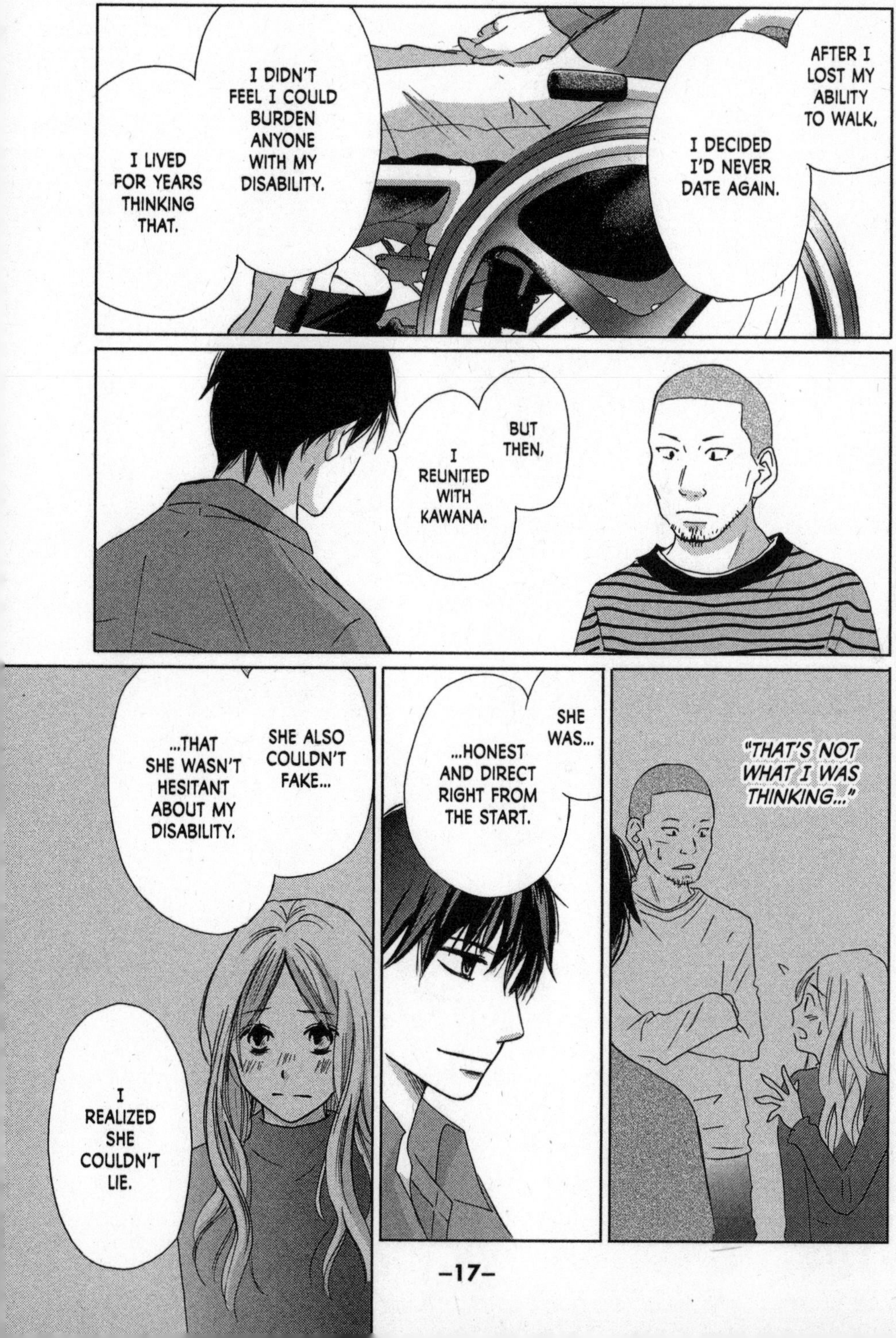
AFTER I LOST MY ABILITY TO WALK,
I DECIDED I'D NEVER DATE AGAIN.
I DIDN'T FEEL I COULD BURDEN ANYONE WITH MY DISABILITY.
I LIVED FOR YEARS THINKING THAT.
BUT THEN,
I REUNITED WITH KAWANA.
"THAT'S NOT WHAT I WAS THINKING..."
SHE WAS...
...HONEST AND DIRECT RIGHT FROM THE START.
SHE ALSO COULDN'T FAKE...
...THAT SHE WASN'T HESITANT ABOUT MY DISABILITY.
I REALIZED SHE COULDN'T LIE.

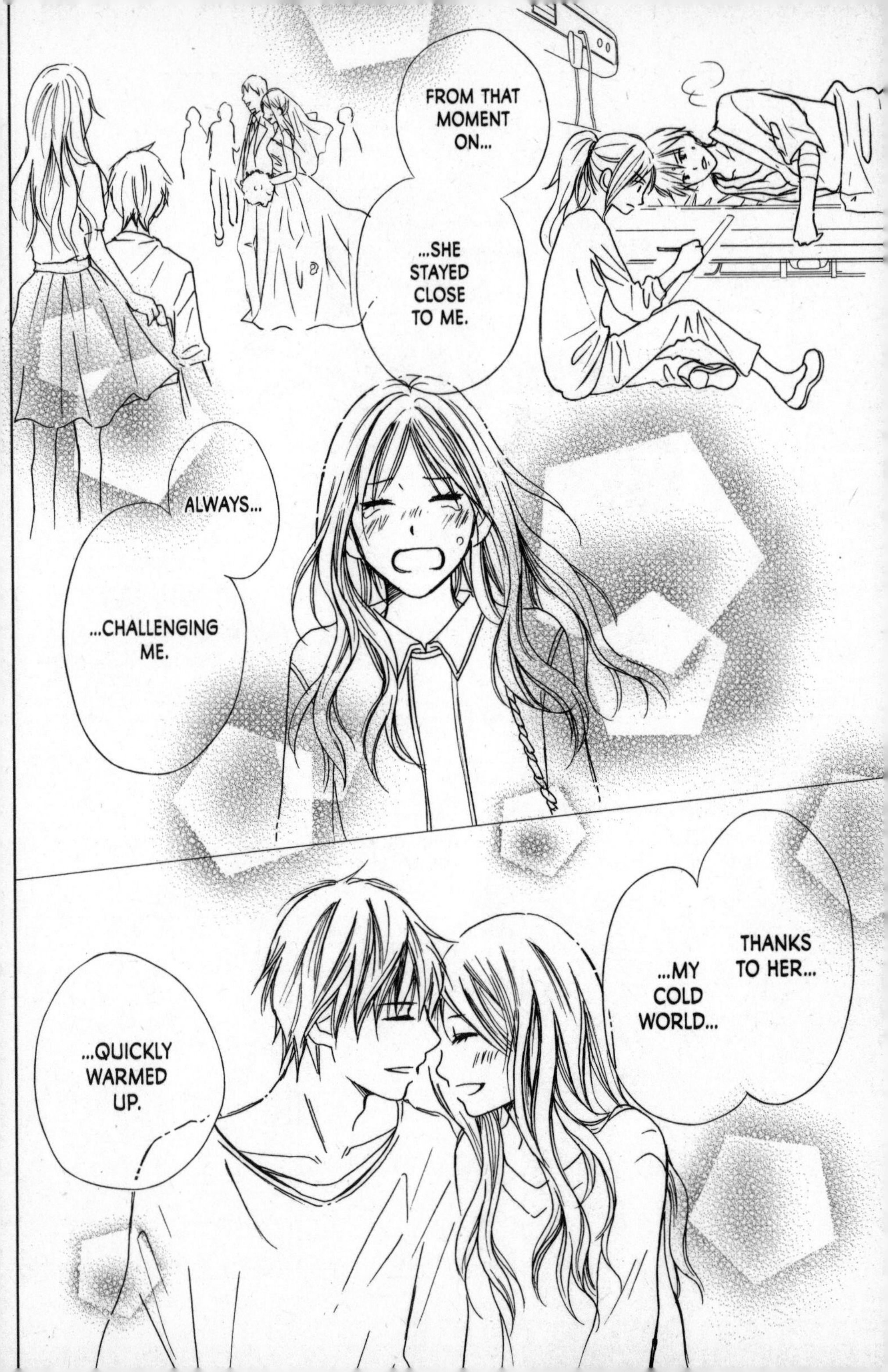
FROM THAT MOMENT ON...
...SHE STAYED CLOSE TO ME.
ALWAYS...
...CHALLENGING ME.
THANKS TO HER...
...MY COLD WORLD...
...QUICKLY WARMED UP.

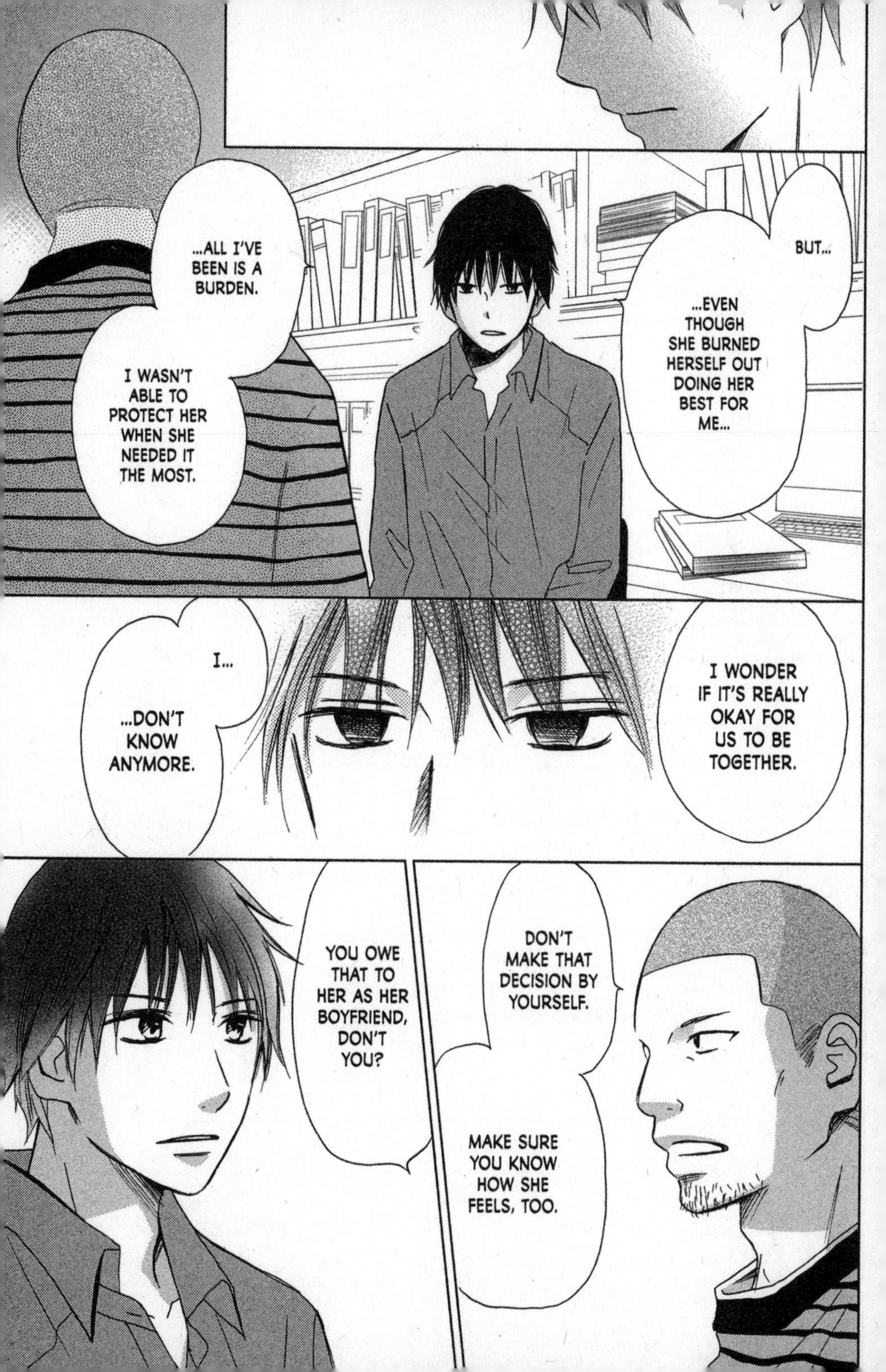
BUT...
...EVEN THOUGH SHE BURNED HERSELF OUT DOING HER BEST FOR ME...
...ALL I'VE BEEN IS A BURDEN.
I WASN'T ABLE TO PROTECT HER WHEN SHE NEEDED IT THE MOST.
I WONDER IF IT'S REALLY OKAY FOR US TO BE TOGETHER.
I...
...DON'T KNOW ANYMORE.
DON'T MAKE THAT DECISION BY YOURSELF.
MAKE SURE YOU KNOW HOW SHE FEELS, TOO.
YOU OWE THAT TO HER AS HER BOYFRIEND, DON'T YOU?

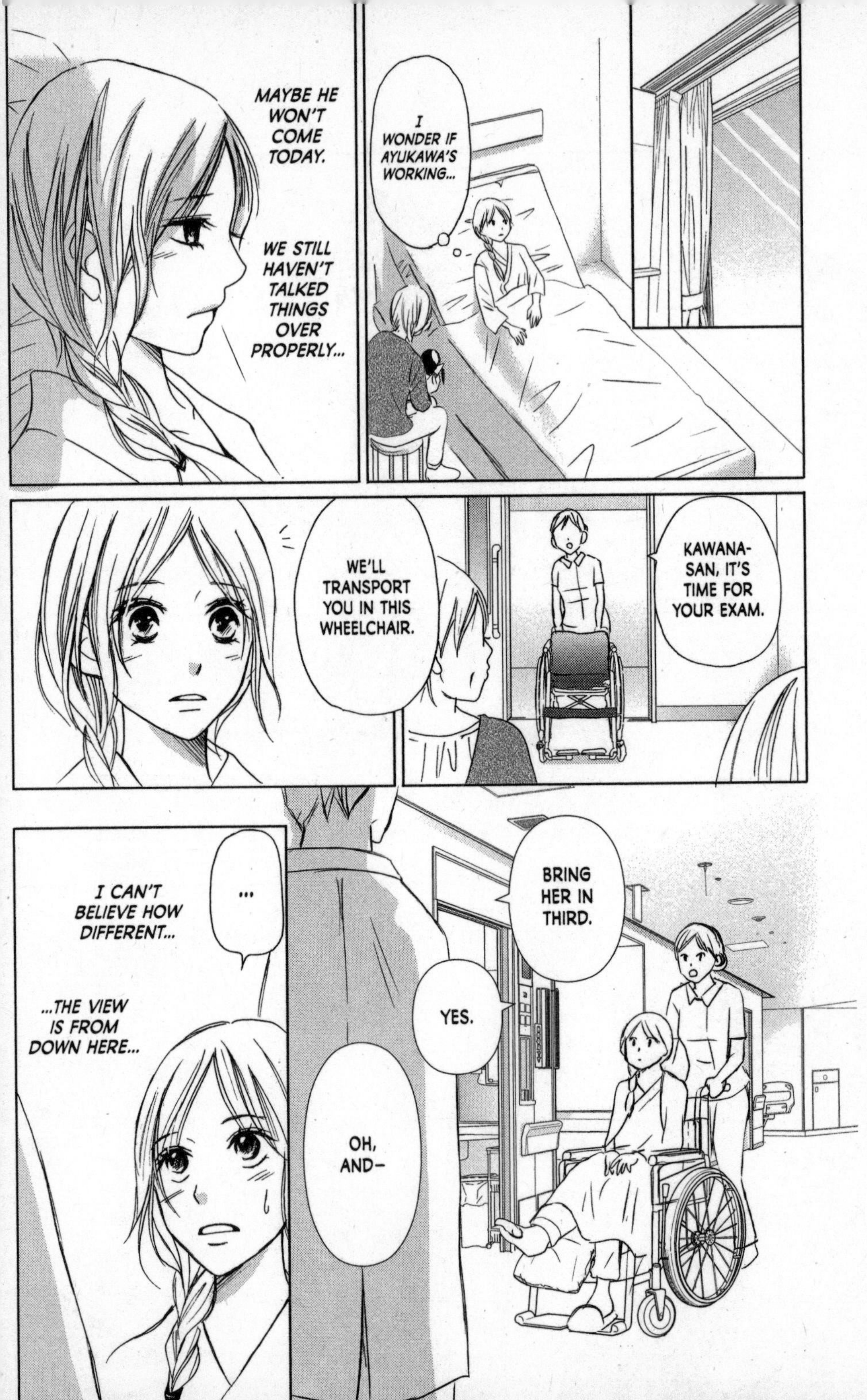
I WONDER IF AYUKAWA'S WORKING...
MAYBE HE WON'T COME TODAY.
WE STILL HAVEN'T TALKED THINGS OVER PROPERLY...
KAWANA-SAN, IT'S TIME FOR YOUR EXAM.
WE'LL TRANSPORT YOU IN THIS WHEELCHAIR.
BRING HER IN THIRD.
YES.
OH, AND–
...
I CAN'T BELIEVE HOW DIFFERENT...
...THE VIEW IS FROM DOWN HERE...

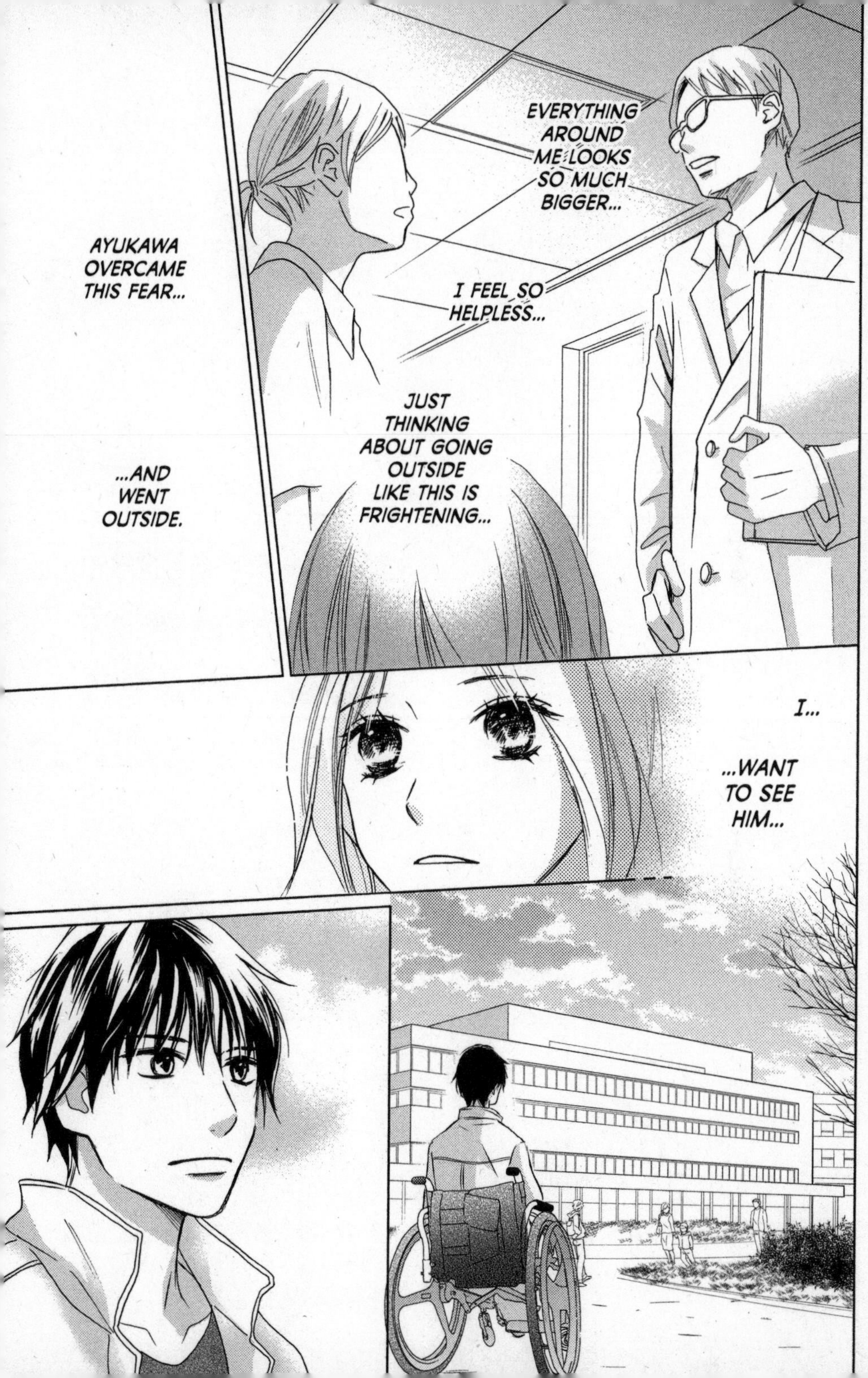
EVERYTHING AROUND ME LOOKS SO MUCH BIGGER...
I FEEL SO HELPLESS...
JUST THINKING ABOUT GOING OUTSIDE LIKE THIS IS FRIGHTENING...
AYUKAWA OVERCAME THIS FEAR...
...AND WENT OUTSIDE.
I...
...WANT TO SEE HIM...

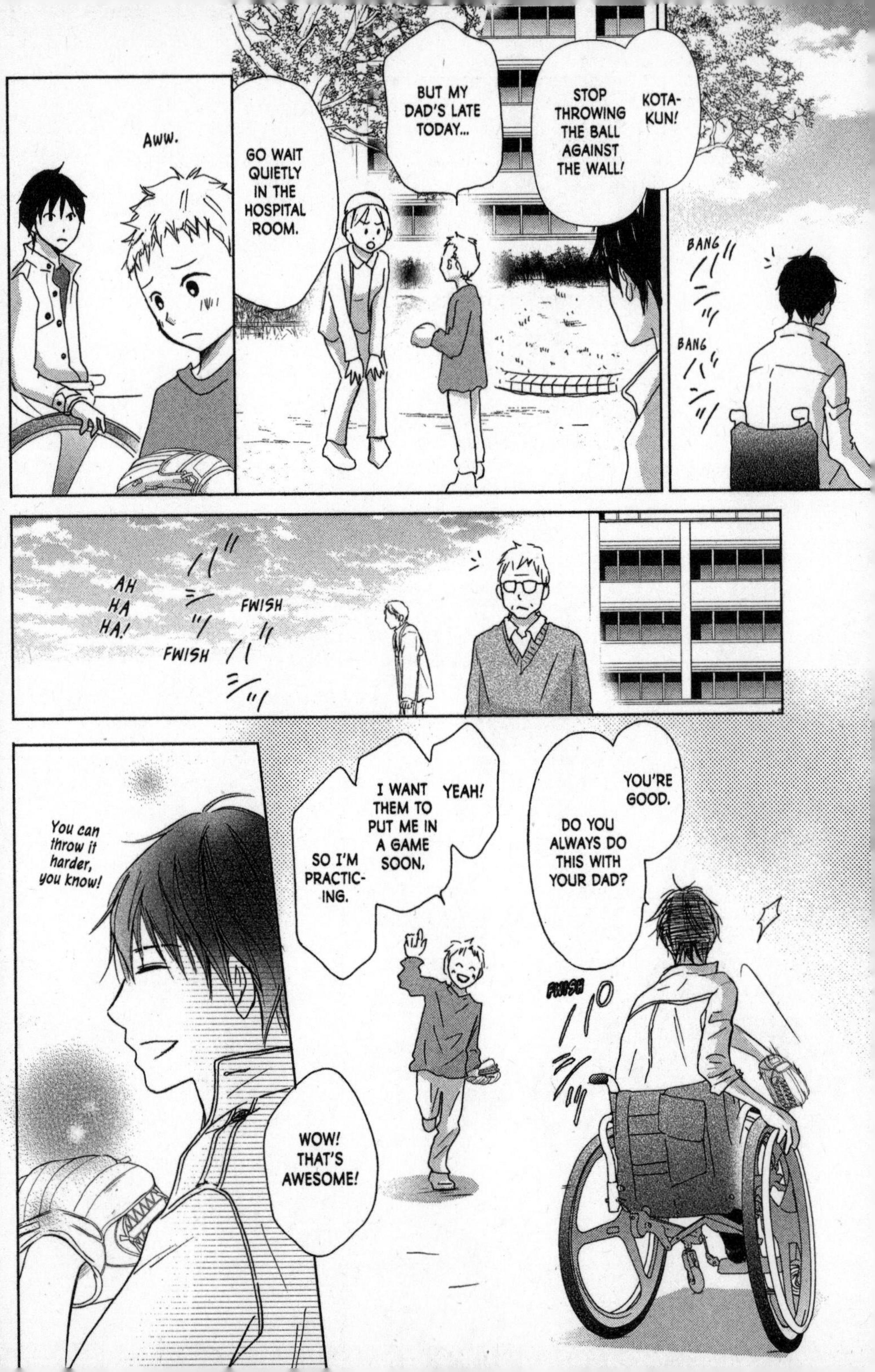
BANG
BANG
KOTA-KUN!
STOP THROWING THE BALL AGAINST THE WALL!
BUT MY DAD'S LATE TODAY...
GO WAIT QUIETLY IN THE HOSPITAL ROOM.
AWW.
FWISH
FWISH
AH HA HA!
FWISH
YOU'RE GOOD.
DO YOU ALWAYS DO THIS WITH YOUR DAD?
YEAH!
I WANT THEM TO PUT ME IN A GAME SOON,
SO I'M PRACTIC-ING.
WOW! THAT'S AWESOME!
You can throw it harder, you know!

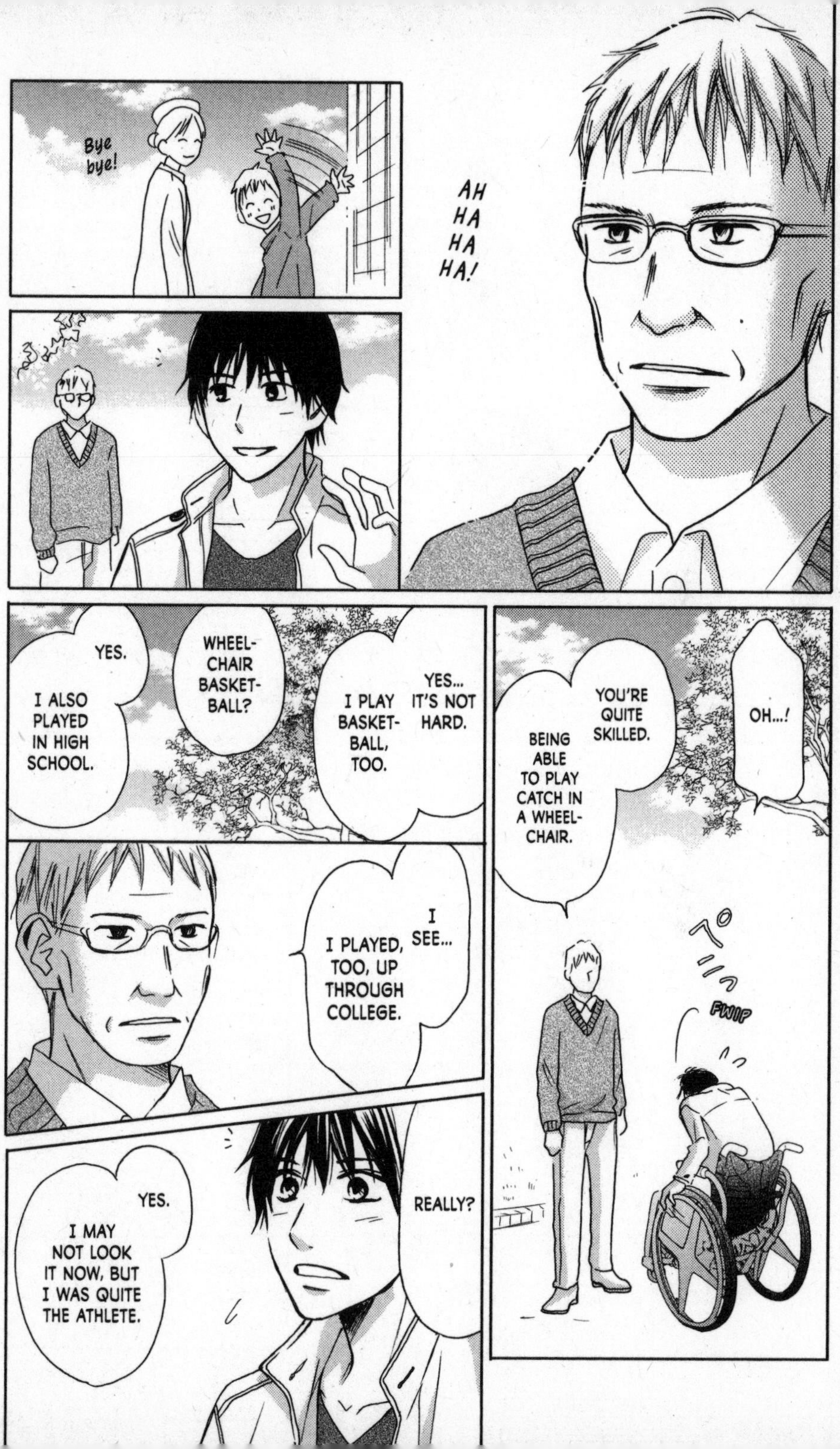
AH HA HA HA!
Bye bye!
OH...!
YOU'RE QUITE SKILLED.
BEING ABLE TO PLAY CATCH IN A WHEEL-CHAIR.
FWIP
YES... IT'S NOT HARD.
I PLAY BASKET-BALL, TOO.
WHEEL-CHAIR BASKET-BALL?
YES.
I ALSO PLAYED IN HIGH SCHOOL.
I SEE...
I PLAYED, TOO, UP THROUGH COLLEGE.
REALLY?
YES.
I MAY NOT LOOK IT NOW, BUT I WAS QUITE THE ATHLETE.

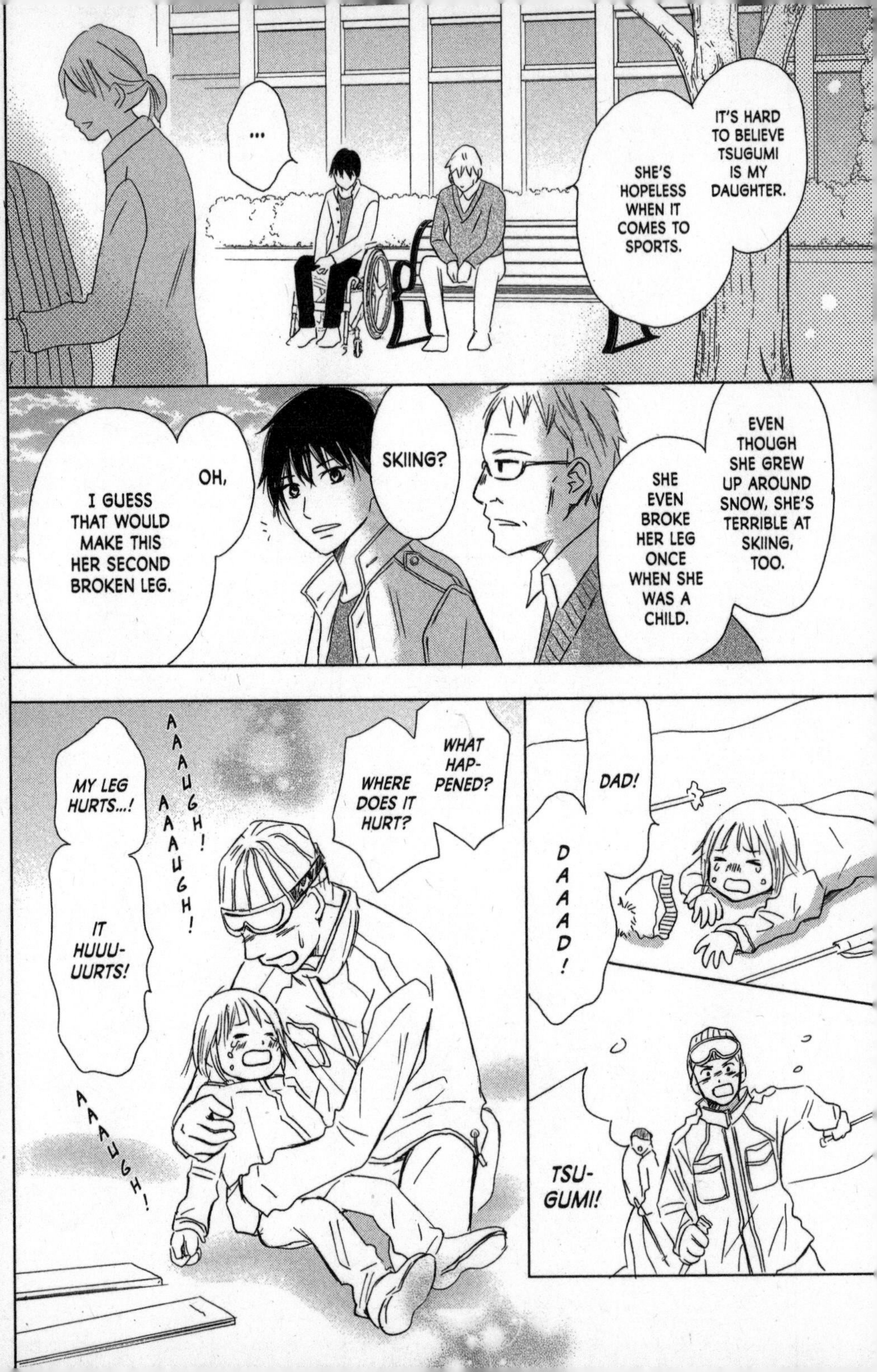
IT'S HARD TO BELIEVE TSUGUMI IS MY DAUGHTER.
SHE'S HOPELESS WHEN IT COMES TO SPORTS.
...
EVEN THOUGH SHE GREW UP AROUND SNOW, SHE'S TERRIBLE AT SKIING, TOO.
SHE EVEN BROKE HER LEG ONCE WHEN SHE WAS A CHILD.
SKIING?
OH,
I GUESS THAT WOULD MAKE THIS HER SECOND BROKEN LEG.
DAD!
DAAAAD!
TSU-GUMI!
WHAT HAP-PENED?
WHERE DOES IT HURT?
AAAUGH!
AAAUGH!
MY LEG HURTS...!
IT HUUU-UURTS!
AAAUGH!

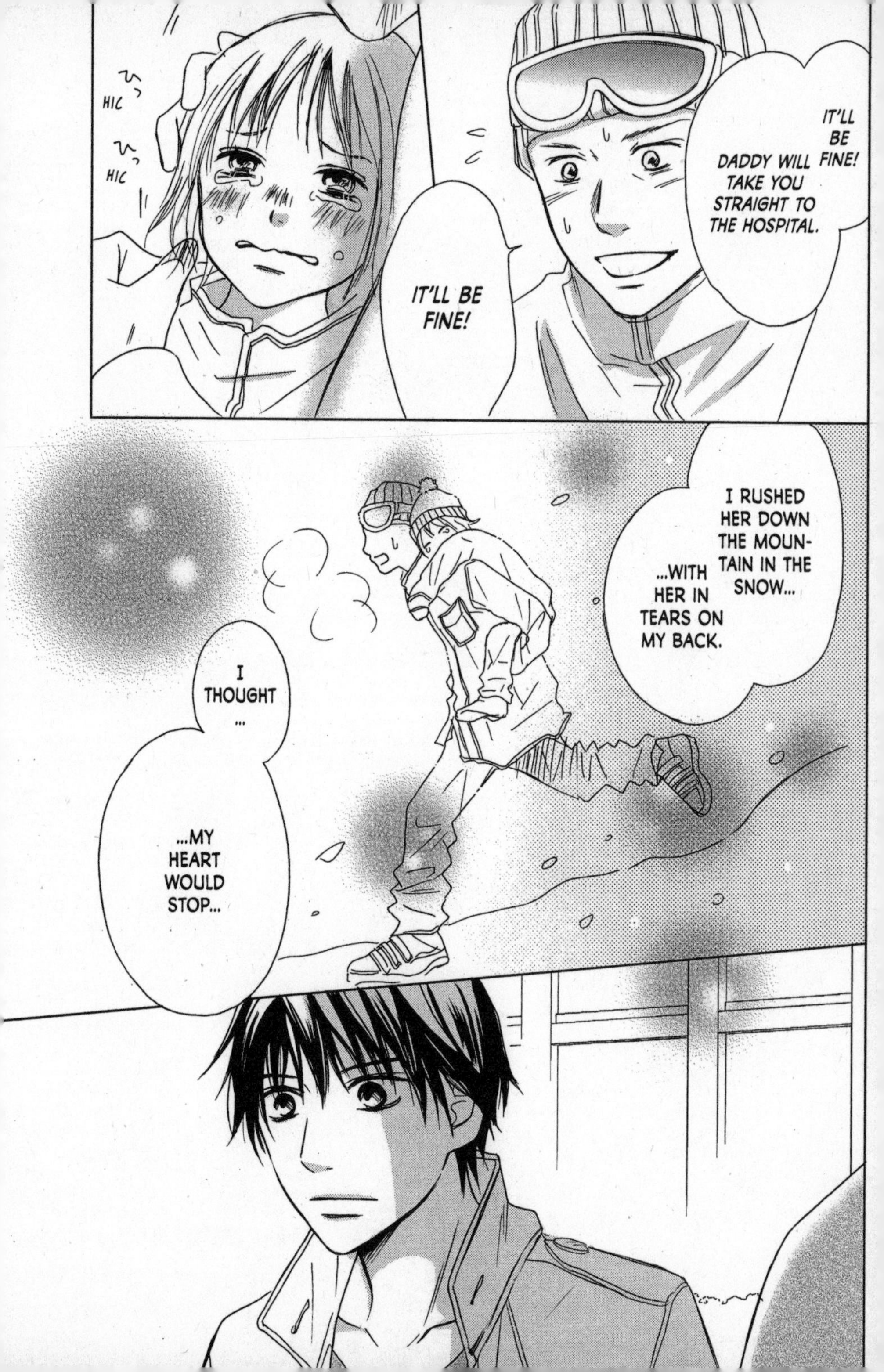
IT'LL BE FINE!
DADDY WILL TAKE YOU STRAIGHT TO THE HOSPITAL.
IT'LL BE FINE!
HIC
HIC
I RUSHED HER DOWN THE MOUN-TAIN IN THE SNOW...
...WITH HER IN TEARS ON MY BACK.
I THOUGHT ...
...MY HEART WOULD STOP...

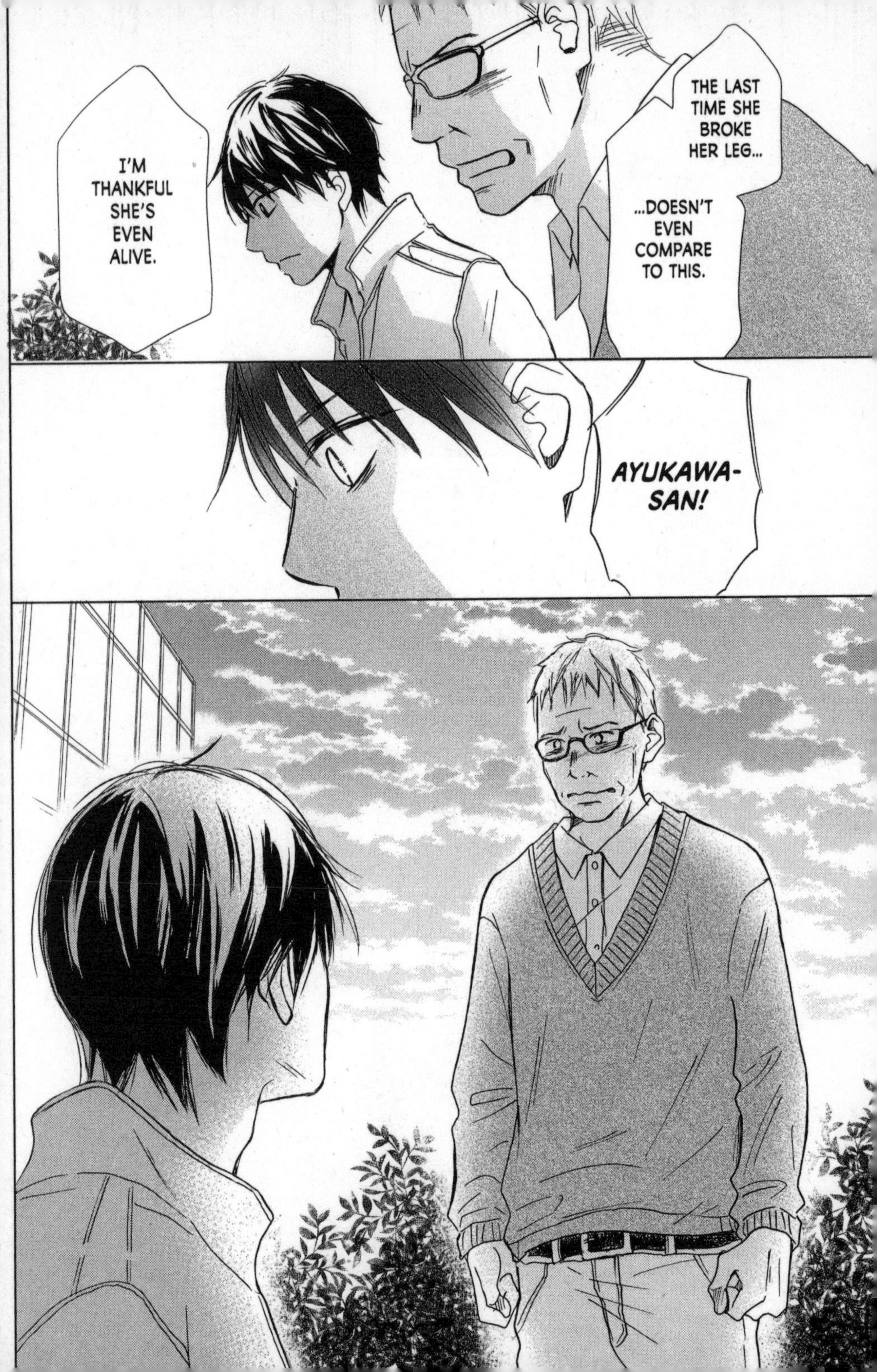
THE LAST TIME SHE BROKE HER LEG...
...DOESN'T EVEN COMPARE TO THIS.
I'M THANKFUL SHE'S EVEN ALIVE.
AYUKAWA-SAN!

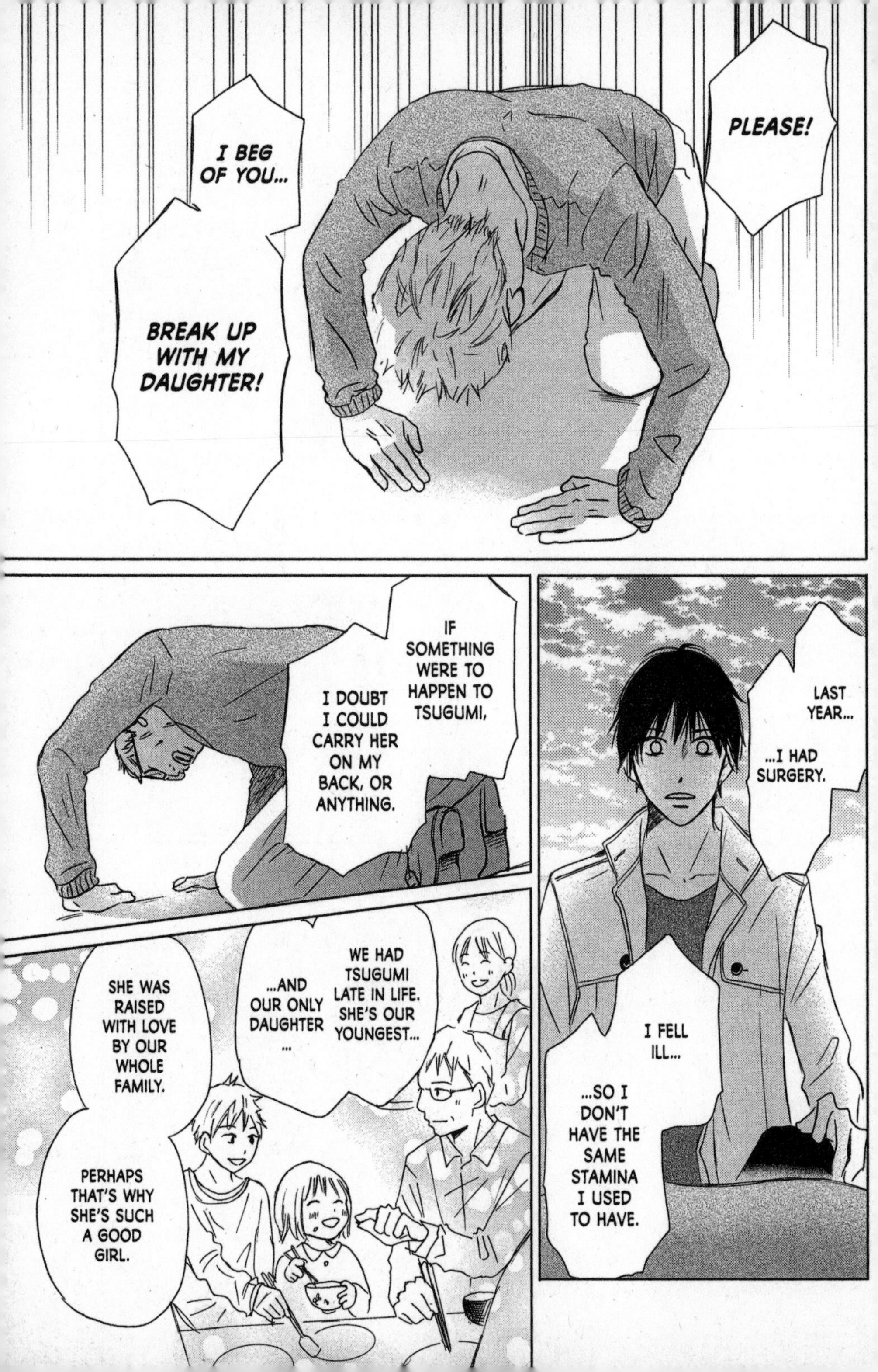
PLEASE!
I BEG OF YOU...
BREAK UP WITH MY DAUGHTER!
LAST YEAR...
...I HAD SURGERY.
I FELL ILL...
...SO I DON'T HAVE THE SAME STAMINA I USED TO HAVE.
IF SOMETHING WERE TO HAPPEN TO TSUGUMI,
I DOUBT I COULD CARRY HER ON MY BACK, OR ANYTHING.
WE HAD TSUGUMI LATE IN LIFE. SHE'S OUR YOUNGEST...
...AND OUR ONLY DAUGHTER ...
SHE WAS RAISED WITH LOVE BY OUR WHOLE FAMILY.
PERHAPS THAT'S WHY SHE'S SUCH A GOOD GIRL.

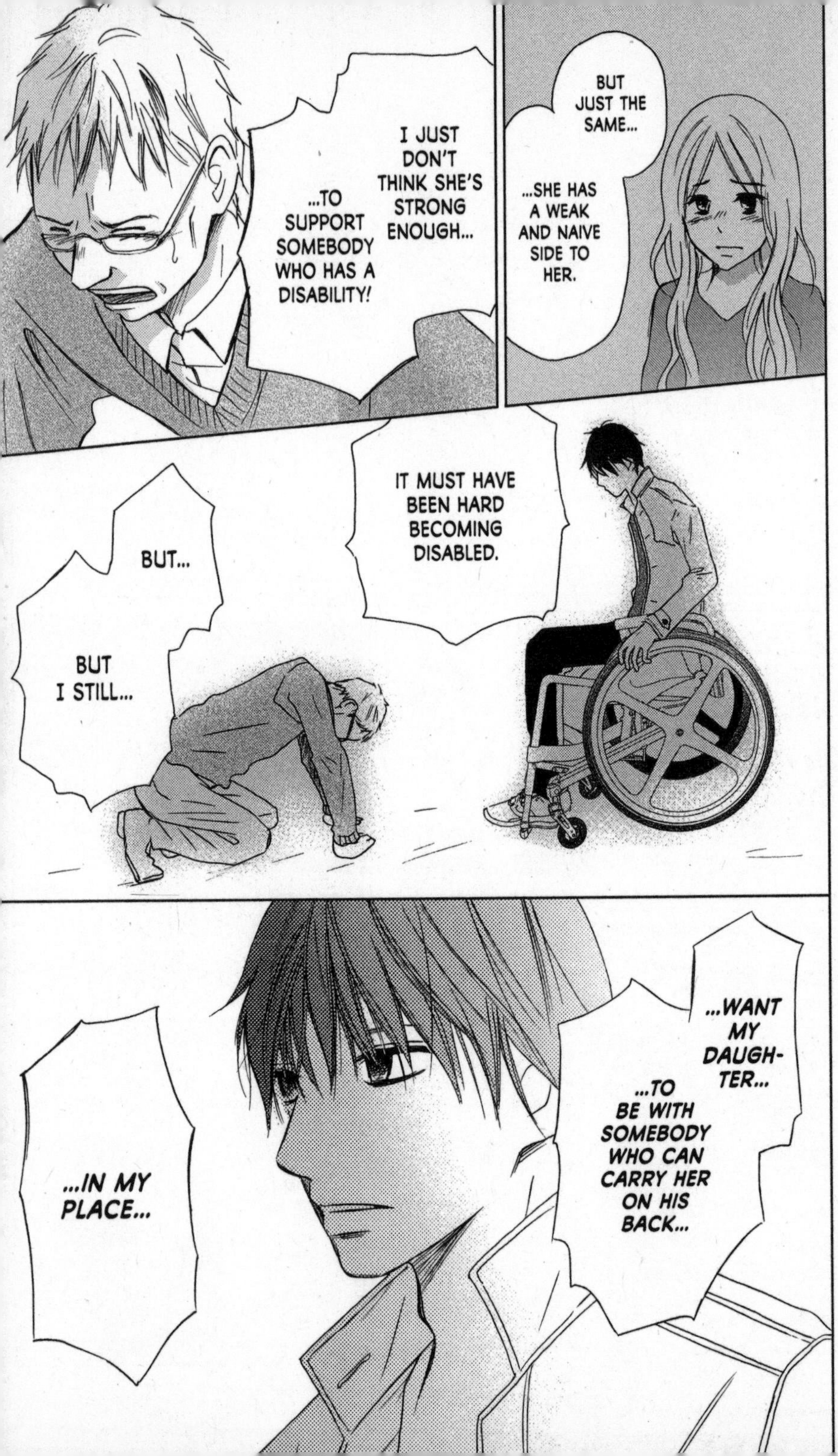
BUT JUST THE SAME...
...SHE HAS A WEAK AND NAIVE SIDE TO HER.
I JUST DON'T THINK SHE'S STRONG ENOUGH...
...TO SUPPORT SOMEBODY WHO HAS A DISABILITY!
IT MUST HAVE BEEN HARD BECOMING DISABLED.
BUT...
BUT I STILL...
...WANT MY DAUGH-TER...
...TO BE WITH SOMEBODY WHO CAN CARRY HER ON HIS BACK...
...IN MY PLACE...

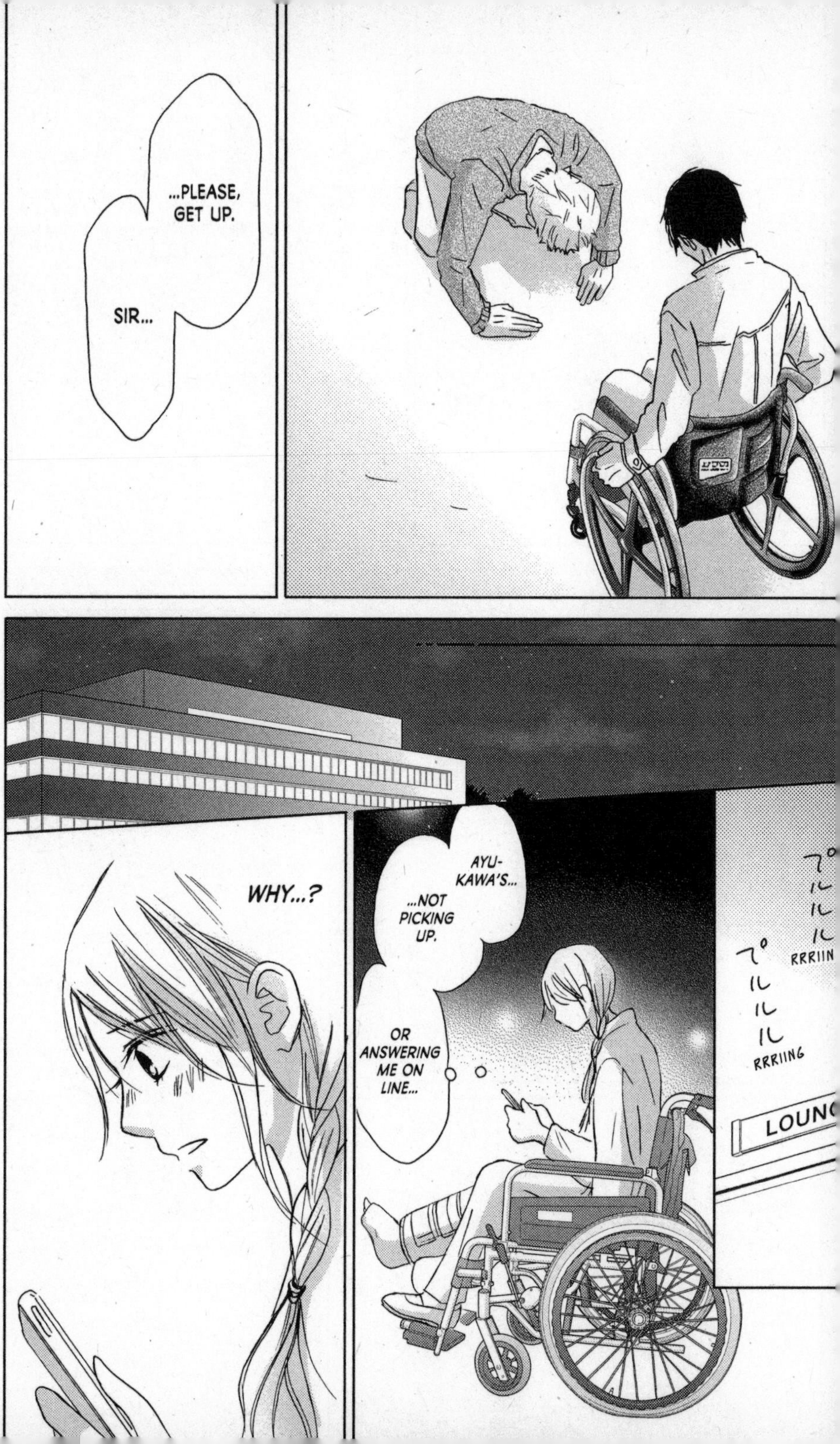
...PLEASE, GET UP.
SIR...
プルルル
RRRIIN
プルルル
RRRIING
LOUNG
AYU-KAWA'S...
...NOT PICKING UP.
OR ANSWERING ME ON LINE...
WHY...?

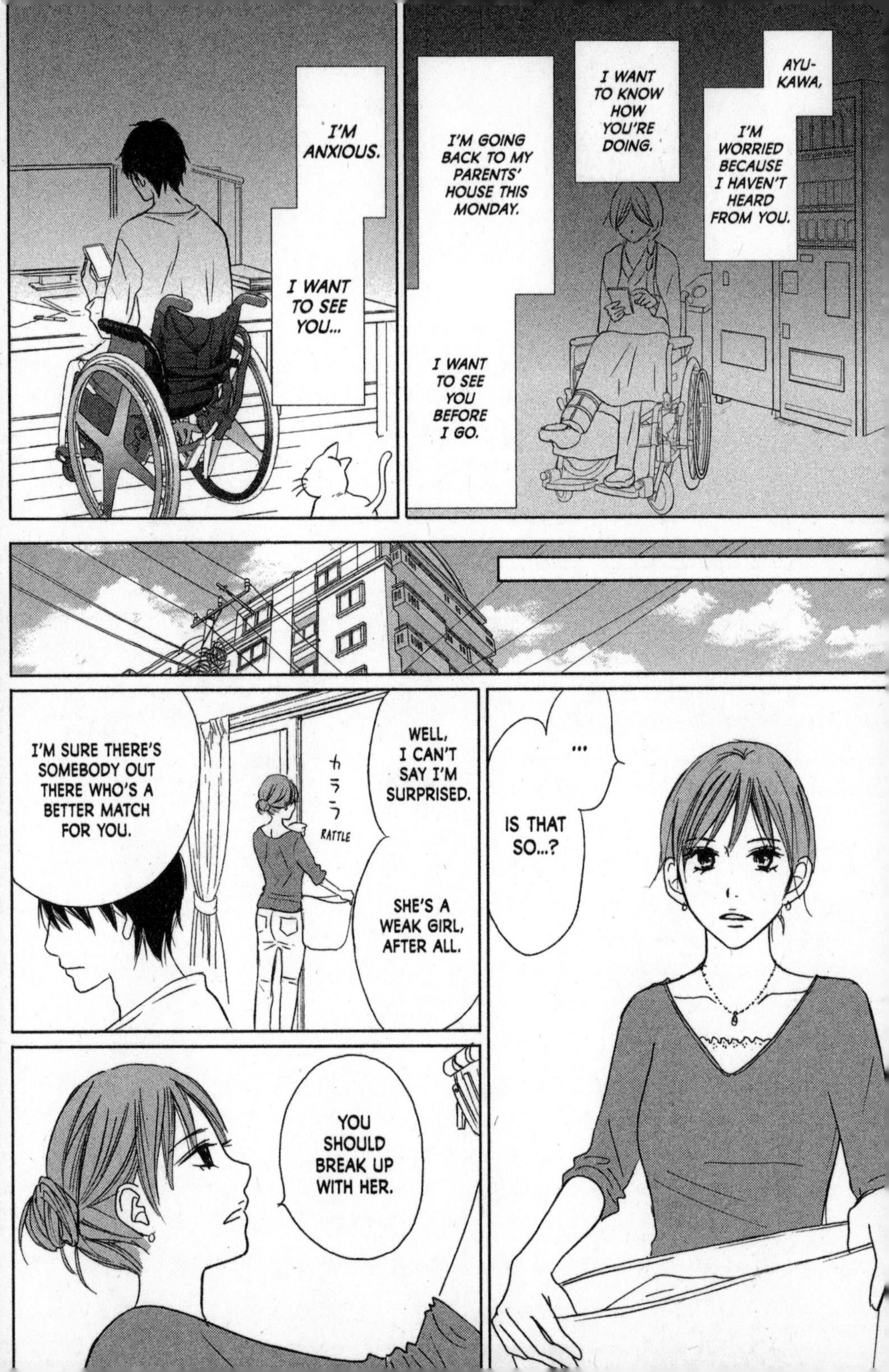

AYU-KAWA,
I'M WORRIED BECAUSE I HAVEN'T HEARD FROM YOU.
I WANT TO KNOW HOW YOU'RE DOING.
I'M GOING BACK TO MY PARENTS' HOUSE THIS MONDAY.
I WANT TO SEE YOU BEFORE I GO.
I'M ANXIOUS.
I WANT TO SEE YOU...
...
IS THAT SO...?
WELL, I CAN'T SAY I'M SURPRISED.
SHE'S A WEAK GIRL, AFTER ALL.
カララ
RATTLE
I'M SURE THERE'S SOMEBODY OUT THERE WHO'S A BETTER MATCH FOR YOU.
YOU SHOULD BREAK UP WITH HER.

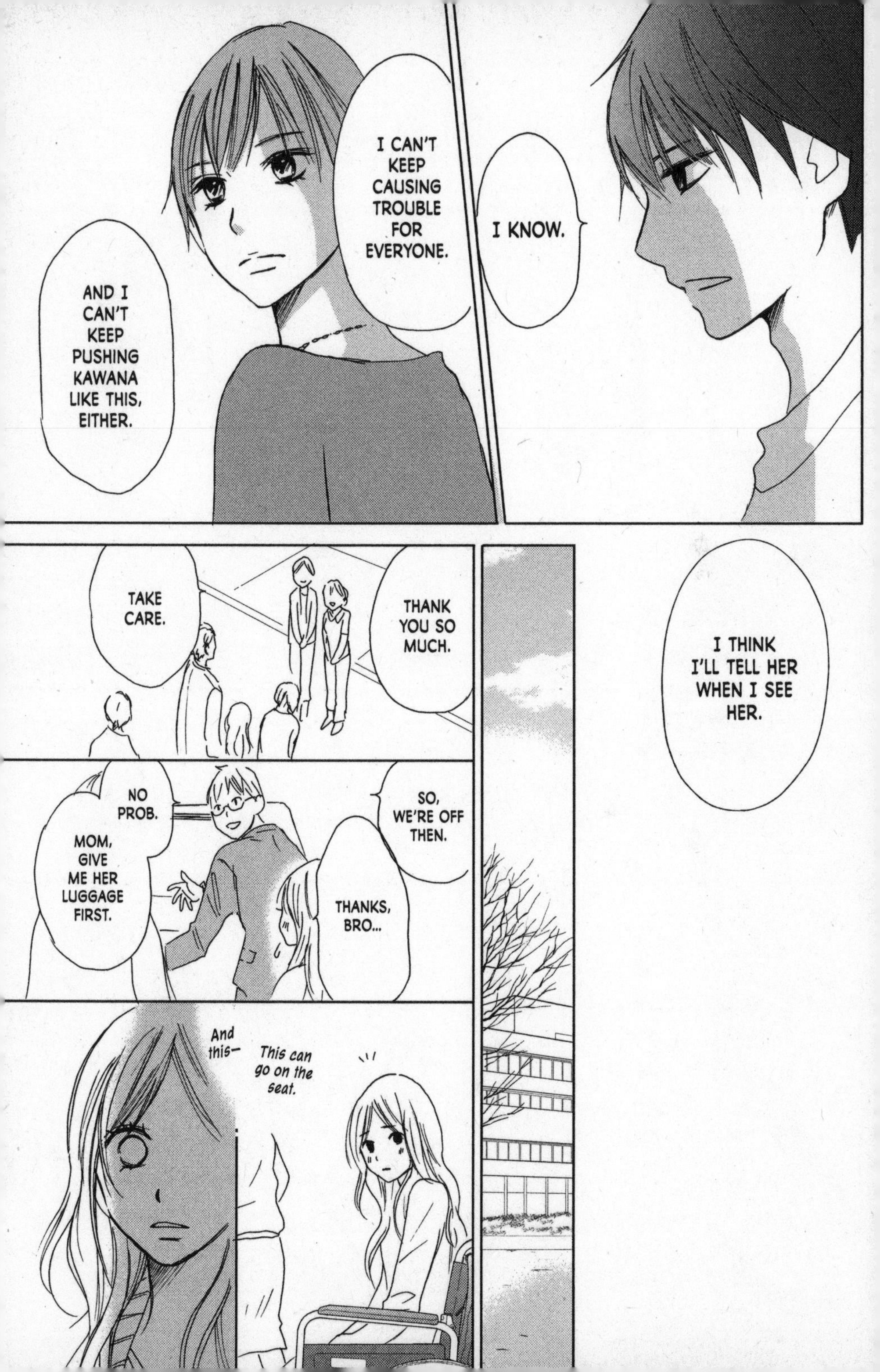
I KNOW.
I CAN'T KEEP CAUSING TROUBLE FOR EVERYONE.
AND I CAN'T KEEP PUSHING KAWANA LIKE THIS, EITHER.
I THINK I'LL TELL HER WHEN I SEE HER.
THANK YOU SO MUCH.
TAKE CARE.
SO, WE'RE OFF THEN.
THANKS, BRO...
NO PROB.
MOM, GIVE ME HER LUGGAGE FIRST.
And this—
This can go on the seat.

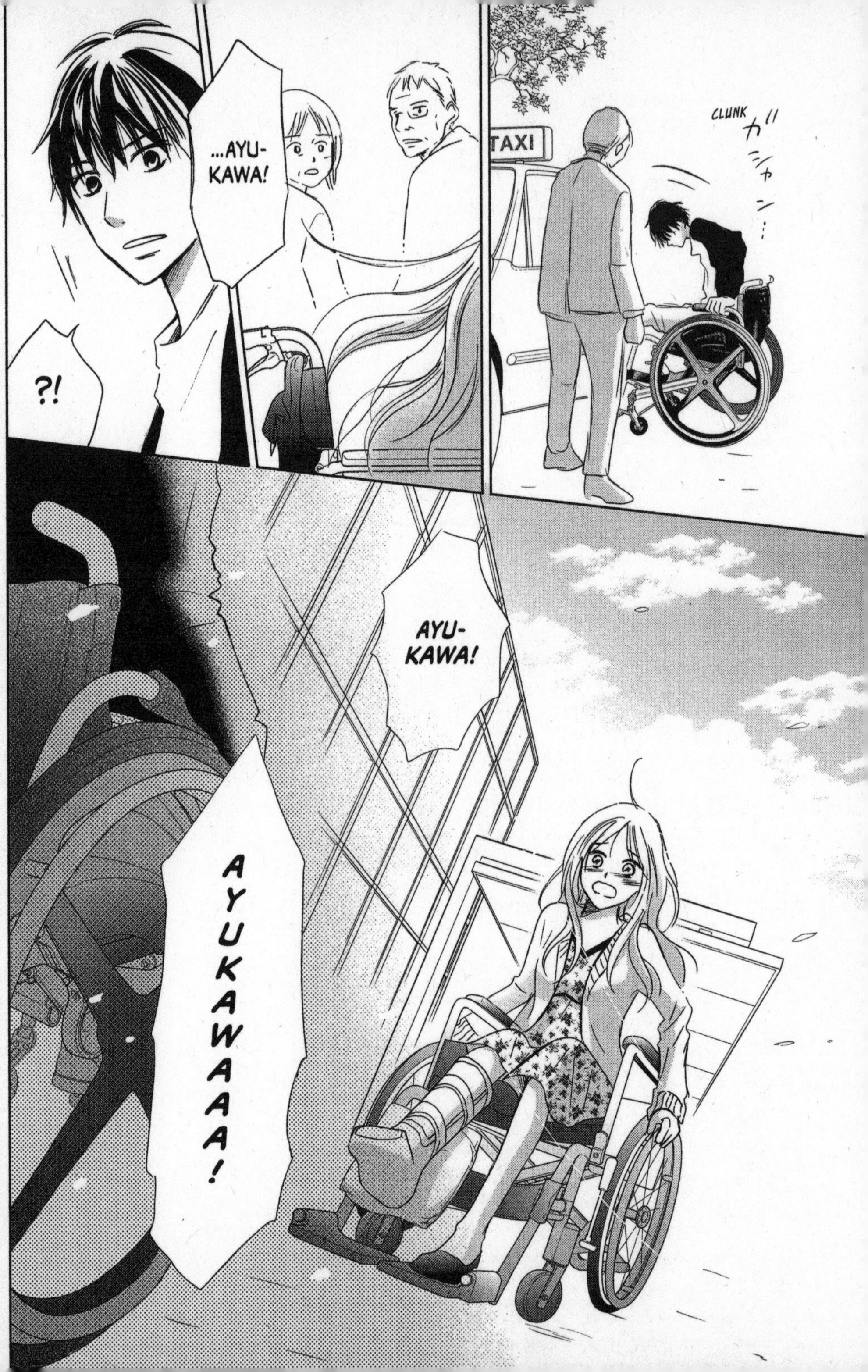
CLUNK
ガシャン…
...AYU-KAWA!
?!
AYU-KAWA!
AYUKAWAAAAA!

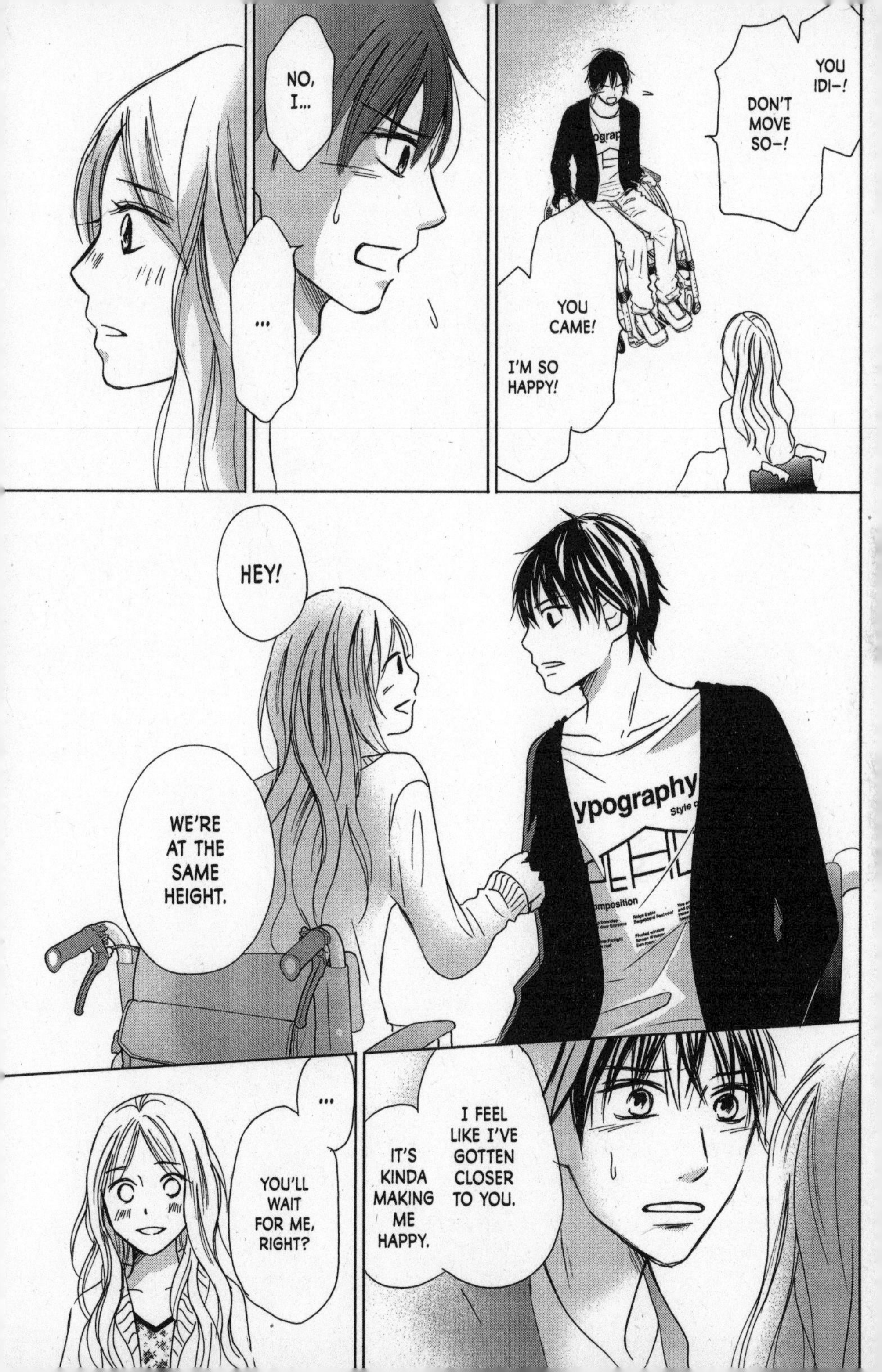
YOU IDI–!
DON'T MOVE SO–!
YOU CAME!
I'M SO HAPPY!
NO, I...
...
HEY!
WE'RE AT THE SAME HEIGHT.
I FEEL LIKE I'VE GOTTEN CLOSER TO YOU.
IT'S KINDA MAKING ME HAPPY.
...
YOU'LL WAIT FOR ME, RIGHT?

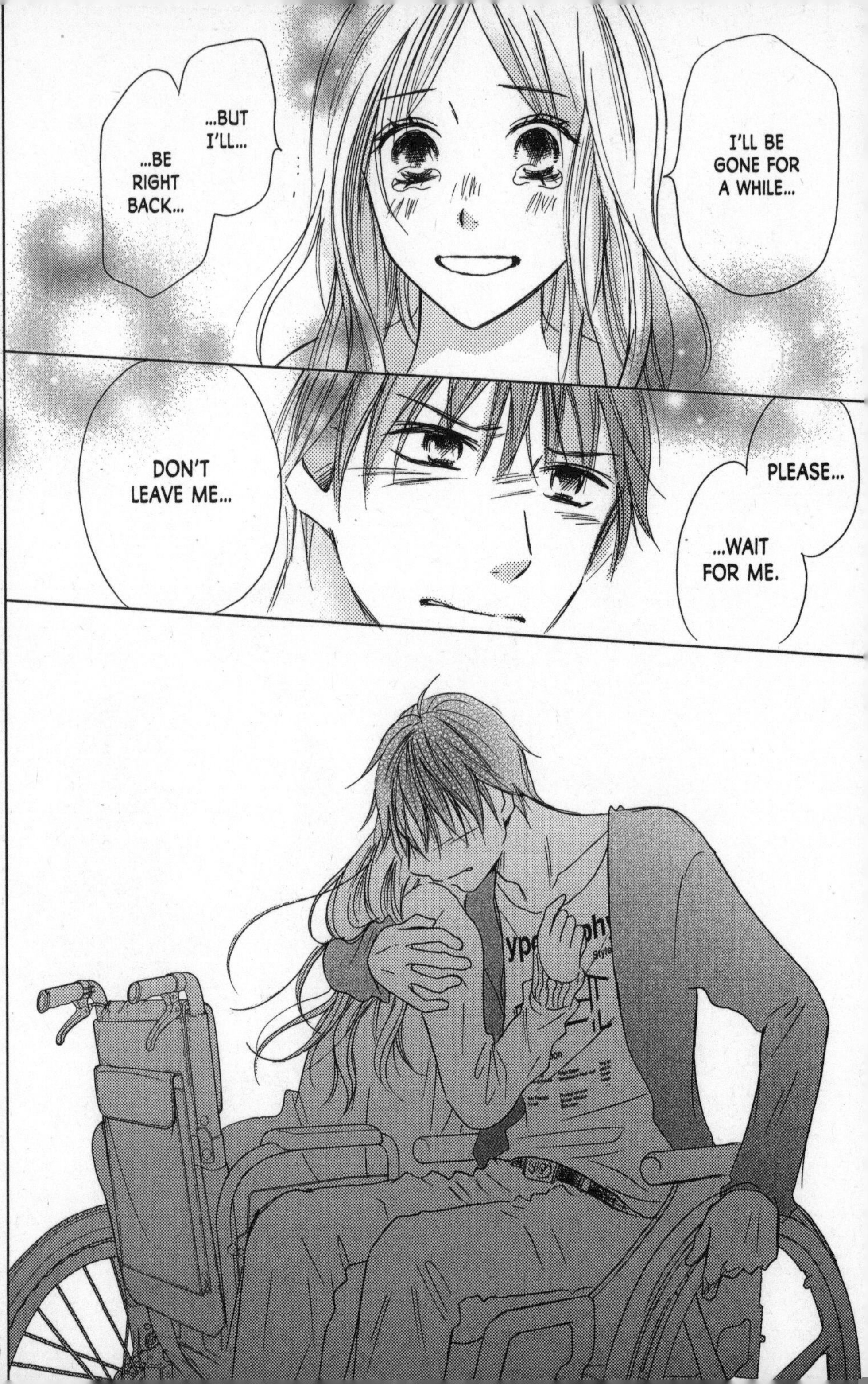
I'LL BE GONE FOR A WHILE...
...BUT I'LL...
...BE RIGHT BACK...
PLEASE...
...WAIT FOR ME.
DON'T LEAVE ME...

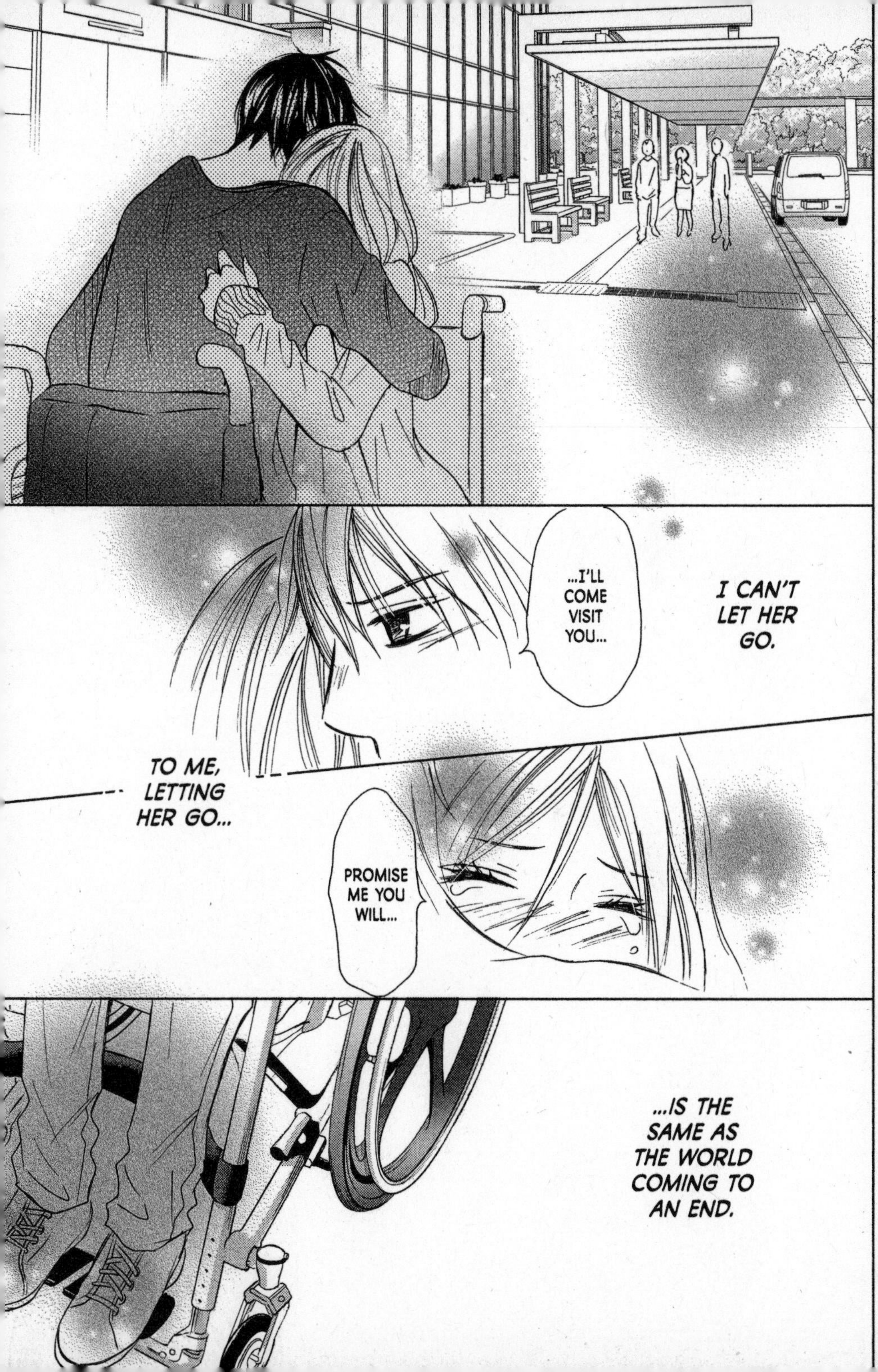
I CAN'T LET HER GO.
...I'LL COME VISIT YOU...
PROMISE ME YOU WILL...
TO ME, LETTING HER GO...
...IS THE SAME AS THE WORLD COMING TO AN END.

PERFECT WORLD

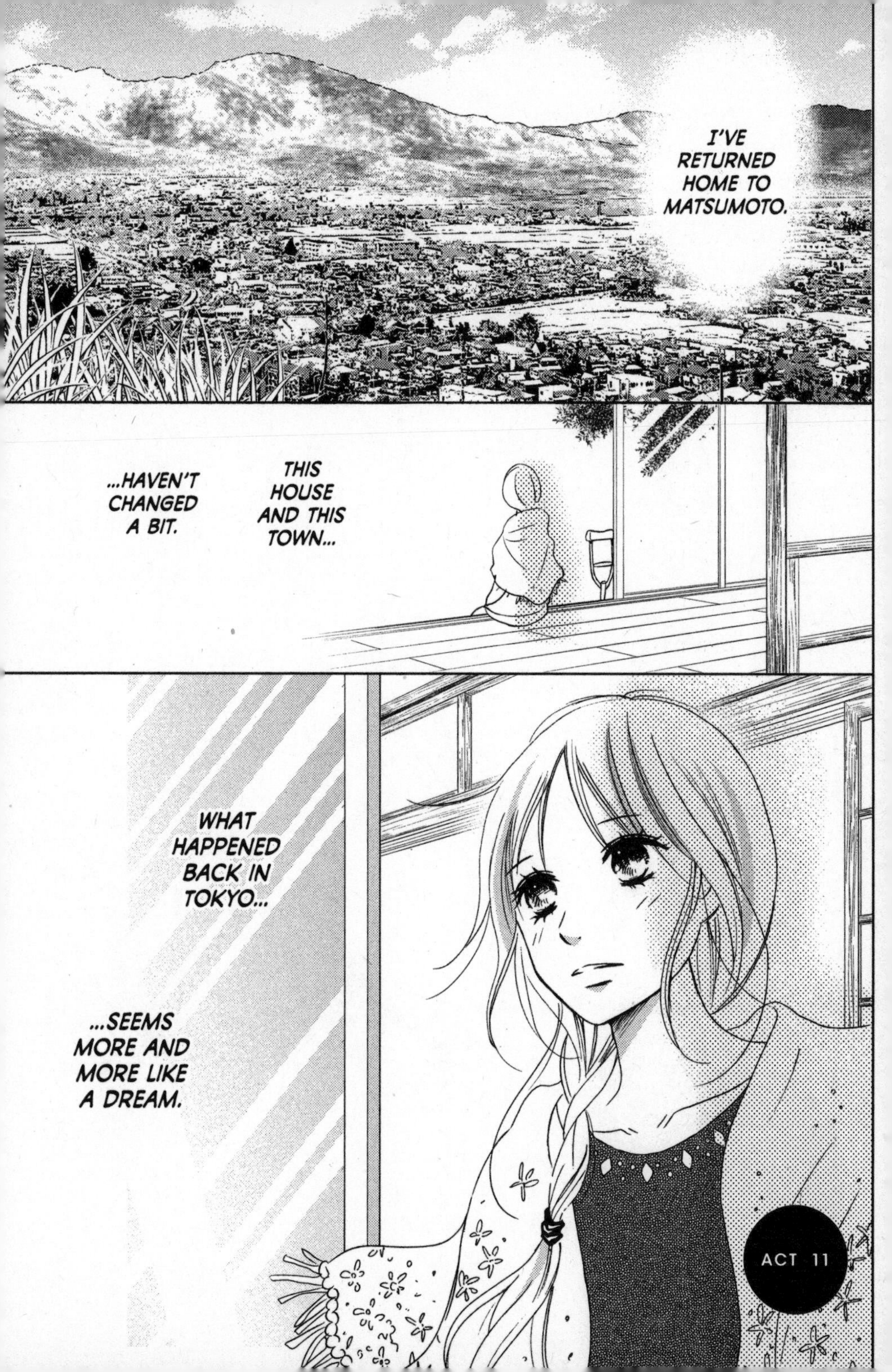
I'VE RETURNED HOME TO MATSUMOTO.
THIS HOUSE AND THIS TOWN...
...HAVEN'T CHANGED A BIT.
WHAT HAPPENED BACK IN TOKYO...
...SEEMS MORE AND MORE LIKE A DREAM.
ACT 11

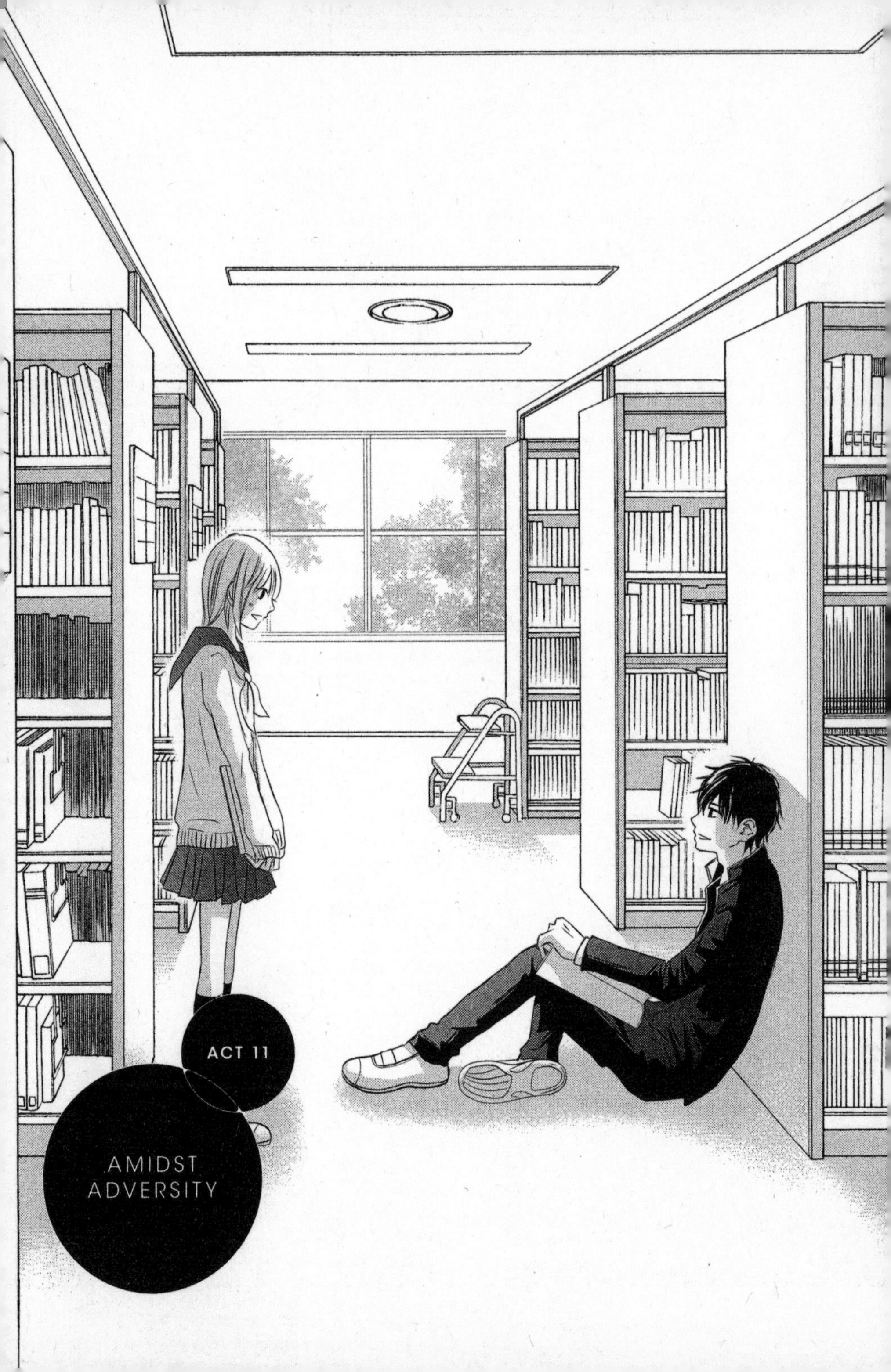
ACT 11
AMIDST ADVERSITY

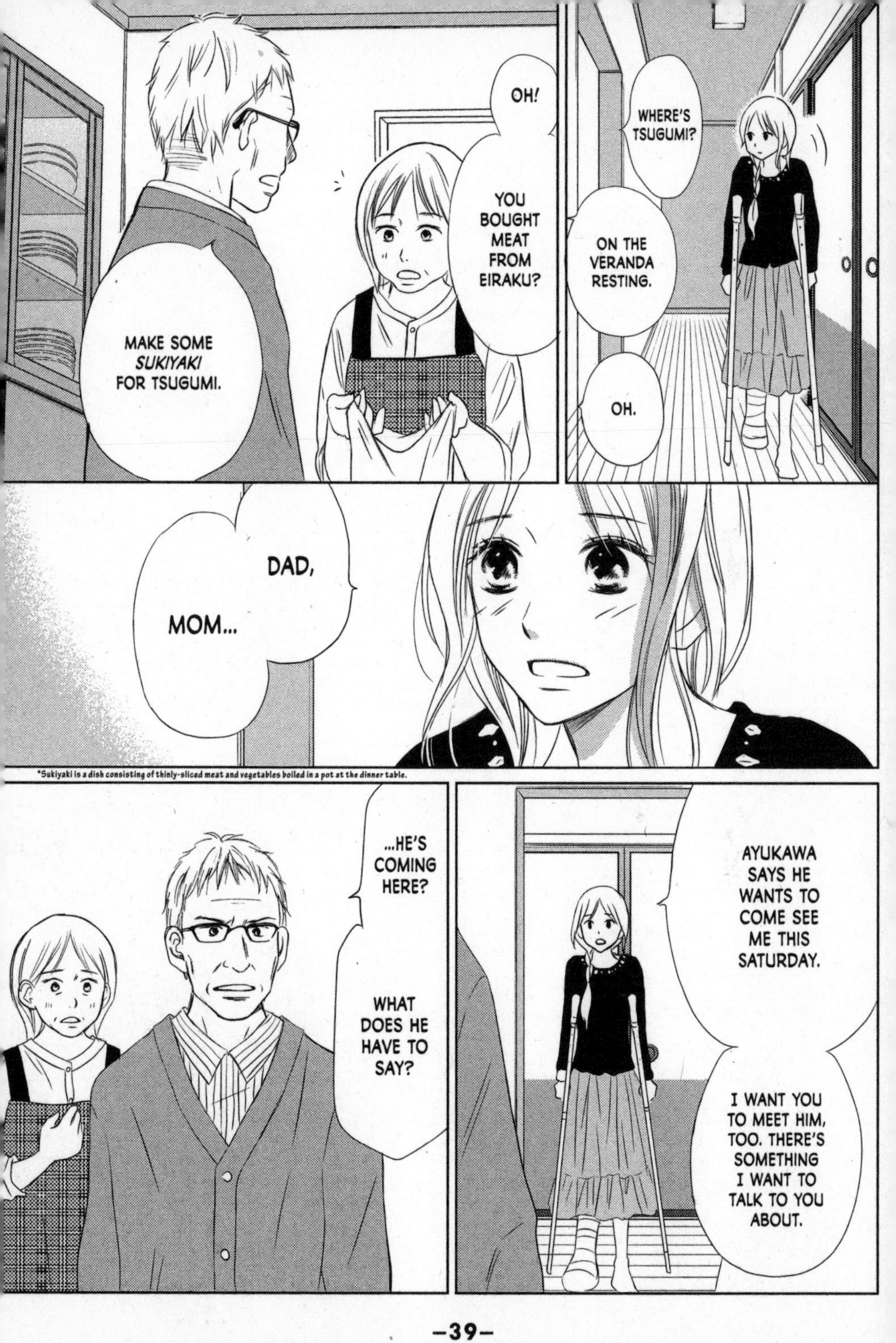
WHERE'S TSUGUMI?
ON THE VERANDA RESTING.
OH.
OH!
YOU BOUGHT MEAT FROM EIRAKU?
MAKE SOME *SUKIYAKI* FOR TSUGUMI.
DAD,
MOM...
AYUKAWA SAYS HE WANTS TO COME SEE ME THIS SATURDAY.
I WANT YOU TO MEET HIM, TOO. THERE'S SOMETHING I WANT TO TALK TO YOU ABOUT.
...HE'S COMING HERE?
WHAT DOES HE HAVE TO SAY?

*Sukiyaki is a dish consisting of thinly-sliced meat and vegetables boiled in a pot at the dinner table.

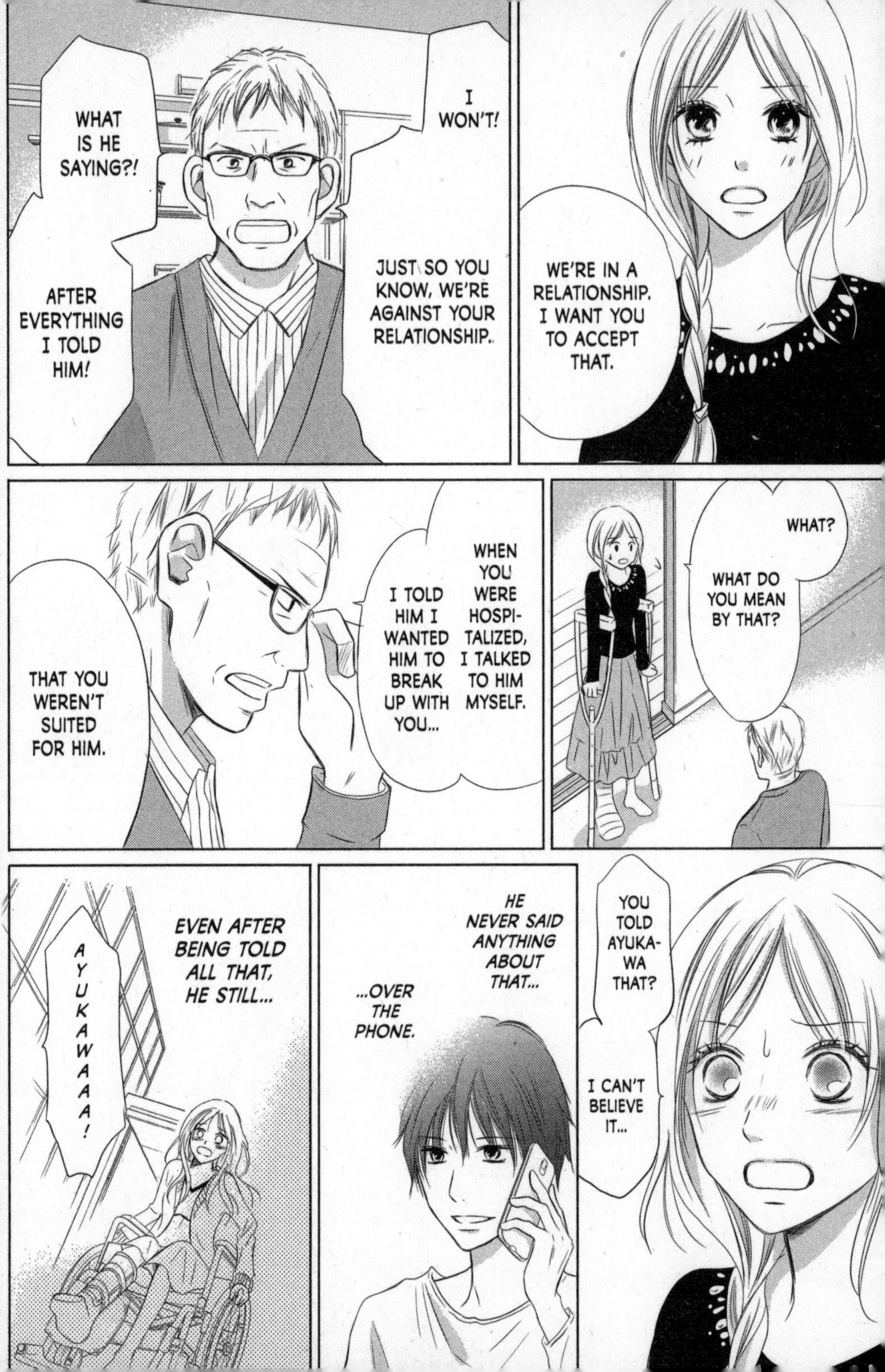
WE'RE IN A RELATIONSHIP. I WANT YOU TO ACCEPT THAT.
I WON'T!
JUST SO YOU KNOW, WE'RE AGAINST YOUR RELATIONSHIP.
WHAT IS HE SAYING?!
AFTER EVERYTHING I TOLD HIM!
WHAT?
WHAT DO YOU MEAN BY THAT?
WHEN YOU WERE HOSPI-TALIZED, I TALKED TO HIM MYSELF.
I TOLD HIM I WANTED HIM TO BREAK UP WITH YOU...
THAT YOU WEREN'T SUITED FOR HIM.
YOU TOLD AYUKA-WA THAT?
I CAN'T BELIEVE IT...
HE NEVER SAID ANYTHING ABOUT THAT...
...OVER THE PHONE.
EVEN AFTER BEING TOLD ALL THAT, HE STILL...
AYUKAWAAAA!

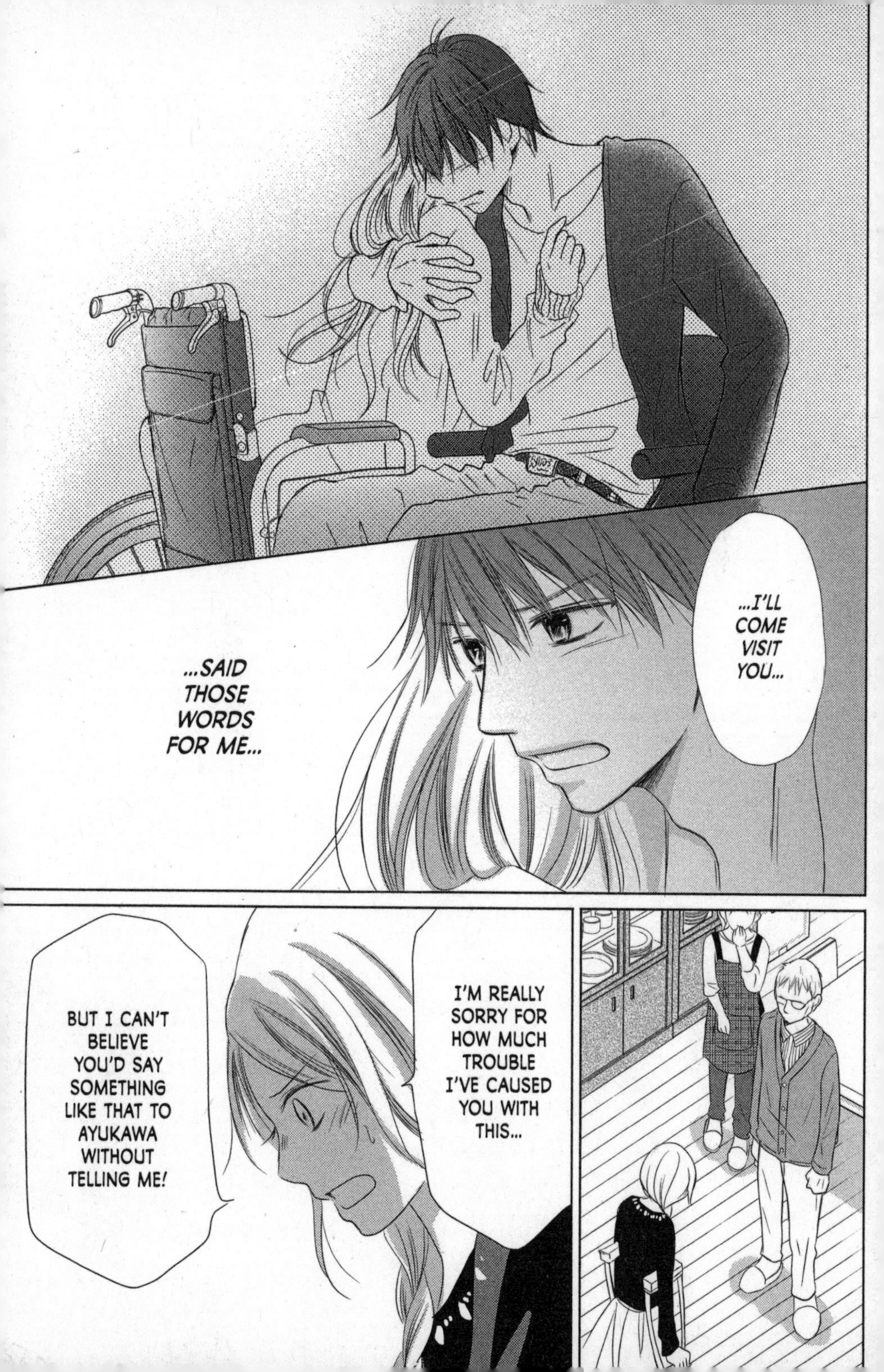
...I'LL COME VISIT YOU...
...SAID THOSE WORDS FOR ME...
I'M REALLY SORRY FOR HOW MUCH TROUBLE I'VE CAUSED YOU WITH THIS...
BUT I CAN'T BELIEVE YOU'D SAY SOMETHING LIKE THAT TO AYUKAWA WITHOUT TELLING ME!

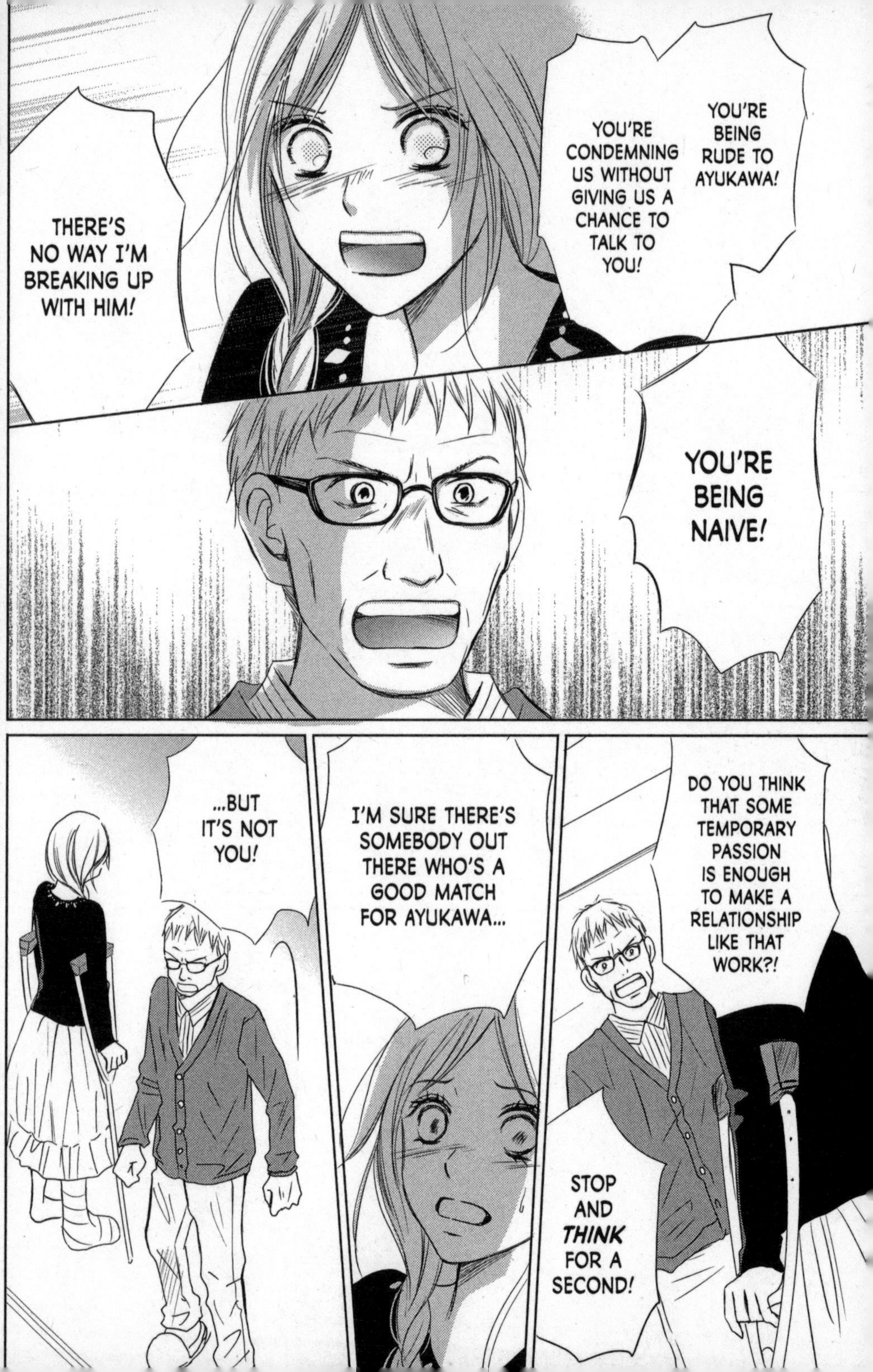
YOU'RE BEING RUDE TO AYUKAWA!
YOU'RE CONDEMNING US WITHOUT GIVING US A CHANCE TO TALK TO YOU!
THERE'S NO WAY I'M BREAKING UP WITH HIM!
YOU'RE BEING NAIVE!
DO YOU THINK THAT SOME TEMPORARY PASSION IS ENOUGH TO MAKE A RELATIONSHIP LIKE THAT WORK?!
STOP AND *THINK* FOR A SECOND!
I'M SURE THERE'S SOMEBODY OUT THERE WHO'S A GOOD MATCH FOR AYUKAWA...
...BUT IT'S NOT YOU!

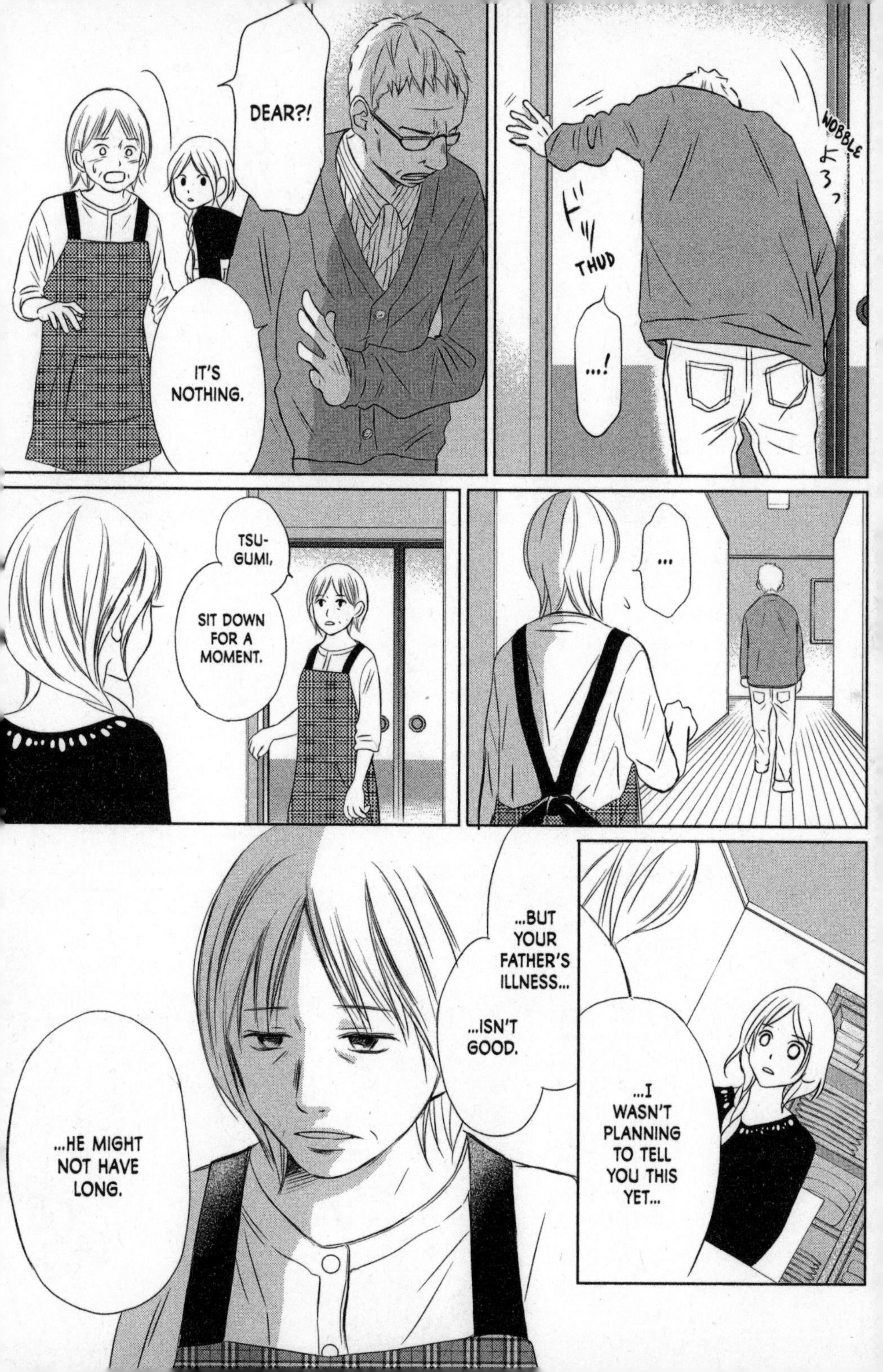
WOBBLE
よろっ
ドッ
THUD
...!
DEAR?!
IT'S NOTHING.
...
TSU-GUMI,
SIT DOWN FOR A MOMENT.
...I WASN'T PLANNING TO TELL YOU THIS YET...
...BUT YOUR FATHER'S ILLNESS...
...ISN'T GOOD.
...HE MIGHT NOT HAVE LONG.

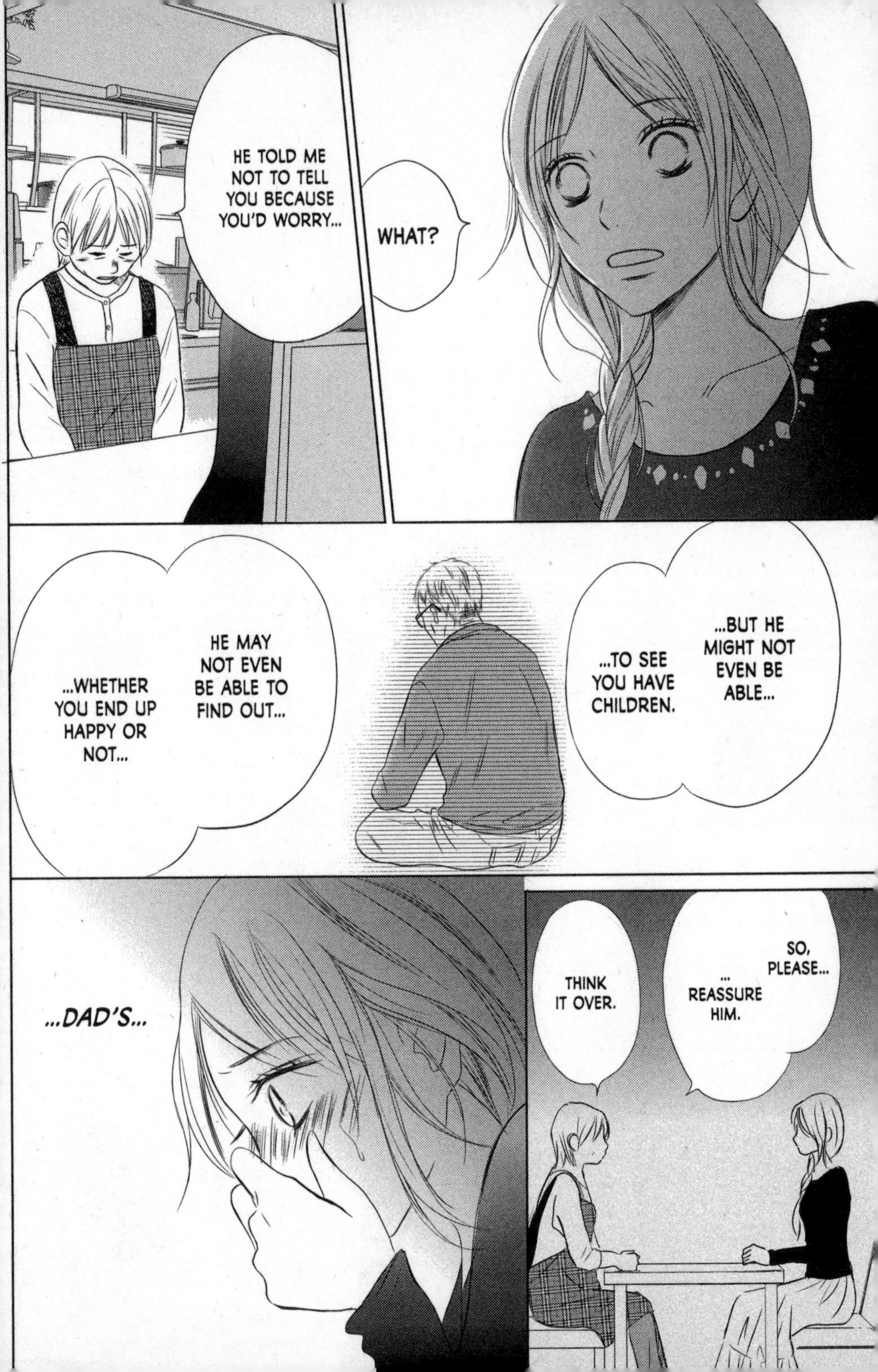
WHAT?
HE TOLD ME NOT TO TELL YOU BECAUSE YOU'D WORRY...
...BUT HE MIGHT NOT EVEN BE ABLE...
...TO SEE YOU HAVE CHILDREN.
HE MAY NOT EVEN BE ABLE TO FIND OUT...
...WHETHER YOU END UP HAPPY OR NOT...
SO, PLEASE...
... REASSURE HIM.
THINK IT OVER.
...DAD'S...

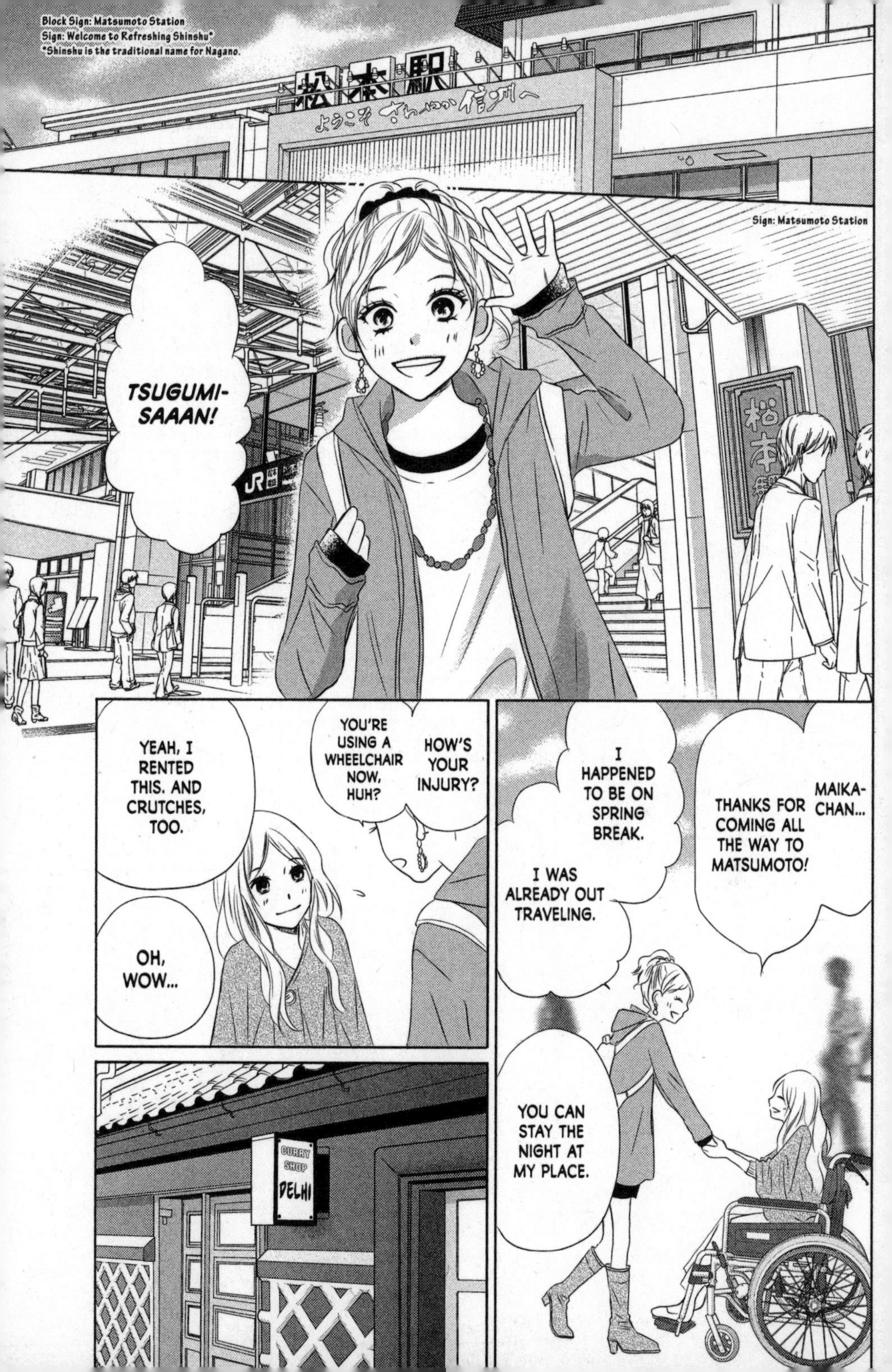
Block Sign: Matsumoto Station
Sign: Welcome to Refreshing Shinshu*
*Shinshu is the traditional name for Nagano.
松本駅
Sign: Matsumoto Station
TSUGUMI-SAAAN!
MAIKA-CHAN... THANKS FOR COMING ALL THE WAY TO MATSUMOTO!
I HAPPENED TO BE ON SPRING BREAK.
I WAS ALREADY OUT TRAVELING.
YOU CAN STAY THE NIGHT AT MY PLACE.
HOW'S YOUR INJURY?
YOU'RE USING A WHEELCHAIR NOW, HUH?
YEAH, I RENTED THIS. AND CRUTCHES, TOO.
OH, WOW...
CURRY SHOP
DELHI

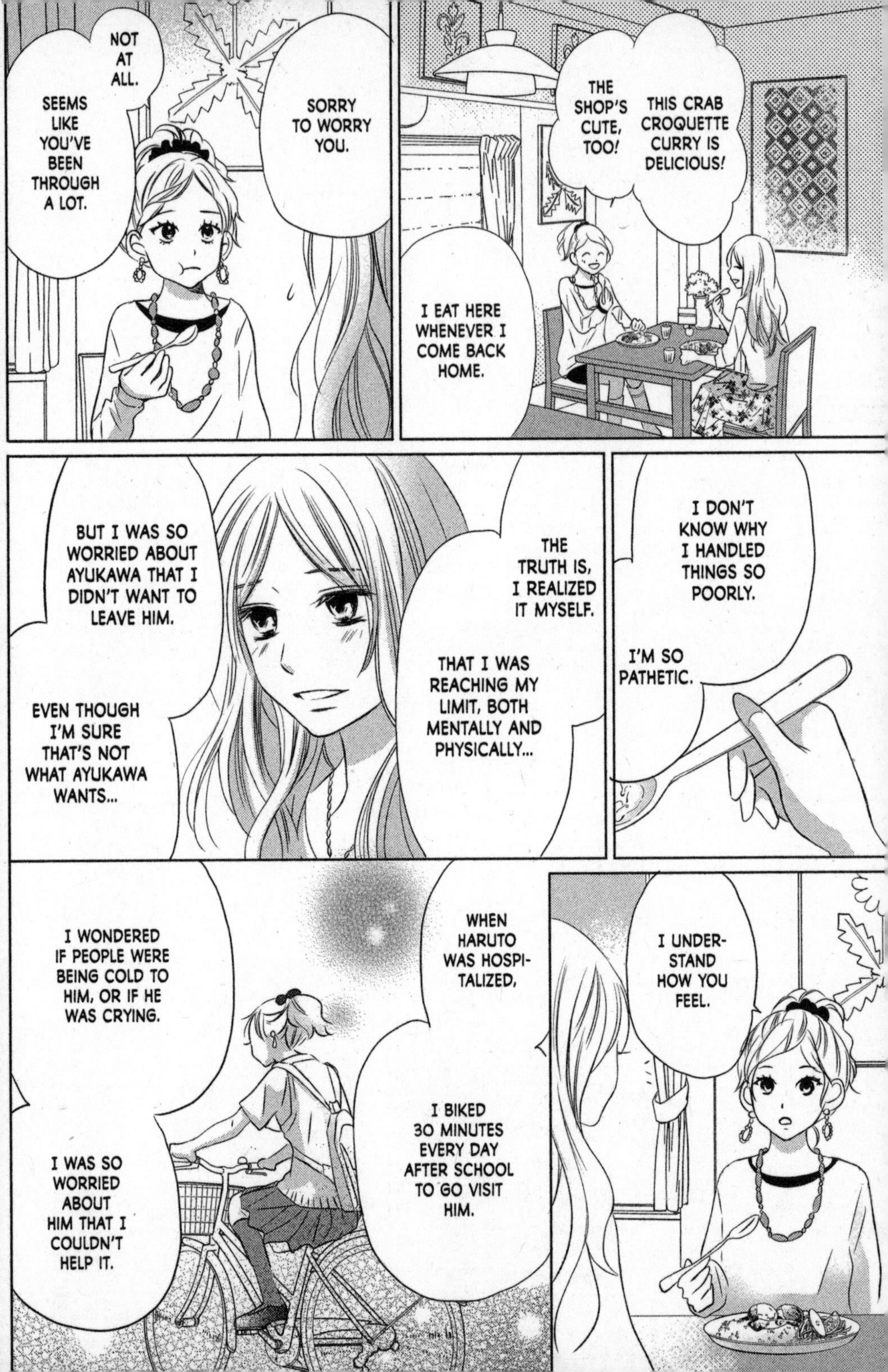
THIS CRAB CROQUETTE CURRY IS DELICIOUS!
THE SHOP'S CUTE, TOO!
I EAT HERE WHENEVER I COME BACK HOME.
SORRY TO WORRY YOU.
NOT AT ALL.
SEEMS LIKE YOU'VE BEEN THROUGH A LOT.
I DON'T KNOW WHY I HANDLED THINGS SO POORLY.
I'M SO PATHETIC.
THE TRUTH IS, I REALIZED IT MYSELF.
THAT I WAS REACHING MY LIMIT, BOTH MENTALLY AND PHYSICALLY...
BUT I WAS SO WORRIED ABOUT AYUKAWA THAT I DIDN'T WANT TO LEAVE HIM.
EVEN THOUGH I'M SURE THAT'S NOT WHAT AYUKAWA WANTS...
I UNDER-STAND HOW YOU FEEL.
WHEN HARUTO WAS HOSPI-TALIZED,
I BIKED 30 MINUTES EVERY DAY AFTER SCHOOL TO GO VISIT HIM.
I WONDERED IF PEOPLE WERE BEING COLD TO HIM, OR IF HE WAS CRYING.
I WAS SO WORRIED ABOUT HIM THAT I COULDN'T HELP IT.

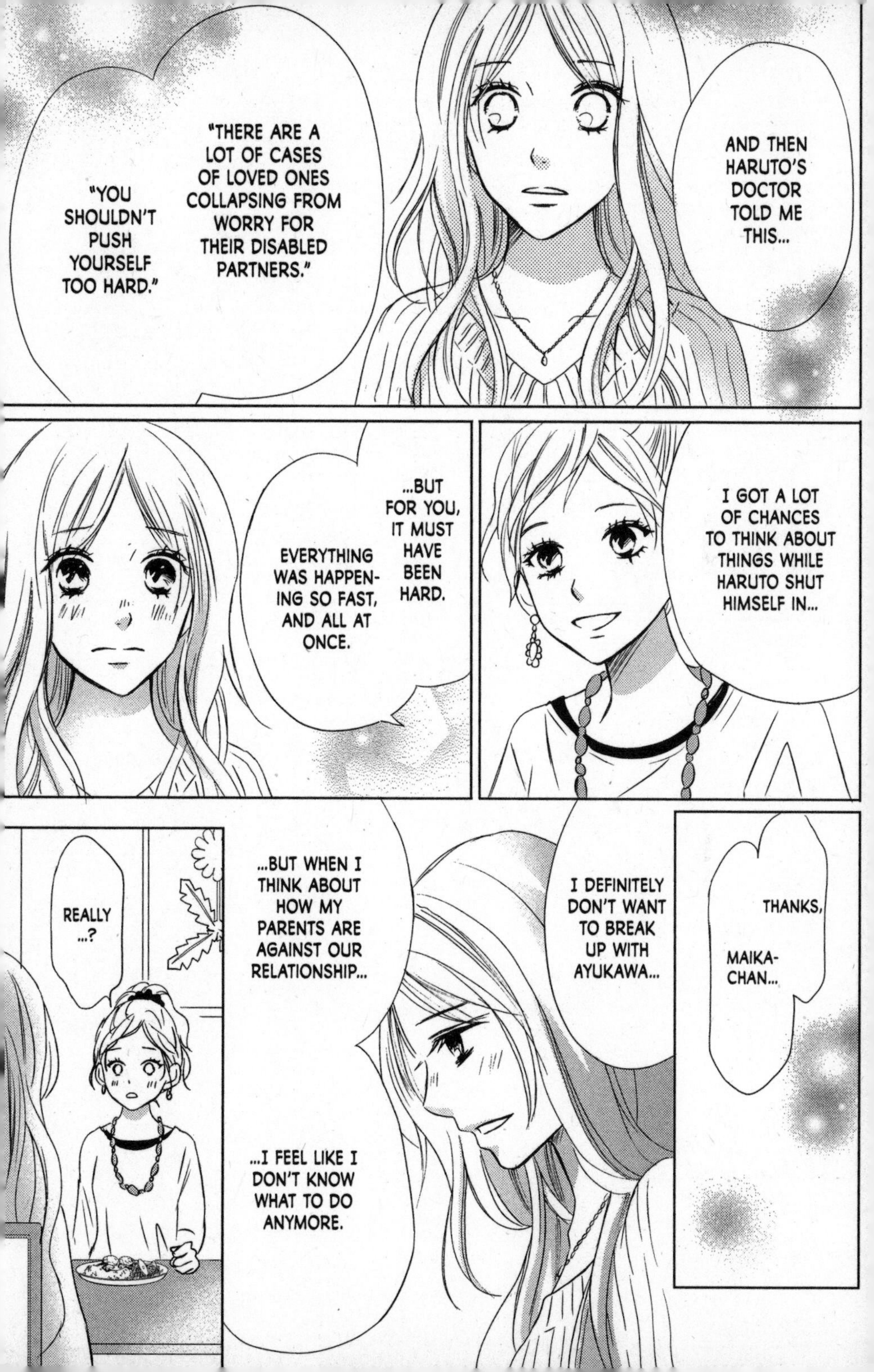
AND THEN HARUTO'S DOCTOR TOLD ME THIS...
"THERE ARE A LOT OF CASES OF LOVED ONES COLLAPSING FROM WORRY FOR THEIR DISABLED PARTNERS."
"YOU SHOULDN'T PUSH YOURSELF TOO HARD."
I GOT A LOT OF CHANCES TO THINK ABOUT THINGS WHILE HARUTO SHUT HIMSELF IN...
...BUT FOR YOU, IT MUST HAVE BEEN HARD.
EVERYTHING WAS HAPPEN-ING SO FAST, AND ALL AT ONCE.
THANKS, MAIKA-CHAN...
I DEFINITELY DON'T WANT TO BREAK UP WITH AYUKAWA...
...BUT WHEN I THINK ABOUT HOW MY PARENTS ARE AGAINST OUR RELATIONSHIP...
...I FEEL LIKE I DON'T KNOW WHAT TO DO ANYMORE.
REALLY ...?

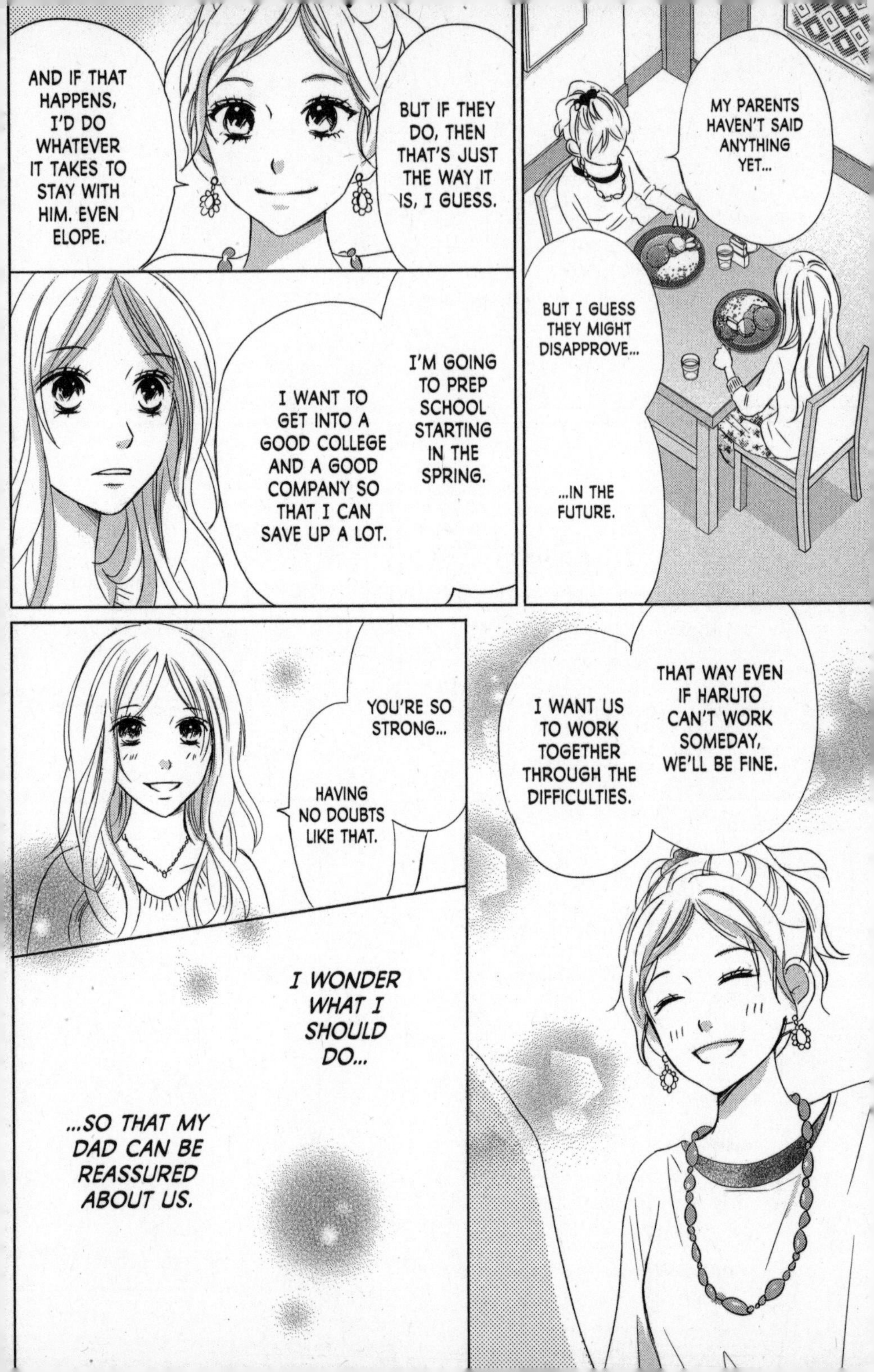
MY PARENTS HAVEN'T SAID ANYTHING YET...
BUT I GUESS THEY MIGHT DISAPPROVE...
...IN THE FUTURE.
BUT IF THEY DO, THEN THAT'S JUST THE WAY IT IS, I GUESS.
AND IF THAT HAPPENS, I'D DO WHATEVER IT TAKES TO STAY WITH HIM. EVEN ELOPE.
I'M GOING TO PREP SCHOOL STARTING IN THE SPRING.
I WANT TO GET INTO A GOOD COLLEGE AND A GOOD COMPANY SO THAT I CAN SAVE UP A LOT.
THAT WAY EVEN IF HARUTO CAN'T WORK SOMEDAY, WE'LL BE FINE.
I WANT US TO WORK TOGETHER THROUGH THE DIFFICULTIES.
YOU'RE SO STRONG...
HAVING NO DOUBTS LIKE THAT.
I WONDER WHAT I SHOULD DO...
...SO THAT MY DAD CAN BE REASSURED ABOUT US.

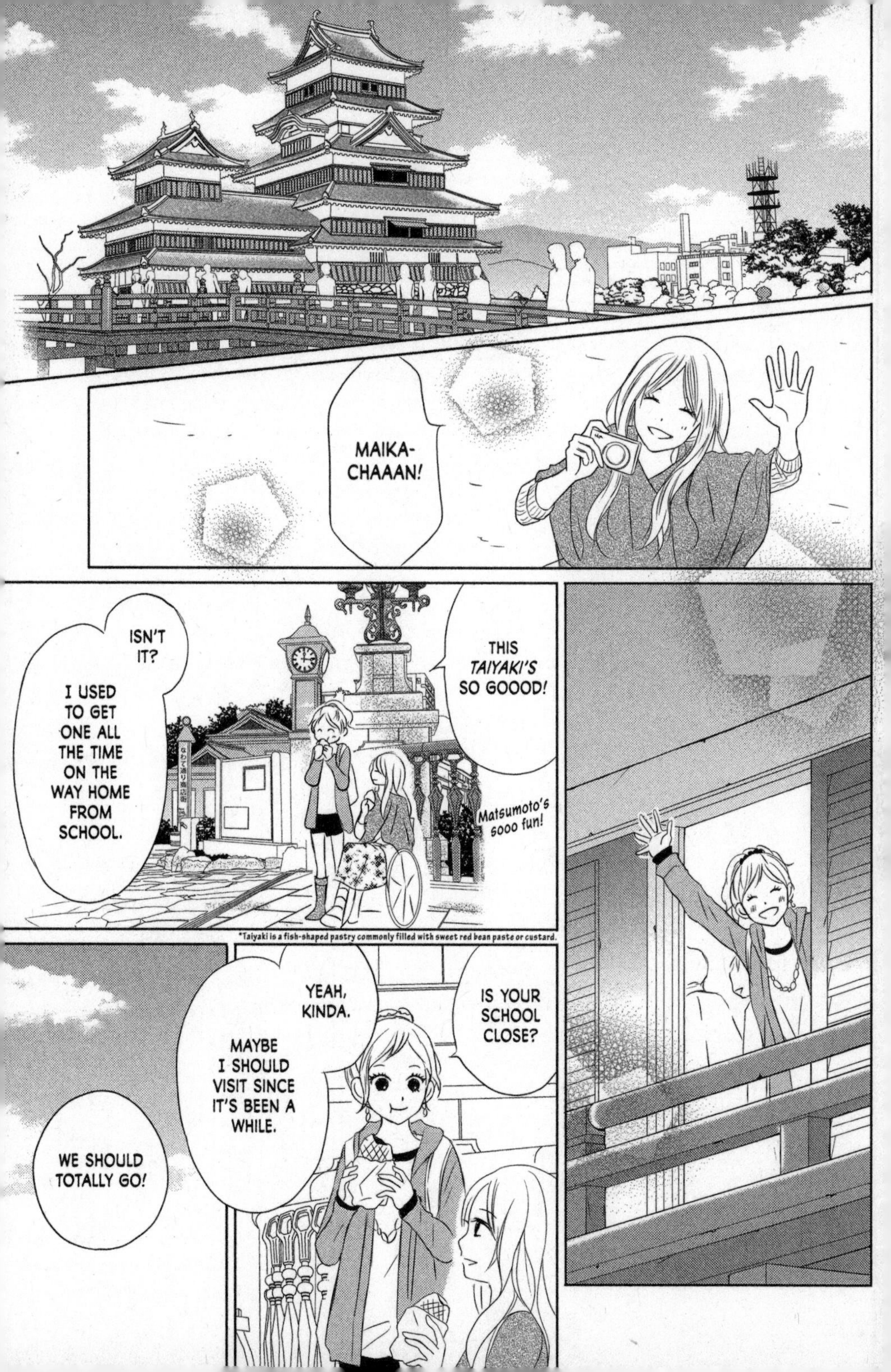
MAIKA-CHAAAN!
THIS *TAIYAKI'S* SO GOOOD!
Matsumoto's sooo fun!
ISN'T IT?
I USED TO GET ONE ALL THE TIME ON THE WAY HOME FROM SCHOOL.
IS YOUR SCHOOL CLOSE?
YEAH, KINDA.
MAYBE I SHOULD VISIT SINCE IT'S BEEN A WHILE.
WE SHOULD TOTALLY GO!

*Taiyaki is a fish-shaped pastry commonly filled with sweet red bean paste or custard.

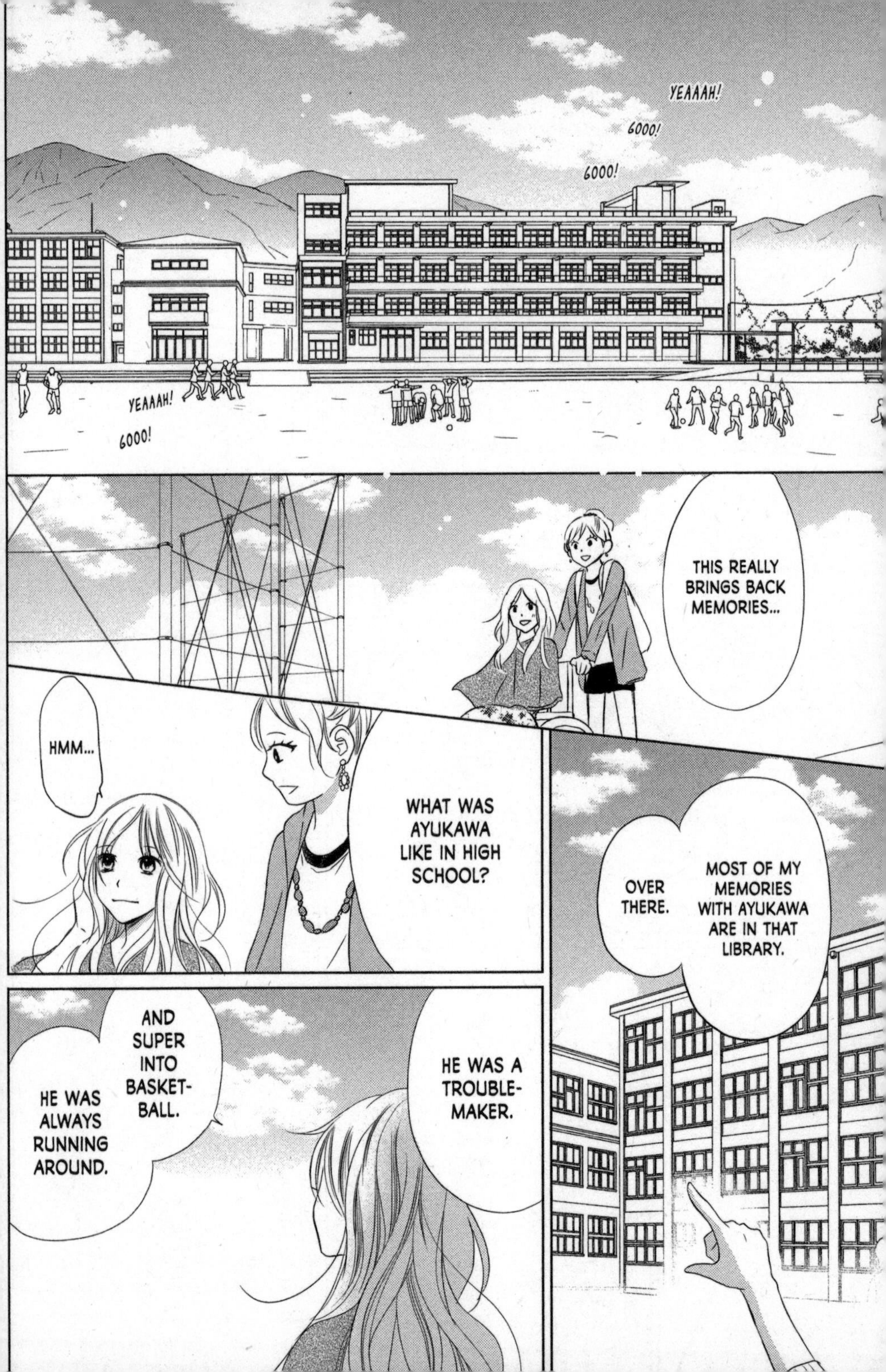
YEAAAH!
GOOO!
GOOO!
YEAAAH!
GOOO!
THIS REALLY BRINGS BACK MEMORIES...
MOST OF MY MEMORIES WITH AYUKAWA ARE IN THAT LIBRARY.
OVER THERE.
WHAT WAS AYUKAWA LIKE IN HIGH SCHOOL?
HMM...
HE WAS A TROUBLE-MAKER.
AND SUPER INTO BASKET-BALL.
HE WAS ALWAYS RUNNING AROUND.

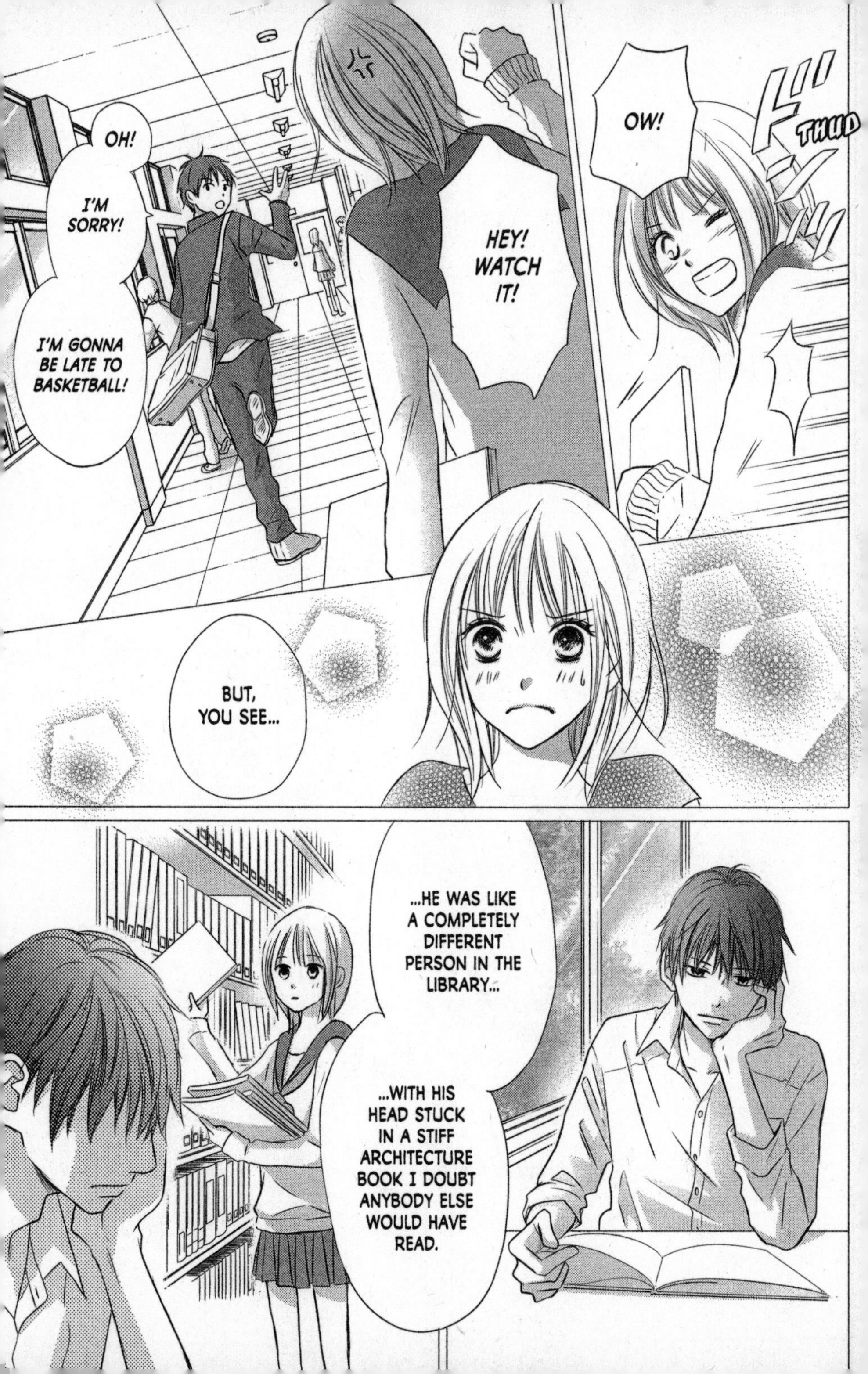
OW!
THUD
OH!
I'M SORRY!
I'M GONNA BE LATE TO BASKETBALL!
HEY! WATCH IT!
BUT, YOU SEE...
...HE WAS LIKE A COMPLETELY DIFFERENT PERSON IN THE LIBRARY...
...WITH HIS HEAD STUCK IN A STIFF ARCHITECTURE BOOK I DOUBT ANYBODY ELSE WOULD HAVE READ.

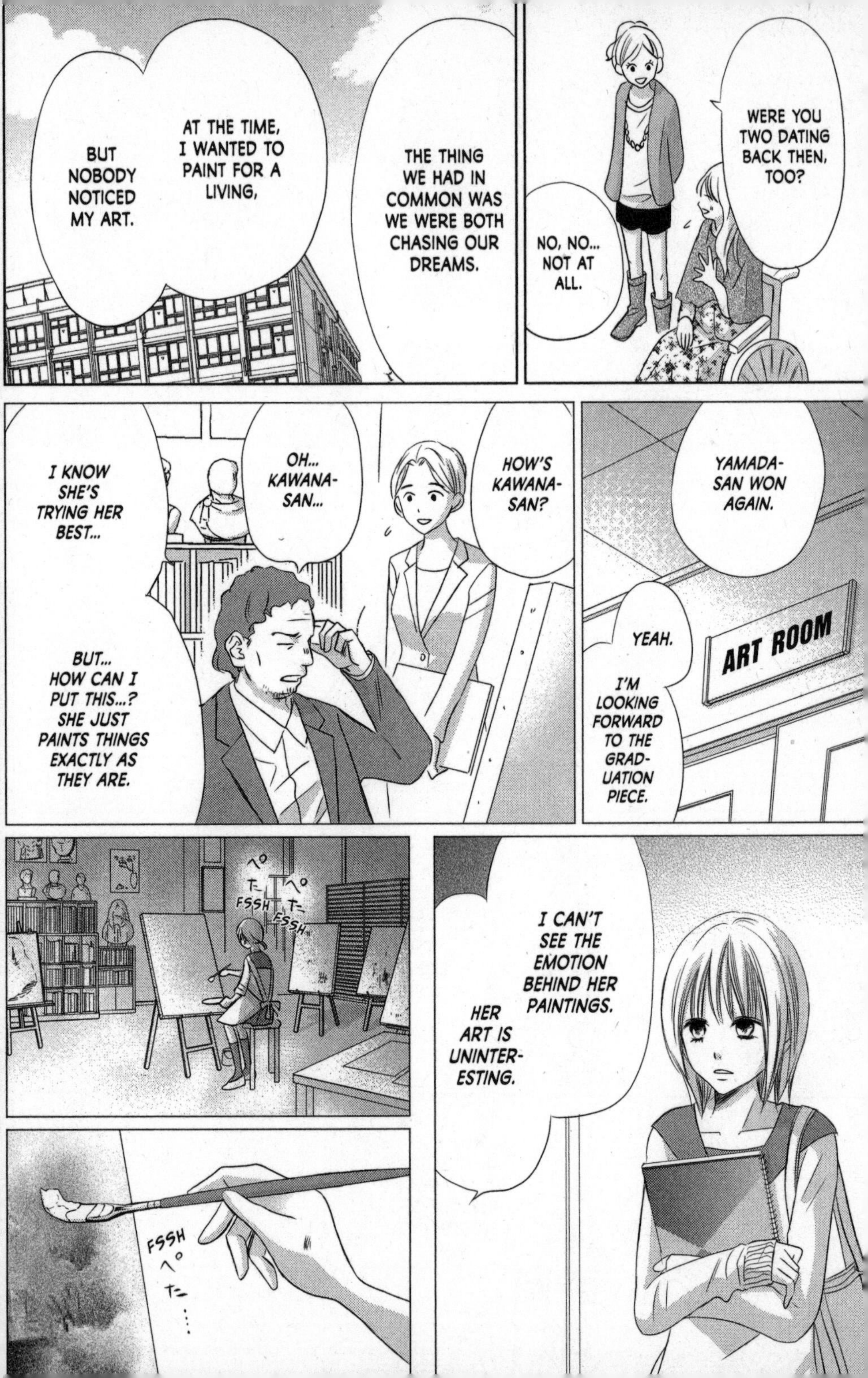
WERE YOU TWO DATING BACK THEN, TOO?
NO, NO... NOT AT ALL.
THE THING WE HAD IN COMMON WAS WE WERE BOTH CHASING OUR DREAMS.
AT THE TIME, I WANTED TO PAINT FOR A LIVING,
BUT NOBODY NOTICED MY ART.
YAMADA-SAN WON AGAIN.
YEAH.
I'M LOOKING FORWARD TO THE GRADUATION PIECE.
ART ROOM
HOW'S KAWANA-SAN?
OH... KAWANA-SAN...
I KNOW SHE'S TRYING HER BEST...
BUT... HOW CAN I PUT THIS...? SHE JUST PAINTS THINGS EXACTLY AS THEY ARE.
I CAN'T SEE THE EMOTION BEHIND HER PAINTINGS.
HER ART IS UNINTERESTING.
ぺた FSSH
ぺた FSSH
FSSH
ぺた....

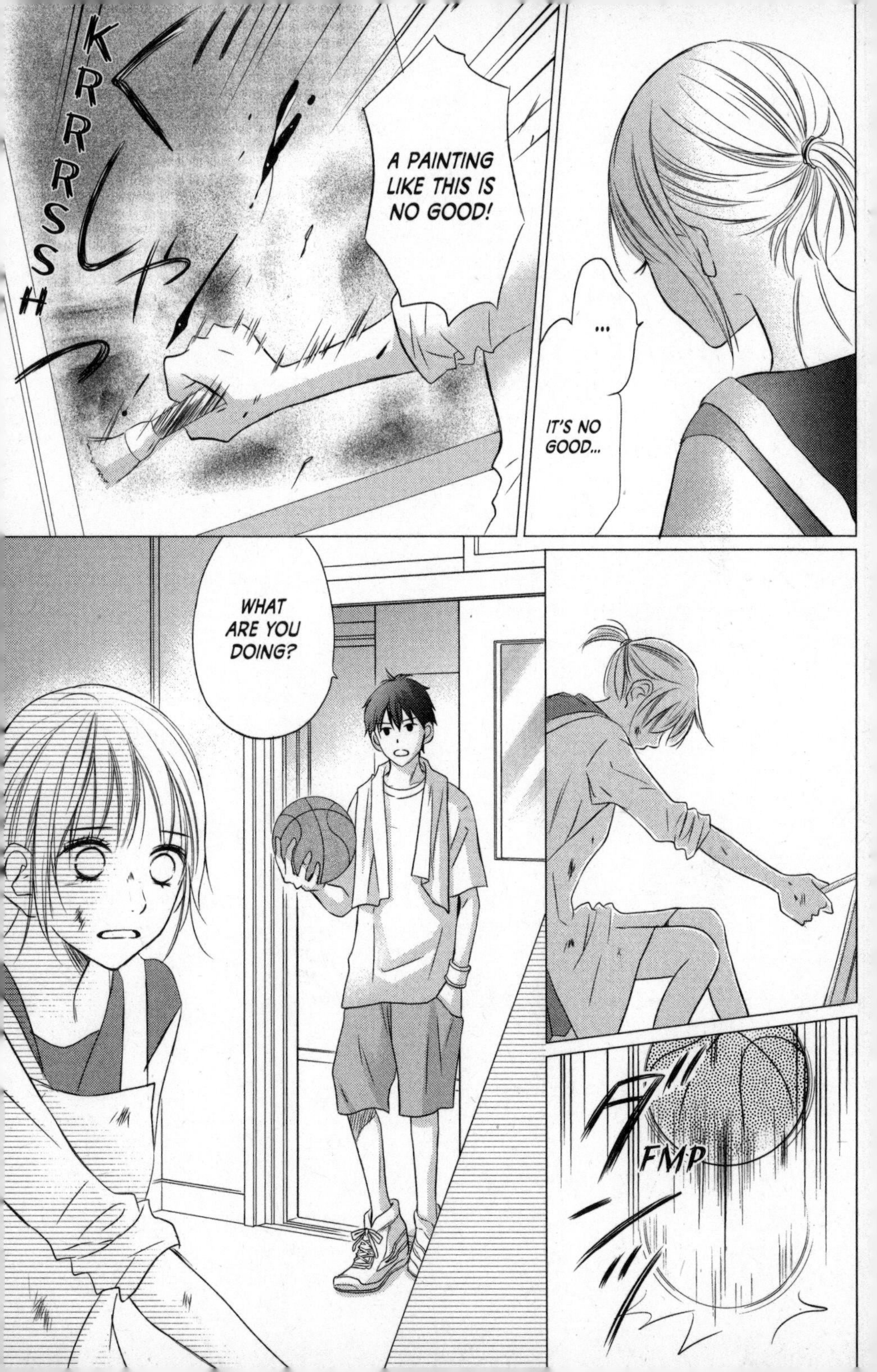
...
IT'S NO GOOD...
A PAINTING LIKE THIS IS NO GOOD!
KRRRSSH
FMP
WHAT ARE YOU DOING?

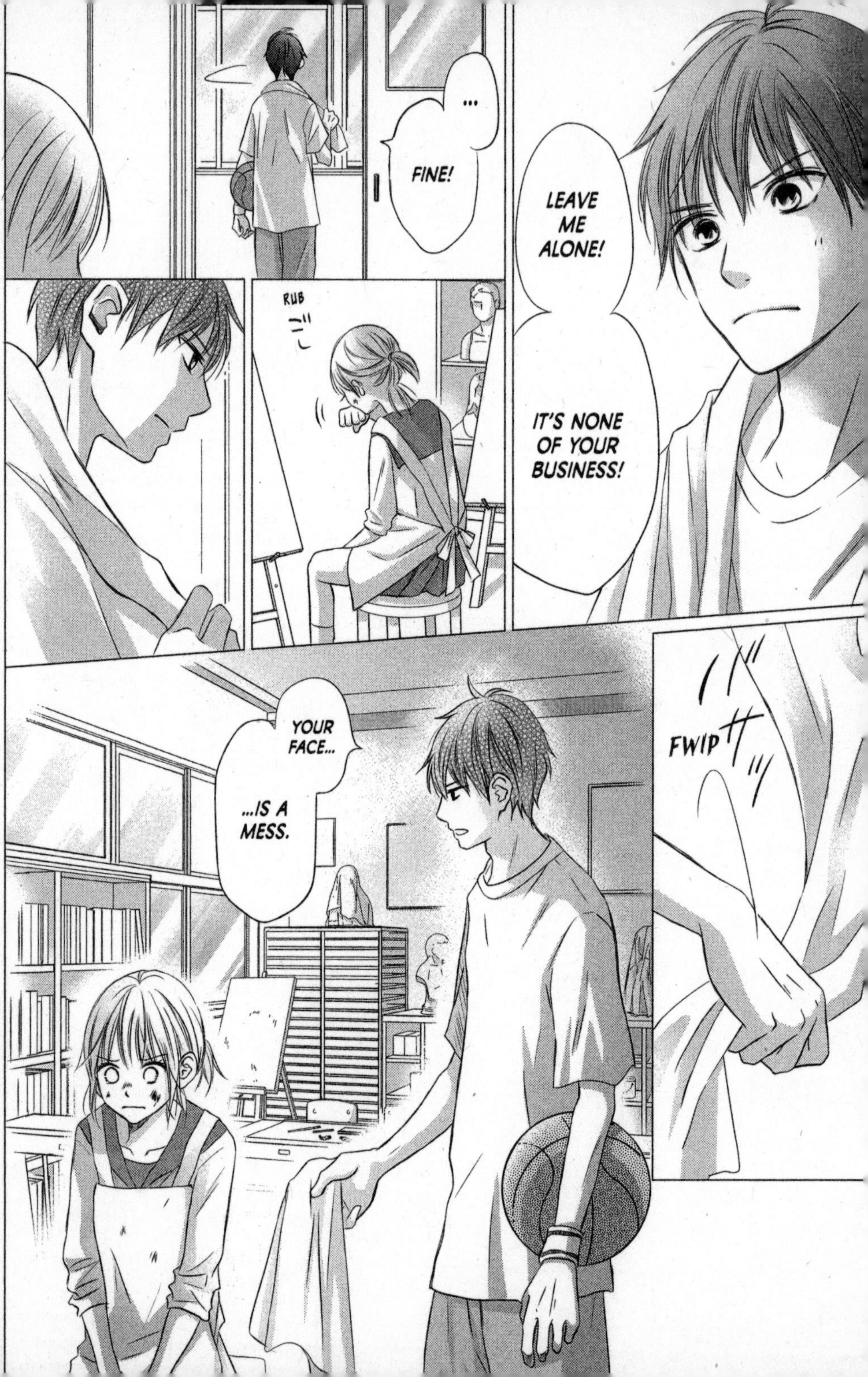
LEAVE ME ALONE!
IT'S NONE OF YOUR BUSINESS!
...
FINE!
RUB
ごし
FWIP
YOUR FACE...
...IS A MESS.

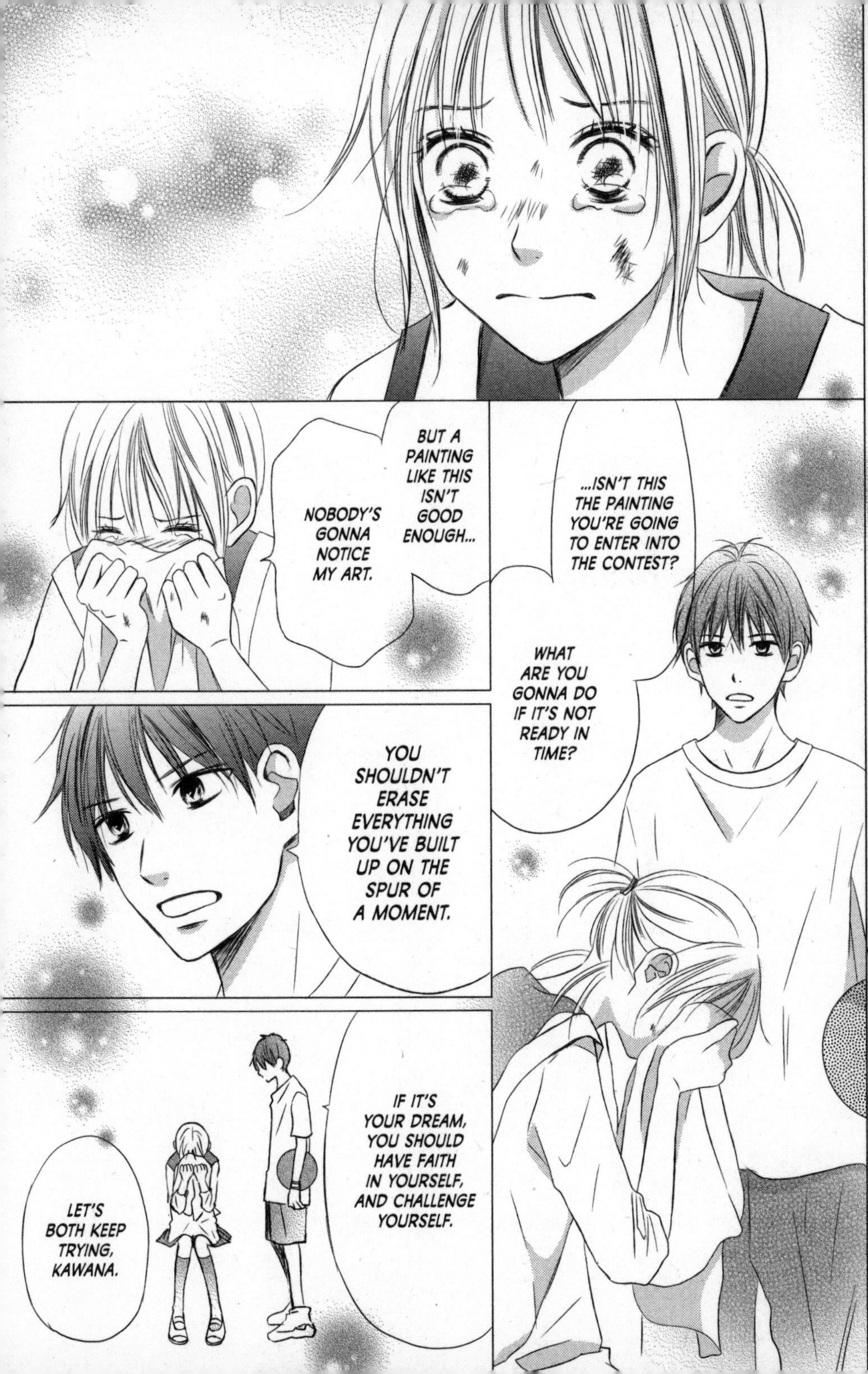
...ISN'T THIS THE PAINTING YOU'RE GOING TO ENTER INTO THE CONTEST?
WHAT ARE YOU GONNA DO IF IT'S NOT READY IN TIME?
BUT A PAINTING LIKE THIS ISN'T GOOD ENOUGH...
NOBODY'S GONNA NOTICE MY ART.
YOU SHOULDN'T ERASE EVERYTHING YOU'VE BUILT UP ON THE SPUR OF A MOMENT.
IF IT'S YOUR DREAM, YOU SHOULD HAVE FAITH IN YOURSELF, AND CHALLENGE YOURSELF.
LET'S BOTH KEEP TRYING, KAWANA.

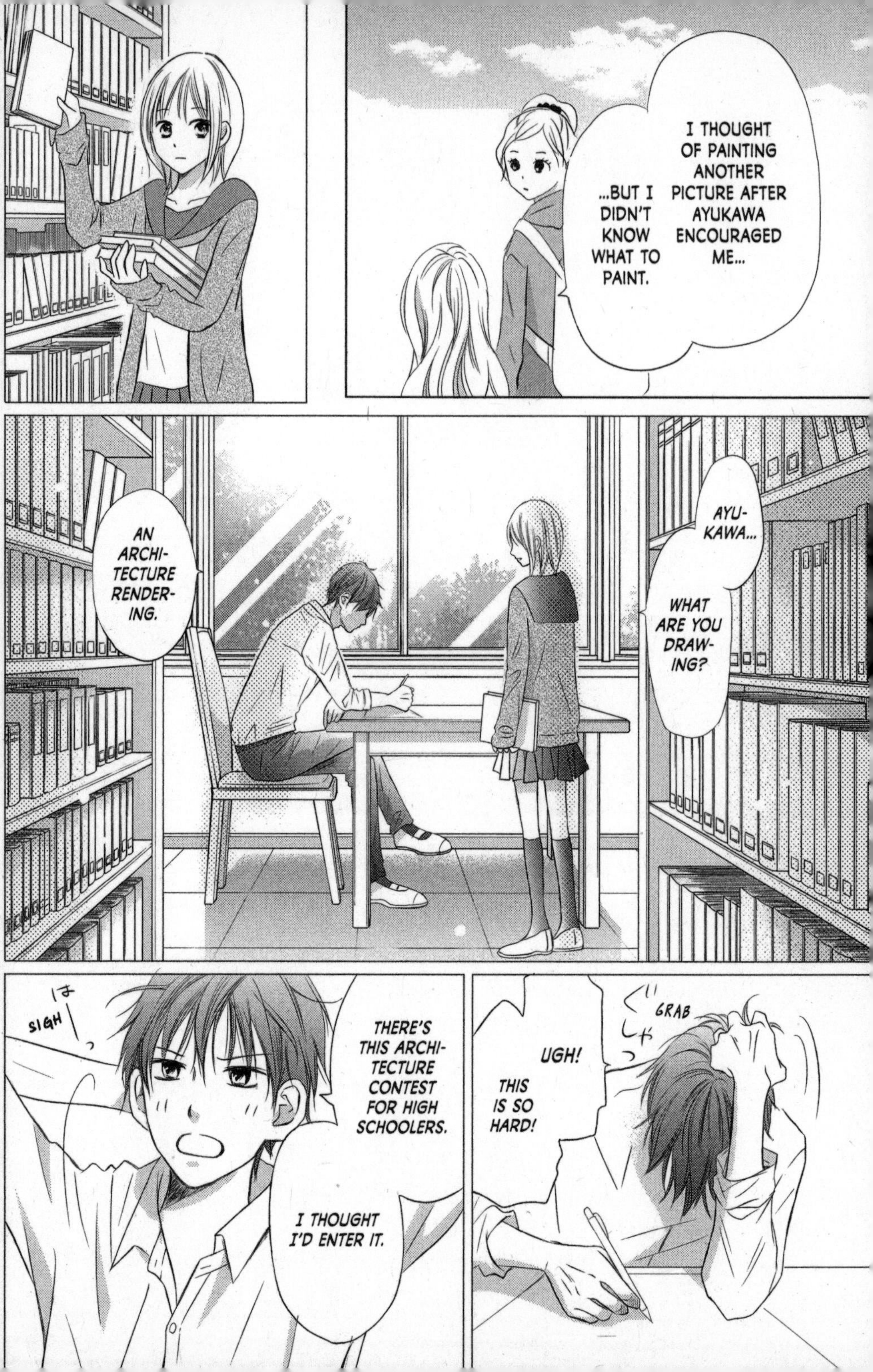
I THOUGHT OF PAINTING ANOTHER PICTURE AFTER AYUKAWA ENCOURAGED ME...
...BUT I DIDN'T KNOW WHAT TO PAINT.
AYU-KAWA...
WHAT ARE YOU DRAW-ING?
AN ARCHI-TECTURE RENDER-ING.
GRAB
UGH!
THIS IS SO HARD!
THERE'S THIS ARCHI-TECTURE CONTEST FOR HIGH SCHOOLERS.
I THOUGHT I'D ENTER IT.
はーっ
SIGH

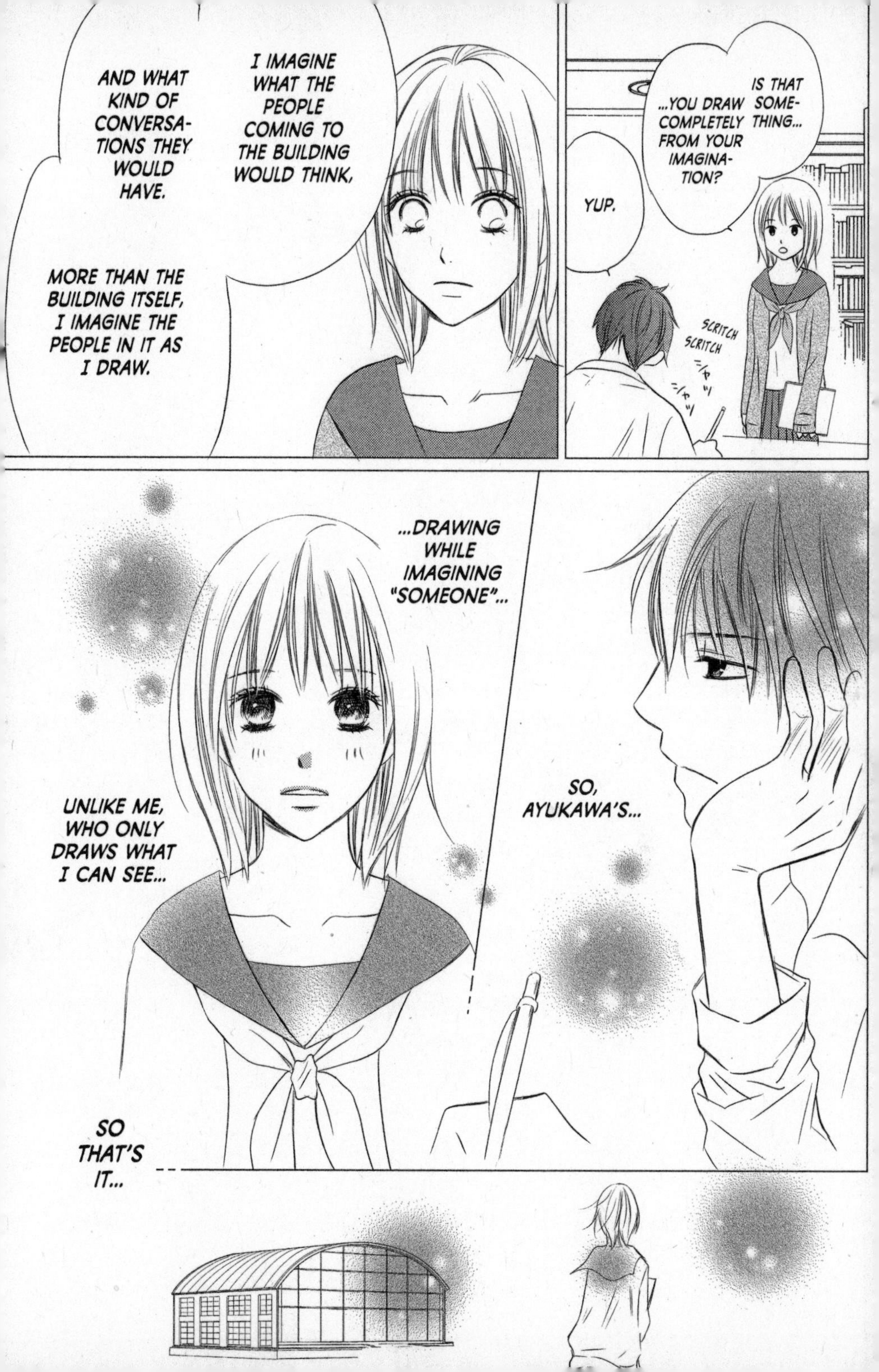
IS THAT SOMETHING...
...YOU DRAW COMPLETELY FROM YOUR IMAGINATION?
YUP.
SCRITCH SCRITCH
I IMAGINE WHAT THE PEOPLE COMING TO THE BUILDING WOULD THINK,
AND WHAT KIND OF CONVERSATIONS THEY WOULD HAVE.
MORE THAN THE BUILDING ITSELF, I IMAGINE THE PEOPLE IN IT AS I DRAW.
SO, AYUKAWA'S...
...DRAWING WHILE IMAGINING "SOMEONE"...
UNLIKE ME, WHO ONLY DRAWS WHAT I CAN SEE...
SO THAT'S IT...

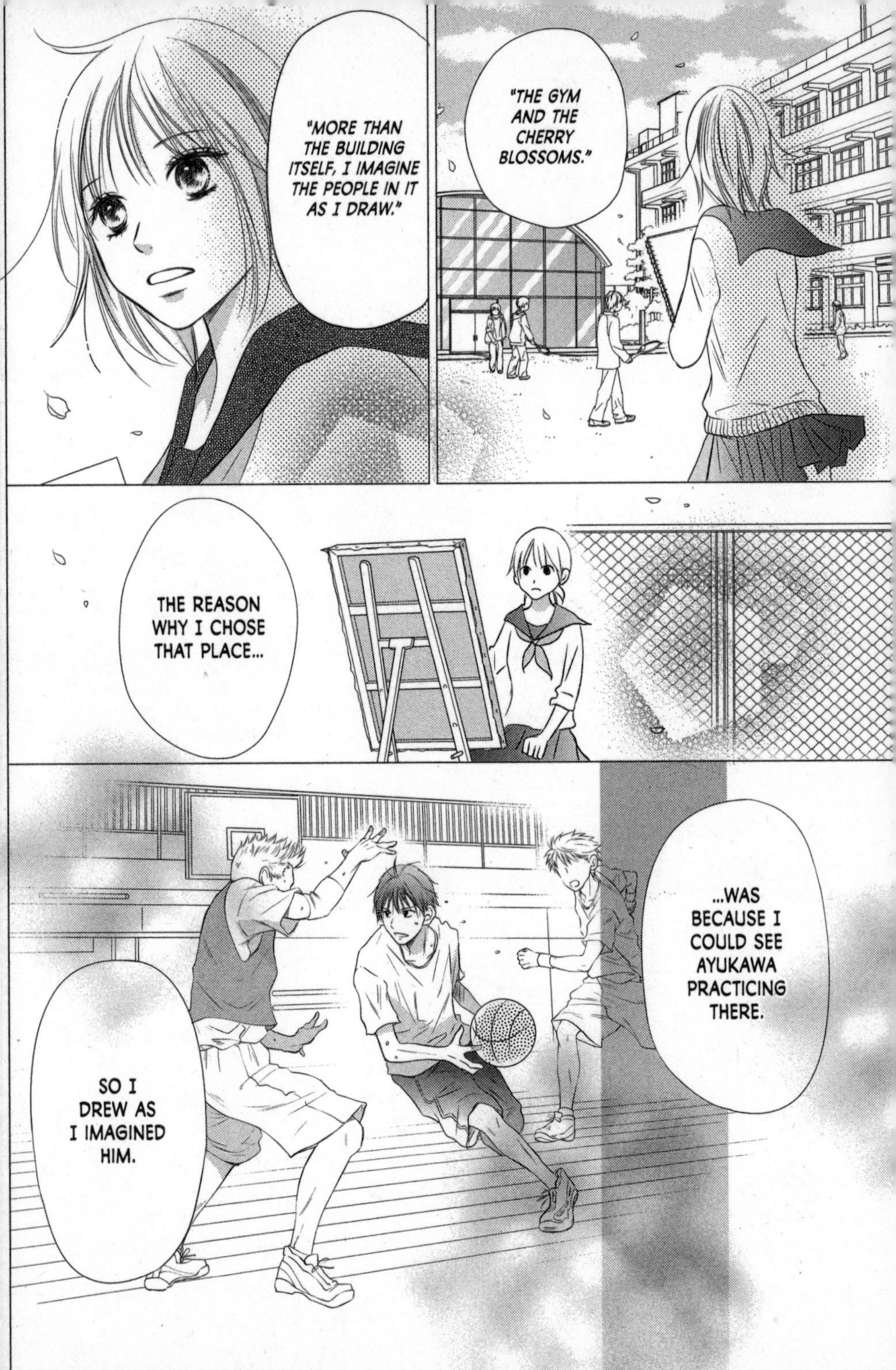
"THE GYM AND THE CHERRY BLOSSOMS."
"MORE THAN THE BUILDING ITSELF, I IMAGINE THE PEOPLE IN IT AS I DRAW."
THE REASON WHY I CHOSE THAT PLACE...
...WAS BECAUSE I COULD SEE AYUKAWA PRACTICING THERE.
SO I DREW AS I IMAGINED HIM.

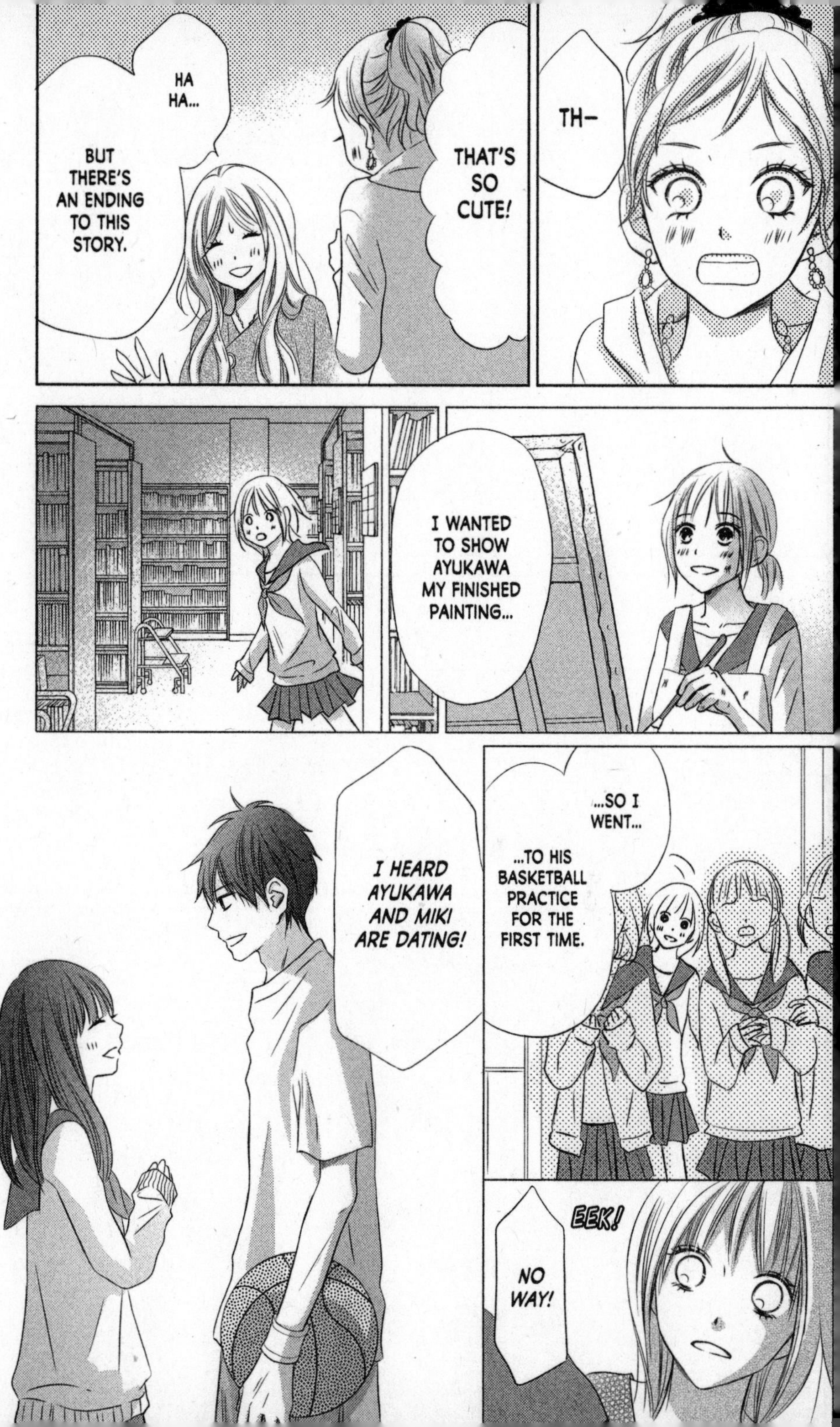
TH–
THAT'S SO CUTE!
HA HA...
BUT THERE'S AN ENDING TO THIS STORY.
I WANTED TO SHOW AYUKAWA MY FINISHED PAINTING...
...SO I WENT...
...TO HIS BASKETBALL PRACTICE FOR THE FIRST TIME.
EEK!
NO WAY!
I HEARD AYUKAWA AND MIKI ARE DATING!

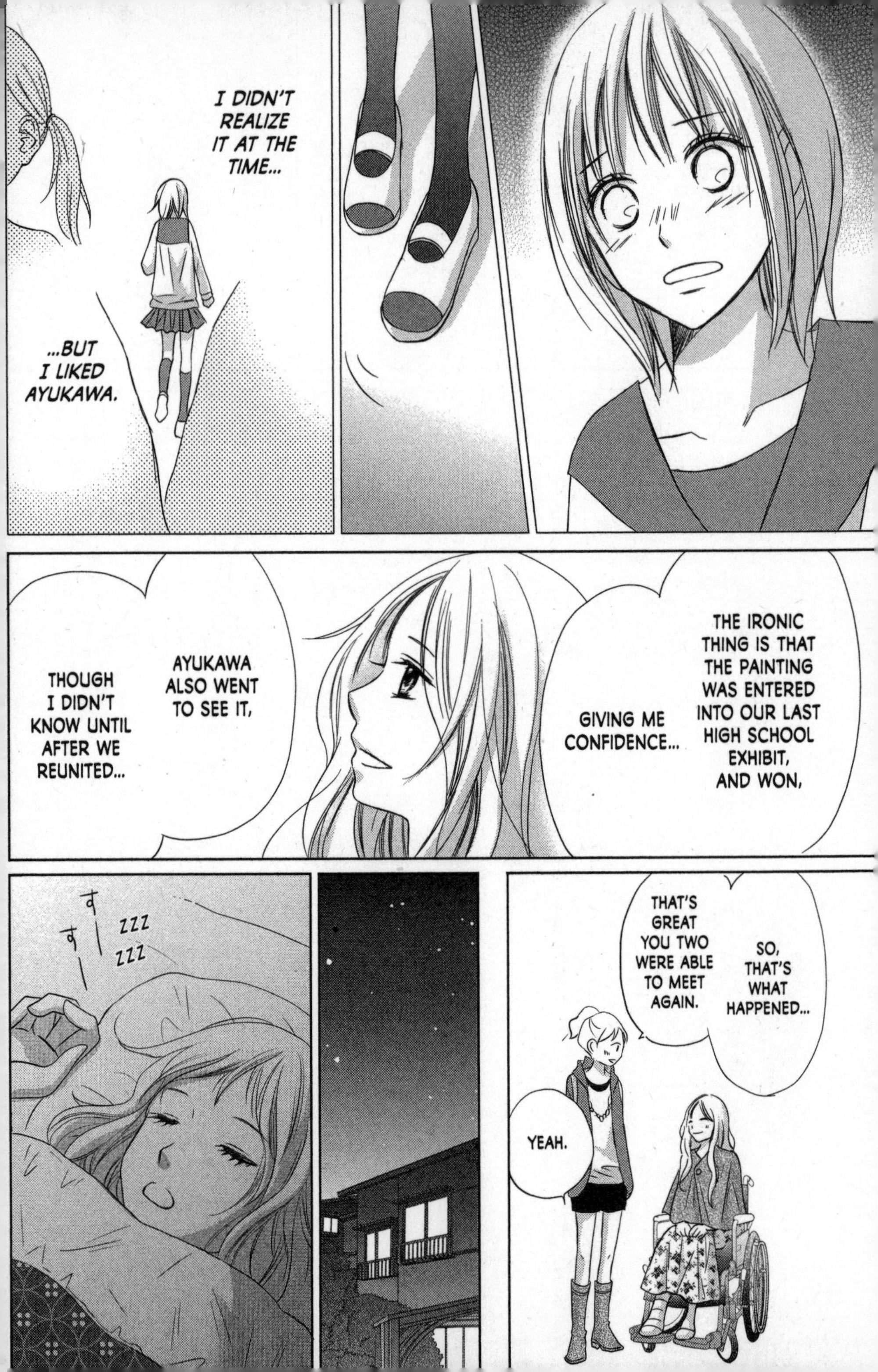
I DIDN'T REALIZE IT AT THE TIME...
...BUT I LIKED AYUKAWA.
THE IRONIC THING IS THAT THE PAINTING WAS ENTERED INTO OUR LAST HIGH SCHOOL EXHIBIT, AND WON,
GIVING ME CONFIDENCE...
AYUKAWA ALSO WENT TO SEE IT,
THOUGH I DIDN'T KNOW UNTIL AFTER WE REUNITED...
SO, THAT'S WHAT HAPPENED...
THAT'S GREAT YOU TWO WERE ABLE TO MEET AGAIN.
YEAH.
すー
すー
ZZZ
ZZZ

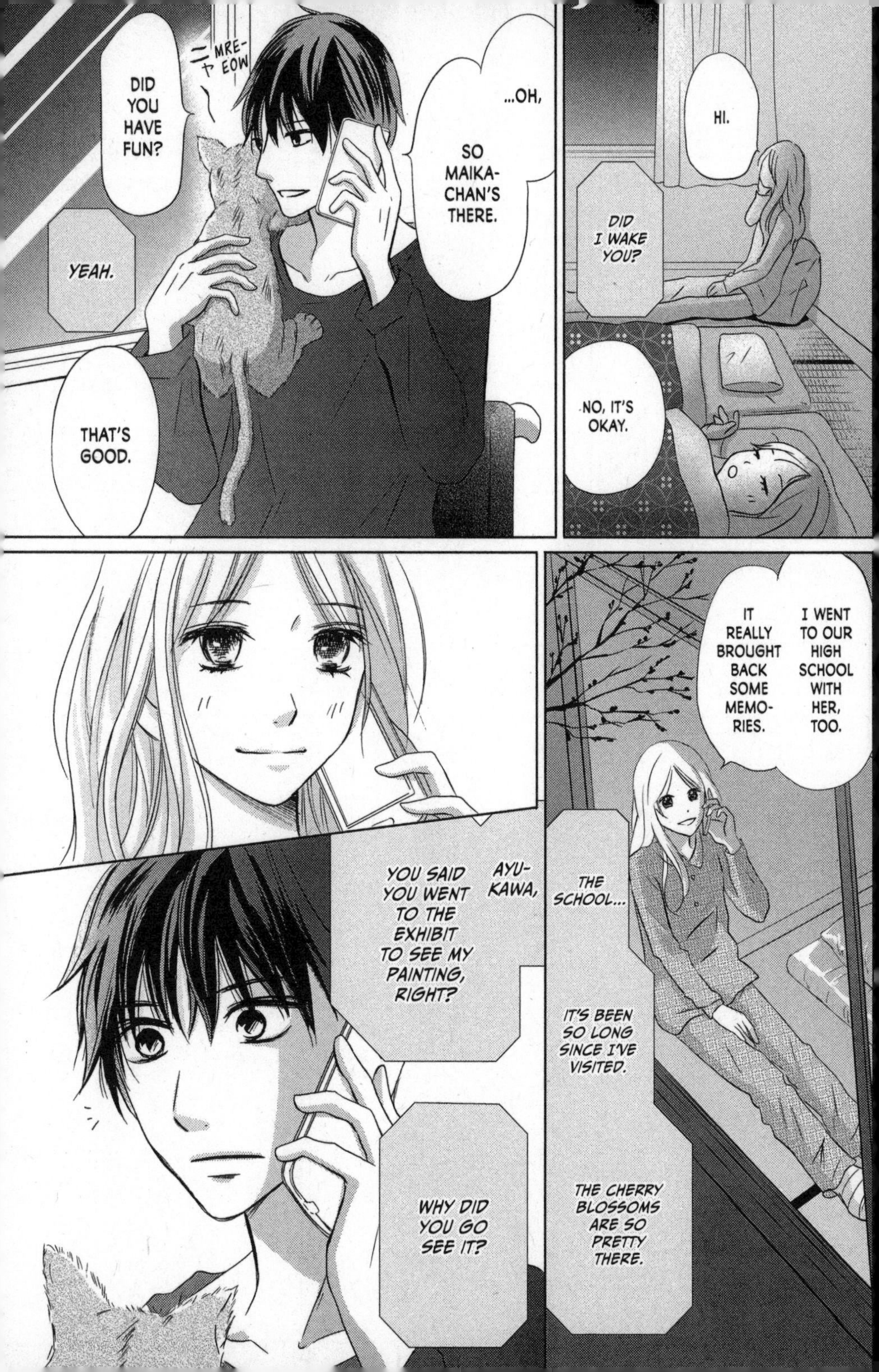
HI.
DID I WAKE YOU?
NO, IT'S OKAY.
ニャ MRE-EOW
...OH, SO MAIKA-CHAN'S THERE.
DID YOU HAVE FUN?
YEAH.
THAT'S GOOD.
I WENT TO OUR HIGH SCHOOL WITH HER, TOO.
IT REALLY BROUGHT BACK SOME MEMORIES.
THE SCHOOL...
IT'S BEEN SO LONG SINCE I'VE VISITED.
THE CHERRY BLOSSOMS ARE SO PRETTY THERE.
AYU-KAWA,
YOU SAID YOU WENT TO THE EXHIBIT TO SEE MY PAINTING, RIGHT?
WHY DID YOU GO SEE IT?

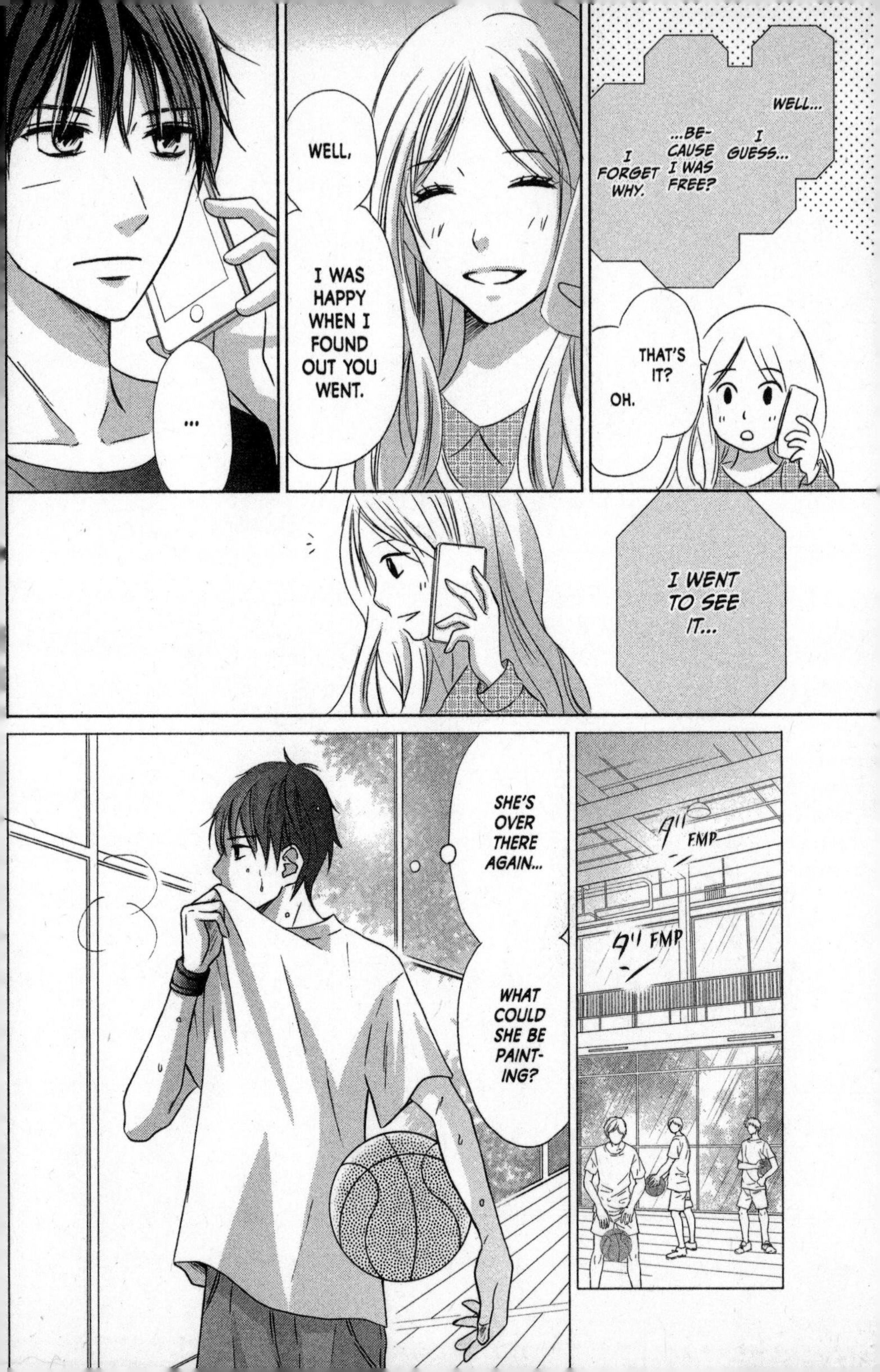
WELL... I GUESS...
...BECAUSE I WAS FREE?
I FORGET WHY.
THAT'S IT?
OH.
WELL,
I WAS HAPPY WHEN I FOUND OUT YOU WENT.
...
I WENT TO SEE IT...
FMP
FMP
SHE'S OVER THERE AGAIN...
WHAT COULD SHE BE PAINTING?

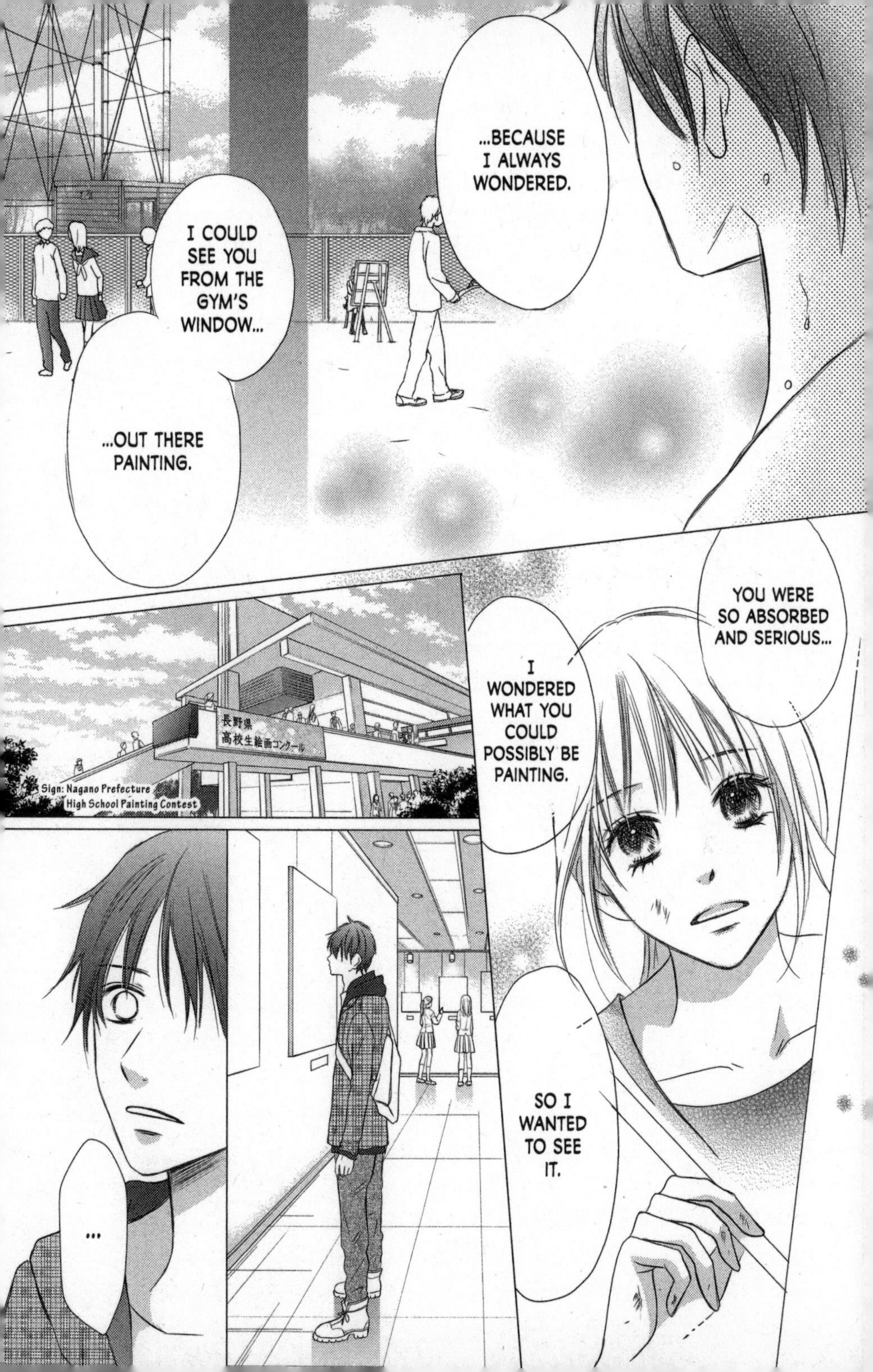
...BECAUSE I ALWAYS WONDERED.
I COULD SEE YOU FROM THE GYM'S WINDOW...
...OUT THERE PAINTING.
YOU WERE SO ABSORBED AND SERIOUS...
I WONDERED WHAT YOU COULD POSSIBLY BE PAINTING.
SO I WANTED TO SEE IT.
長野県
高校生絵画コンクール
Sign: Nagano Prefecture
High School Painting Contest
...

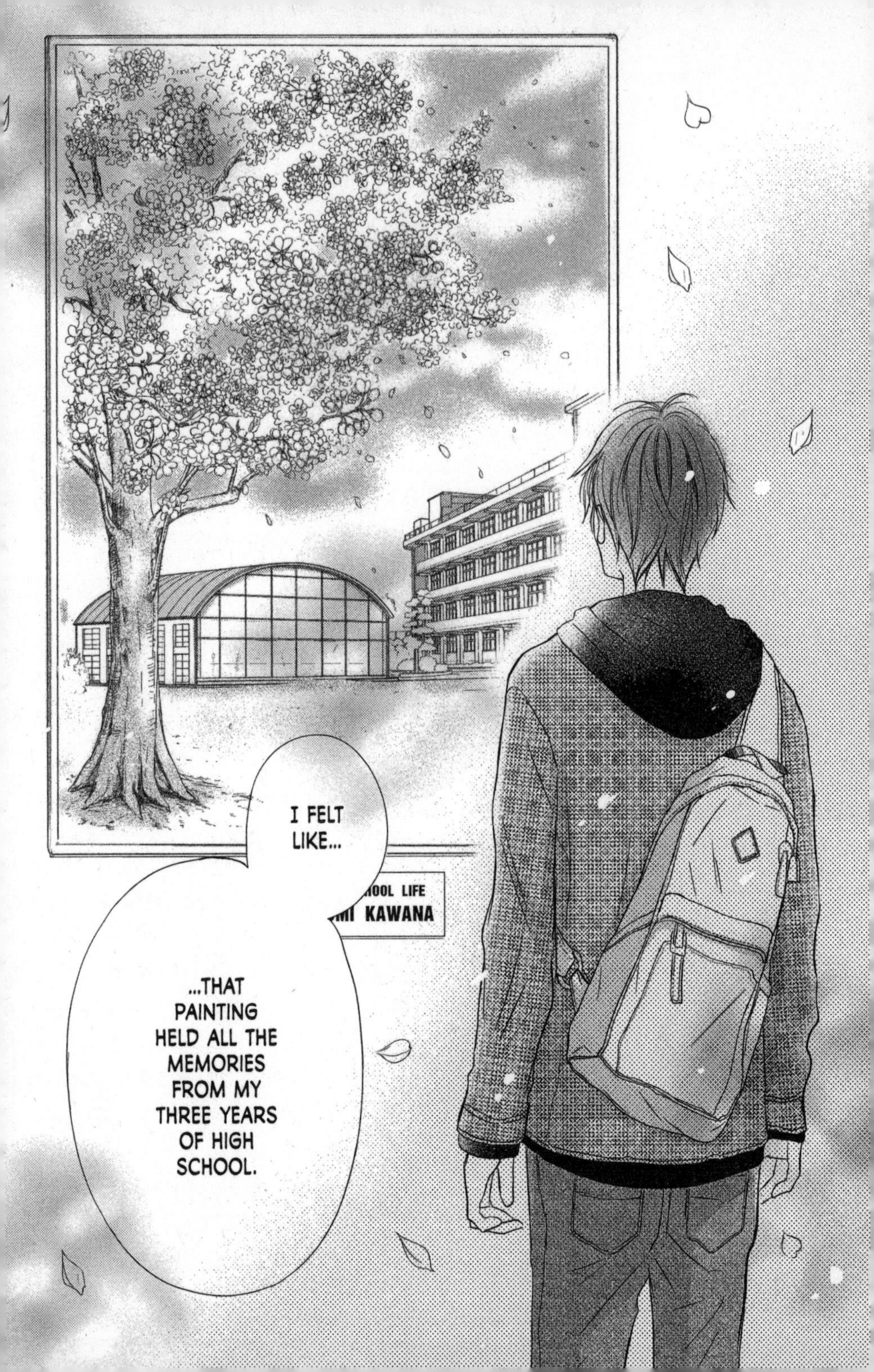
I FELT LIKE...
OOL LIFE
MI KAWANA
...THAT PAINTING HELD ALL THE MEMORIES FROM MY THREE YEARS OF HIGH SCHOOL.

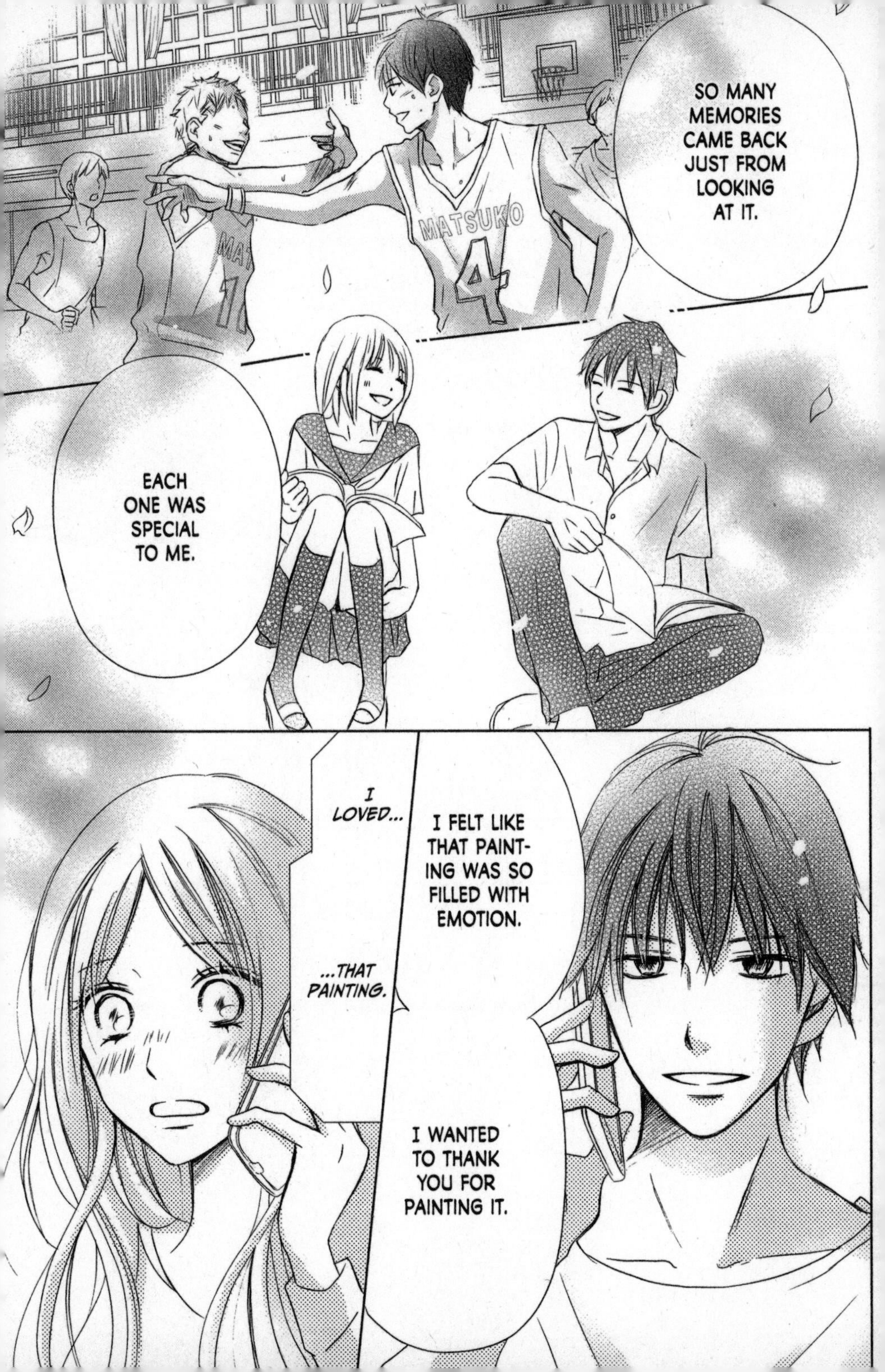
SO MANY MEMORIES CAME BACK JUST FROM LOOKING AT IT.
MATSUKO
4
EACH ONE WAS SPECIAL TO ME.
I FELT LIKE THAT PAINT-ING WAS SO FILLED WITH EMOTION.
I LOVED...
...THAT PAINTING.
I WANTED TO THANK YOU FOR PAINTING IT.

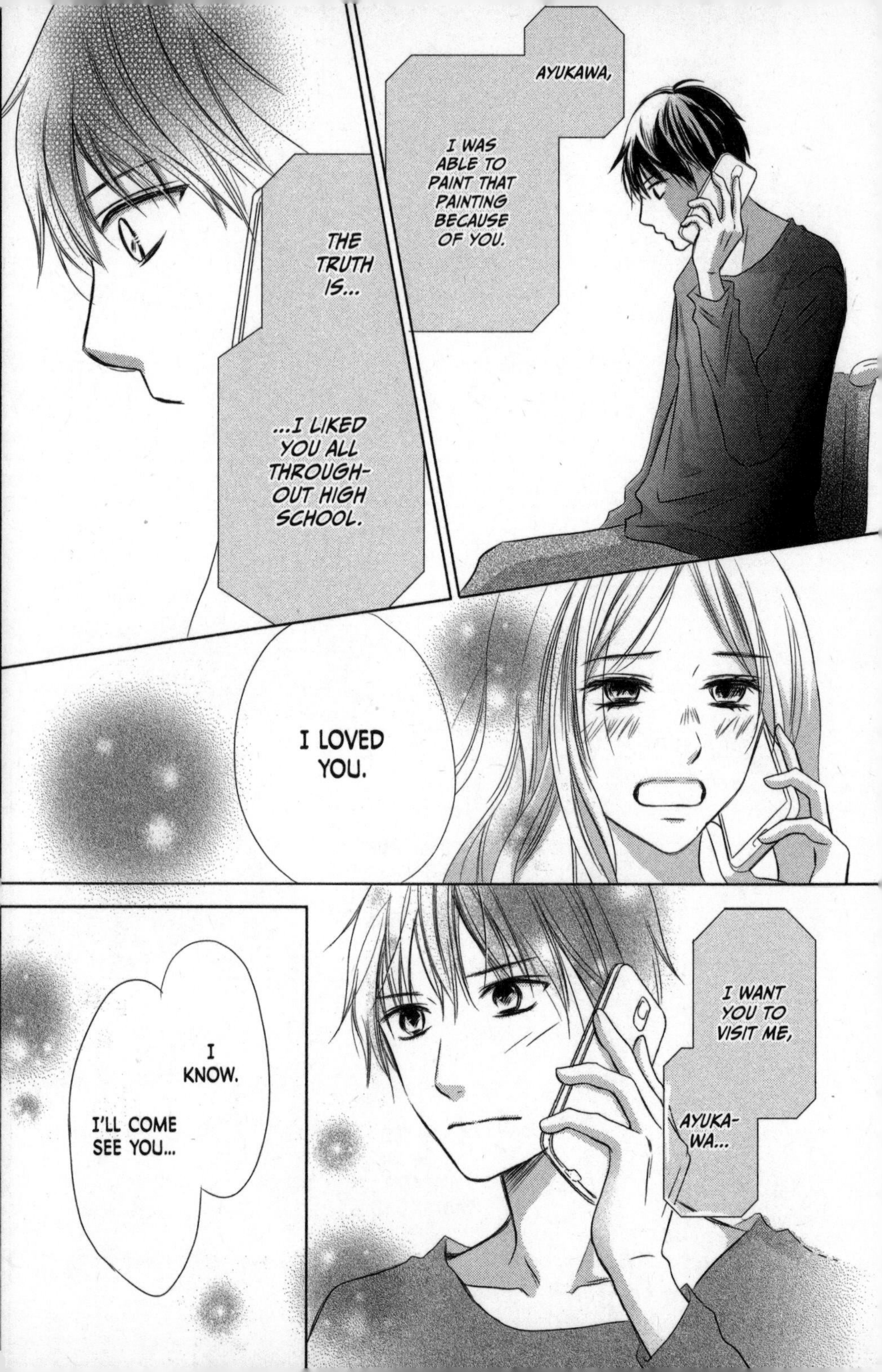
AYUKAWA,
I WAS ABLE TO PAINT THAT PAINTING BECAUSE OF YOU.
THE TRUTH IS...
...I LIKED YOU ALL THROUGH-OUT HIGH SCHOOL.
I LOVED YOU.
I WANT YOU TO VISIT ME,
AYUKA-WA...
I KNOW.
I'LL COME SEE YOU...

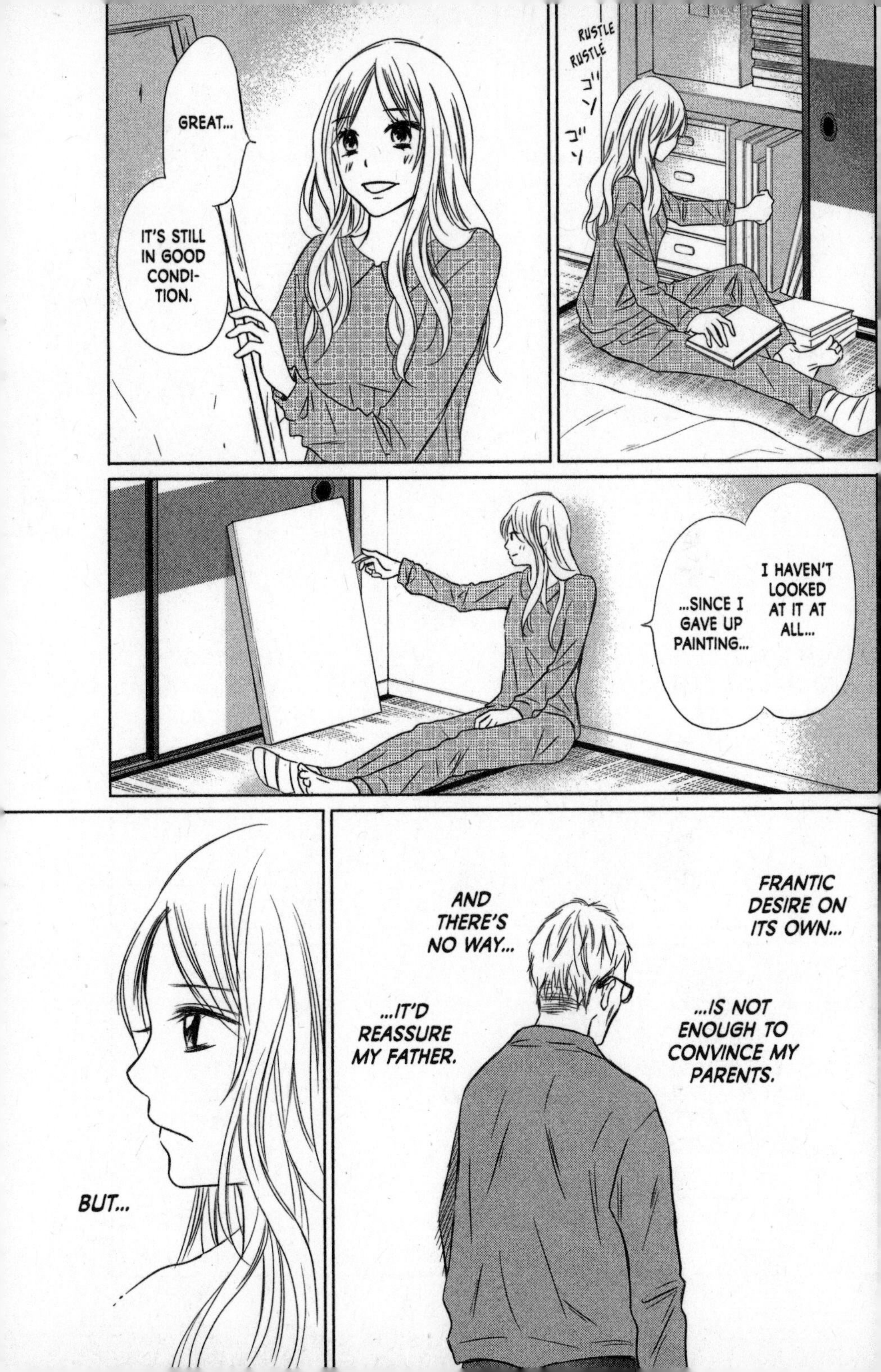
RUSTLE RUSTLE
ゴソゴソ
GREAT...
IT'S STILL IN GOOD CONDITION.
I HAVEN'T LOOKED AT IT AT ALL...
...SINCE I GAVE UP PAINTING...
FRANTIC DESIRE ON ITS OWN...
...IS NOT ENOUGH TO CONVINCE MY PARENTS.
AND THERE'S NO WAY...
...IT'D REASSURE MY FATHER.
BUT...

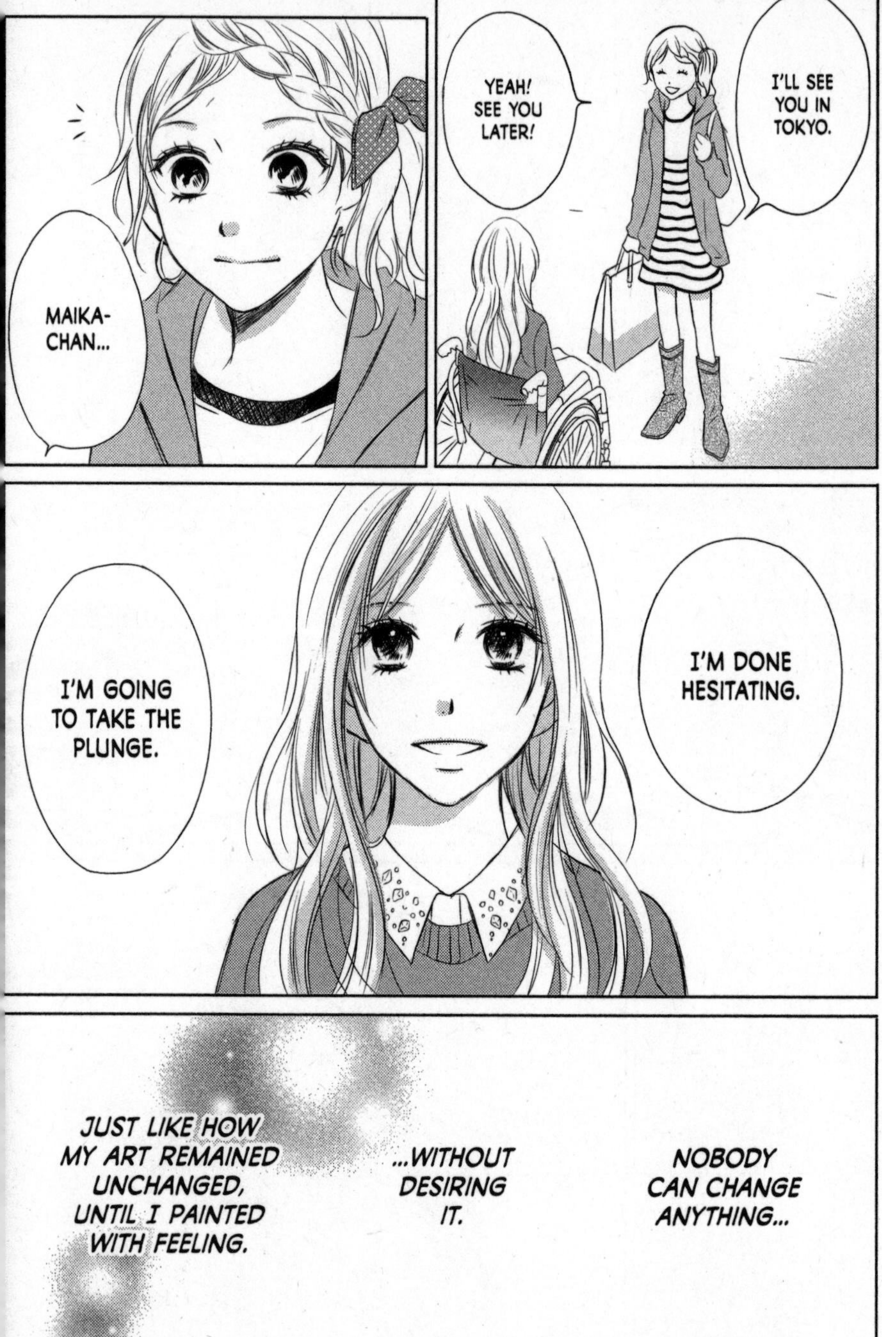
I'LL SEE YOU IN TOKYO.
YEAH! SEE YOU LATER!
MAIKA-CHAN...
I'M DONE HESITATING.
I'M GOING TO TAKE THE PLUNGE.
NOBODY CAN CHANGE ANYTHING...
...WITHOUT DESIRING IT.
JUST LIKE HOW MY ART REMAINED UNCHANGED, UNTIL I PAINTED WITH FEELING.

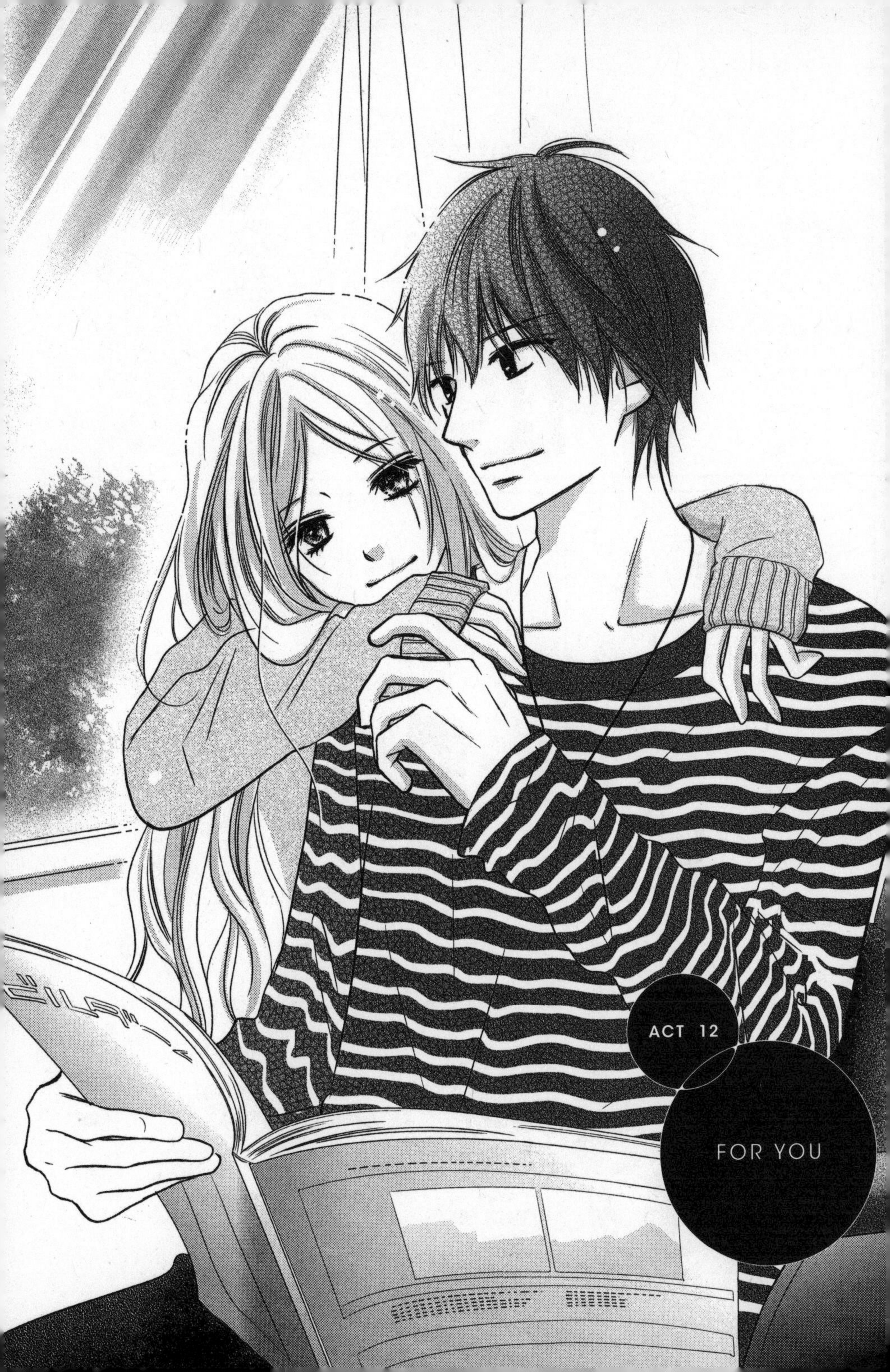
ACT 12
FOR YOU

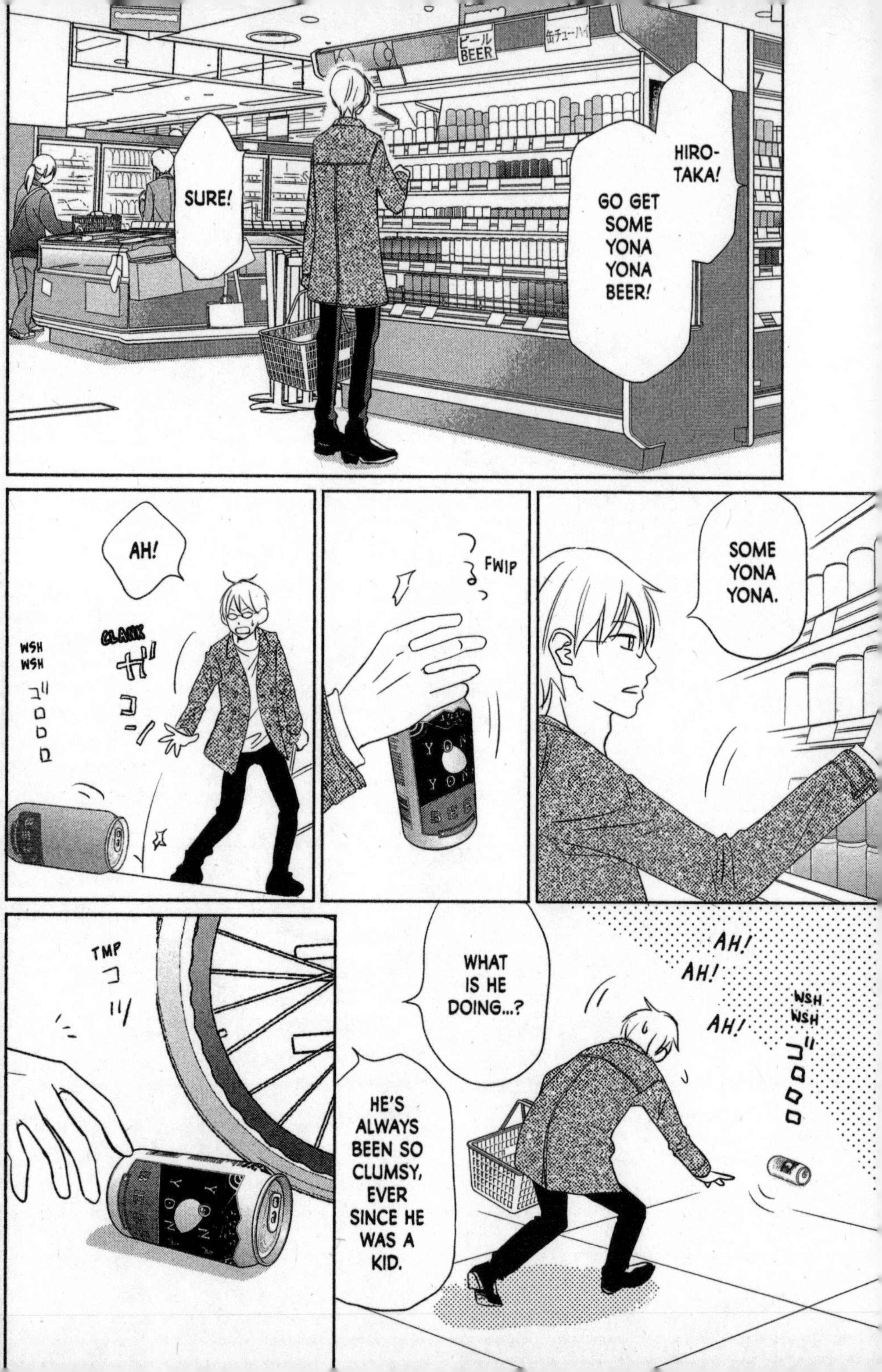
ビール
BEER
缶チューハイ
HIRO-TAKA!
GO GET SOME YONA YONA BEER!
SURE!
SOME YONA YONA.
FWIP
AH!
CLANK
ガッ
コーン
WSH WSH
ゴロロロ
WHAT IS HE DOING...?
HE'S ALWAYS BEEN SO CLUMSY, EVER SINCE HE WAS A KID.
AH!
AH!
AH!
WSH WSH
ゴロロロ
TMP
コツ

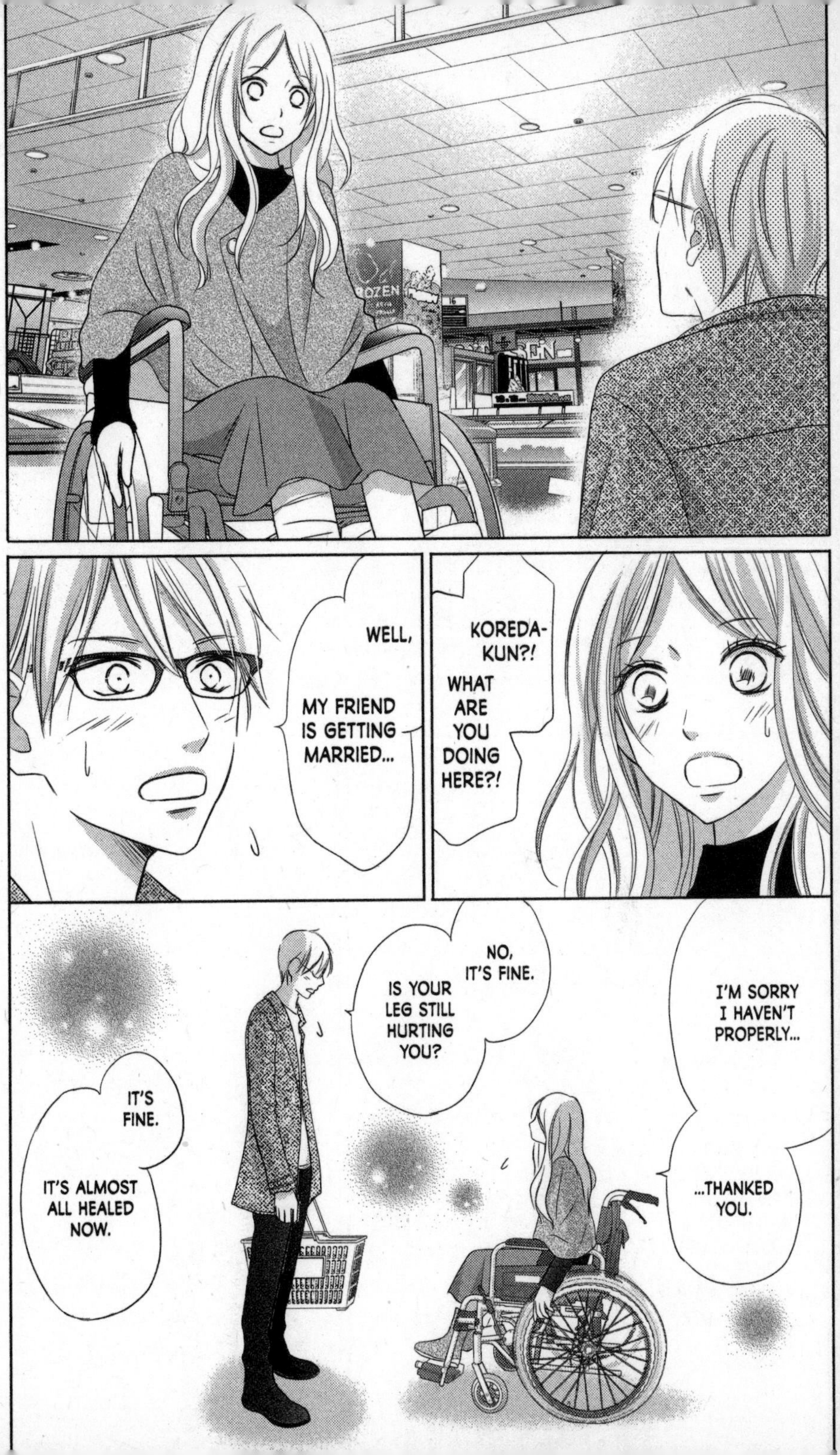
KOREDA-KUN?!
WHAT ARE YOU DOING HERE?!
WELL,
MY FRIEND IS GETTING MARRIED...
I'M SORRY I HAVEN'T PROPERLY...
...THANKED YOU.
NO, IT'S FINE.
IS YOUR LEG STILL HURTING YOU?
IT'S FINE.
IT'S ALMOST ALL HEALED NOW.

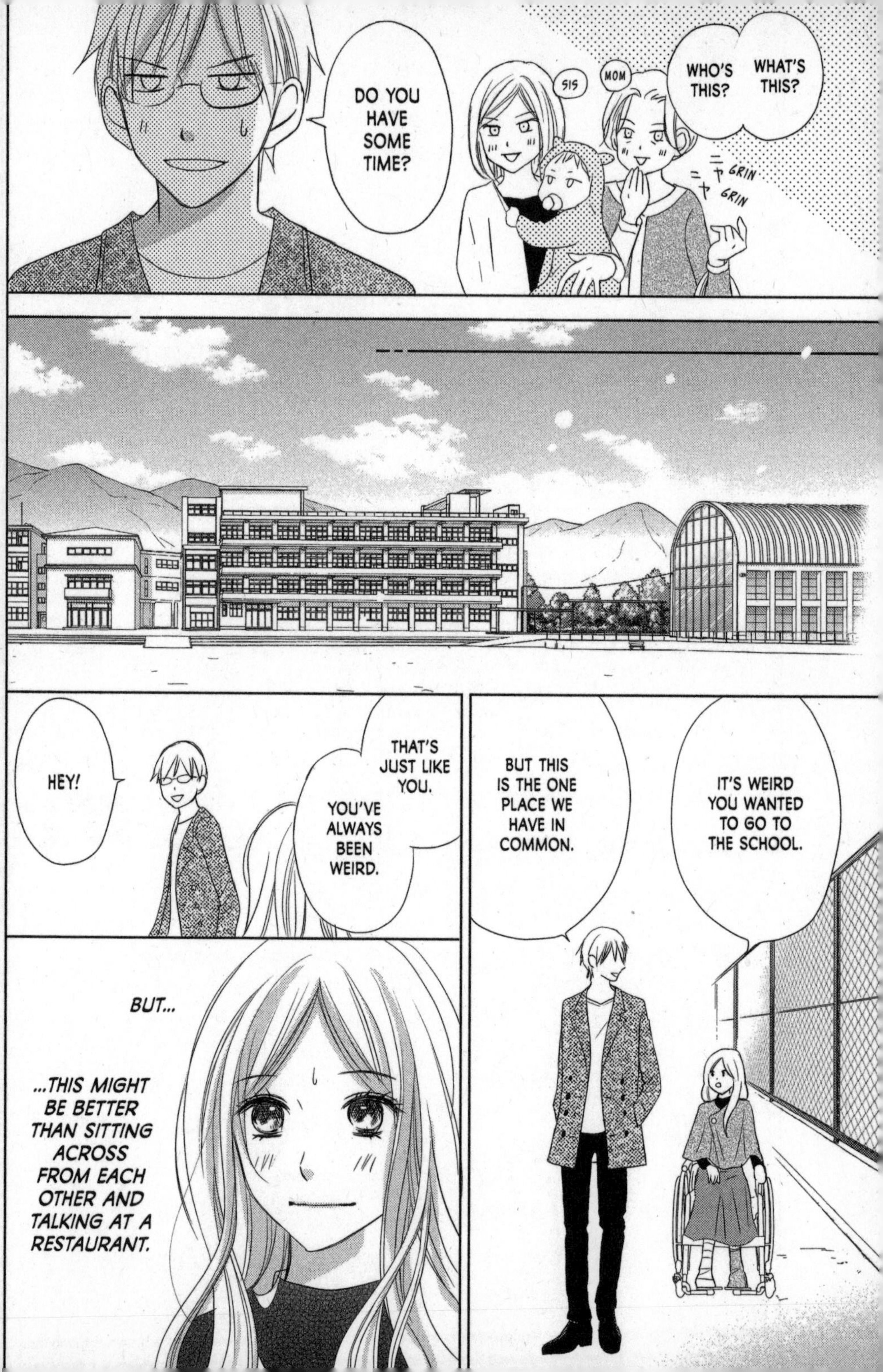
WHAT'S THIS?
WHO'S THIS?
MOM
SIS
ニヤ GRIN
ニヤ GRIN
DO YOU HAVE SOME TIME?
IT'S WEIRD YOU WANTED TO GO TO THE SCHOOL.
BUT THIS IS THE ONE PLACE WE HAVE IN COMMON.
THAT'S JUST LIKE YOU.
YOU'VE ALWAYS BEEN WEIRD.
HEY!
BUT...
...THIS MIGHT BE BETTER THAN SITTING ACROSS FROM EACH OTHER AND TALKING AT A RESTAURANT.

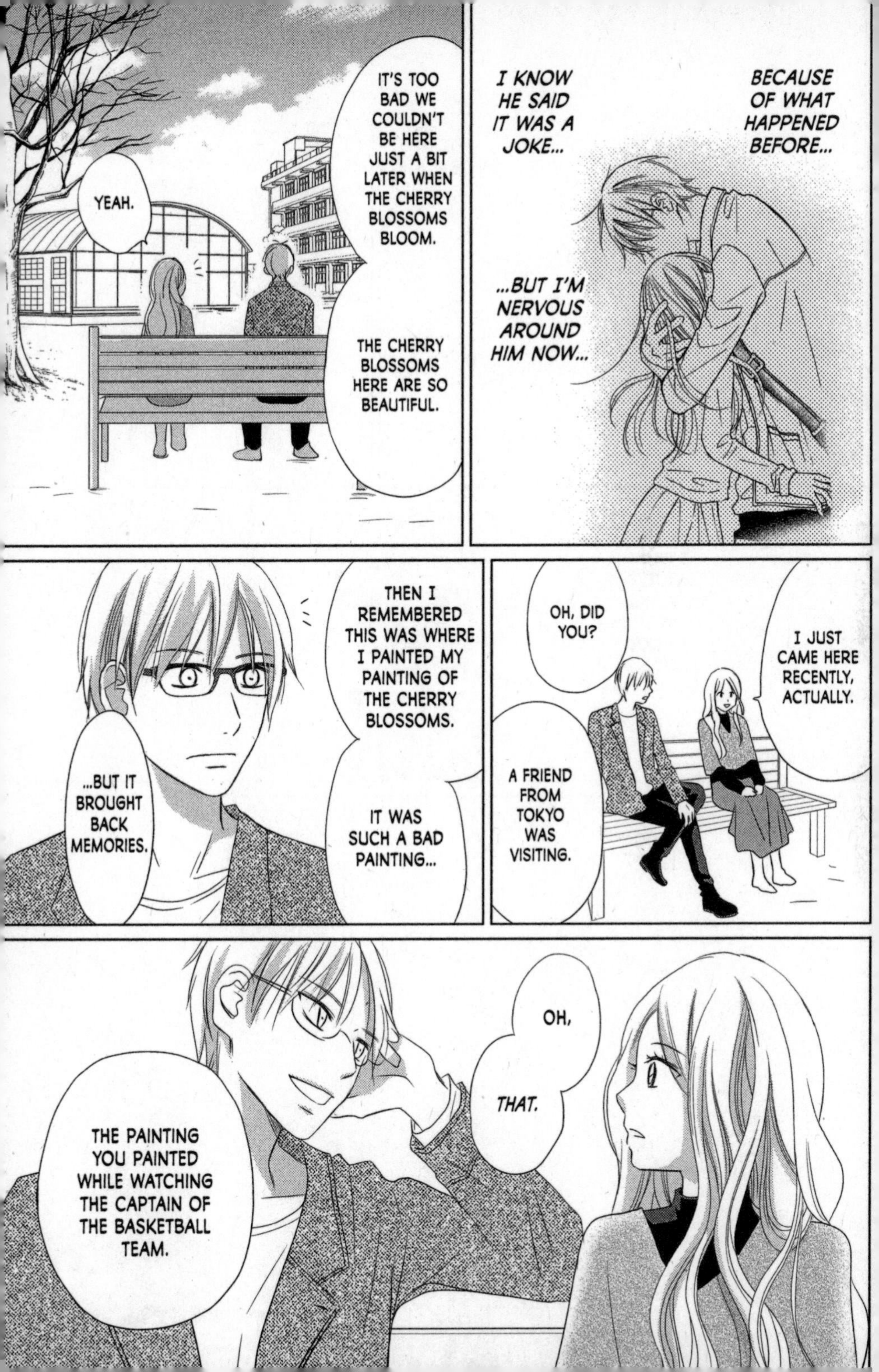
BECAUSE OF WHAT HAPPENED BEFORE...
I KNOW HE SAID IT WAS A JOKE...
...BUT I'M NERVOUS AROUND HIM NOW...
IT'S TOO BAD WE COULDN'T BE HERE JUST A BIT LATER WHEN THE CHERRY BLOSSOMS BLOOM.
YEAH.
THE CHERRY BLOSSOMS HERE ARE SO BEAUTIFUL.
I JUST CAME HERE RECENTLY, ACTUALLY.
OH, DID YOU?
A FRIEND FROM TOKYO WAS VISITING.
THEN I REMEMBERED THIS WAS WHERE I PAINTED MY PAINTING OF THE CHERRY BLOSSOMS.
IT WAS SUCH A BAD PAINTING...
...BUT IT BROUGHT BACK MEMORIES.
OH,
THAT.
THE PAINTING YOU PAINTED WHILE WATCHING THE CAPTAIN OF THE BASKETBALL TEAM.

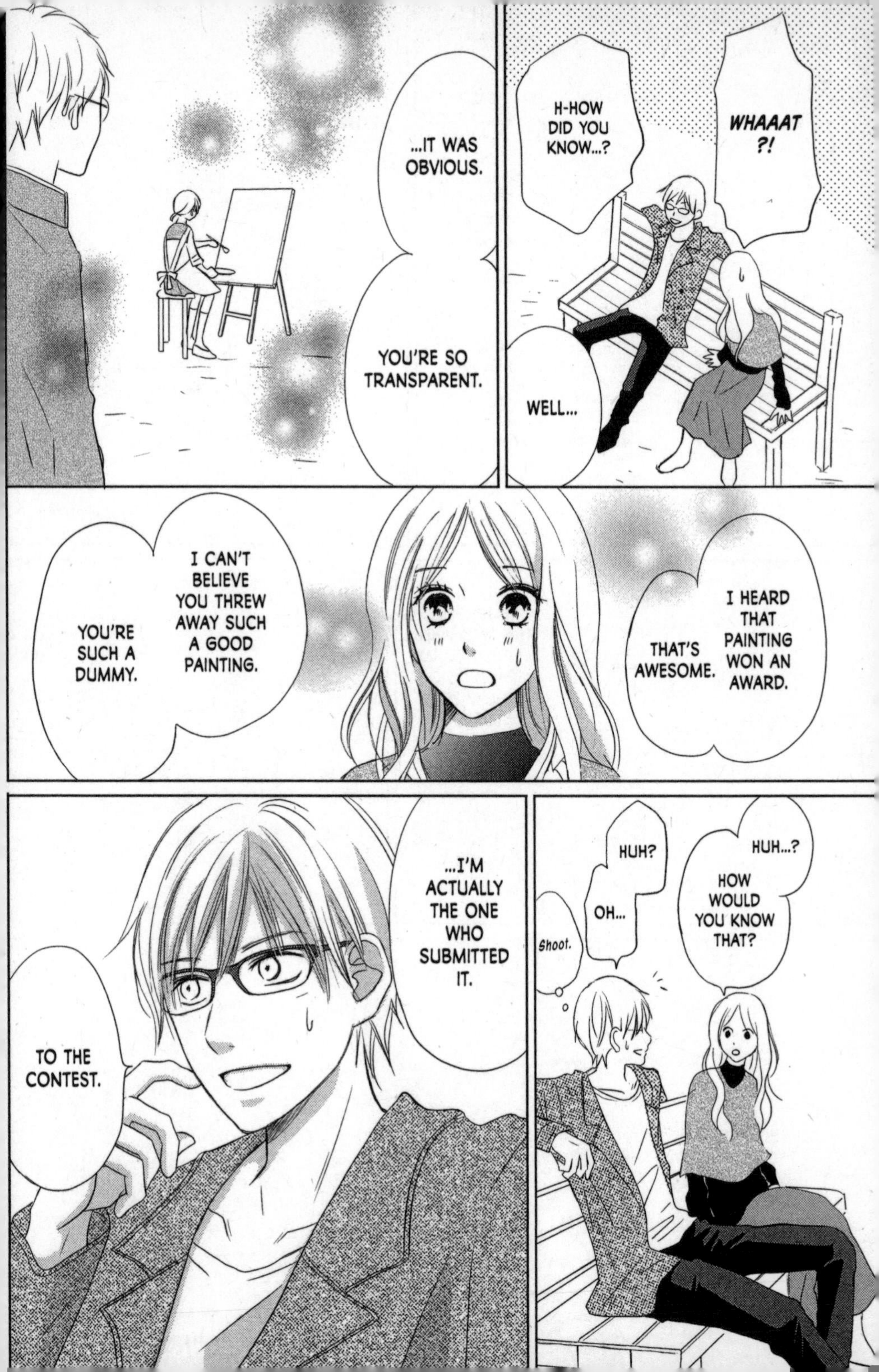
WHAAAT?!
H-HOW DID YOU KNOW...?
WELL...
...IT WAS OBVIOUS.
YOU'RE SO TRANSPARENT.
I HEARD THAT PAINTING WON AN AWARD.
THAT'S AWESOME.
I CAN'T BELIEVE YOU THREW AWAY SUCH A GOOD PAINTING.
YOU'RE SUCH A DUMMY.
HUH...?
HOW WOULD YOU KNOW THAT?
HUH?
OH...
Shoot.
...I'M ACTUALLY THE ONE WHO SUBMITTED IT.
TO THE CONTEST.

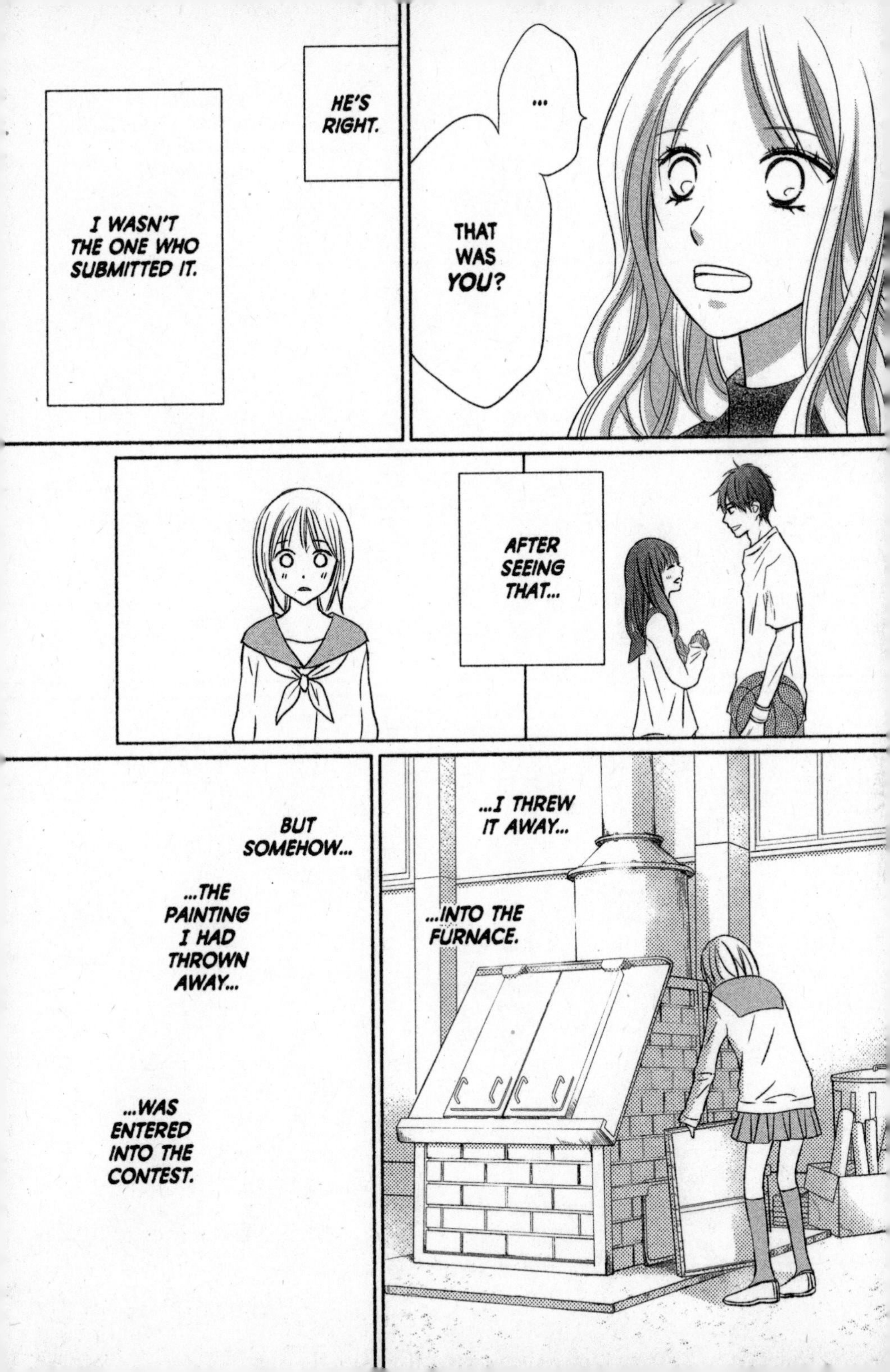
...
THAT WAS YOU?
HE'S RIGHT.
I WASN'T THE ONE WHO SUBMITTED IT.
AFTER SEEING THAT...
...I THREW IT AWAY...
...INTO THE FURNACE.
BUT SOMEHOW...
...THE PAINTING I HAD THROWN AWAY...
...WAS ENTERED INTO THE CONTEST.

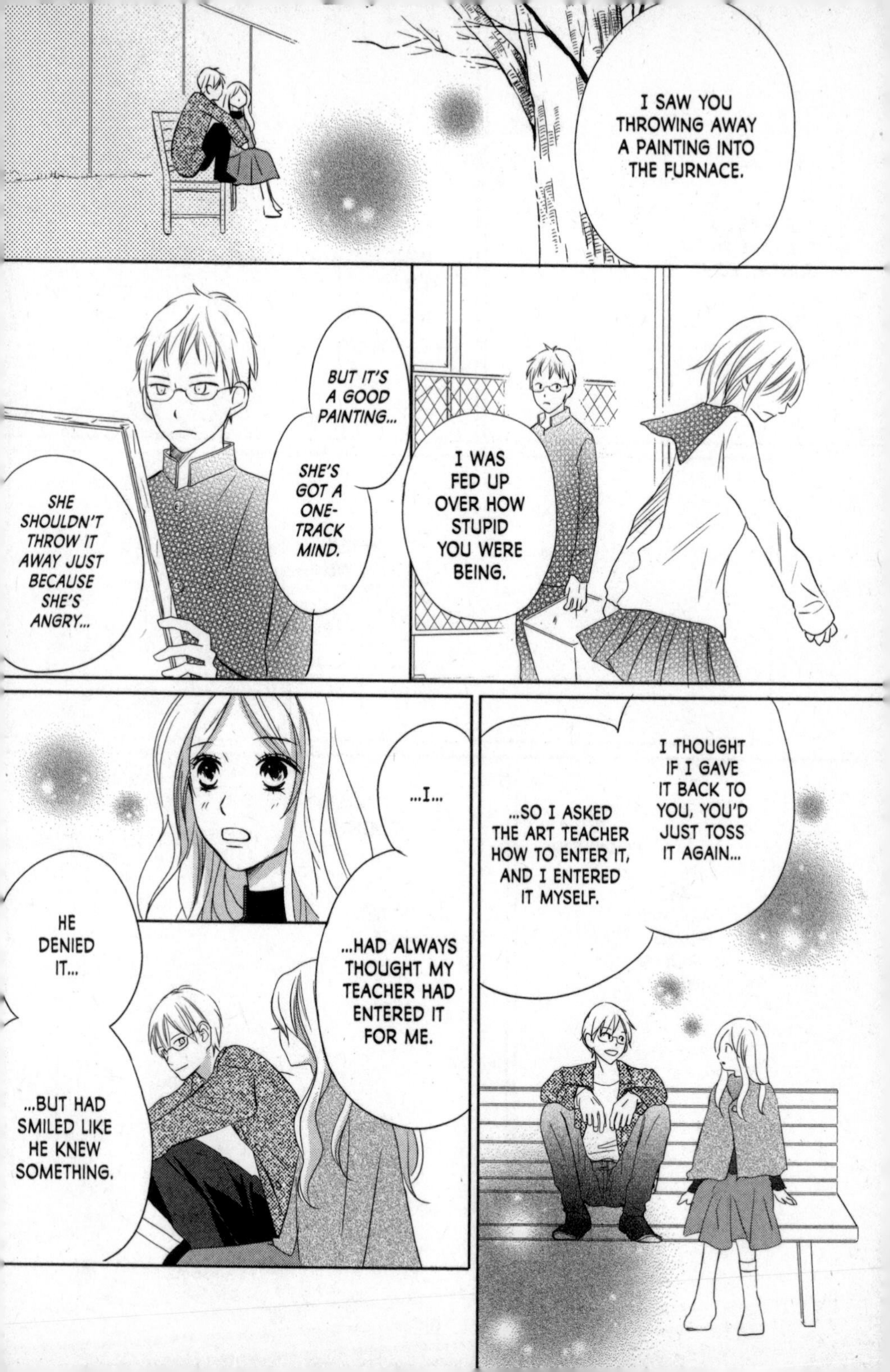
I SAW YOU THROWING AWAY A PAINTING INTO THE FURNACE.
I WAS FED UP OVER HOW STUPID YOU WERE BEING.
BUT IT'S A GOOD PAINTING...
SHE'S GOT A ONE-TRACK MIND.
SHE SHOULDN'T THROW IT AWAY JUST BECAUSE SHE'S ANGRY...
I THOUGHT IF I GAVE IT BACK TO YOU, YOU'D JUST TOSS IT AGAIN...
...SO I ASKED THE ART TEACHER HOW TO ENTER IT, AND I ENTERED IT MYSELF.
...I...
...HAD ALWAYS THOUGHT MY TEACHER HAD ENTERED IT FOR ME.
HE DENIED IT...
...BUT HAD SMILED LIKE HE KNEW SOMETHING.

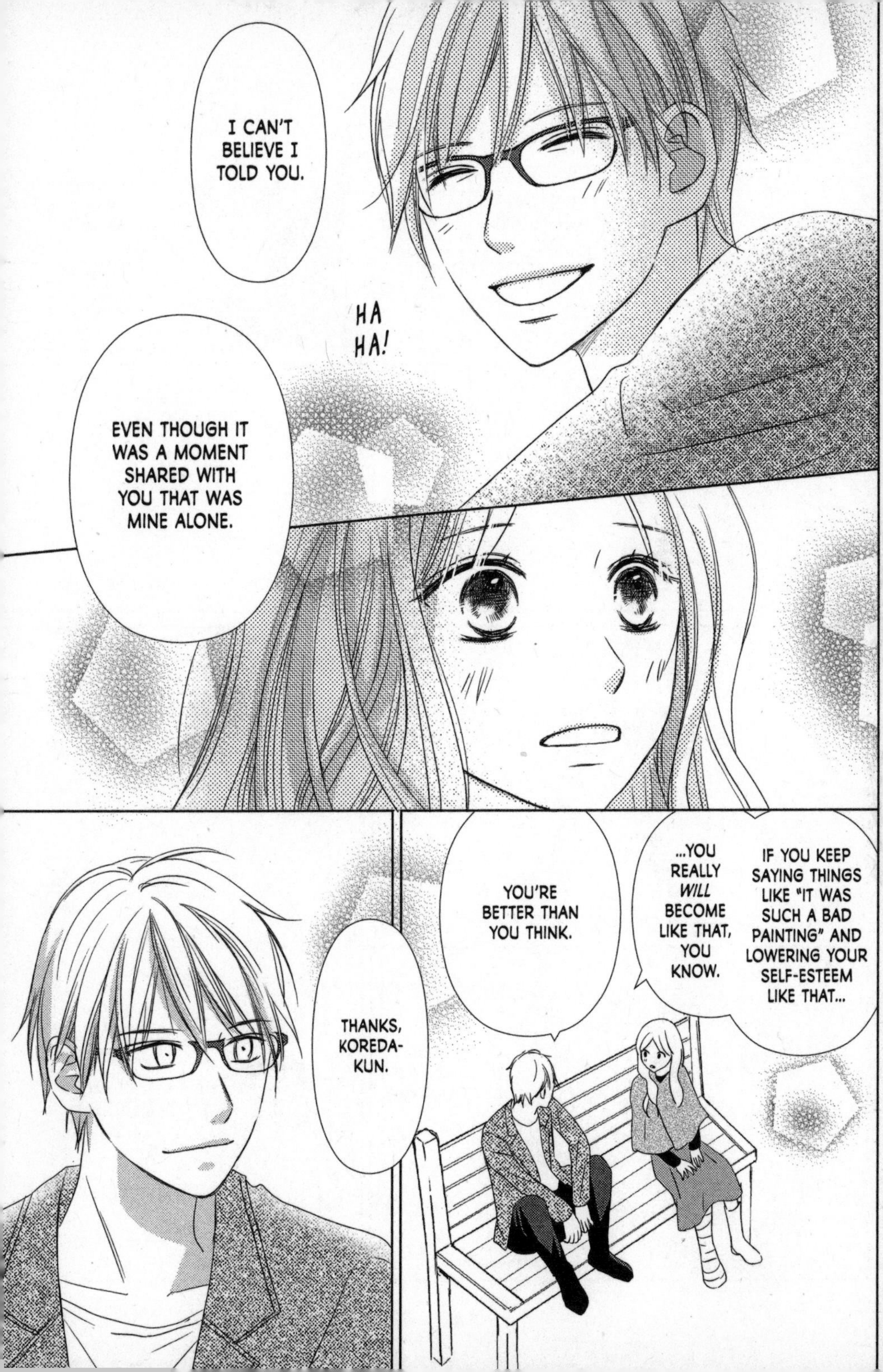
I CAN'T BELIEVE I TOLD YOU.
HA HA!
EVEN THOUGH IT WAS A MOMENT SHARED WITH YOU THAT WAS MINE ALONE.
IF YOU KEEP SAYING THINGS LIKE "IT WAS SUCH A BAD PAINTING" AND LOWERING YOUR SELF-ESTEEM LIKE THAT...
...YOU REALLY *WILL* BECOME LIKE THAT, YOU KNOW.
YOU'RE BETTER THAN YOU THINK.
THANKS, KOREDA-KUN.

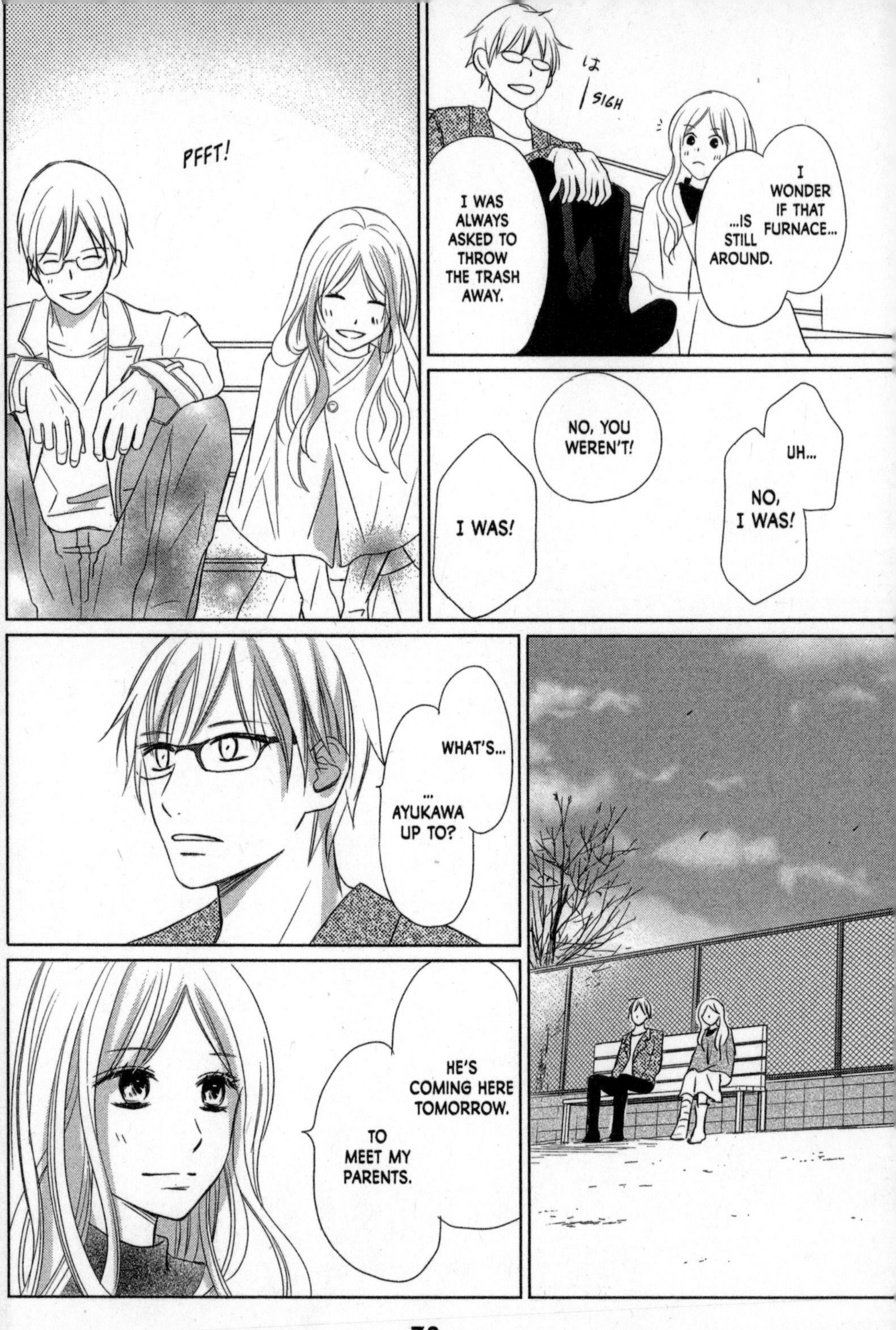
は
SIGH
I WONDER IF THAT FURNACE...
...IS STILL AROUND.
I WAS ALWAYS ASKED TO THROW THE TRASH AWAY.
UH...
NO, I WAS!
NO, YOU WEREN'T!
I WAS!
PFFT!
WHAT'S...
...AYUKAWA UP TO?
HE'S COMING HERE TOMORROW.
TO MEET MY PARENTS.

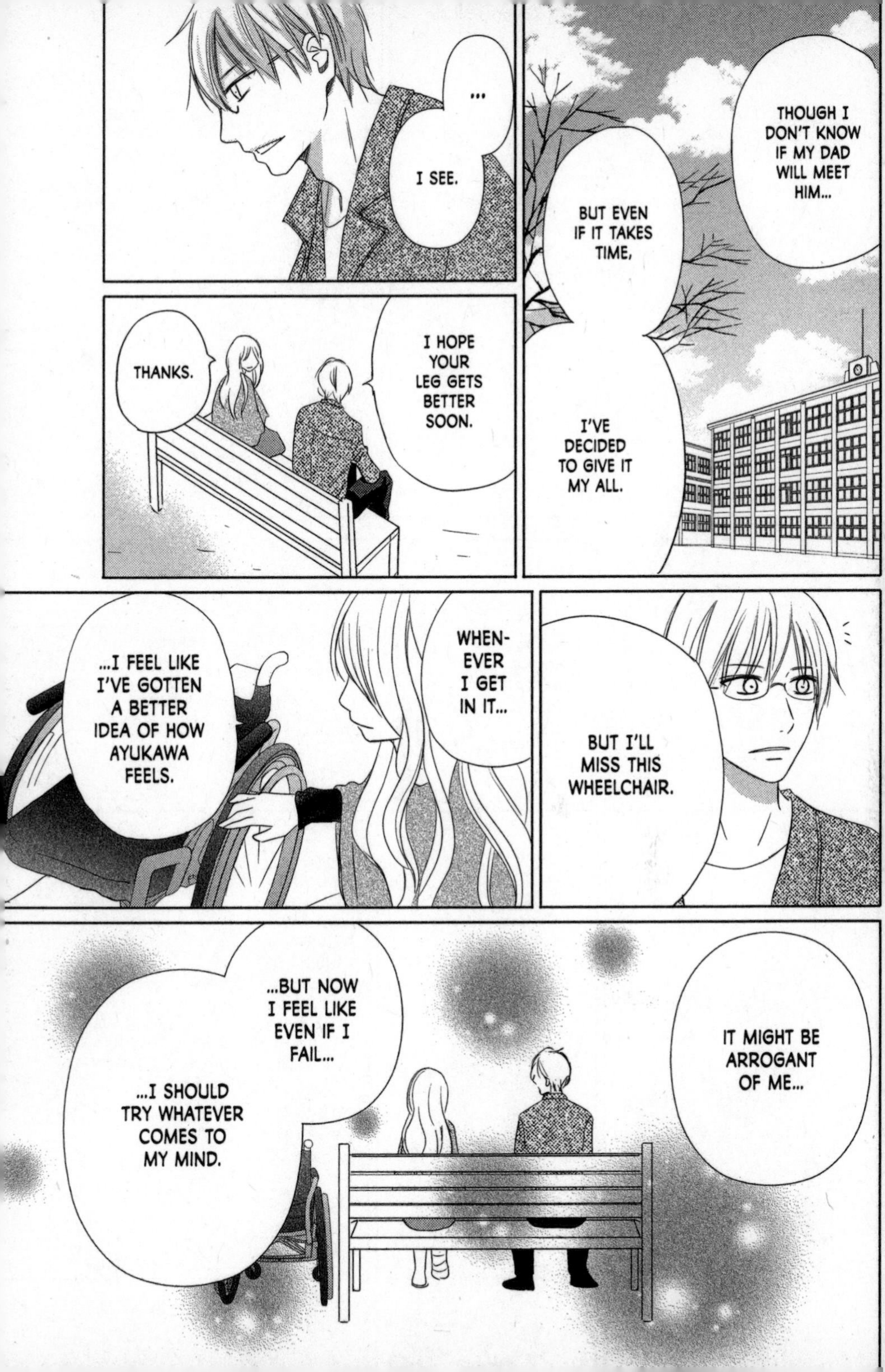
THOUGH I DON'T KNOW IF MY DAD WILL MEET HIM...
BUT EVEN IF IT TAKES TIME,
I'VE DECIDED TO GIVE IT MY ALL.
...
I SEE.
I HOPE YOUR LEG GETS BETTER SOON.
THANKS.
BUT I'LL MISS THIS WHEELCHAIR.
WHEN-EVER I GET IN IT...
...I FEEL LIKE I'VE GOTTEN A BETTER IDEA OF HOW AYUKAWA FEELS.
IT MIGHT BE ARROGANT OF ME...
...BUT NOW I FEEL LIKE EVEN IF I FAIL...
...I SHOULD TRY WHATEVER COMES TO MY MIND.

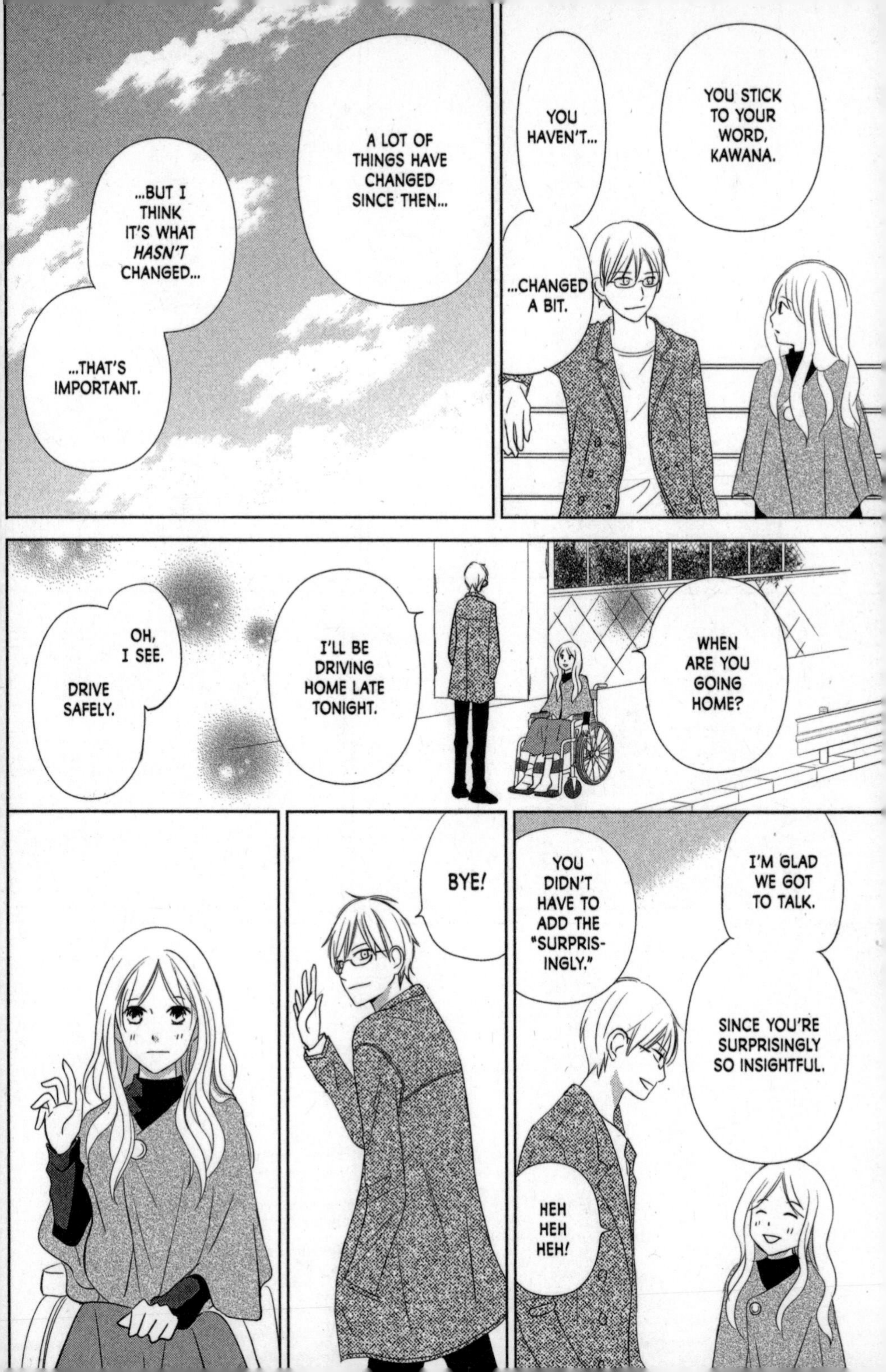
YOU STICK TO YOUR WORD, KAWANA.
YOU HAVEN'T...
...CHANGED A BIT.
A LOT OF THINGS HAVE CHANGED SINCE THEN...
...BUT I THINK IT'S WHAT *HASN'T* CHANGED...
...THAT'S IMPORTANT.
WHEN ARE YOU GOING HOME?
I'LL BE DRIVING HOME LATE TONIGHT.
OH, I SEE.
DRIVE SAFELY.
I'M GLAD WE GOT TO TALK.
SINCE YOU'RE SURPRISINGLY SO INSIGHTFUL.
YOU DIDN'T HAVE TO ADD THE "SURPRIS-INGLY."
HEH HEH HEH!
BYE!

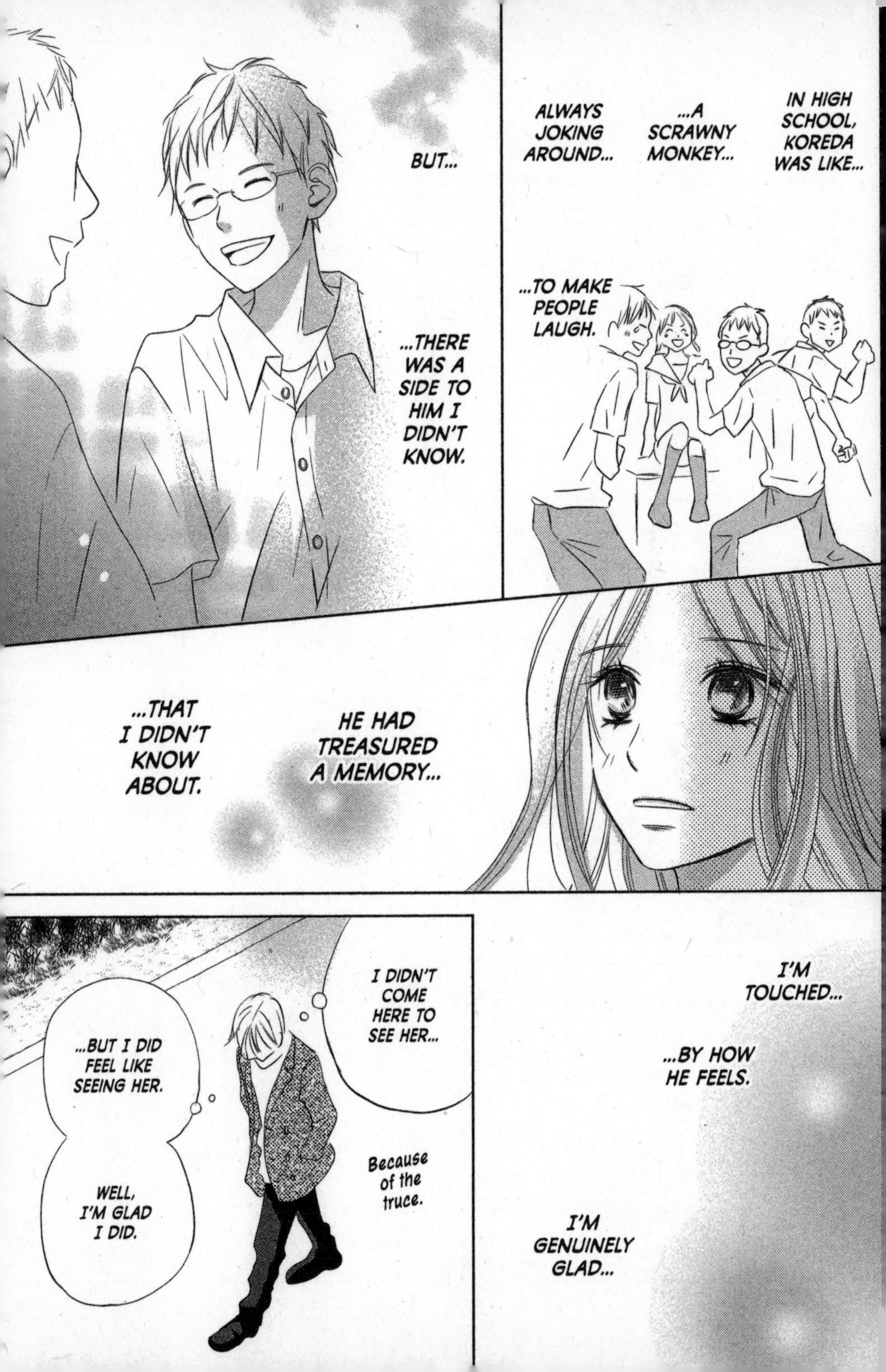
IN HIGH SCHOOL, KOREDA WAS LIKE...
...A SCRAWNY MONKEY...
ALWAYS JOKING AROUND...
...TO MAKE PEOPLE LAUGH.
BUT...
...THERE WAS A SIDE TO HIM I DIDN'T KNOW.
HE HAD TREASURED A MEMORY...
...THAT I DIDN'T KNOW ABOUT.
I'M TOUCHED...
...BY HOW HE FEELS.
I'M GENUINELY GLAD...
I DIDN'T COME HERE TO SEE HER...
Because of the truce.
...BUT I DID FEEL LIKE SEEING HER.
WELL, I'M GLAD I DID.

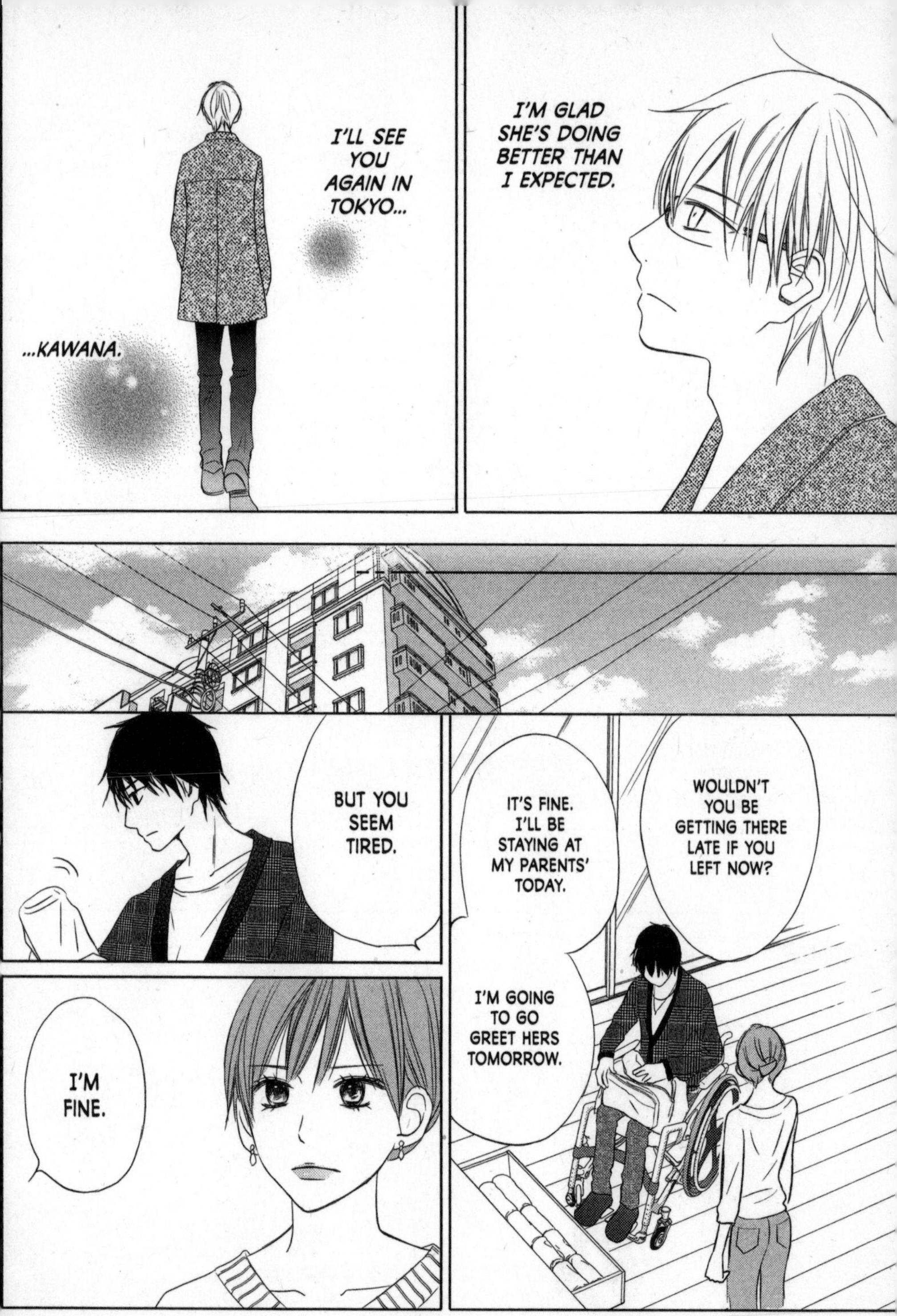
I'M GLAD SHE'S DOING BETTER THAN I EXPECTED.
I'LL SEE YOU AGAIN IN TOKYO...
...KAWANA.
WOULDN'T YOU BE GETTING THERE LATE IF YOU LEFT NOW?
IT'S FINE. I'LL BE STAYING AT MY PARENTS' TODAY.
I'M GOING TO GO GREET HERS TOMORROW.
BUT YOU SEEM TIRED.
I'M FINE.

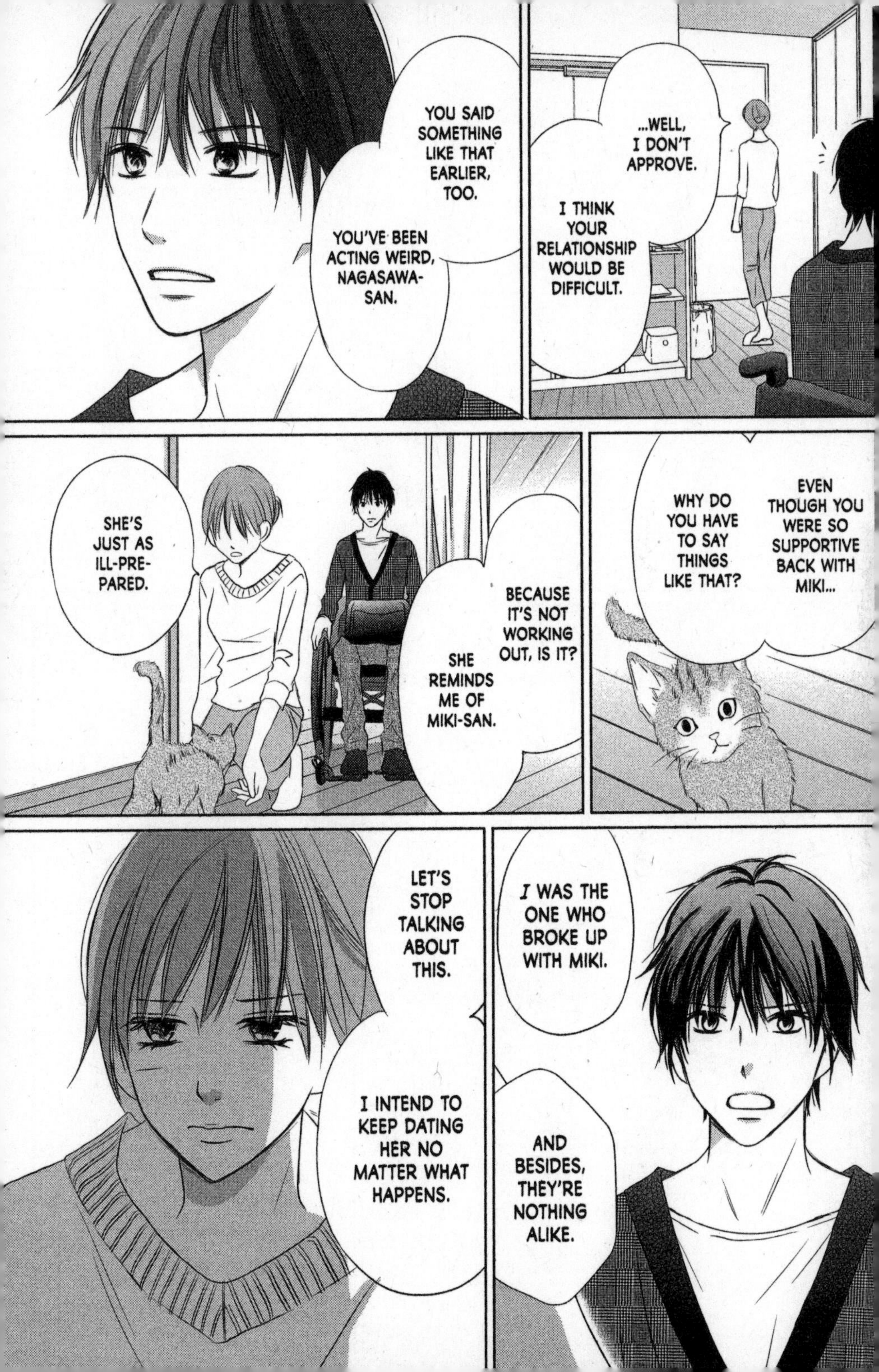
...WELL, I DON'T APPROVE.
I THINK YOUR RELATIONSHIP WOULD BE DIFFICULT.
YOU SAID SOMETHING LIKE THAT EARLIER, TOO.
YOU'VE BEEN ACTING WEIRD, NAGASAWA-SAN.
EVEN THOUGH YOU WERE SO SUPPORTIVE BACK WITH MIKI...
WHY DO YOU HAVE TO SAY THINGS LIKE THAT?
BECAUSE IT'S NOT WORKING OUT, IS IT?
SHE REMINDS ME OF MIKI-SAN.
SHE'S JUST AS ILL-PRE-PARED.
I WAS THE ONE WHO BROKE UP WITH MIKI.
AND BESIDES, THEY'RE NOTHING ALIKE.
LET'S STOP TALKING ABOUT THIS.
I INTEND TO KEEP DATING HER NO MATTER WHAT HAPPENS.

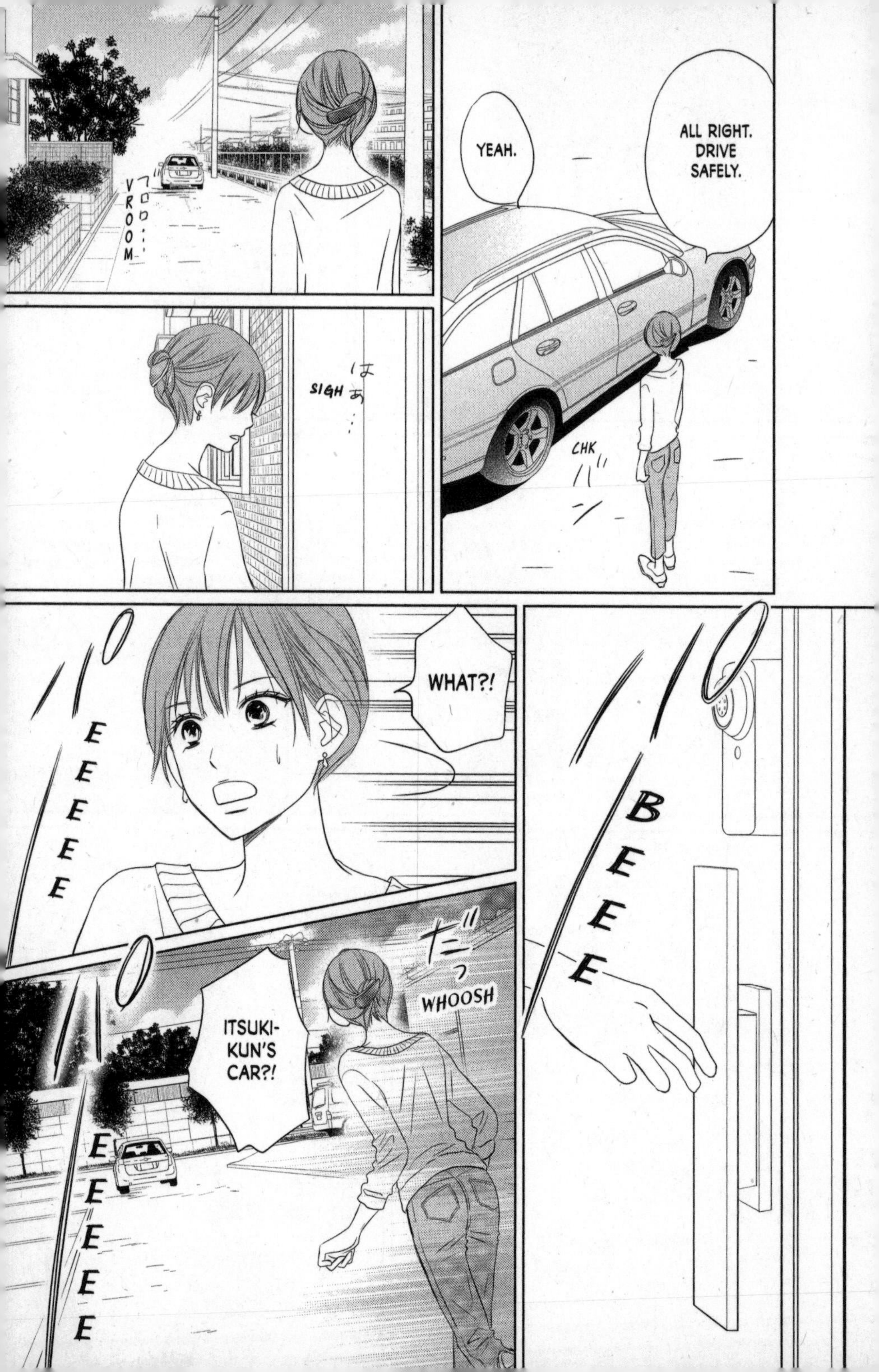
ALL RIGHT. DRIVE SAFELY.
YEAH.
CHK
ブロロ…
VROOM
はあ…
SIGH
BEEE
E
WHAT?!
EEEEE
だっ
WHOOSH
ITSUKI-KUN'S CAR?!
EEEEEE

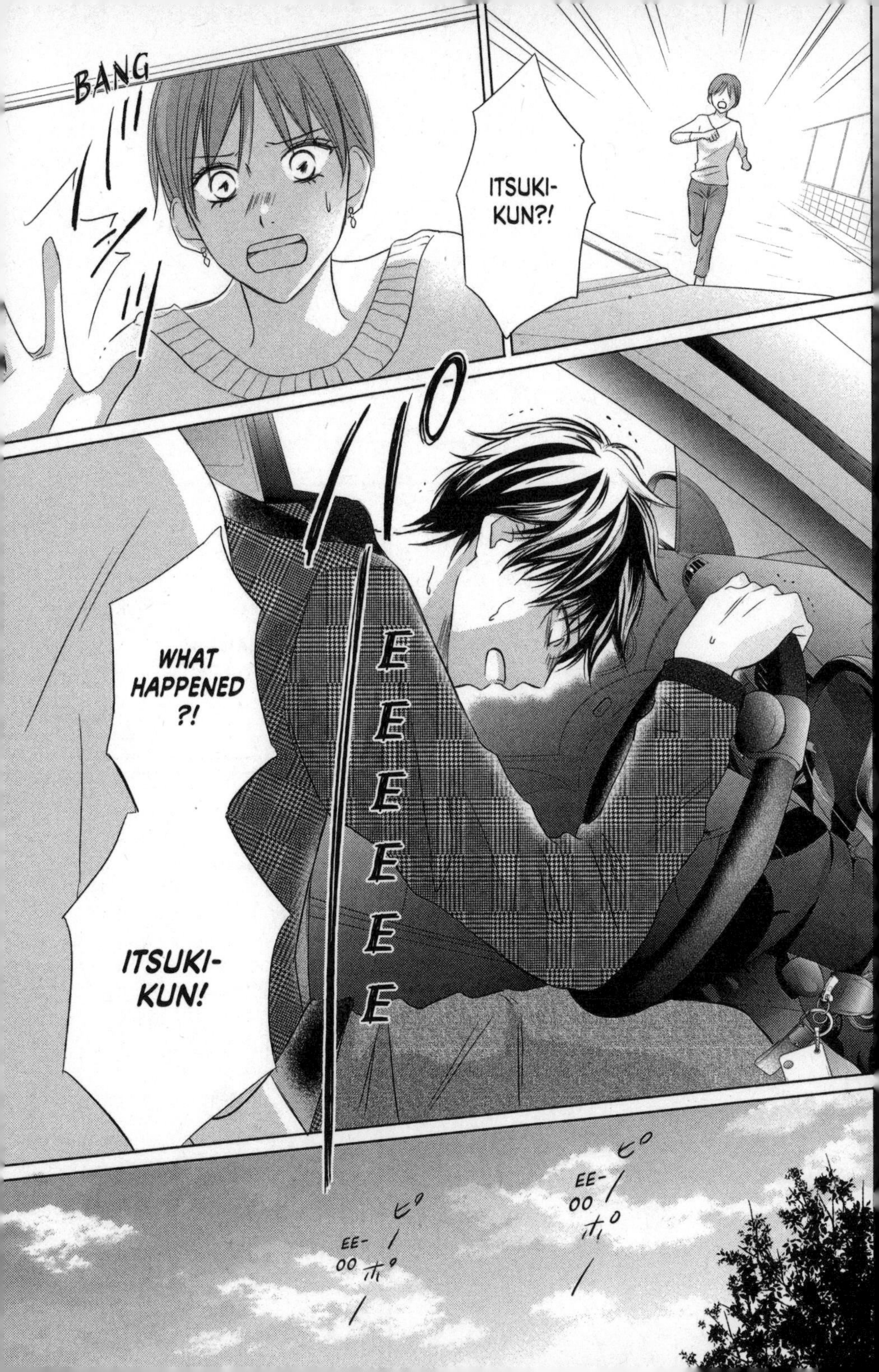
ITSUKI-KUN?!
BANG
WHAT HAPPENED?!
ITSUKI-KUN!
EEEEEE
EE-OO
EE-OO

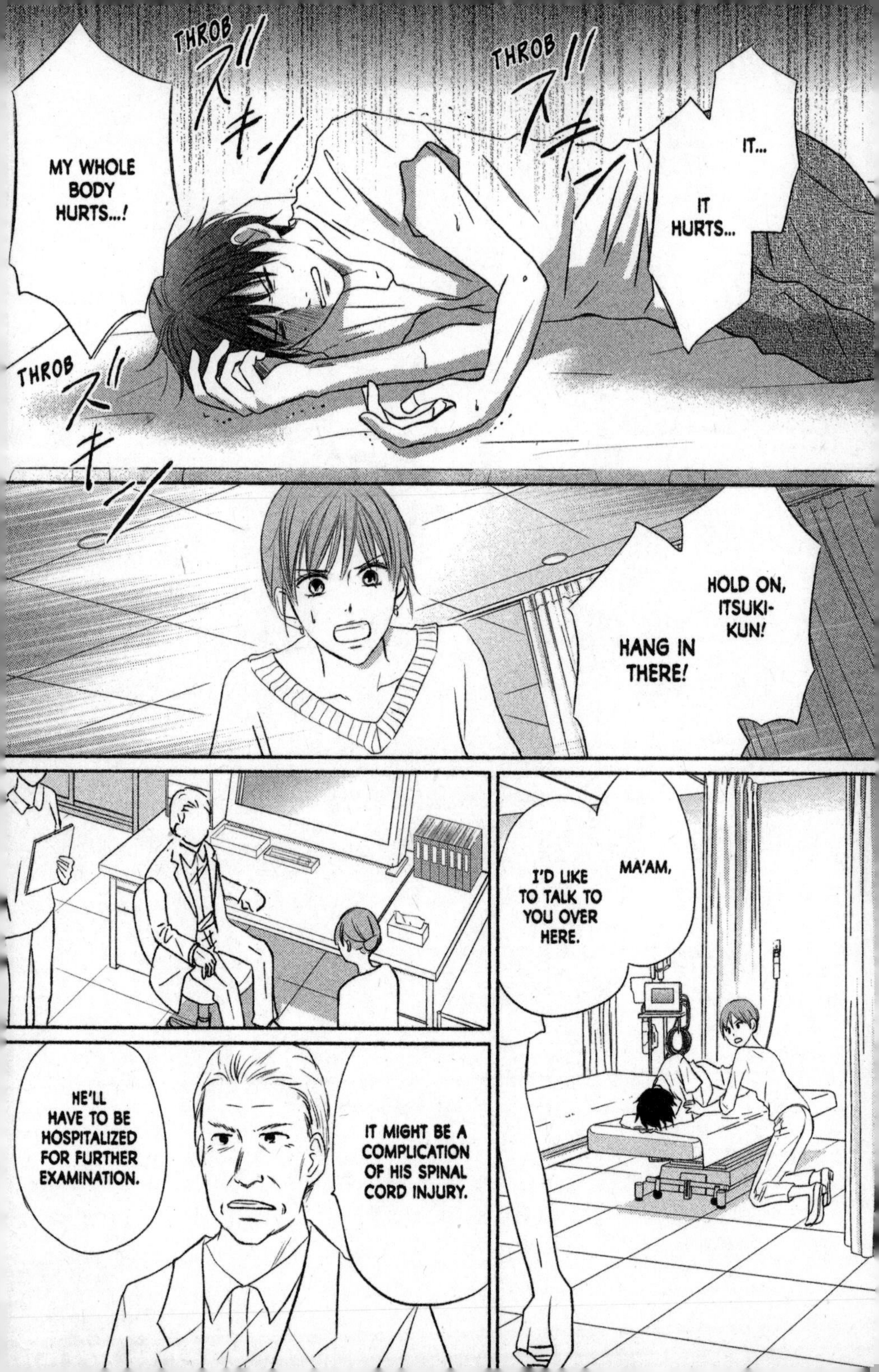
IT...
IT HURTS...
THROB ズキン
THROB ズキン
MY WHOLE BODY HURTS...!
THROB ズキン
HOLD ON, ITSUKI-KUN!
HANG IN THERE!
MA'AM,
I'D LIKE TO TALK TO YOU OVER HERE.
IT MIGHT BE A COMPLICATION OF HIS SPINAL CORD INJURY.
HE'LL HAVE TO BE HOSPITALIZED FOR FURTHER EXAMINATION.

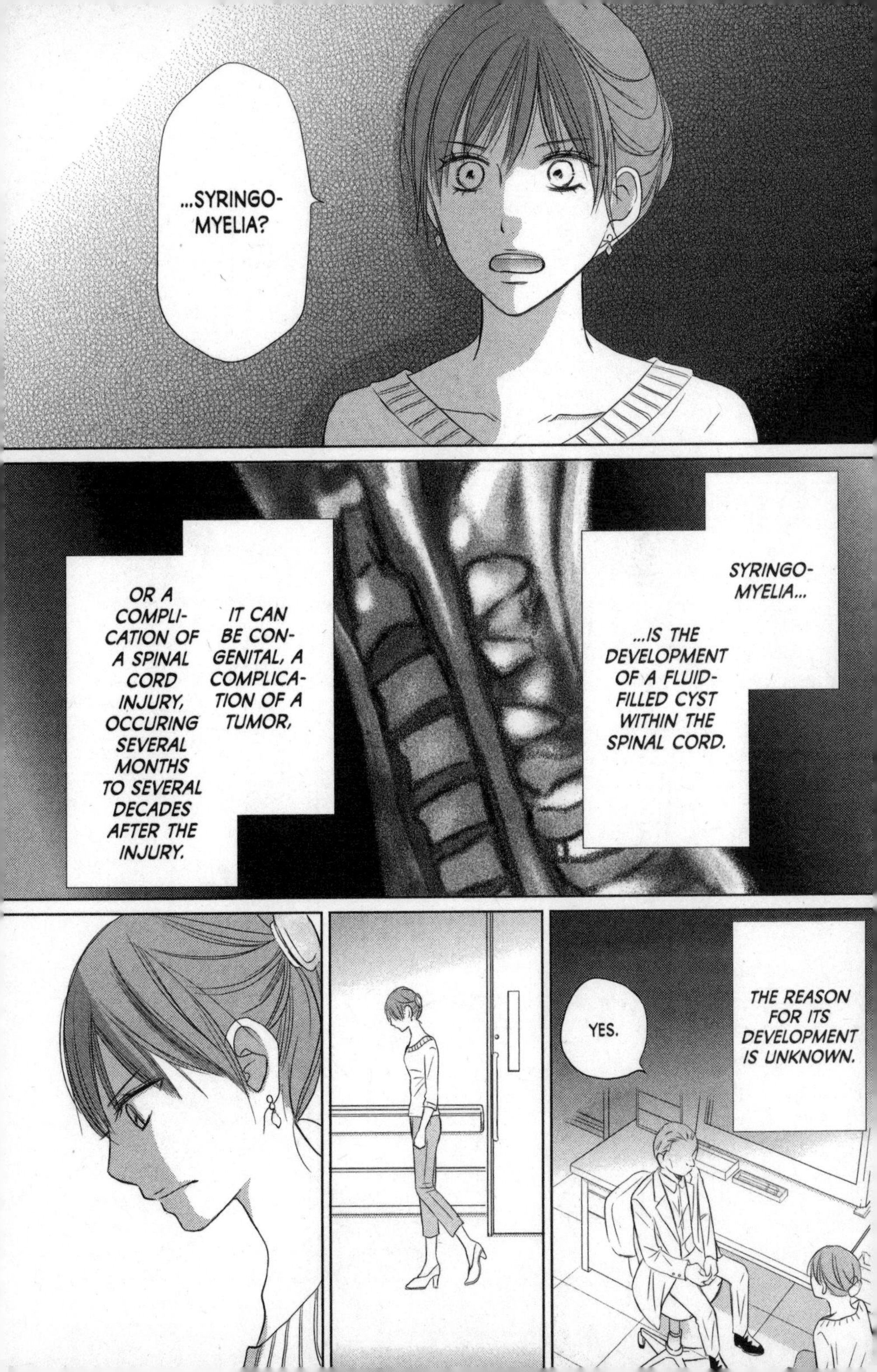
...SYRINGO-MYELIA?
SYRINGO-MYELIA...
...IS THE DEVELOPMENT OF A FLUID-FILLED CYST WITHIN THE SPINAL CORD.
IT CAN BE CON-GENITAL, A COMPLICA-TION OF A TUMOR,
OR A COMPLI-CATION OF A SPINAL CORD INJURY, OCCURING SEVERAL MONTHS TO SEVERAL DECADES AFTER THE INJURY.
THE REASON FOR ITS DEVELOPMENT IS UNKNOWN.
YES.

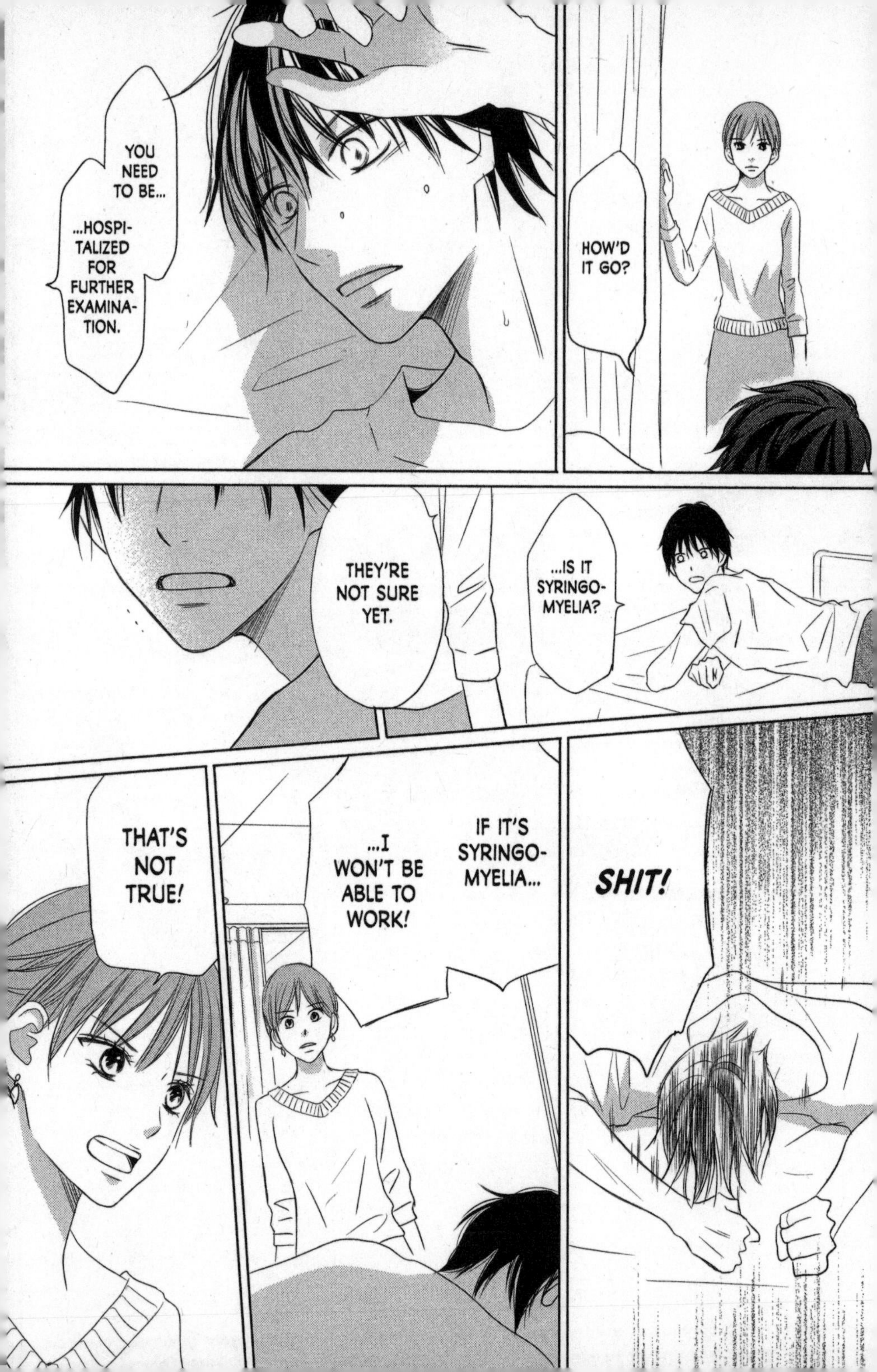
HOW'D IT GO?
YOU NEED TO BE...
...HOSPITALIZED FOR FURTHER EXAMINATION.
...IS IT SYRINGOMYELIA?
THEY'RE NOT SURE YET.
SHIT!
IF IT'S SYRINGOMYELIA...
...I WON'T BE ABLE TO WORK!
THAT'S NOT TRUE!

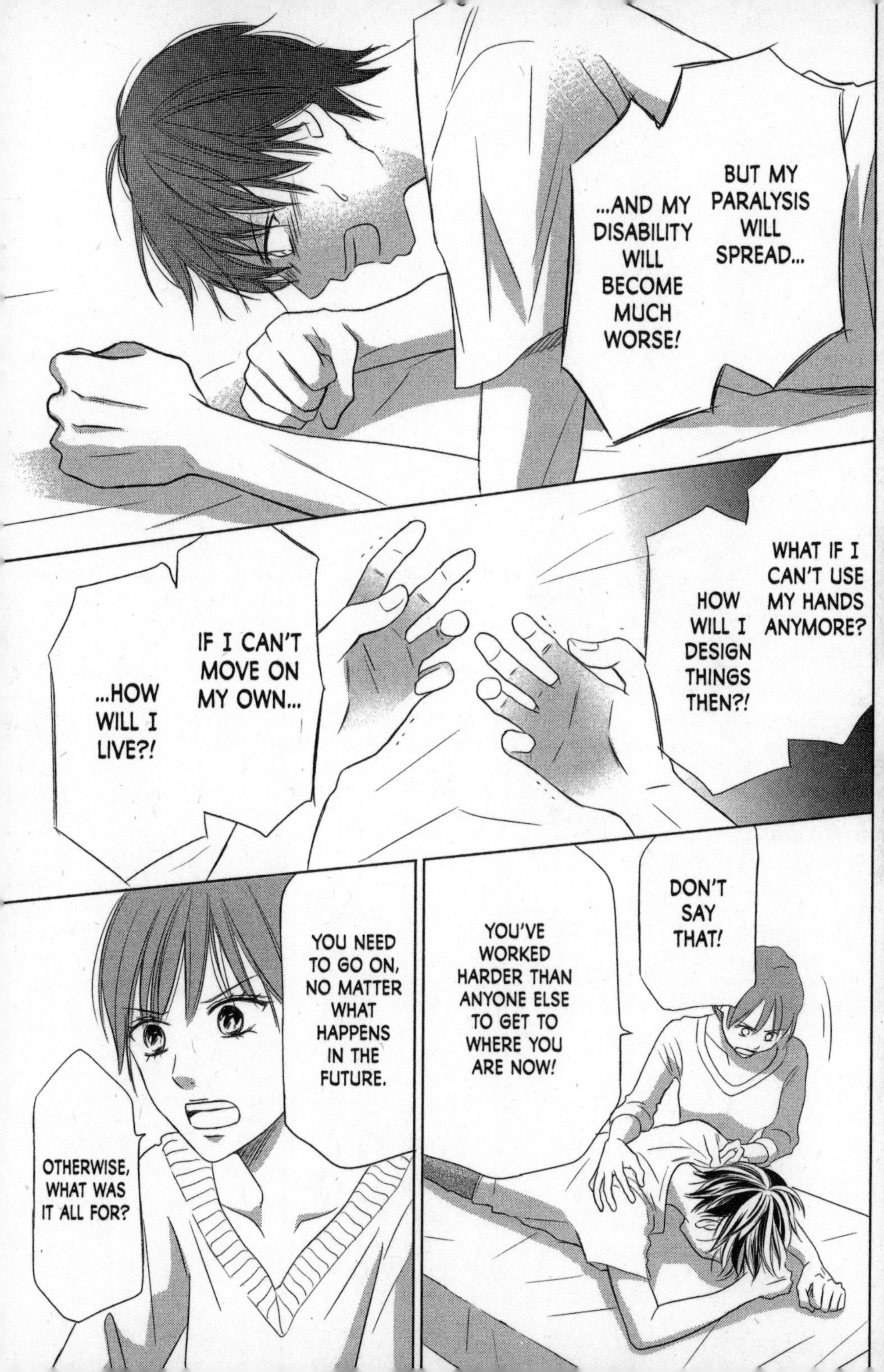
BUT MY PARALYSIS WILL SPREAD...
...AND MY DISABILITY WILL BECOME MUCH WORSE!
WHAT IF I CAN'T USE MY HANDS ANYMORE?
HOW WILL I DESIGN THINGS THEN?!
IF I CAN'T MOVE ON MY OWN...
...HOW WILL I LIVE?!
DON'T SAY THAT!
YOU'VE WORKED HARDER THAN ANYONE ELSE TO GET TO WHERE YOU ARE NOW!
YOU NEED TO GO ON, NO MATTER WHAT HAPPENS IN THE FUTURE.
OTHERWISE, WHAT WAS IT ALL FOR?

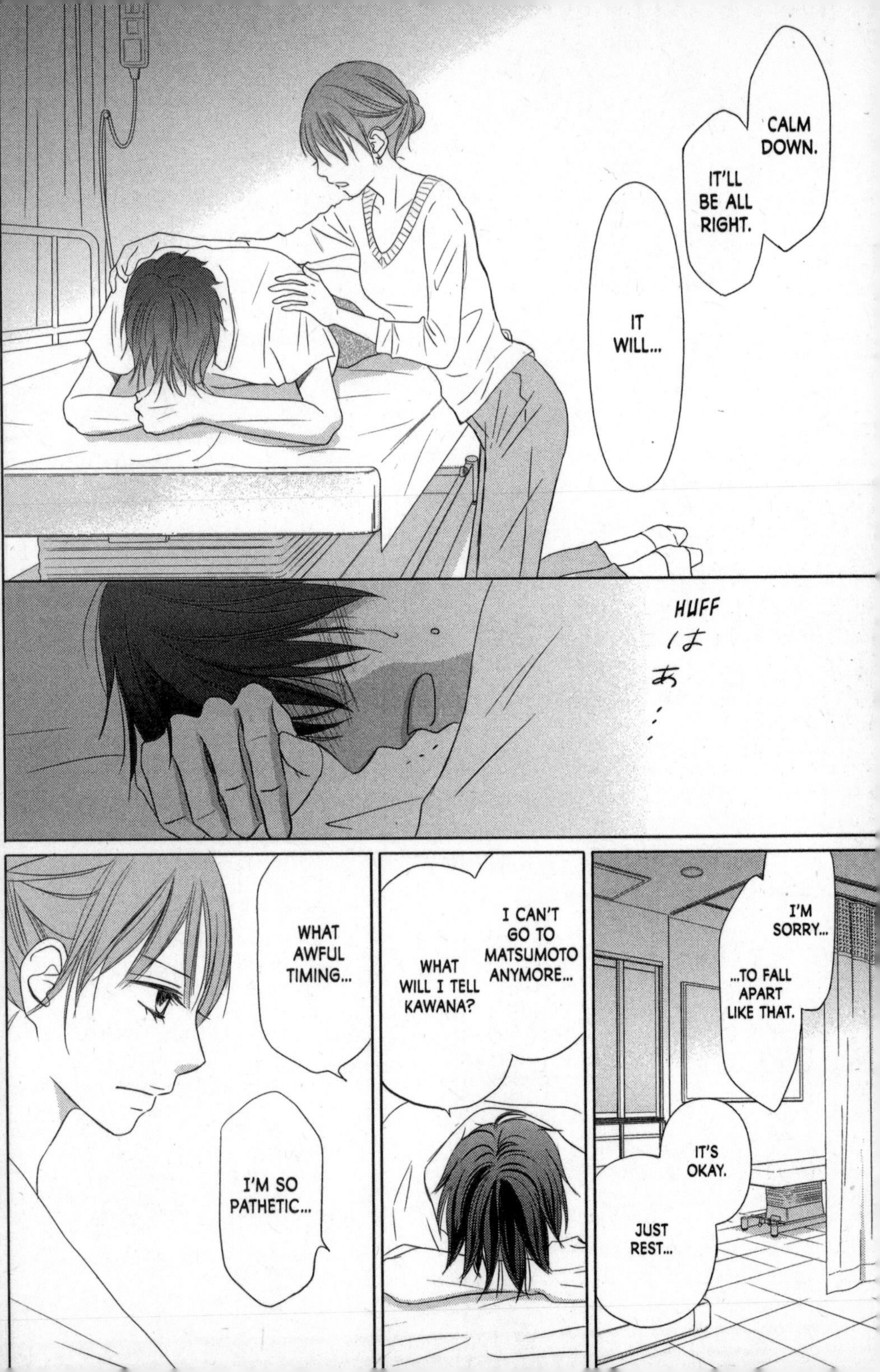
CALM DOWN.
IT'LL BE ALL RIGHT.
IT WILL...
HUFF
はあ・・・
I'M SORRY...
...TO FALL APART LIKE THAT.
IT'S OKAY.
JUST REST...
I CAN'T GO TO MATSUMOTO ANYMORE...
WHAT WILL I TELL KAWANA?
WHAT AWFUL TIMING...
I'M SO PATHETIC...

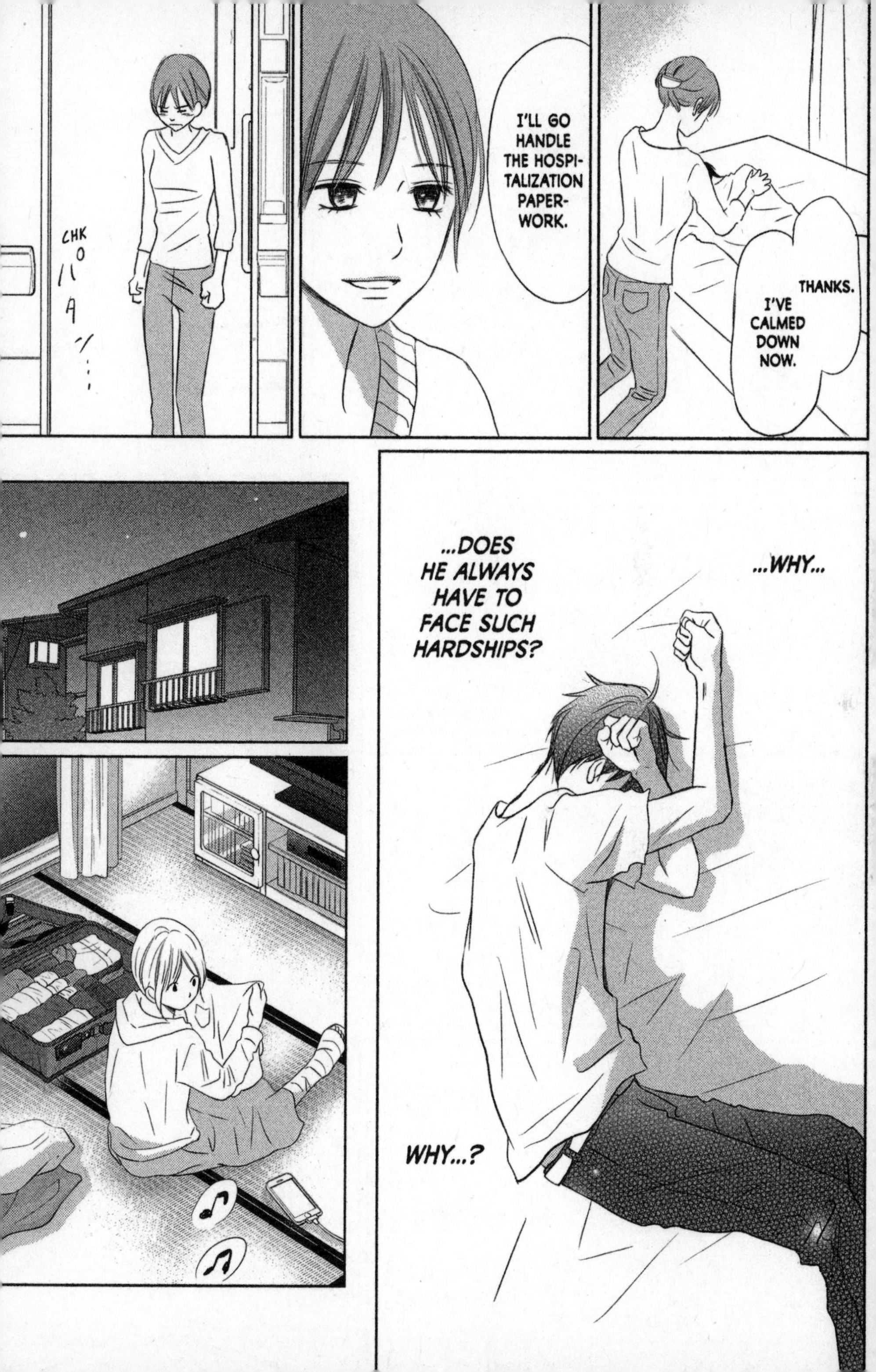
THANKS. I'VE CALMED DOWN NOW.
I'LL GO HANDLE THE HOSPITALIZATION PAPERWORK.
CHK
パタン…
...WHY...
...DOES HE ALWAYS HAVE TO FACE SUCH HARDSHIPS?
WHY...?

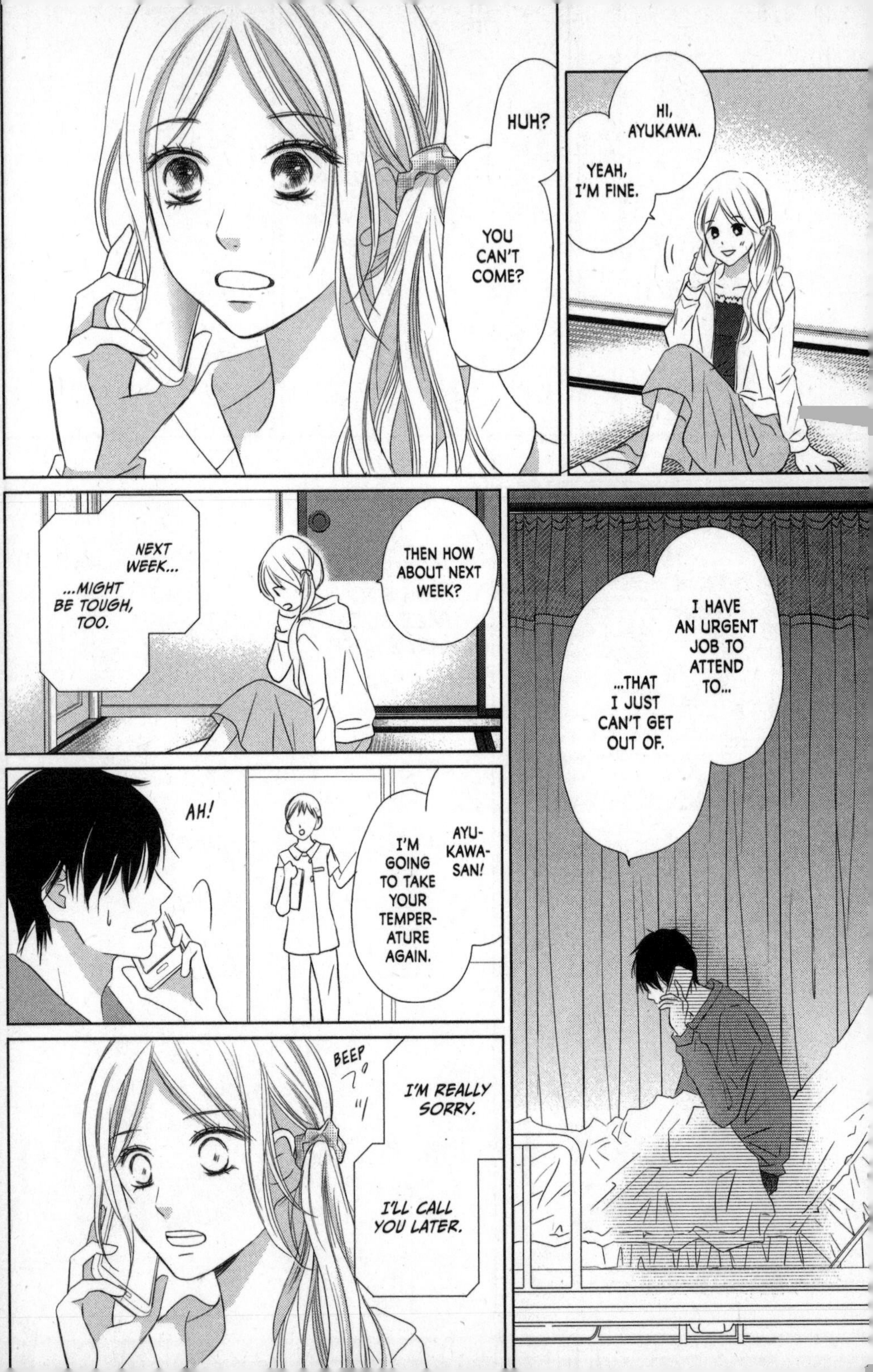
HI, AYUKAWA.
YEAH, I'M FINE.
HUH?
YOU CAN'T COME?
I HAVE AN URGENT JOB TO ATTEND TO...
...THAT I JUST CAN'T GET OUT OF.
THEN HOW ABOUT NEXT WEEK?
NEXT WEEK...
...MIGHT BE TOUGH, TOO.
AYU-KAWA-SAN!
I'M GOING TO TAKE YOUR TEMPER-ATURE AGAIN.
AH!
BEEP
I'M REALLY SORRY.
I'LL CALL YOU LATER.

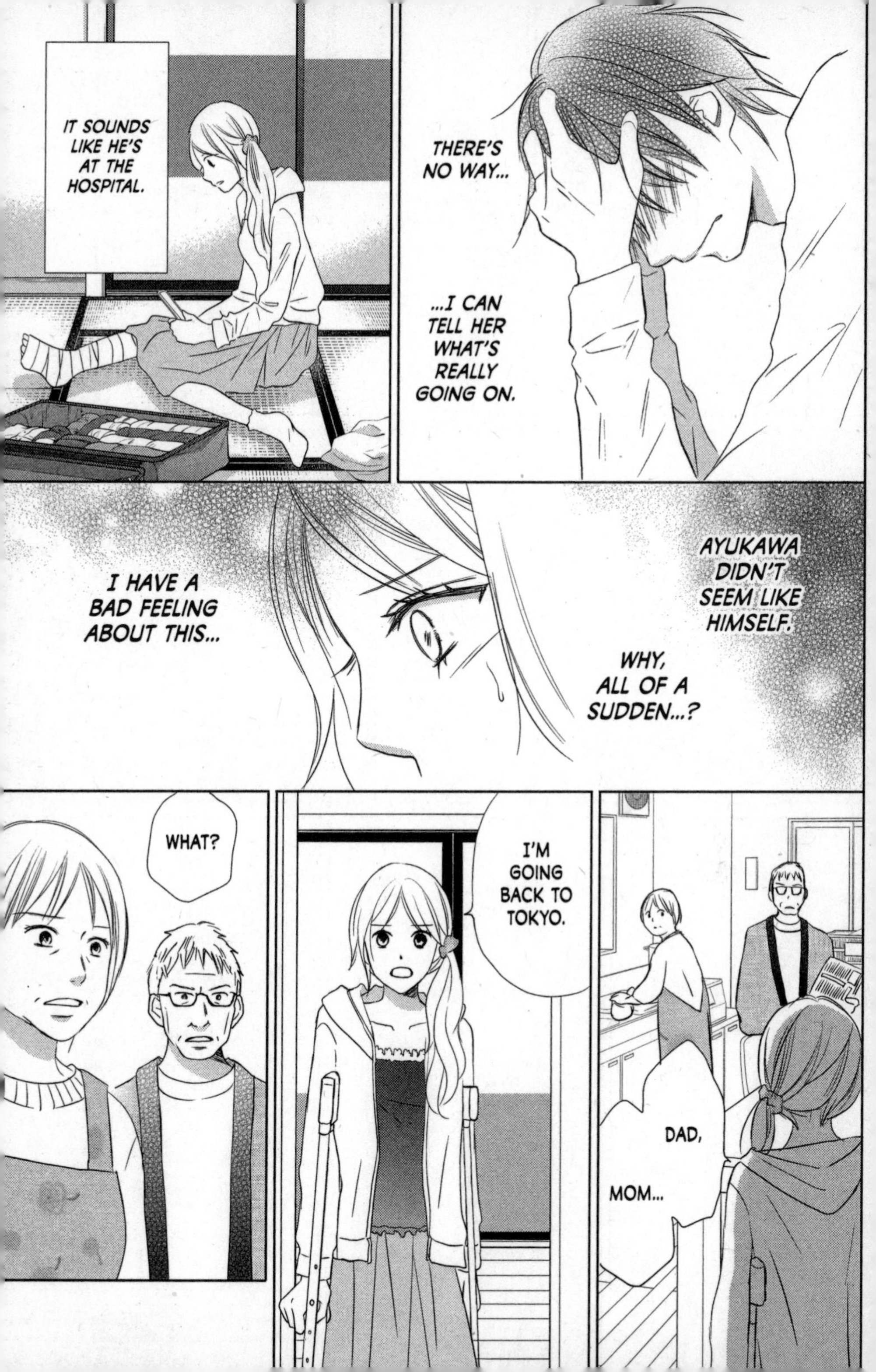
THERE'S NO WAY...
...I CAN TELL HER WHAT'S REALLY GOING ON.
IT SOUNDS LIKE HE'S AT THE HOSPITAL.
AYUKAWA DIDN'T SEEM LIKE HIMSELF.
WHY, ALL OF A SUDDEN...?
I HAVE A BAD FEELING ABOUT THIS...
DAD,
MOM...
I'M GOING BACK TO TOKYO.
WHAT?

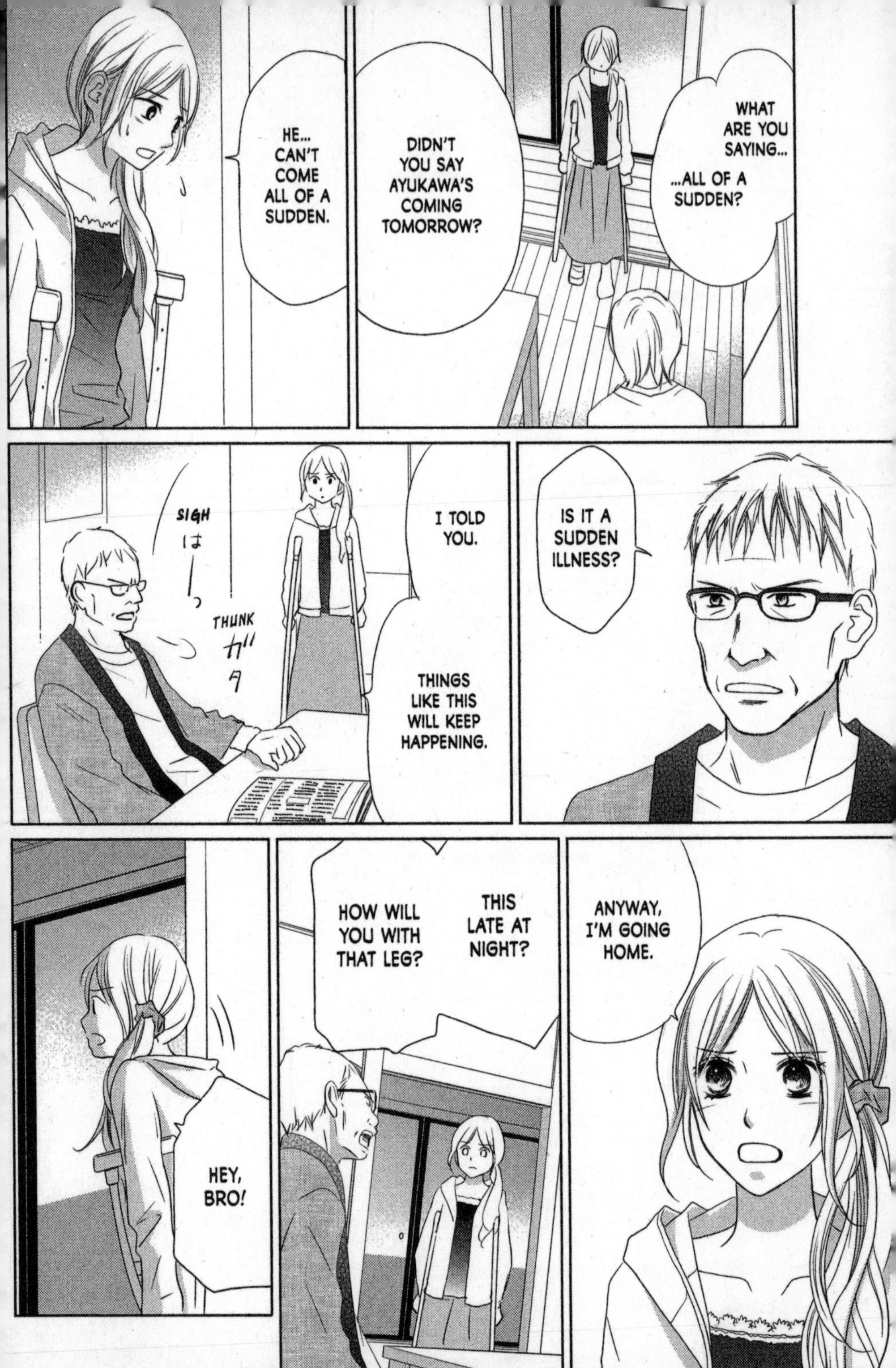
WHAT ARE YOU SAYING... ...ALL OF A SUDDEN?
DIDN'T YOU SAY AYUKAWA'S COMING TOMORROW?
HE... CAN'T COME ALL OF A SUDDEN.
IS IT A SUDDEN ILLNESS?
I TOLD YOU.
THINGS LIKE THIS WILL KEEP HAPPENING.
SIGH
はーっ
THUNK
ガタ
ANYWAY, I'M GOING HOME.
THIS LATE AT NIGHT?
HOW WILL YOU WITH THAT LEG?
HEY, BRO!

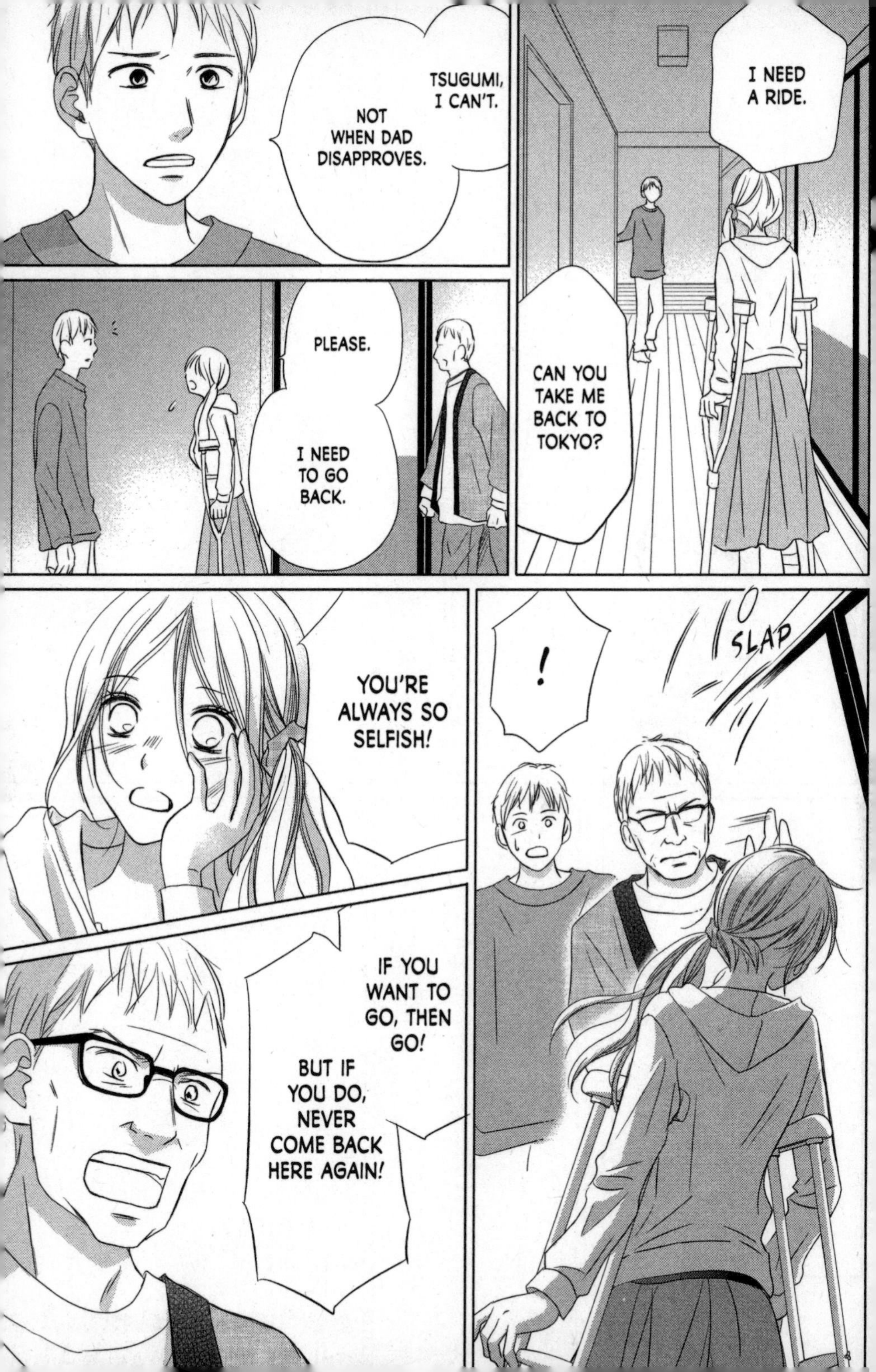
I NEED A RIDE.
CAN YOU TAKE ME BACK TO TOKYO?
TSUGUMI, I CAN'T.
NOT WHEN DAD DISAPPROVES.
PLEASE.
I NEED TO GO BACK.
SLAP
!
YOU'RE ALWAYS SO SELFISH!
IF YOU WANT TO GO, THEN GO!
BUT IF YOU DO, NEVER COME BACK HERE AGAIN!

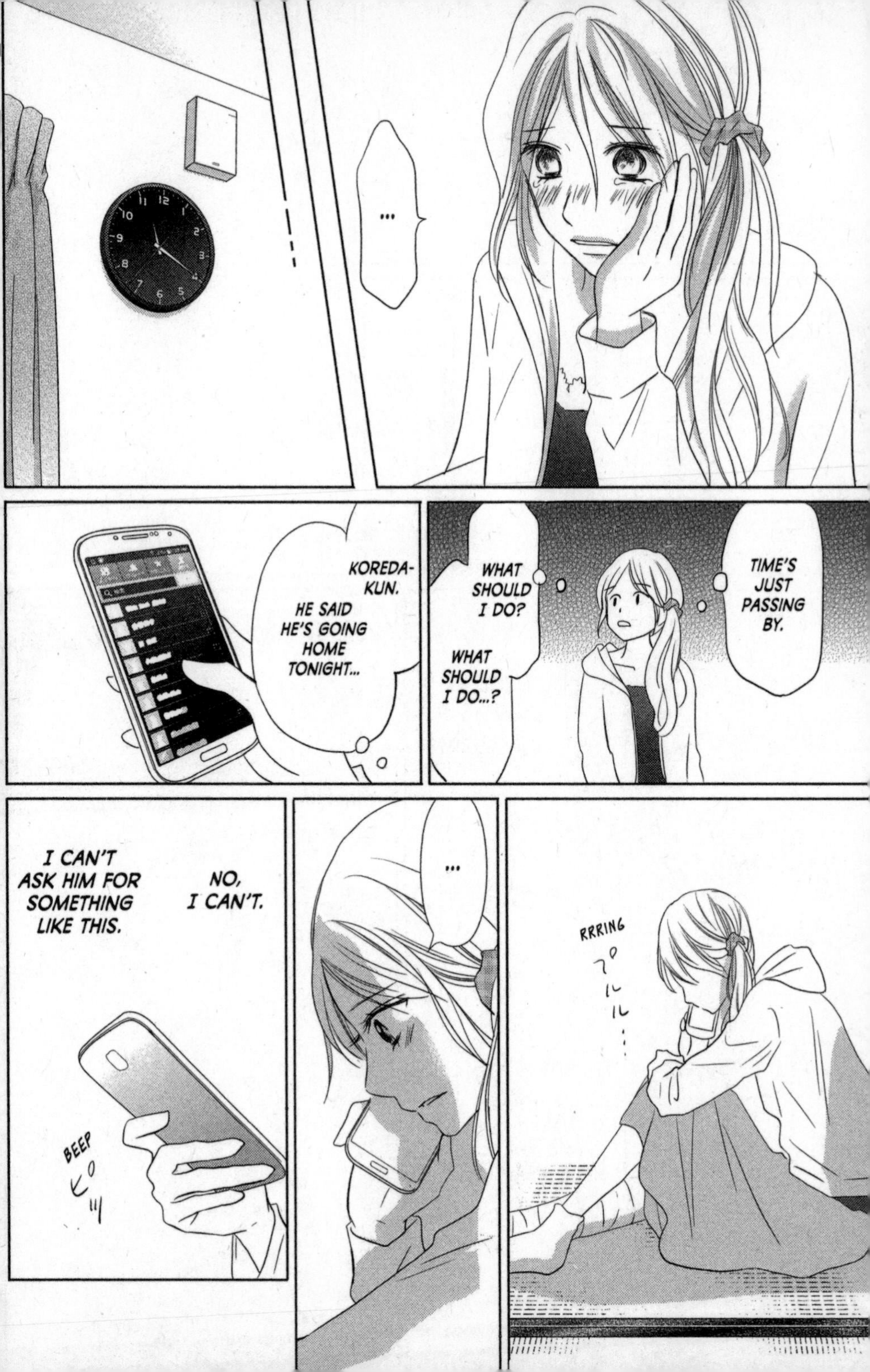
...
TIME'S JUST PASSING BY.
WHAT SHOULD I DO?
WHAT SHOULD I DO...?
KOREDA-KUN.
HE SAID HE'S GOING HOME TONIGHT...
RRRING
プルル…
...
NO, I CAN'T.
I CAN'T ASK HIM FOR SOMETHING LIKE THIS.
BEEP
ピッ

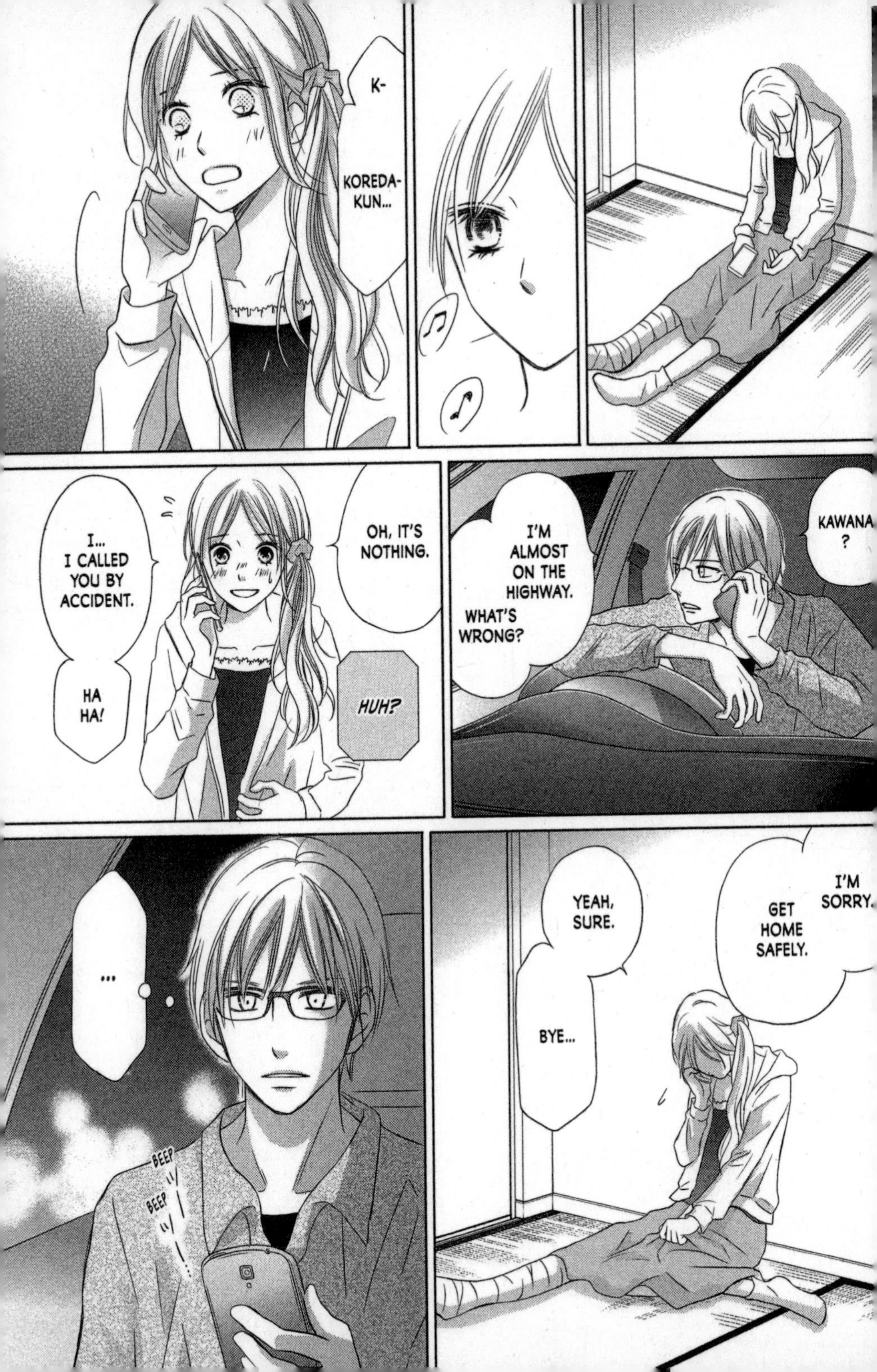
K-
KOREDA-KUN...
KAWANA?
I'M ALMOST ON THE HIGHWAY.
WHAT'S WRONG?
HUH?
OH, IT'S NOTHING.
I... I CALLED YOU BY ACCIDENT.
HA HA!
I'M SORRY.
GET HOME SAFELY.
YEAH, SURE.
BYE...
...
BEEP
BEEP

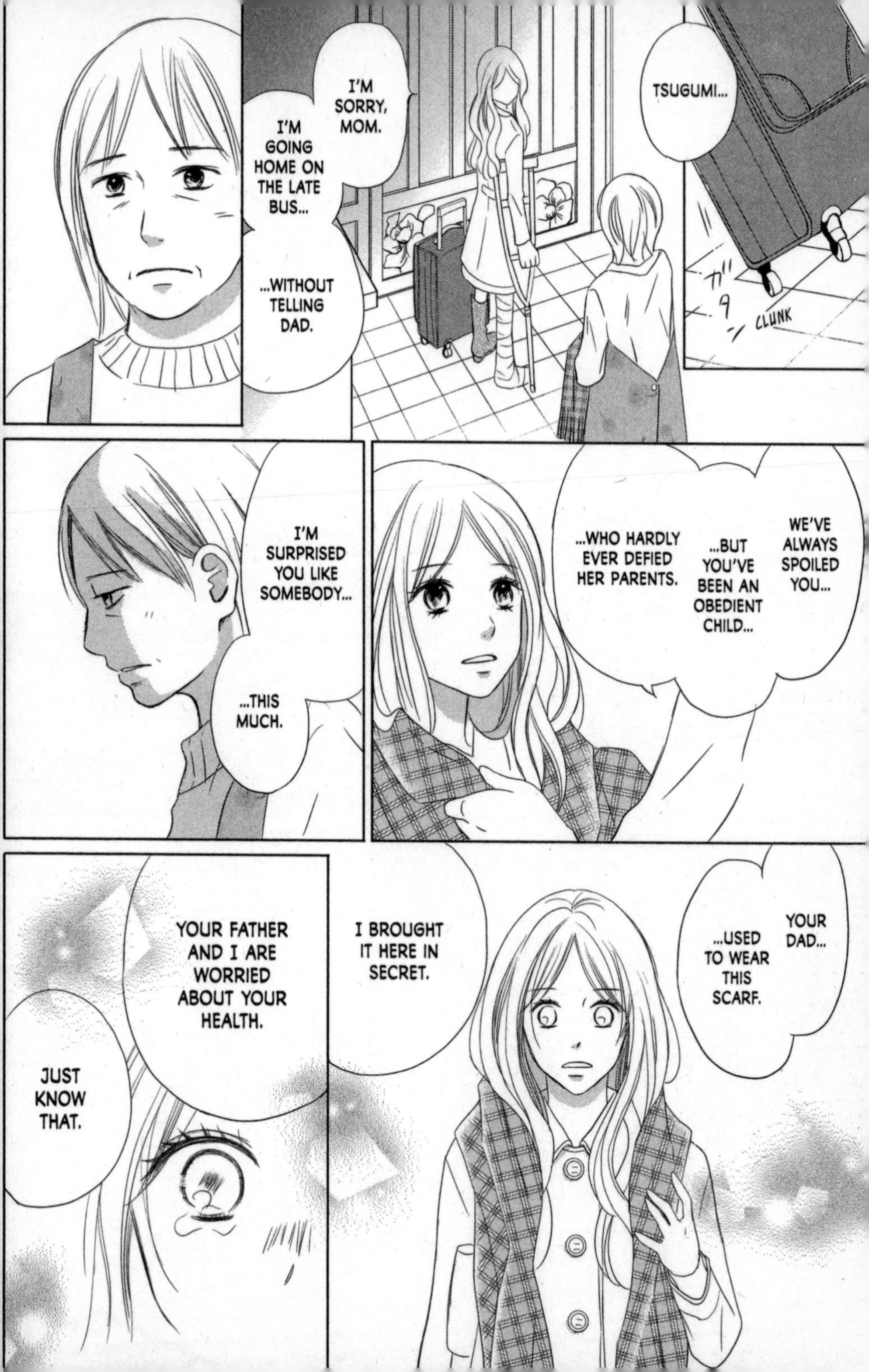
TSUGUMI...
ガタ
CLUNK
I'M SORRY, MOM.
I'M GOING HOME ON THE LATE BUS...
...WITHOUT TELLING DAD.
WE'VE ALWAYS SPOILED YOU...
...BUT YOU'VE BEEN AN OBEDIENT CHILD...
...WHO HARDLY EVER DEFIED HER PARENTS.
I'M SURPRISED YOU LIKE SOMEBODY...
...THIS MUCH.
YOUR DAD...
...USED TO WEAR THIS SCARF.
I BROUGHT IT HERE IN SECRET.
YOUR FATHER AND I ARE WORRIED ABOUT YOUR HEALTH.
JUST KNOW THAT.

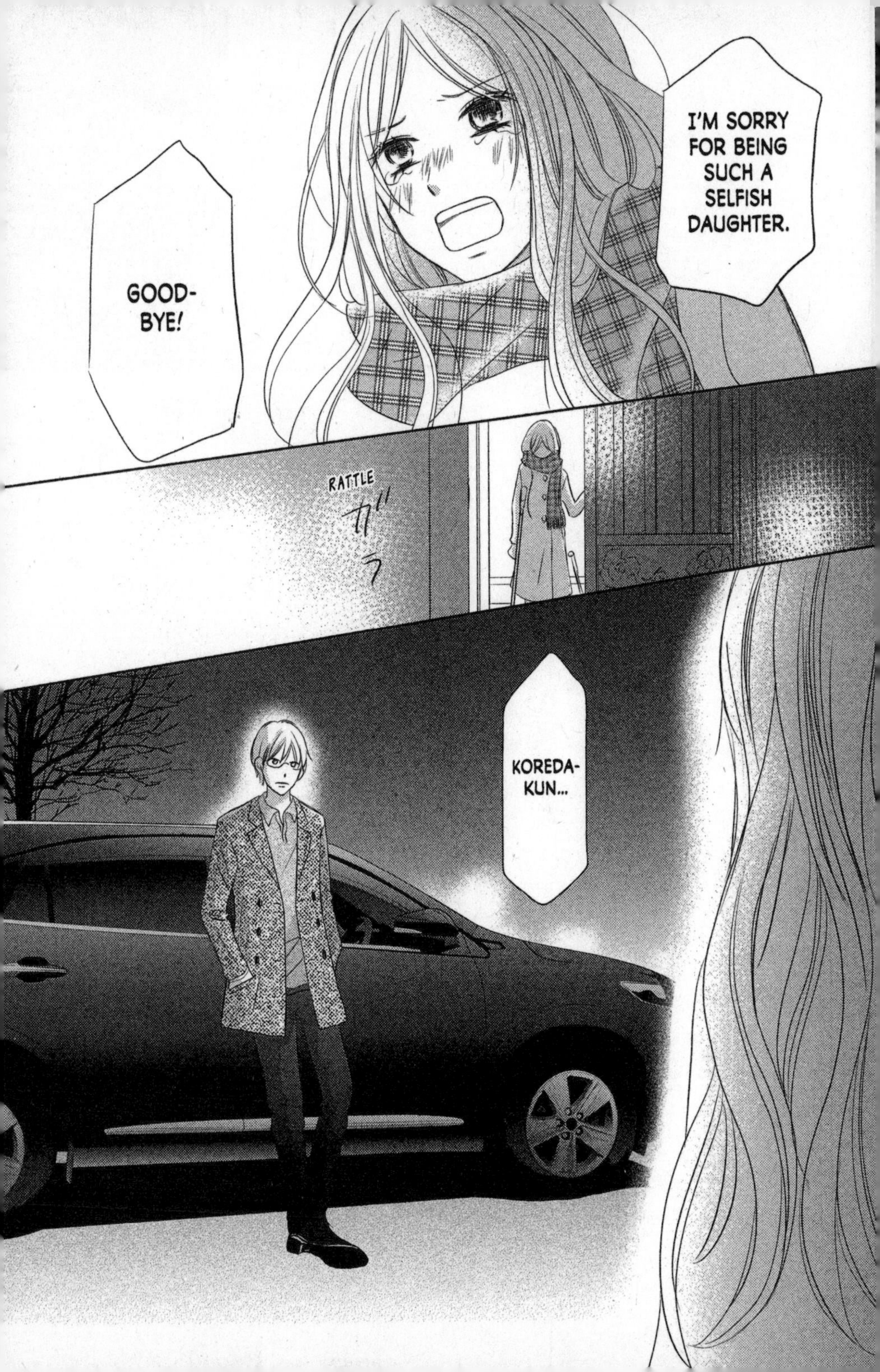
I'M SORRY FOR BEING SUCH A SELFISH DAUGHTER.
GOOD-BYE!
RATTLE
ガラ
KOREDA-KUN...

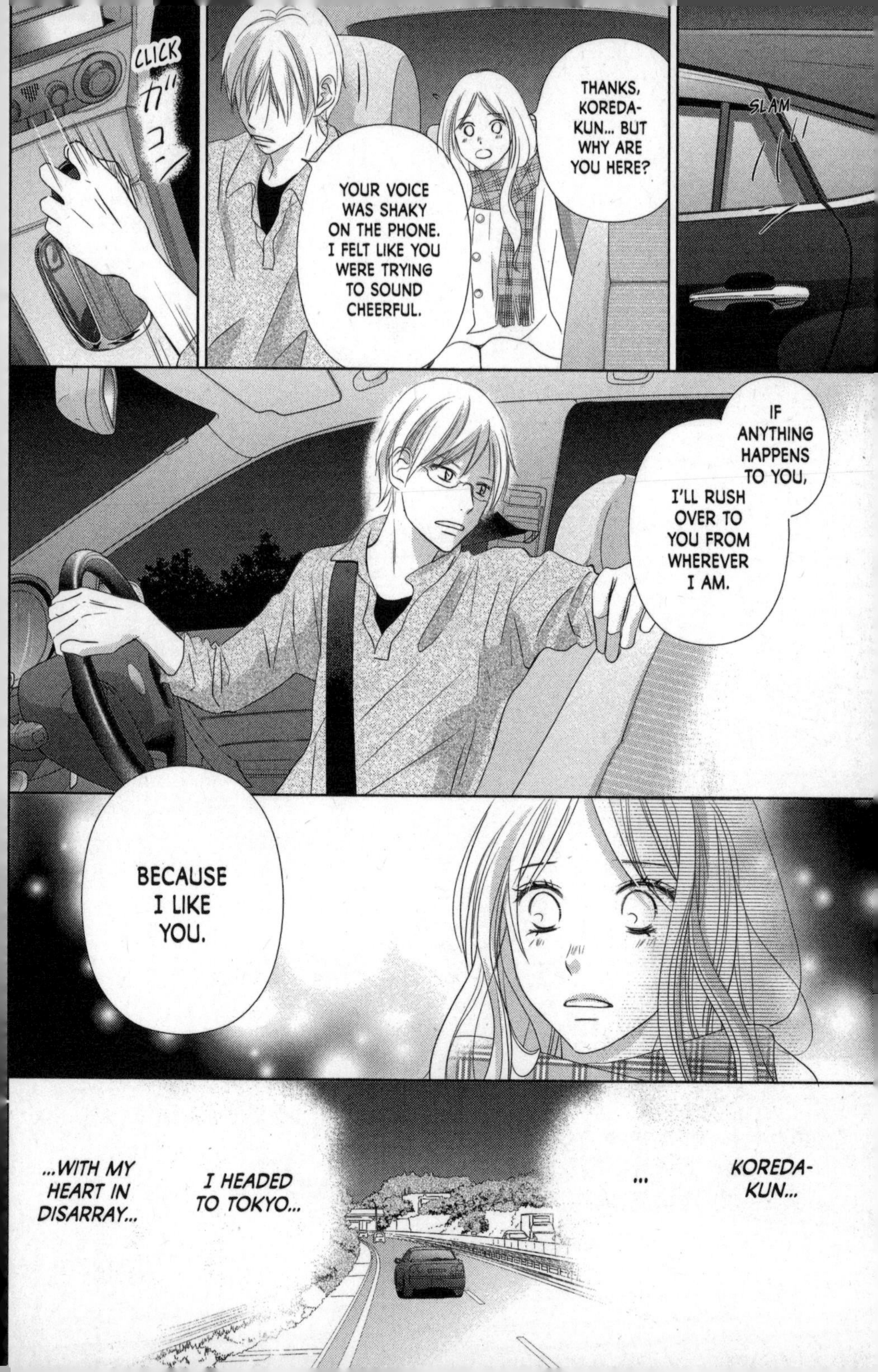
SLAM
THANKS, KOREDA-KUN... BUT WHY ARE YOU HERE?
YOUR VOICE WAS SHAKY ON THE PHONE. I FELT LIKE YOU WERE TRYING TO SOUND CHEERFUL.
CLICK
ガコ
IF ANYTHING HAPPENS TO YOU, I'LL RUSH OVER TO YOU FROM WHEREVER I AM.
BECAUSE I LIKE YOU.
KOREDA-KUN...
...
I HEADED TO TOKYO...
...WITH MY HEART IN DISARRAY...

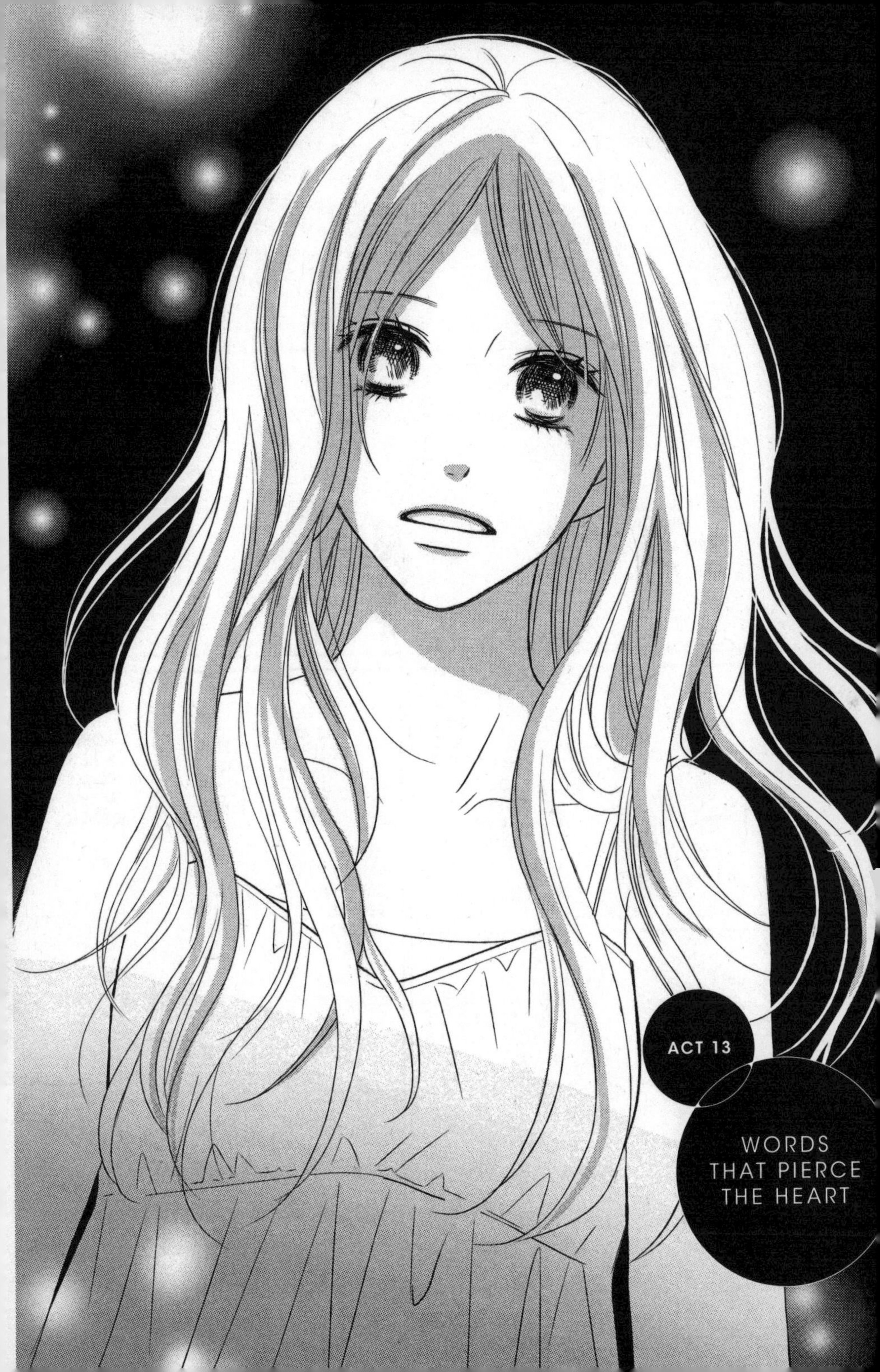
ACT 13
WORDS THAT PIERCE THE HEART

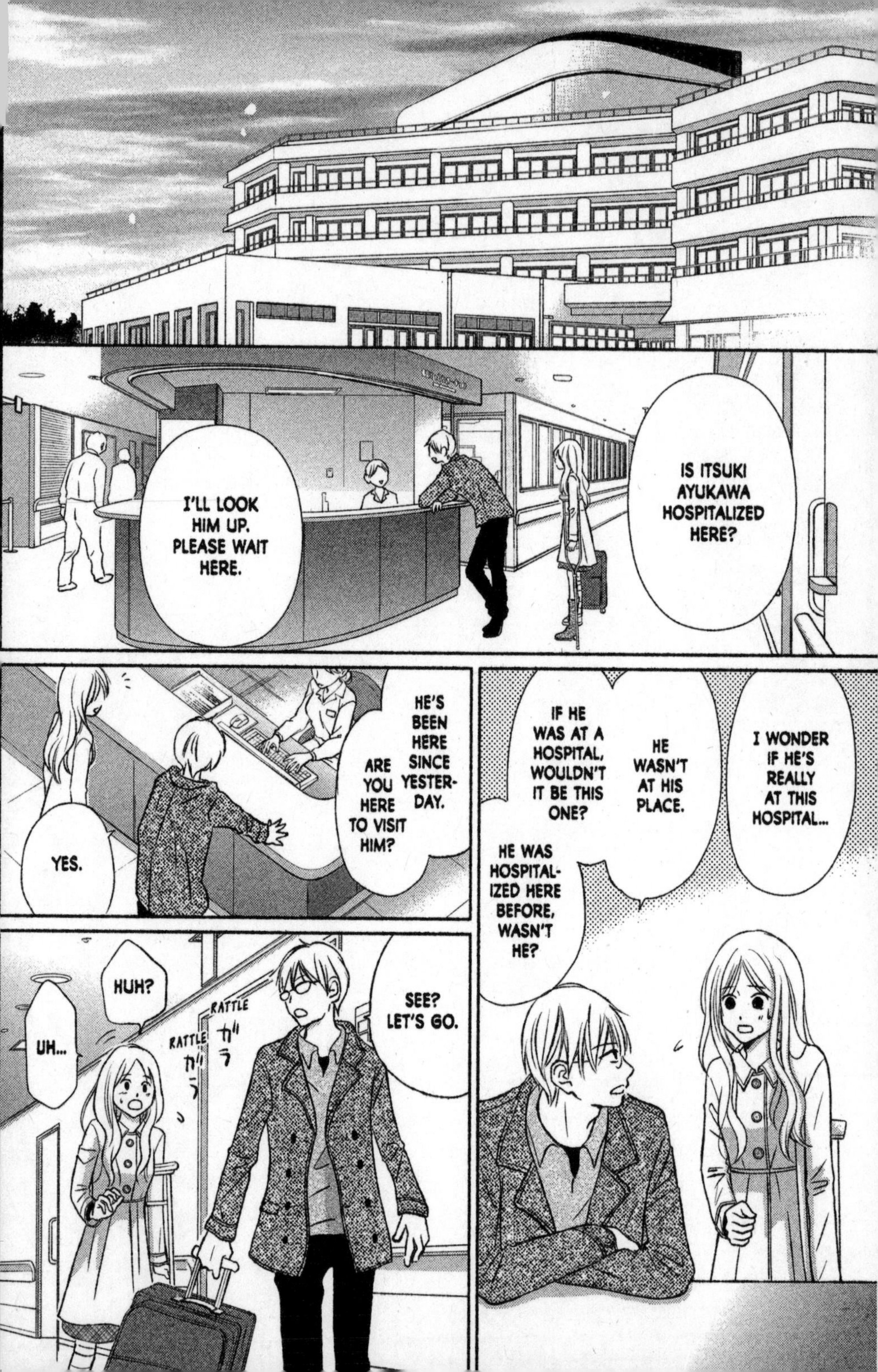
IS ITSUKI AYUKAWA HOSPITALIZED HERE?
I'LL LOOK HIM UP. PLEASE WAIT HERE.
I WONDER IF HE'S REALLY AT THIS HOSPITAL...
HE WASN'T AT HIS PLACE.
IF HE WAS AT A HOSPITAL, WOULDN'T IT BE THIS ONE?
HE WAS HOSPITALIZED HERE BEFORE, WASN'T HE?
HE'S BEEN HERE SINCE YESTERDAY.
ARE YOU HERE TO VISIT HIM?
YES.
SEE? LET'S GO.
HUH?
RATTLE ガラ
RATTLE ガラ
UH...

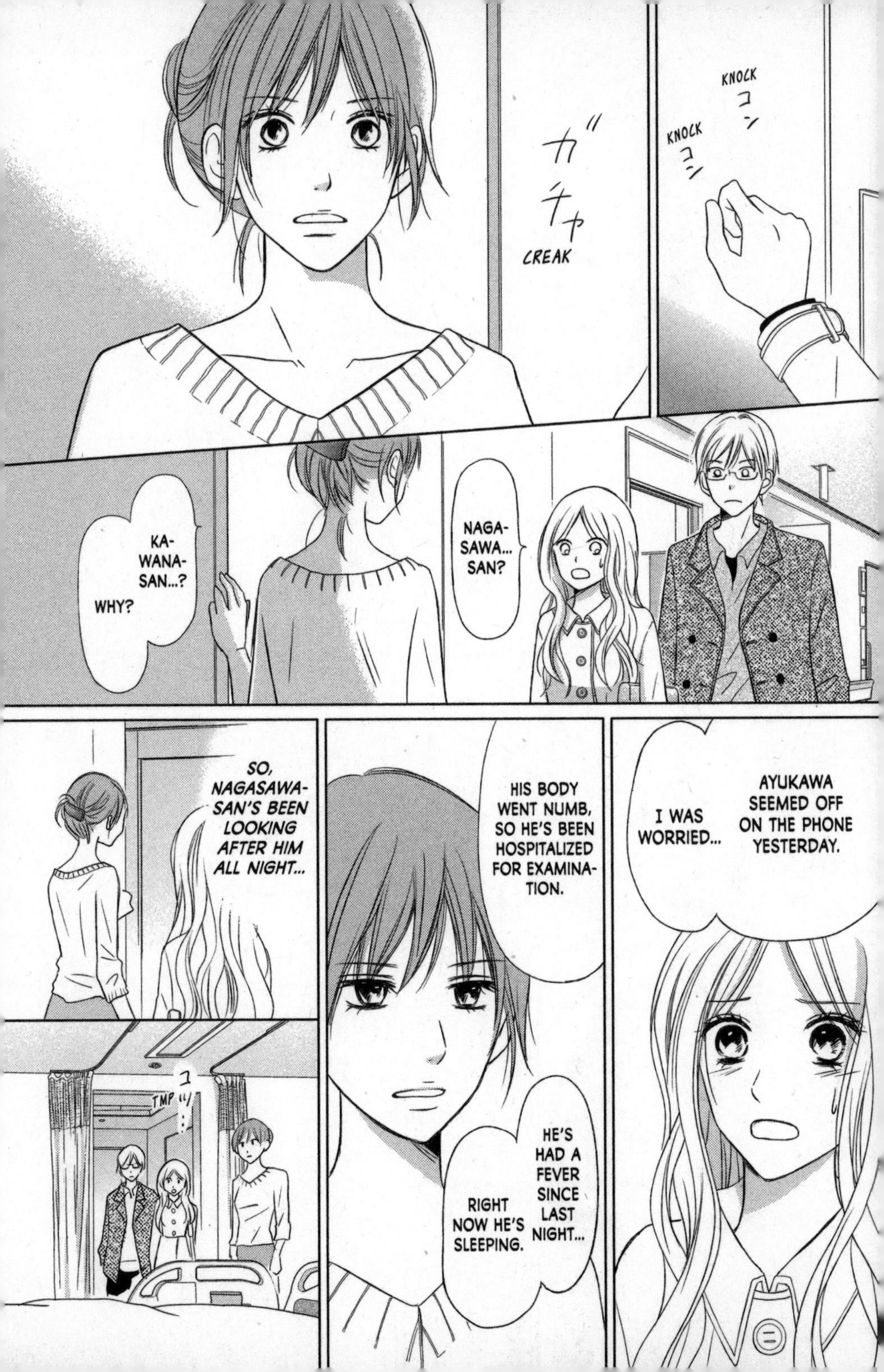
KNOCK
コン
KNOCK
コン
ガチャ
CREAK
NAGA-SAWA... SAN?
KA-WANA-SAN...?
WHY?
AYUKAWA SEEMED OFF ON THE PHONE YESTERDAY.
I WAS WORRIED...
HIS BODY WENT NUMB, SO HE'S BEEN HOSPITALIZED FOR EXAMINA-TION.
HE'S HAD A FEVER SINCE LAST NIGHT...
RIGHT NOW HE'S SLEEPING.
SO, NAGASAWA-SAN'S BEEN LOOKING AFTER HIM ALL NIGHT...
TMP
コツ...

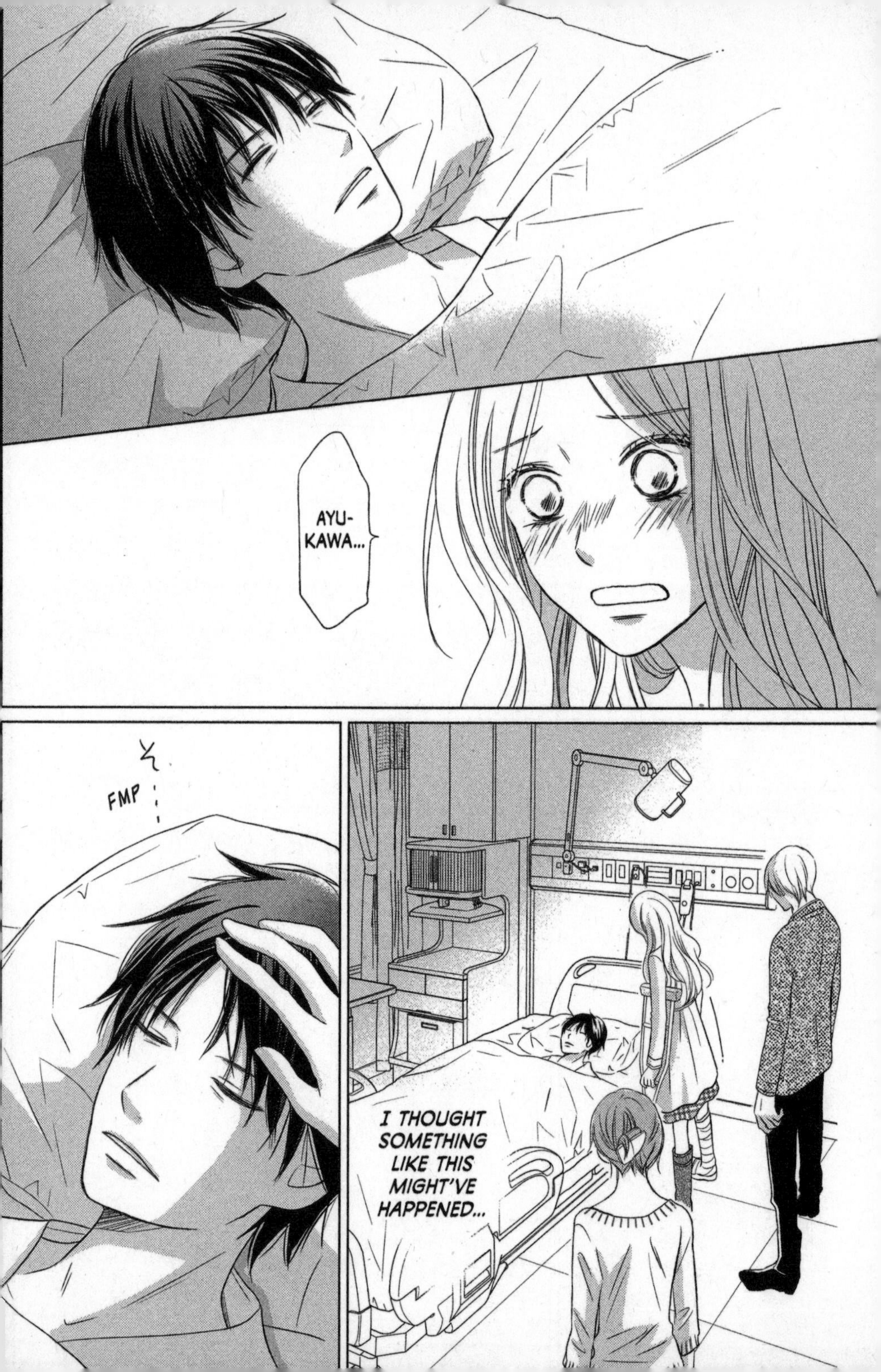
AYU-
KAWA...
I THOUGHT SOMETHING LIKE THIS MIGHT'VE HAPPENED...
FMP

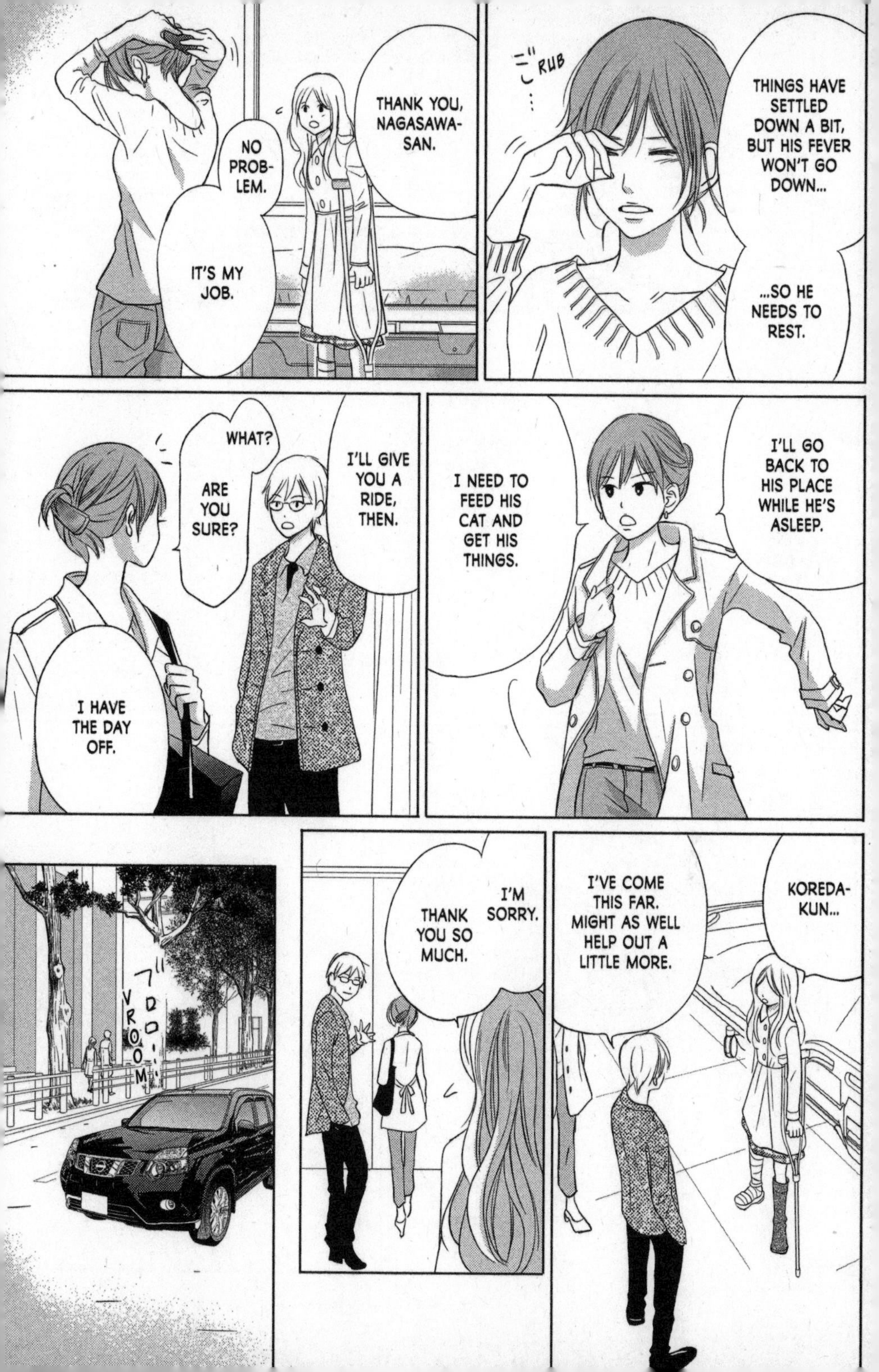
RUB
THINGS HAVE SETTLED DOWN A BIT, BUT HIS FEVER WON'T GO DOWN...
...SO HE NEEDS TO REST.
THANK YOU, NAGASAWA-SAN.
NO PROB-LEM.
IT'S MY JOB.
I'LL GO BACK TO HIS PLACE WHILE HE'S ASLEEP.
I NEED TO FEED HIS CAT AND GET HIS THINGS.
I'LL GIVE YOU A RIDE, THEN.
WHAT?
ARE YOU SURE?
I HAVE THE DAY OFF.
KOREDA-KUN...
I'VE COME THIS FAR. MIGHT AS WELL HELP OUT A LITTLE MORE.
I'M SORRY.
THANK YOU SO MUCH.
VROOM

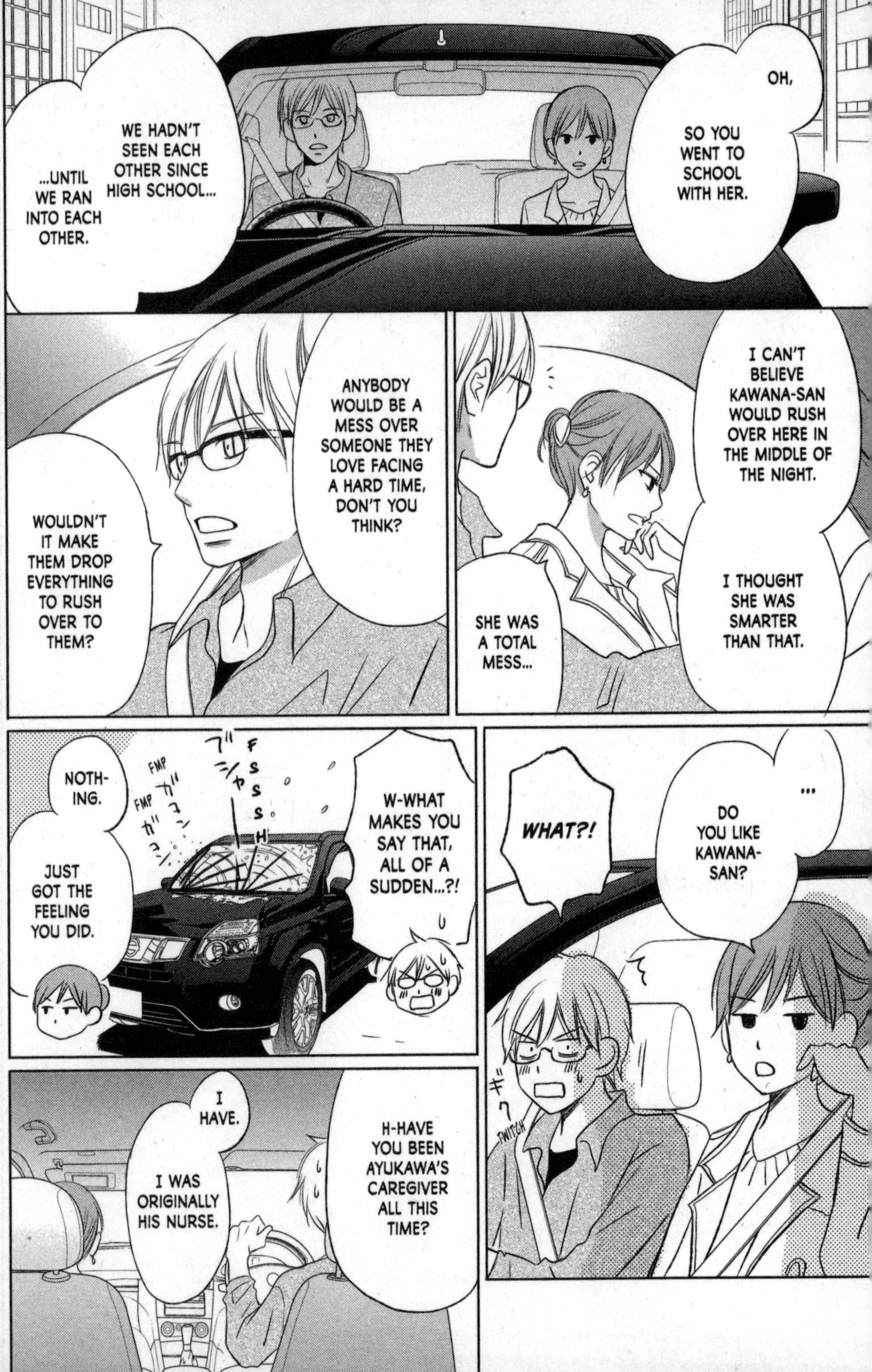
OH,
SO YOU WENT TO SCHOOL WITH HER.
WE HADN'T SEEN EACH OTHER SINCE HIGH SCHOOL...
...UNTIL WE RAN INTO EACH OTHER.
I CAN'T BELIEVE KAWANA-SAN WOULD RUSH OVER HERE IN THE MIDDLE OF THE NIGHT.
I THOUGHT SHE WAS SMARTER THAN THAT.
SHE WAS A TOTAL MESS...
ANYBODY WOULD BE A MESS OVER SOMEONE THEY LOVE FACING A HARD TIME, DON'T YOU THINK?
WOULDN'T IT MAKE THEM DROP EVERYTHING TO RUSH OVER TO THEM?
...
DO YOU LIKE KAWANA-SAN?
WHAT?!
TWITCH
W-WHAT MAKES YOU SAY THAT, ALL OF A SUDDEN...?!
FSSSH
FMP
FMP
NOTH-ING.
JUST GOT THE FEELING YOU DID.
H-HAVE YOU BEEN AYUKAWA'S CAREGIVER ALL THIS TIME?
I HAVE.
I WAS ORIGINALLY HIS NURSE.

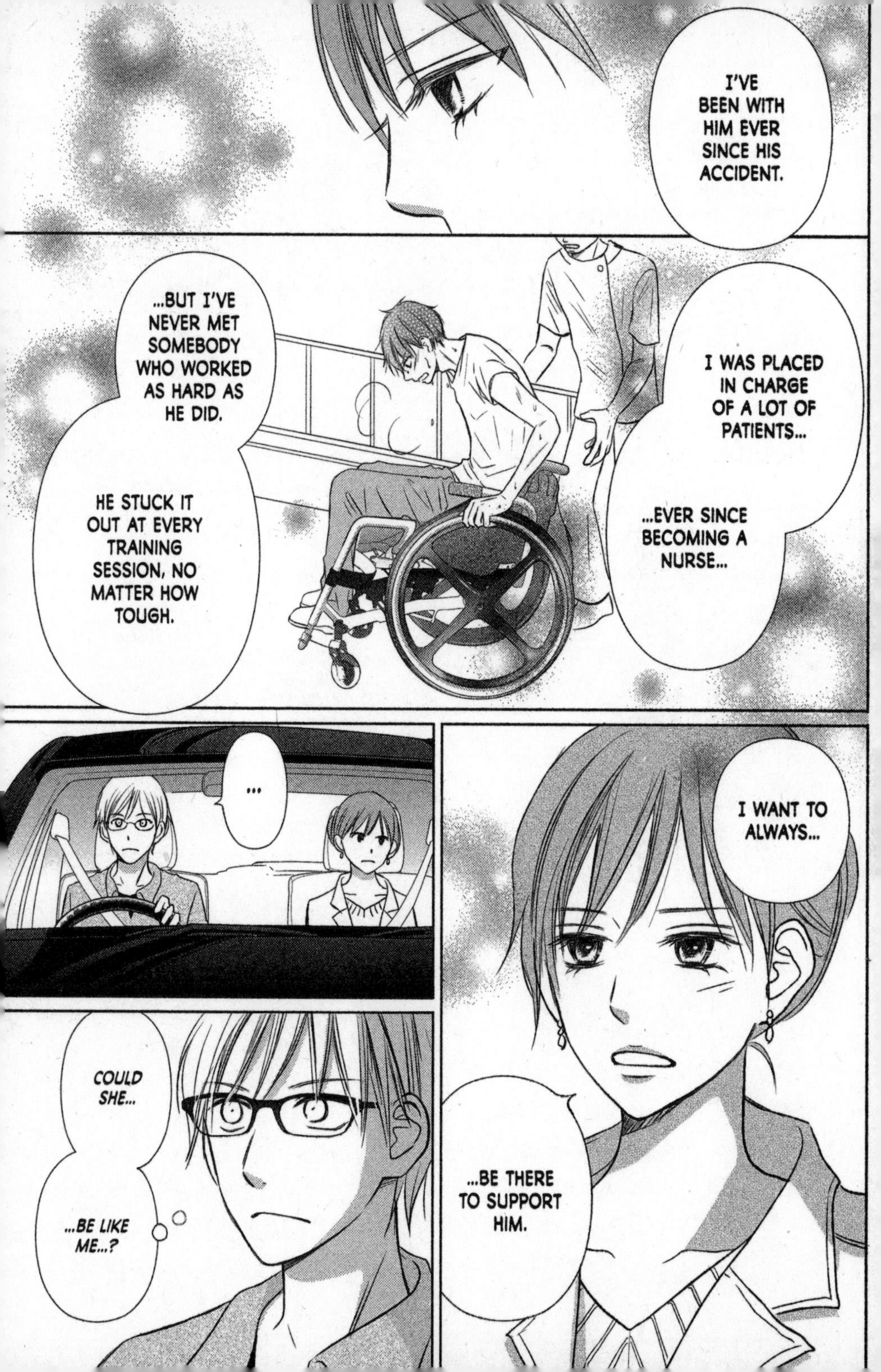
I'VE BEEN WITH HIM EVER SINCE HIS ACCIDENT.
I WAS PLACED IN CHARGE OF A LOT OF PATIENTS...
...EVER SINCE BECOMING A NURSE...
...BUT I'VE NEVER MET SOMEBODY WHO WORKED AS HARD AS HE DID.
HE STUCK IT OUT AT EVERY TRAINING SESSION, NO MATTER HOW TOUGH.
I WANT TO ALWAYS...
...BE THERE TO SUPPORT HIM.
...
COULD SHE...
...BE LIKE ME...?

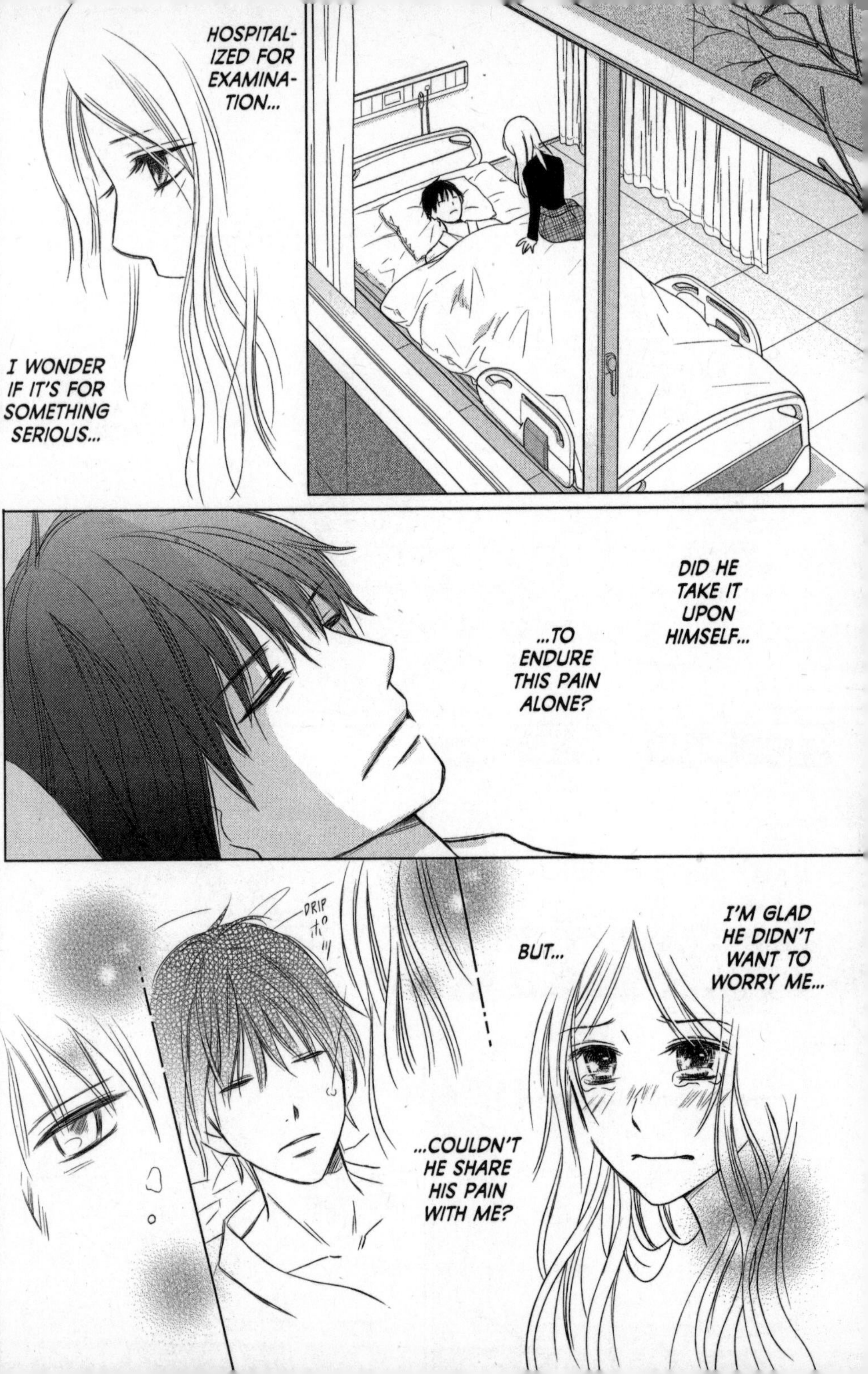
HOSPITAL-IZED FOR EXAMINA-TION...
I WONDER IF IT'S FOR SOMETHING SERIOUS...
DID HE TAKE IT UPON HIMSELF...
...TO ENDURE THIS PAIN ALONE?
I'M GLAD HE DIDN'T WANT TO WORRY ME...
BUT...
DRIP
ポツ
...COULDN'T HE SHARE HIS PAIN WITH ME?

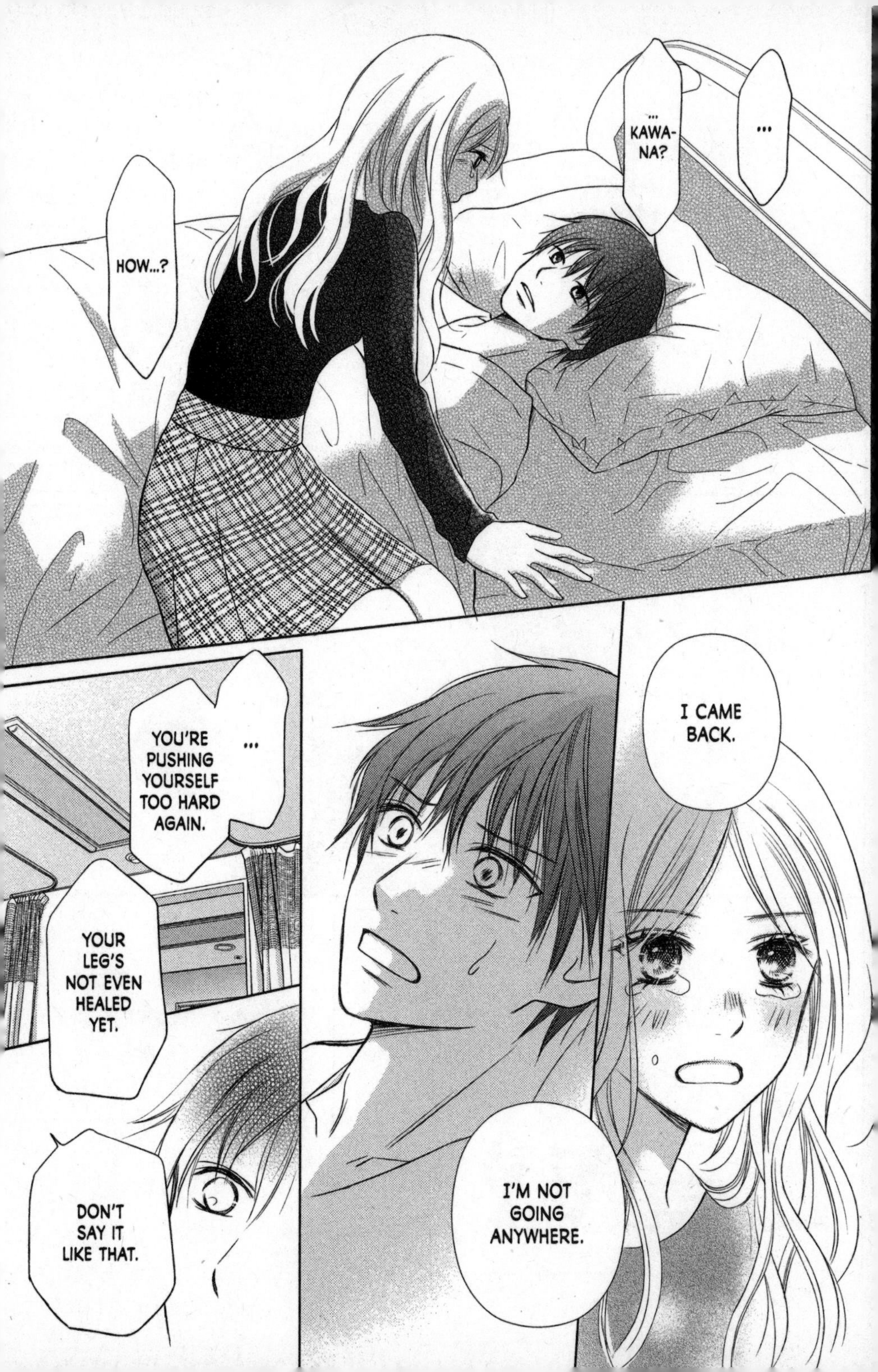
...
... KAWANA?
HOW...?
I CAME BACK.
I'M NOT GOING ANYWHERE.
...
YOU'RE PUSHING YOURSELF TOO HARD AGAIN.
YOUR LEG'S NOT EVEN HEALED YET.
DON'T SAY IT LIKE THAT.

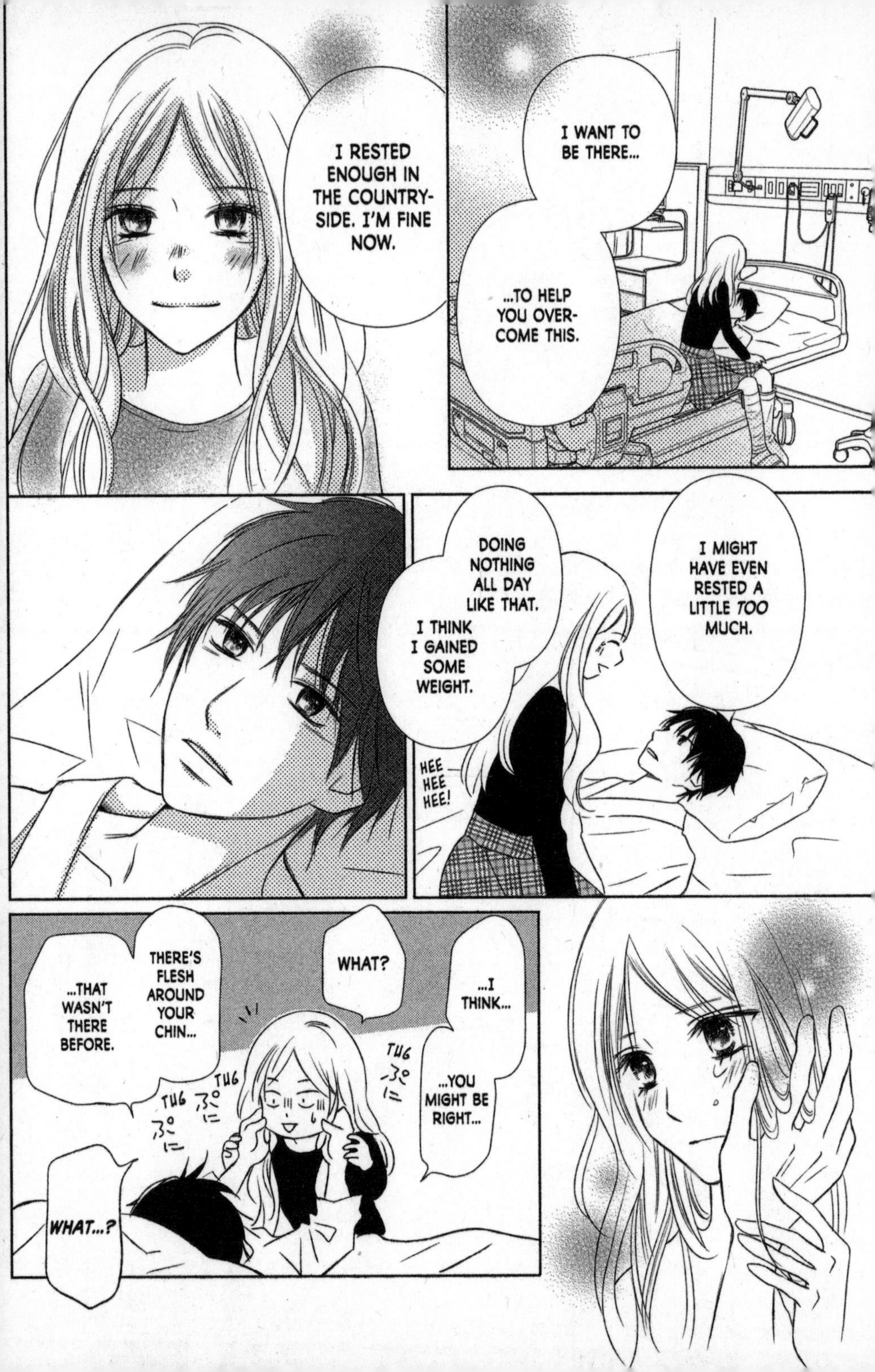
I WANT TO BE THERE...
...TO HELP YOU OVER-COME THIS.
I RESTED ENOUGH IN THE COUNTRY-SIDE. I'M FINE NOW.
I MIGHT HAVE EVEN RESTED A LITTLE *TOO* MUCH.
DOING NOTHING ALL DAY LIKE THAT.
I THINK I GAINED SOME WEIGHT.
HEE HEE HEE!
...I THINK...
...YOU MIGHT BE RIGHT...
WHAT?
TUG ぷに
TUG ぷに
TUG ぷに
THERE'S FLESH AROUND YOUR CHIN...
...THAT WASN'T THERE BEFORE.
WHAT...?

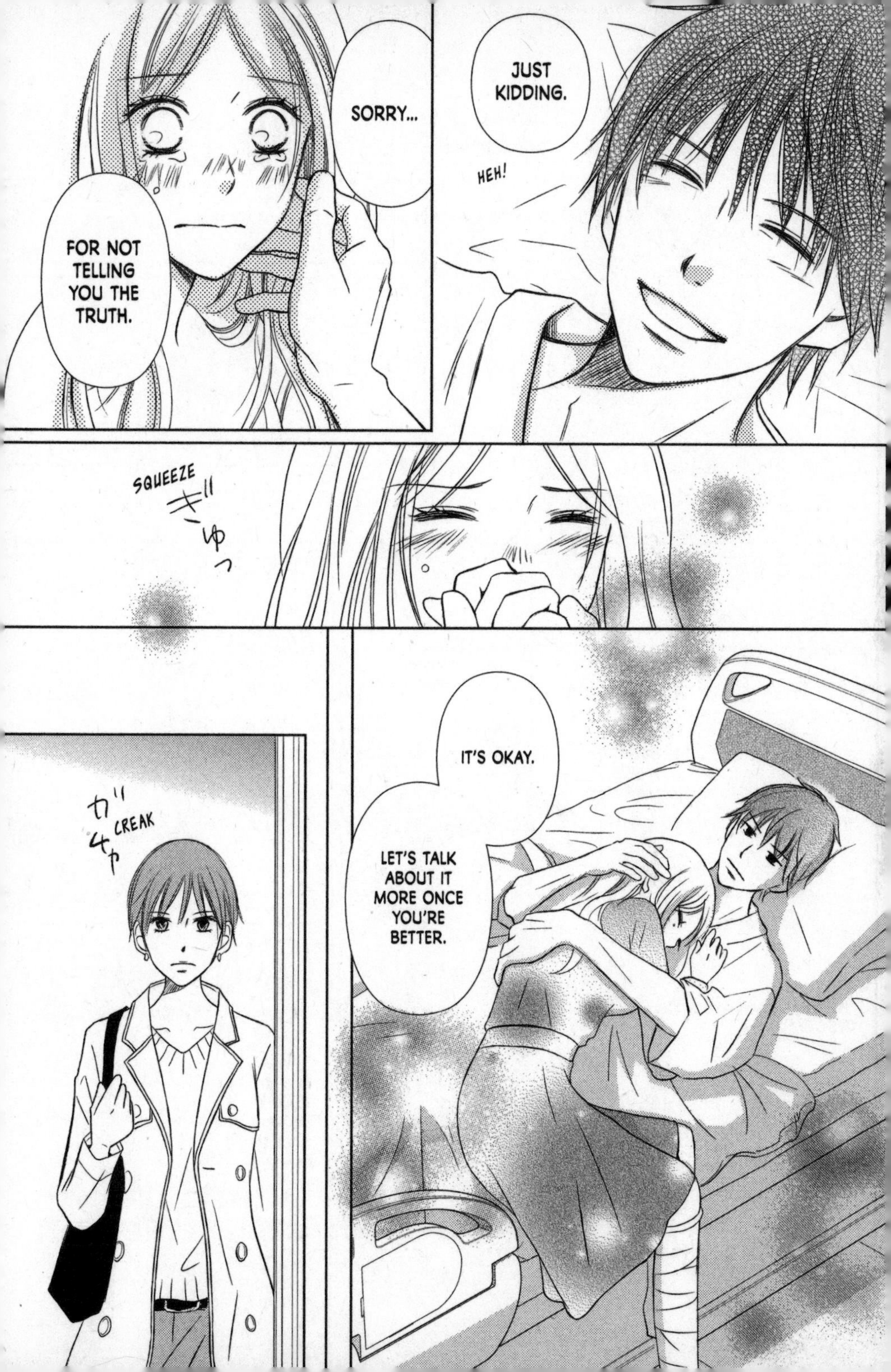
JUST KIDDING.
HEH!
SORRY...
FOR NOT TELLING YOU THE TRUTH.
SQUEEZE
ぎゅっ
IT'S OKAY.
LET'S TALK ABOUT IT MORE ONCE YOU'RE BETTER.
ガチャ
CREAK

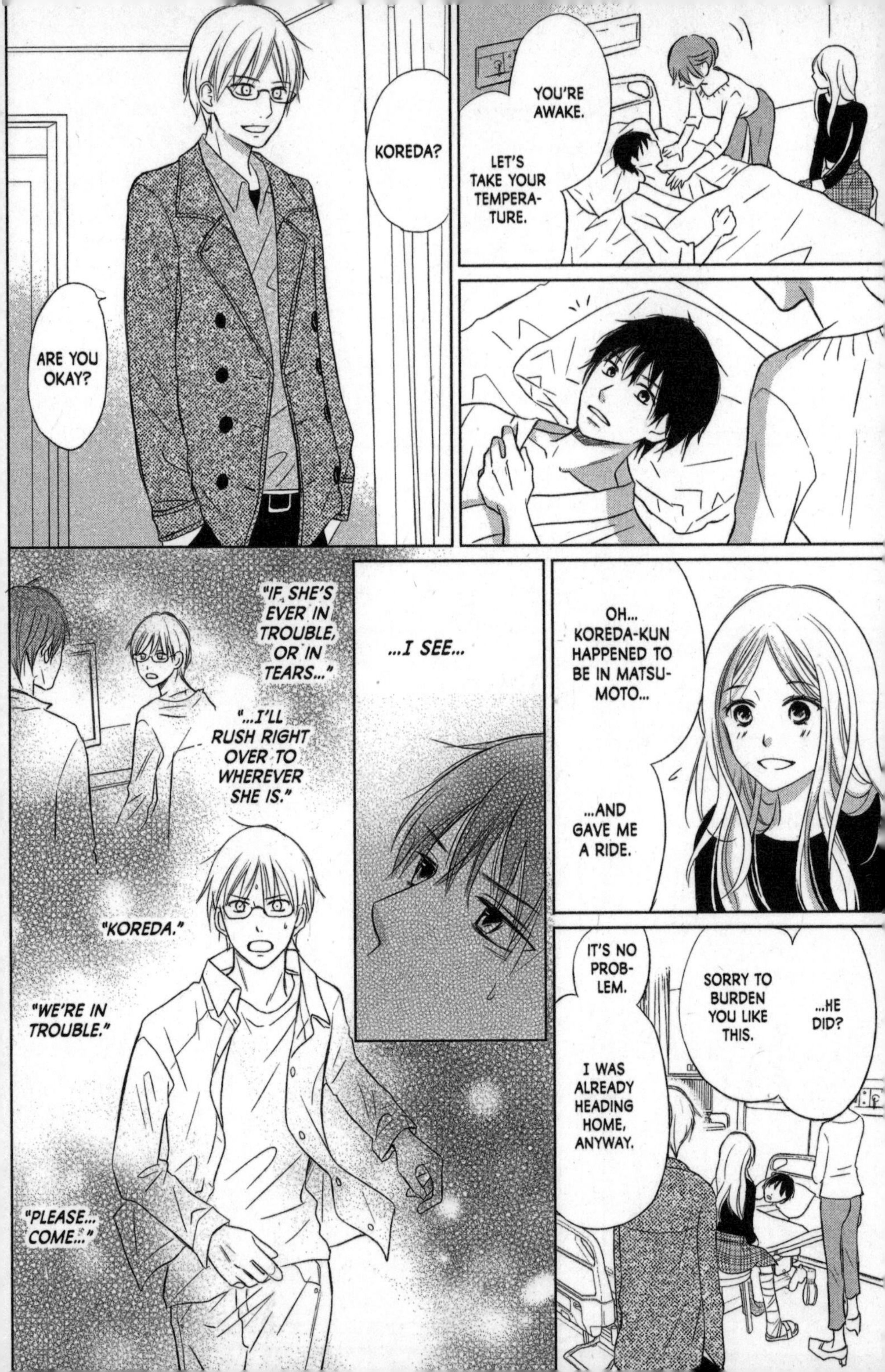
YOU'RE AWAKE.
LET'S TAKE YOUR TEMPERA-TURE.
KOREDA?
ARE YOU OKAY?
OH... KOREDA-KUN HAPPENED TO BE IN MATSU-MOTO...
...AND GAVE ME A RIDE.
...HE DID?
SORRY TO BURDEN YOU LIKE THIS.
IT'S NO PROB-LEM.
I WAS ALREADY HEADING HOME, ANYWAY.
...I SEE...
"IF SHE'S EVER IN TROUBLE, OR IN TEARS..."
"...I'LL RUSH RIGHT OVER TO WHEREVER SHE IS."
"KOREDA."
"WE'RE IN TROUBLE."
"PLEASE... COME..."

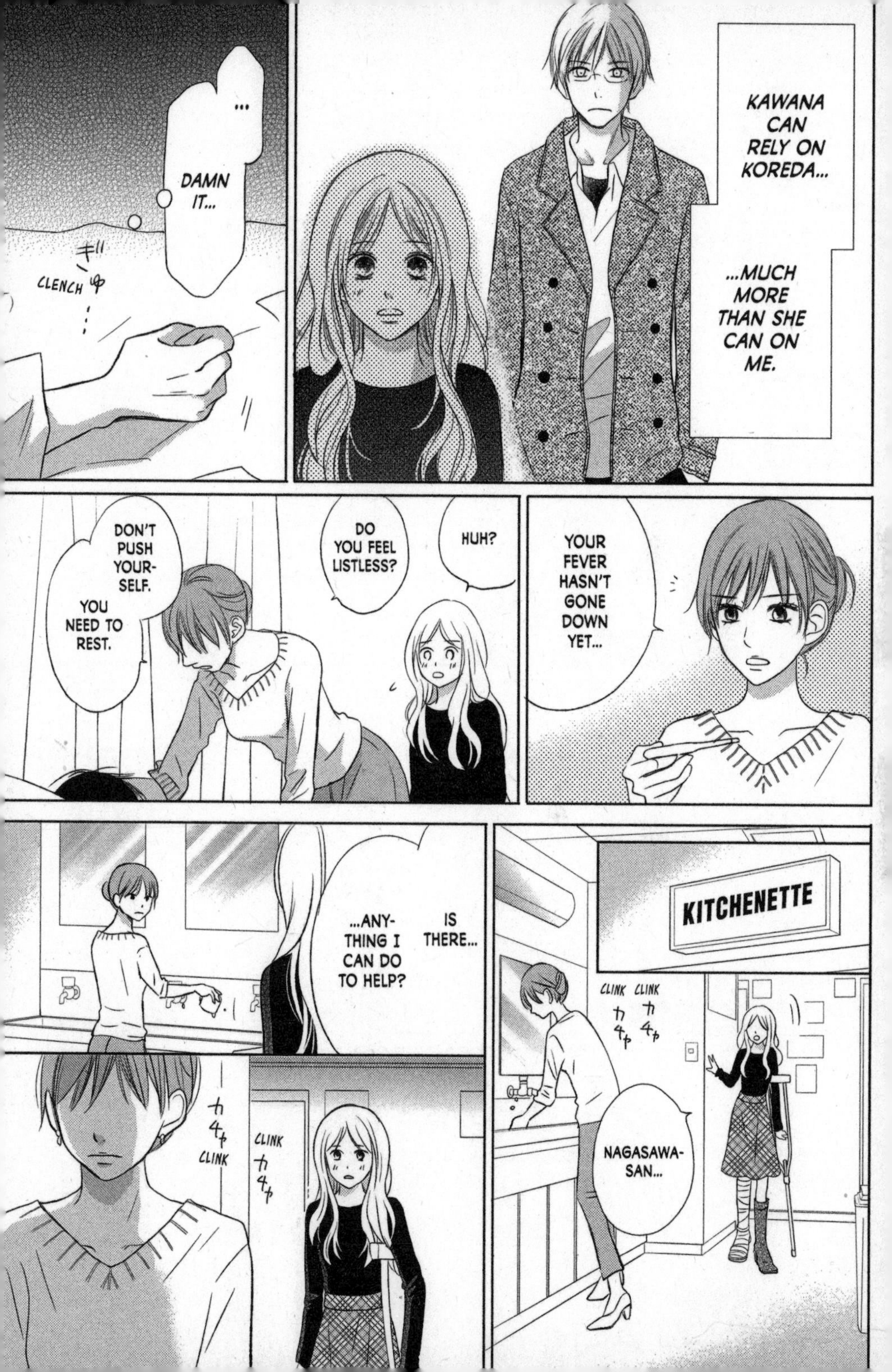
KAWANA CAN RELY ON KOREDA...
...MUCH MORE THAN SHE CAN ON ME.
...
DAMN IT...
CLENCH
YOUR FEVER HASN'T GONE DOWN YET...
HUH?
DO YOU FEEL LISTLESS?
DON'T PUSH YOURSELF.
YOU NEED TO REST.
KITCHENETTE
CLINK CLINK
NAGASAWA-SAN...
IS THERE...
...ANYTHING I CAN DO TO HELP?
CLINK
CLINK

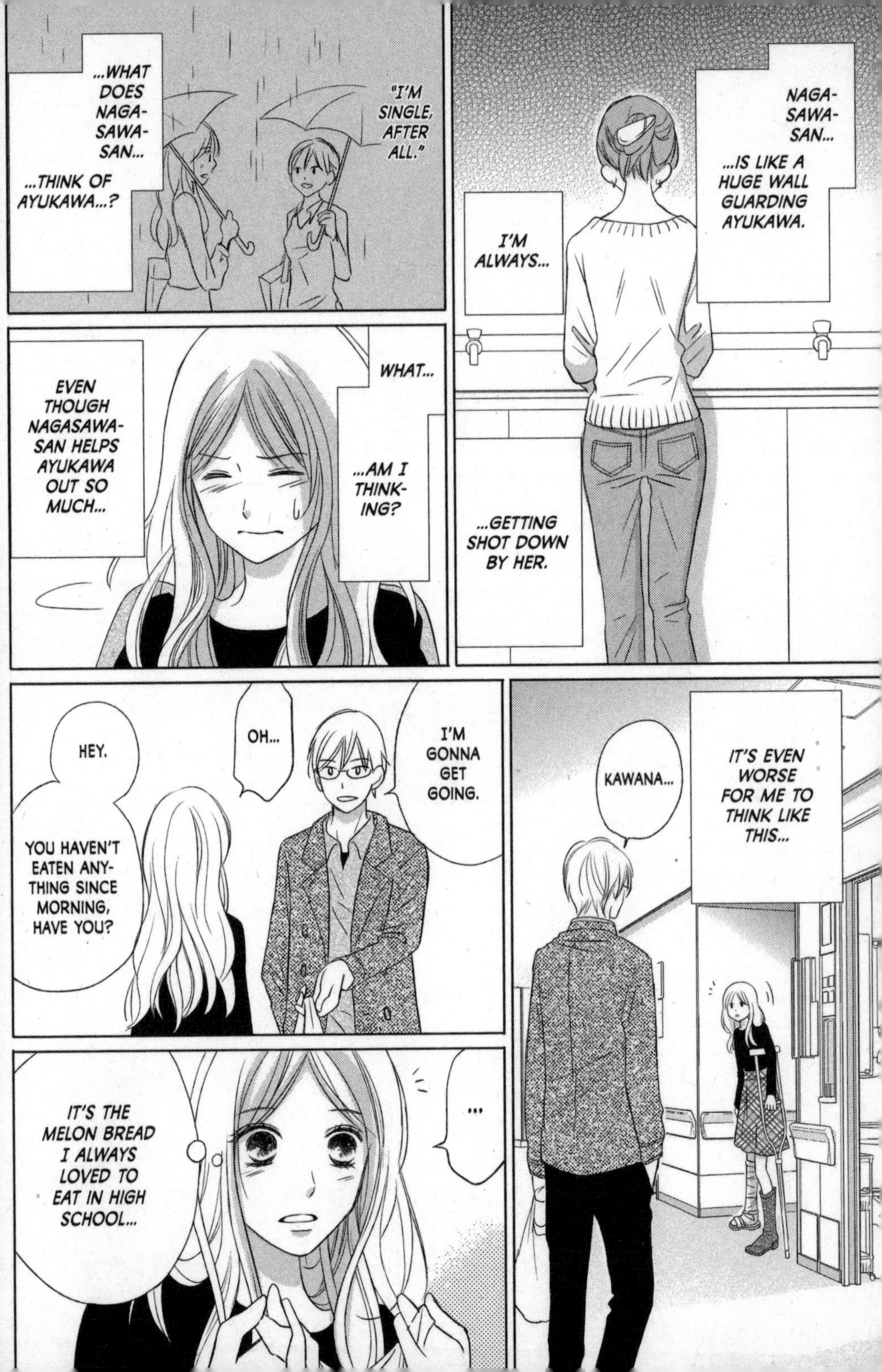
NAGA-SAWA-SAN...
...IS LIKE A HUGE WALL GUARDING AYUKAWA.
I'M ALWAYS...
...GETTING SHOT DOWN BY HER.
"I'M SINGLE, AFTER ALL."
...WHAT DOES NAGA-SAWA-SAN...
...THINK OF AYUKAWA...?
WHAT...
...AM I THINK-ING?
EVEN THOUGH NAGASAWA-SAN HELPS AYUKAWA OUT SO MUCH...
IT'S EVEN WORSE FOR ME TO THINK LIKE THIS...
KAWANA...
I'M GONNA GET GOING.
OH...
HEY.
YOU HAVEN'T EATEN ANY-THING SINCE MORNING, HAVE YOU?
...
IT'S THE MELON BREAD I ALWAYS LOVED TO EAT IN HIGH SCHOOL...

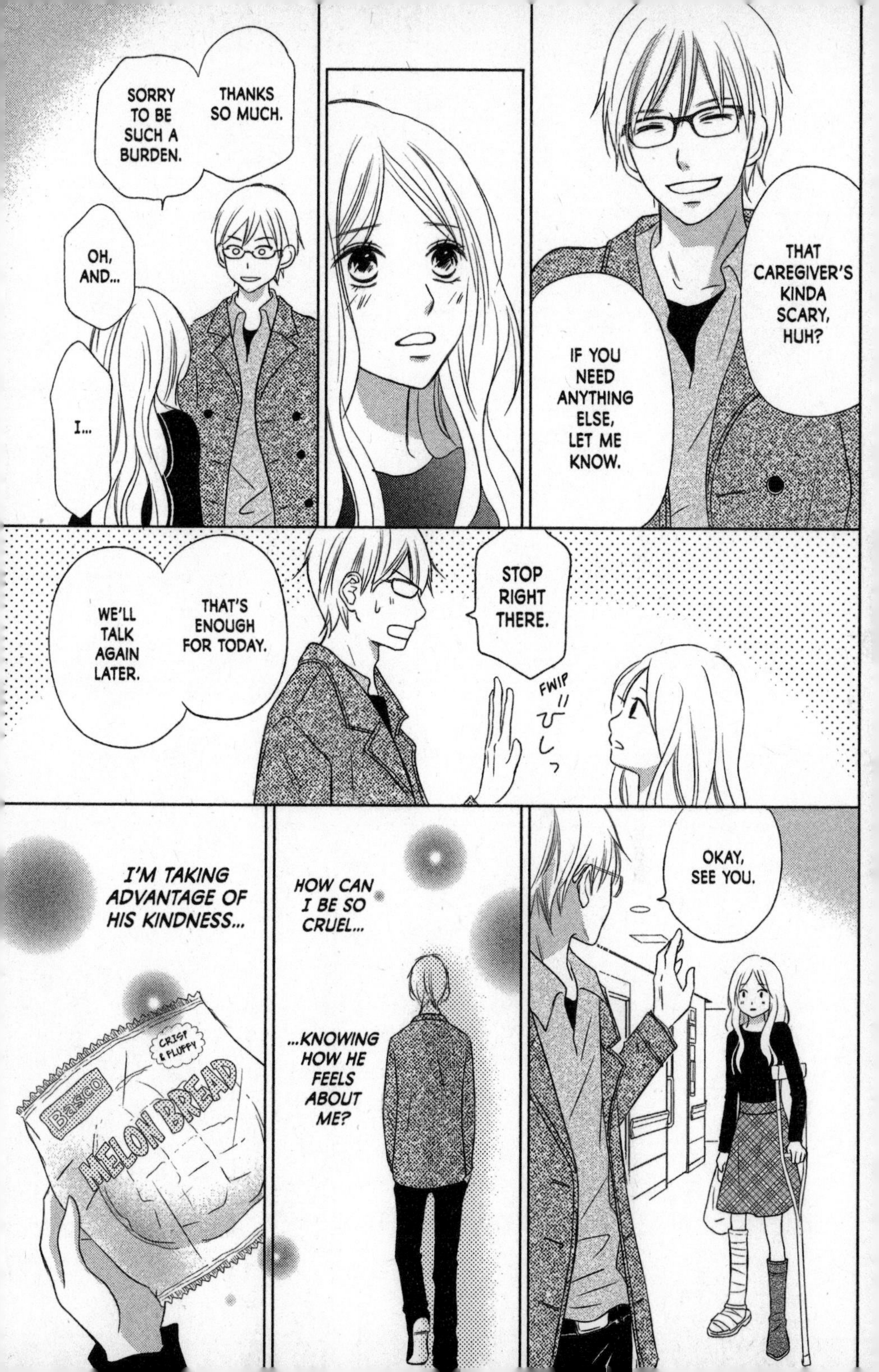
THAT CAREGIVER'S KINDA SCARY, HUH?
IF YOU NEED ANYTHING ELSE, LET ME KNOW.
THANKS SO MUCH.
SORRY TO BE SUCH A BURDEN.
OH, AND...
I...
STOP RIGHT THERE.
FWIP
びしっ
THAT'S ENOUGH FOR TODAY.
WE'LL TALK AGAIN LATER.
OKAY, SEE YOU.
HOW CAN I BE SO CRUEL...
...KNOWING HOW HE FEELS ABOUT ME?
I'M TAKING ADVANTAGE OF HIS KINDNESS...
CRISP & FLUFFY
Basco
MELON BREAD

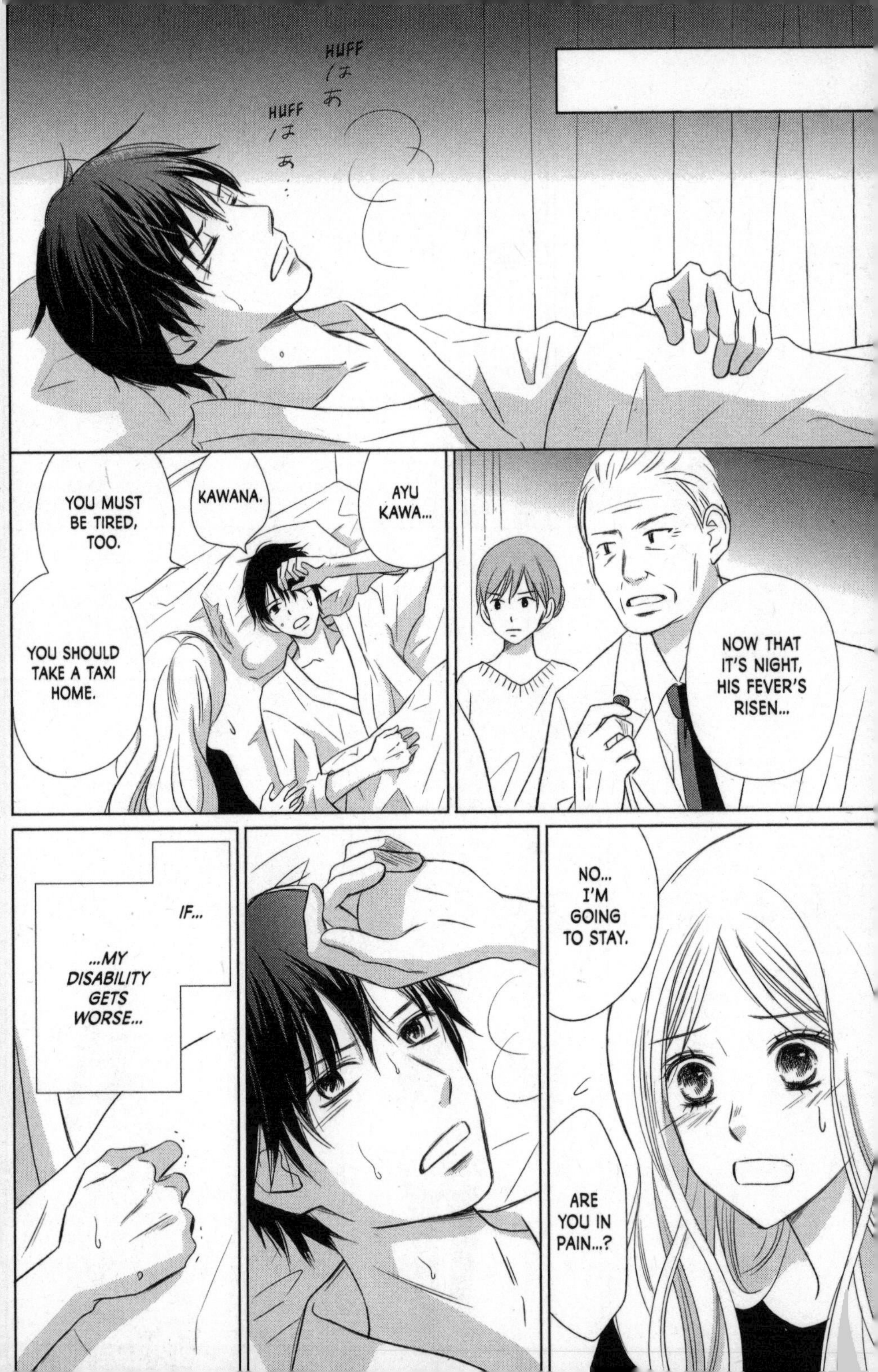
HUFF はあ
HUFF はあ…
NOW THAT IT'S NIGHT, HIS FEVER'S RISEN...
AYU KAWA...
KAWANA.
YOU MUST BE TIRED, TOO.
YOU SHOULD TAKE A TAXI HOME.
NO... I'M GOING TO STAY.
ARE YOU IN PAIN...?
IF...
...MY DISABILITY GETS WORSE...

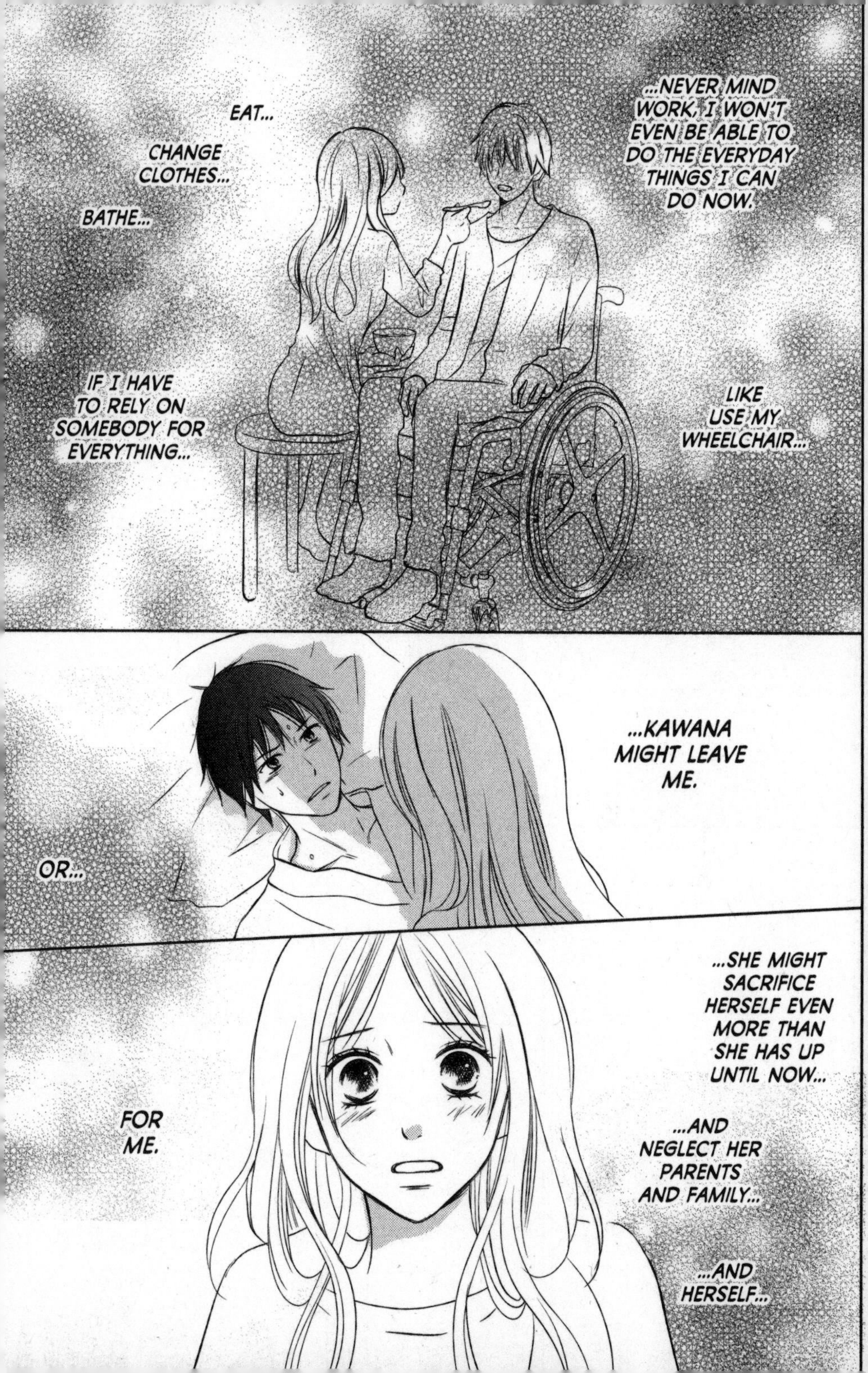
...NEVER MIND WORK, I WON'T EVEN BE ABLE TO DO THE EVERYDAY THINGS I CAN DO NOW.
EAT...
CHANGE CLOTHES...
BATHE...
LIKE USE MY WHEELCHAIR...
IF I HAVE TO RELY ON SOMEBODY FOR EVERYTHING...
...KAWANA MIGHT LEAVE ME.
OR...
...SHE MIGHT SACRIFICE HERSELF EVEN MORE THAN SHE HAS UP UNTIL NOW...
...AND NEGLECT HER PARENTS AND FAMILY...
...AND HERSELF...
FOR ME.

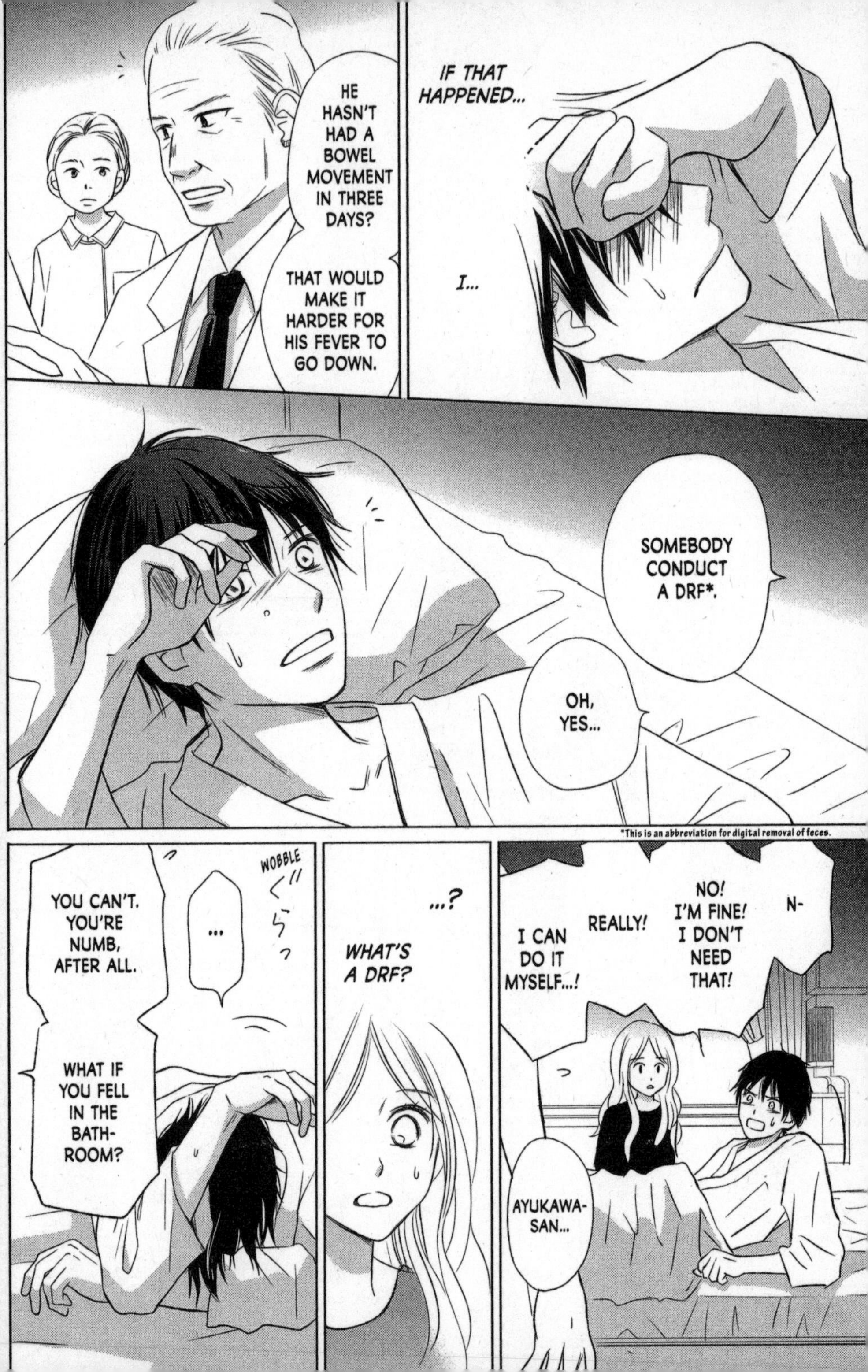
IF THAT HAPPENED...
I...
HE HASN'T HAD A BOWEL MOVEMENT IN THREE DAYS?
THAT WOULD MAKE IT HARDER FOR HIS FEVER TO GO DOWN.
SOMEBODY CONDUCT A DRF*.
OH, YES...
N-
NO! I'M FINE! I DON'T NEED THAT!
REALLY!
I CAN DO IT MYSELF...!
AYUKAWA-SAN...
...?
WHAT'S A DRF?
WOBBLE
...
YOU CAN'T. YOU'RE NUMB, AFTER ALL.
WHAT IF YOU FELL IN THE BATH-ROOM?

*This is an abbreviation for digital removal of feces.

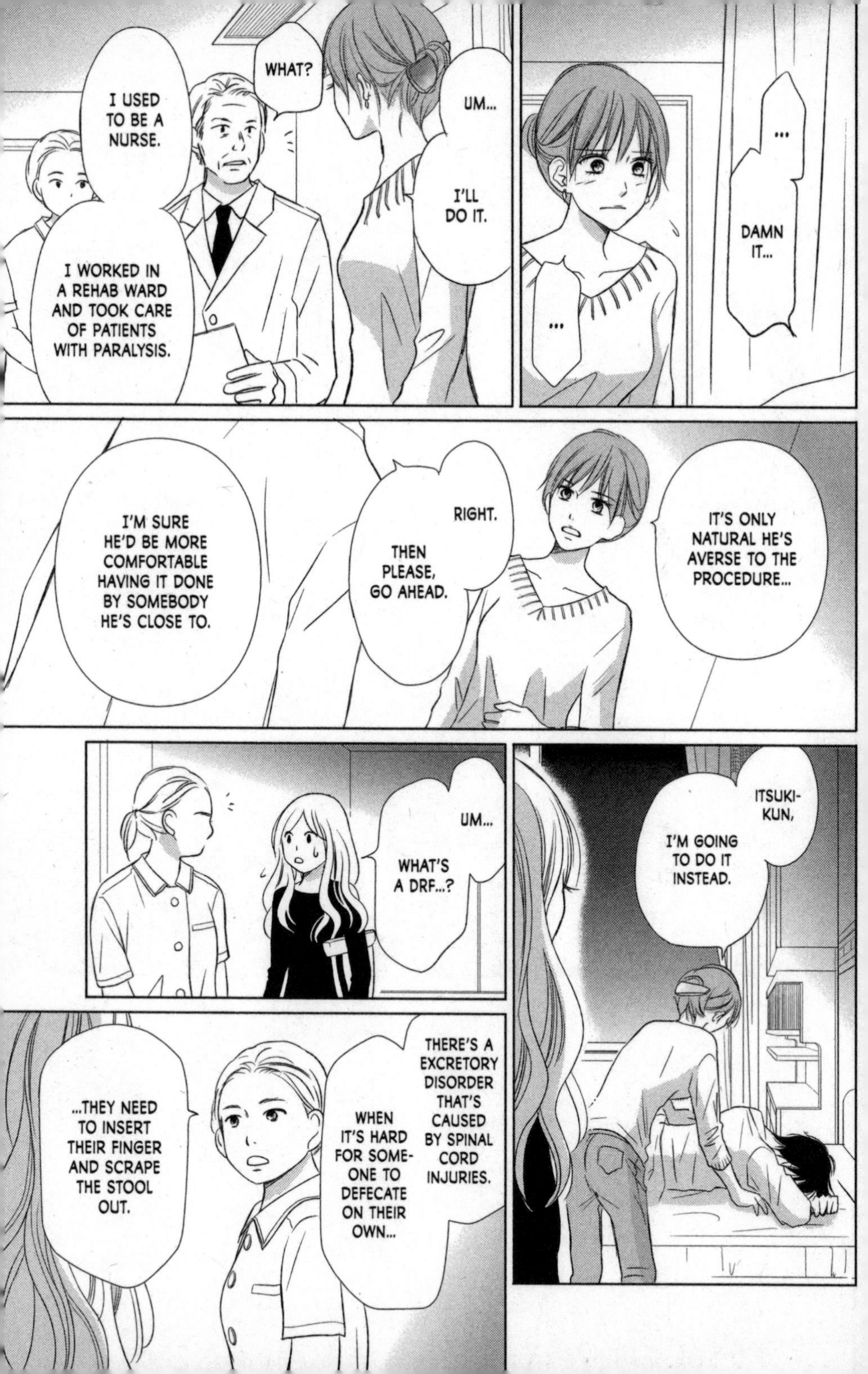
...
DAMN IT...
...
UM...
I'LL DO IT.
WHAT?
I USED TO BE A NURSE.
I WORKED IN A REHAB WARD AND TOOK CARE OF PATIENTS WITH PARALYSIS.
IT'S ONLY NATURAL HE'S AVERSE TO THE PROCEDURE...
RIGHT.
THEN PLEASE, GO AHEAD.
I'M SURE HE'D BE MORE COMFORTABLE HAVING IT DONE BY SOMEBODY HE'S CLOSE TO.
ITSUKI-KUN,
I'M GOING TO DO IT INSTEAD.
UM...
WHAT'S A DRF...?
THERE'S A EXCRETORY DISORDER THAT'S CAUSED BY SPINAL CORD INJURIES.
WHEN IT'S HARD FOR SOME-ONE TO DEFECATE ON THEIR OWN...
...THEY NEED TO INSERT THEIR FINGER AND SCRAPE THE STOOL OUT.

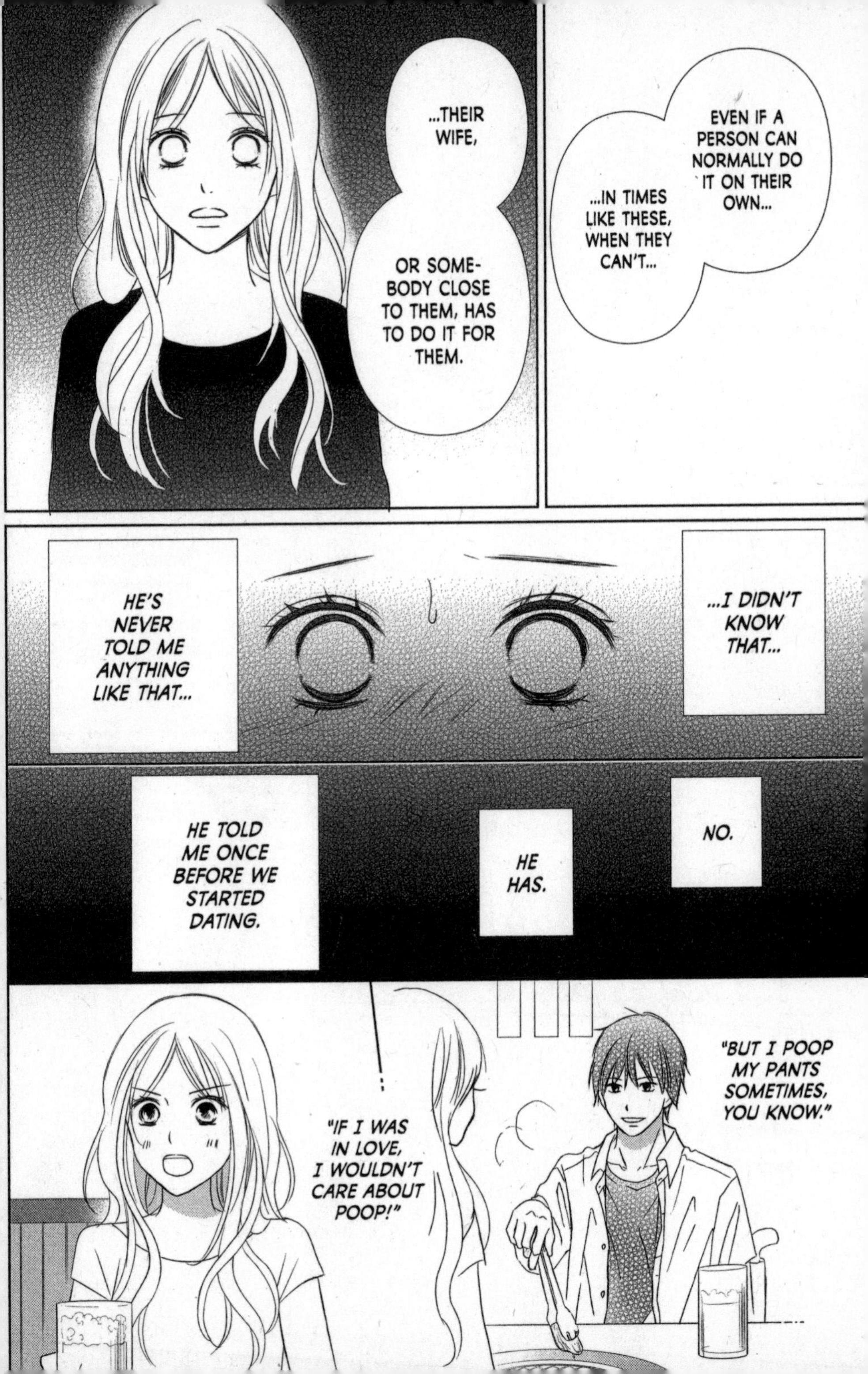
EVEN IF A PERSON CAN NORMALLY DO IT ON THEIR OWN...
...IN TIMES LIKE THESE, WHEN THEY CAN'T...
...THEIR WIFE,
OR SOME-BODY CLOSE TO THEM, HAS TO DO IT FOR THEM.
...I DIDN'T KNOW THAT...
HE'S NEVER TOLD ME ANYTHING LIKE THAT...
NO.
HE HAS.
HE TOLD ME ONCE BEFORE WE STARTED DATING.
"BUT I POOP MY PANTS SOMETIMES, YOU KNOW."
"IF I WAS IN LOVE, I WOULDN'T CARE ABOUT POOP!"

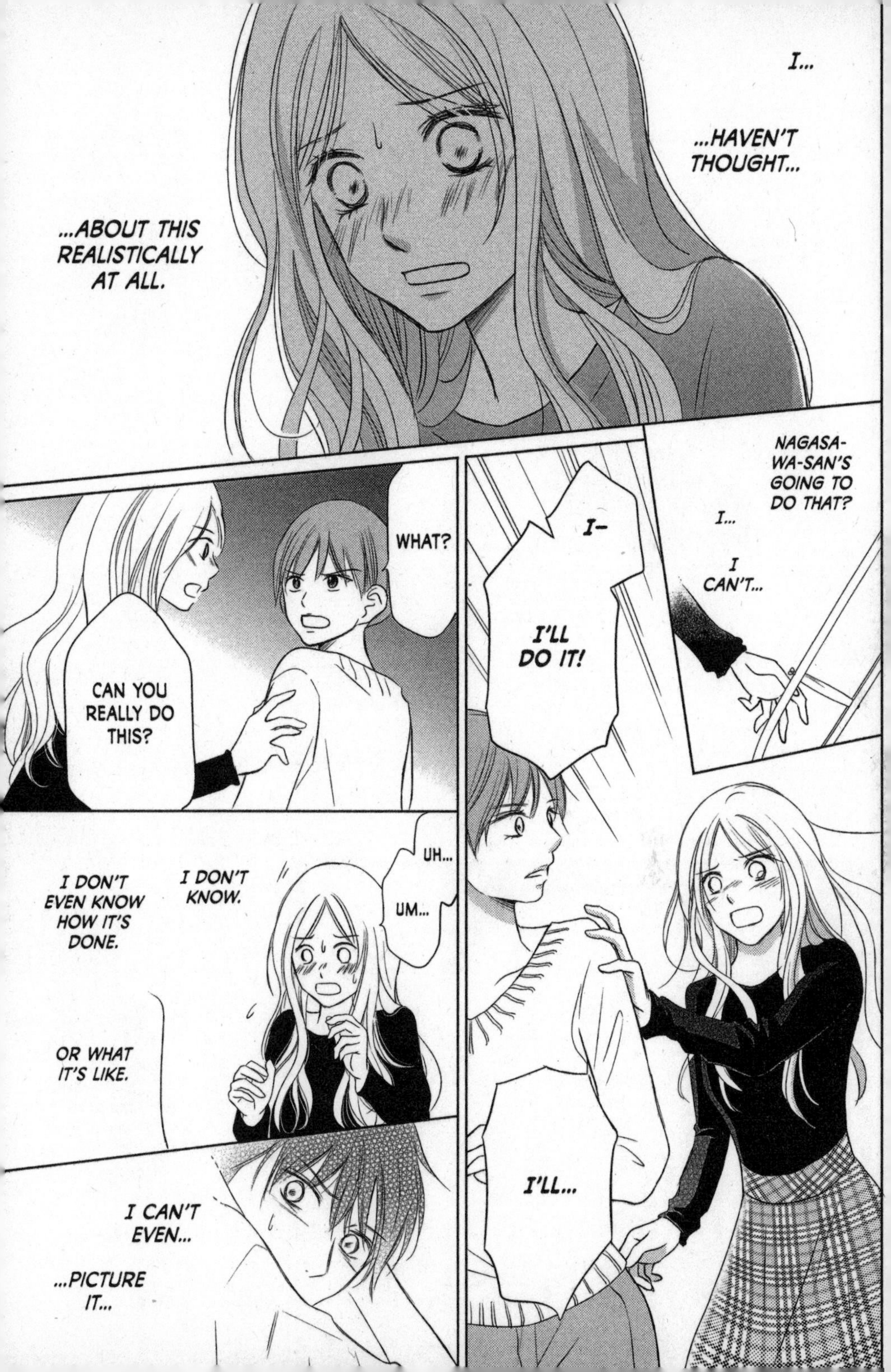
I...
...HAVEN'T THOUGHT...
...ABOUT THIS REALISTICALLY AT ALL.
NAGASA-WA-SAN'S GOING TO DO THAT?
I...
I CAN'T...
I-
I'LL DO IT!
I'LL...
WHAT?
CAN YOU REALLY DO THIS?
UH...
UM...
I DON'T KNOW.
I DON'T EVEN KNOW HOW IT'S DONE.
OR WHAT IT'S LIKE.
I CAN'T EVEN...
...PICTURE IT...

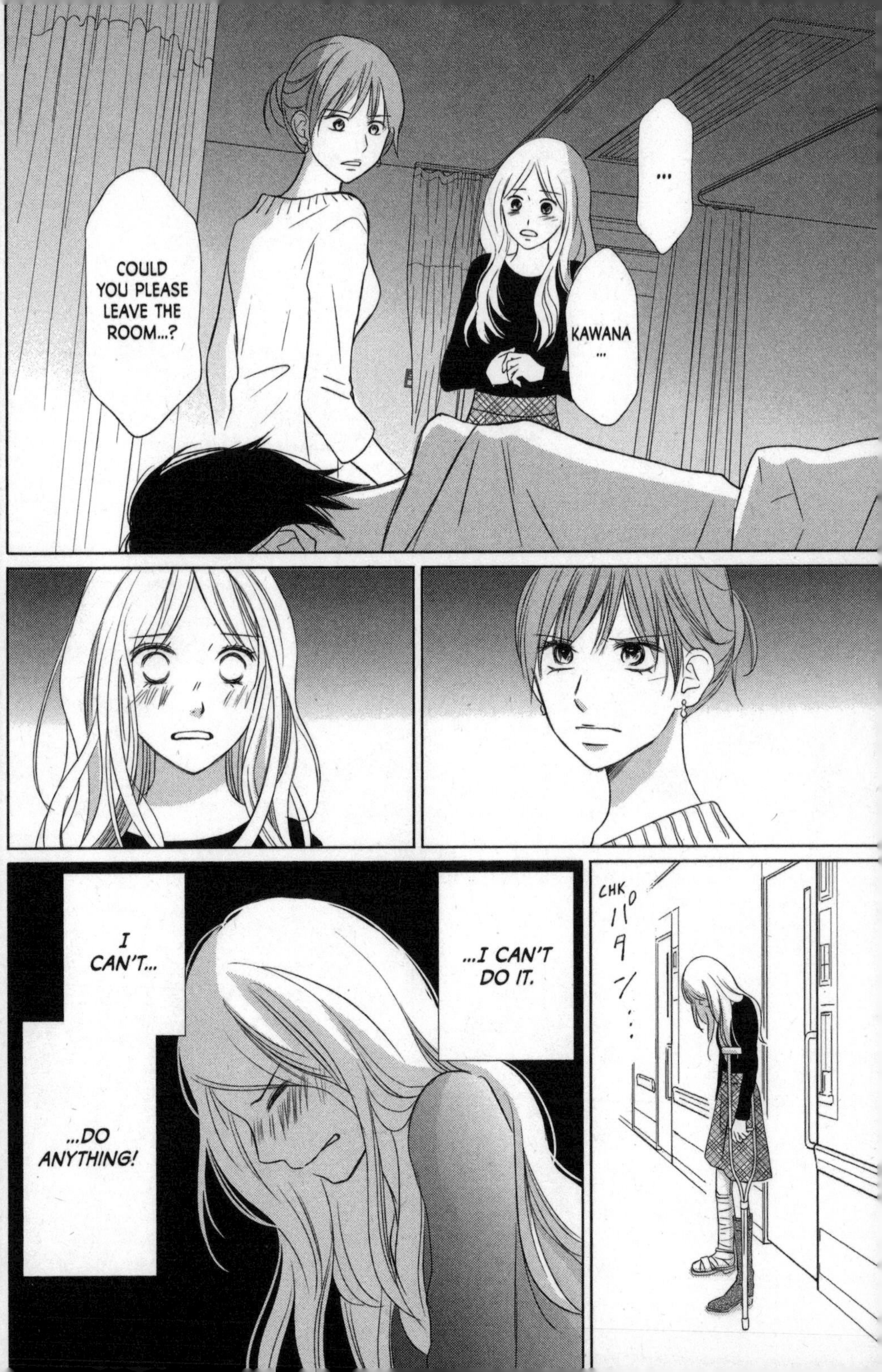
...
KAWANA ...
COULD YOU PLEASE LEAVE THE ROOM...?
CHK
パタン…
...I CAN'T DO IT.
I CAN'T...
...DO ANYTHING!

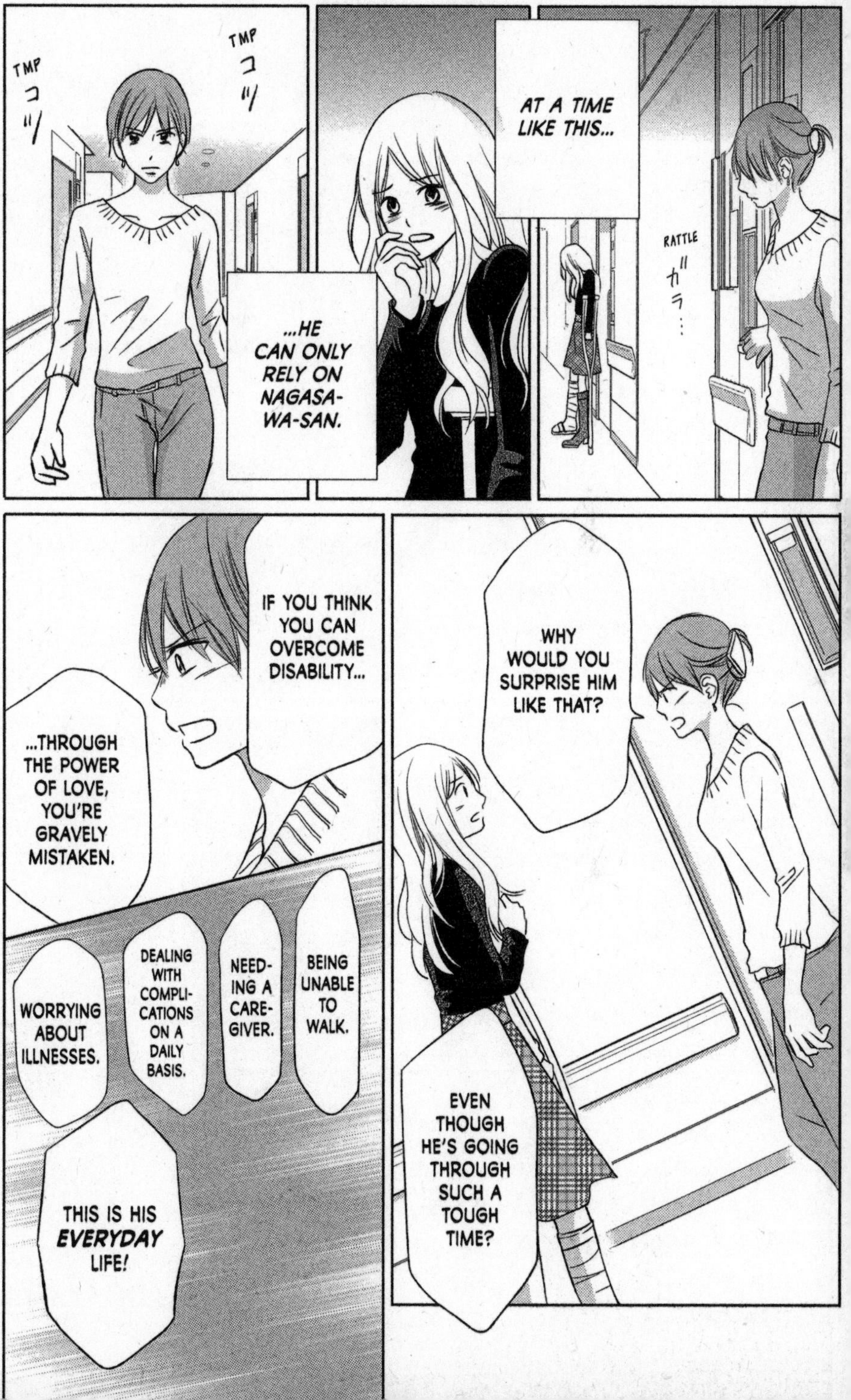
AT A TIME LIKE THIS...
RATTLE
ガラ…
...HE CAN ONLY RELY ON NAGASA-WA-SAN.
TMP
コツ
TMP
コツ
WHY WOULD YOU SURPRISE HIM LIKE THAT?
EVEN THOUGH HE'S GOING THROUGH SUCH A TOUGH TIME?
IF YOU THINK YOU CAN OVERCOME DISABILITY...
...THROUGH THE POWER OF LOVE, YOU'RE GRAVELY MISTAKEN.
BEING UNABLE TO WALK.
NEED-ING A CARE-GIVER.
DEALING WITH COMPLI-CATIONS ON A DAILY BASIS.
WORRYING ABOUT ILLNESSES.
THIS IS HIS *EVERYDAY* LIFE!

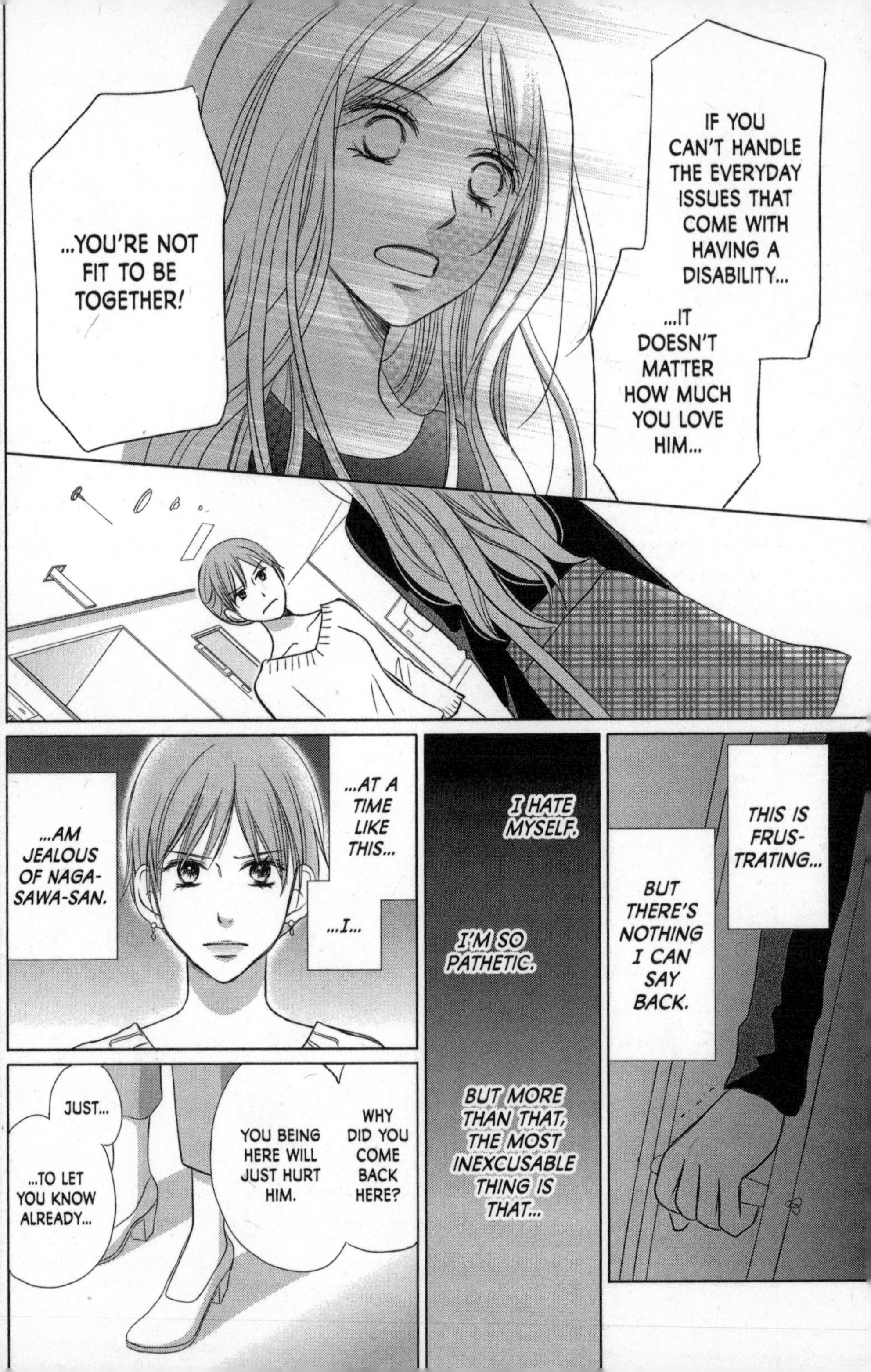
IF YOU CAN'T HANDLE THE EVERYDAY ISSUES THAT COME WITH HAVING A DISABILITY...
...IT DOESN'T MATTER HOW MUCH YOU LOVE HIM...
...YOU'RE NOT FIT TO BE TOGETHER!
THIS IS FRUS-TRATING...
BUT THERE'S NOTHING I CAN SAY BACK.
I HATE MYSELF.
I'M SO PATHETIC.
BUT MORE THAN THAT, THE MOST INEXCUSABLE THING IS THAT...
...AT A TIME LIKE THIS...
...I...
...AM JEALOUS OF NAGA-SAWA-SAN.
WHY DID YOU COME BACK HERE?
YOU BEING HERE WILL JUST HURT HIM.
JUST...
...TO LET YOU KNOW ALREADY...

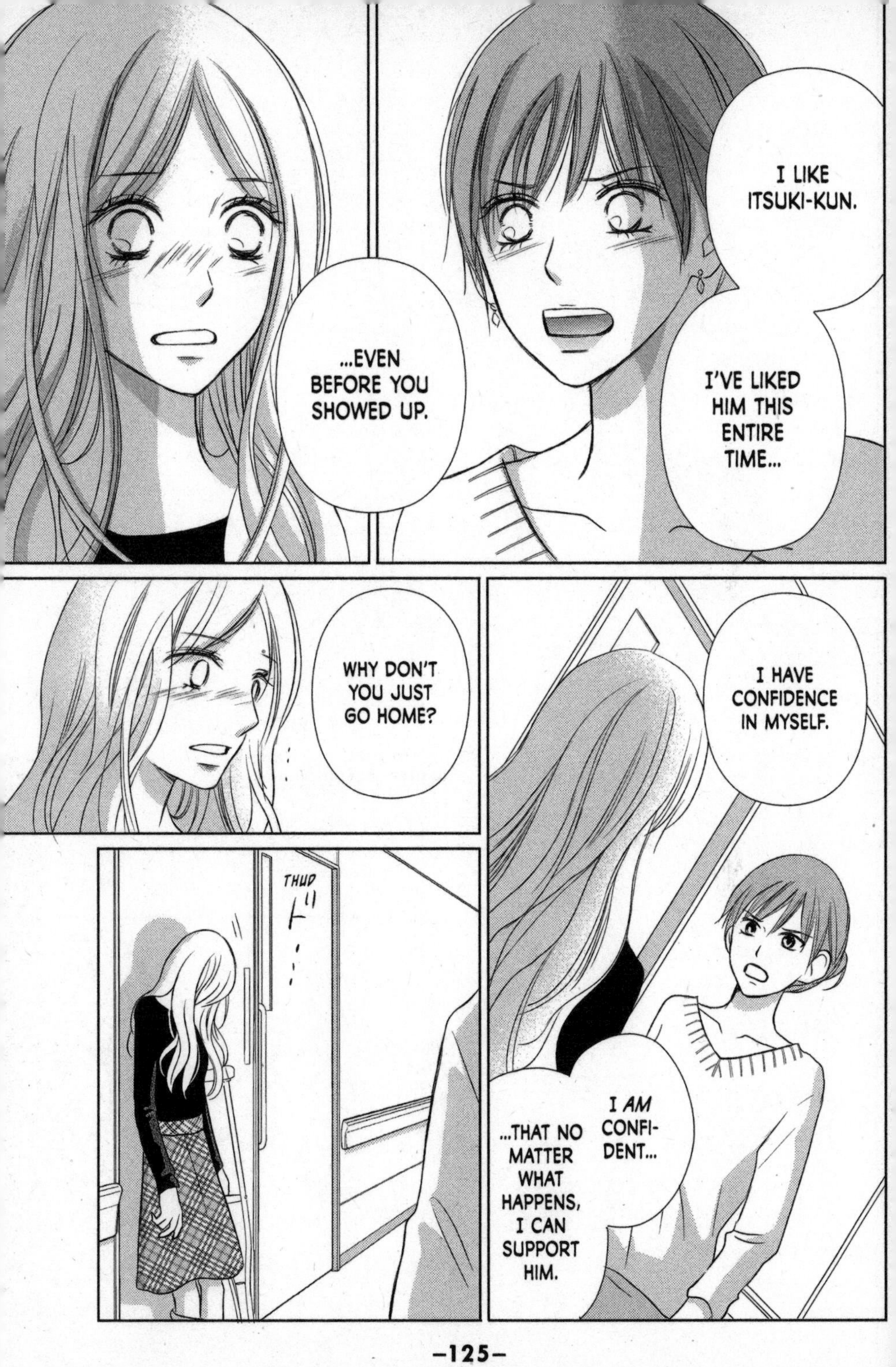
I LIKE ITSUKI-KUN.
I'VE LIKED HIM THIS ENTIRE TIME...
...EVEN BEFORE YOU SHOWED UP.
I HAVE CONFIDENCE IN MYSELF.
I *AM* CONFIDENT...
...THAT NO MATTER WHAT HAPPENS, I CAN SUPPORT HIM.
WHY DON'T YOU JUST GO HOME?
THUD

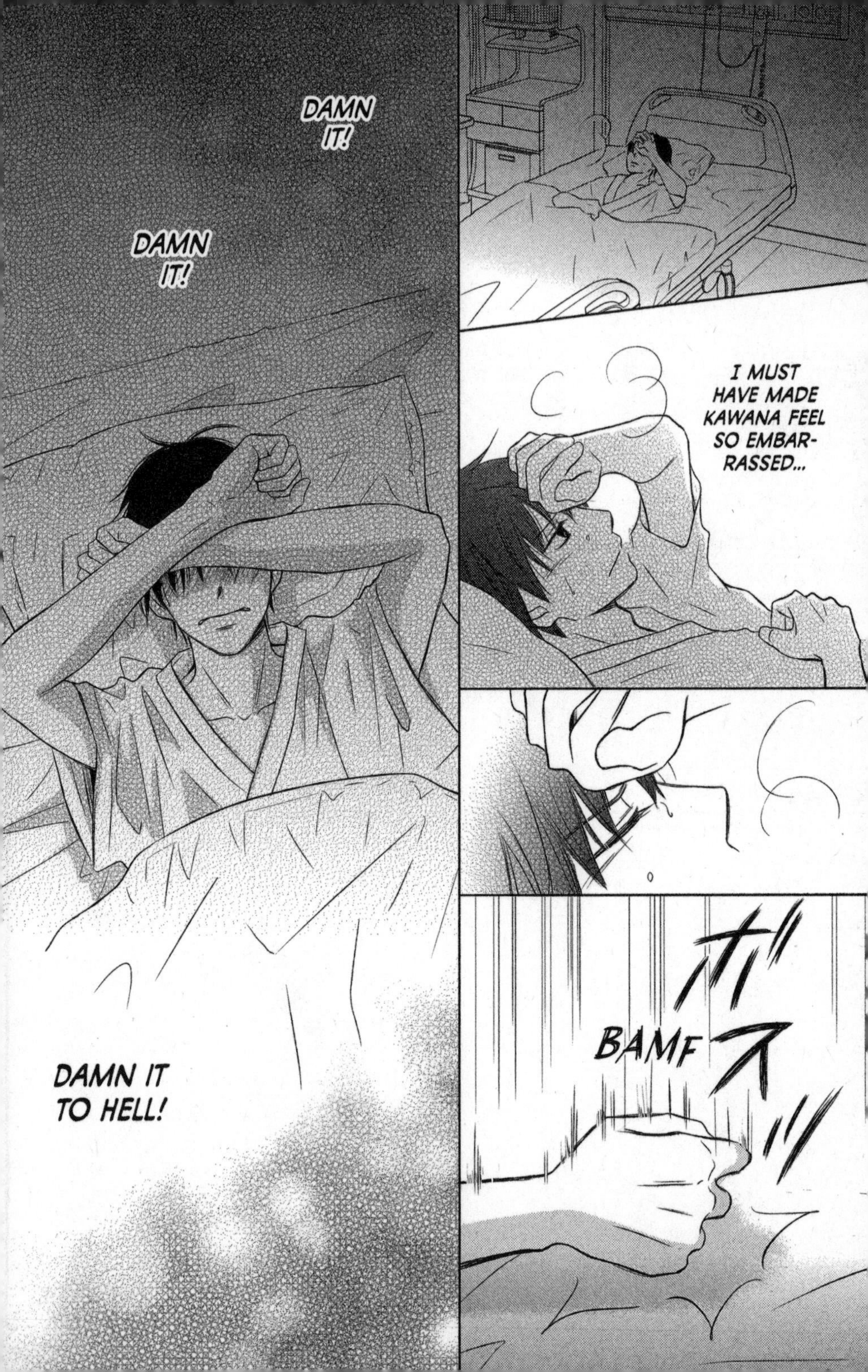
I MUST HAVE MADE KAWANA FEEL SO EMBAR-RASSED...
BAMF
ガスッ
DAMN IT!
DAMN IT!
DAMN IT TO HELL!

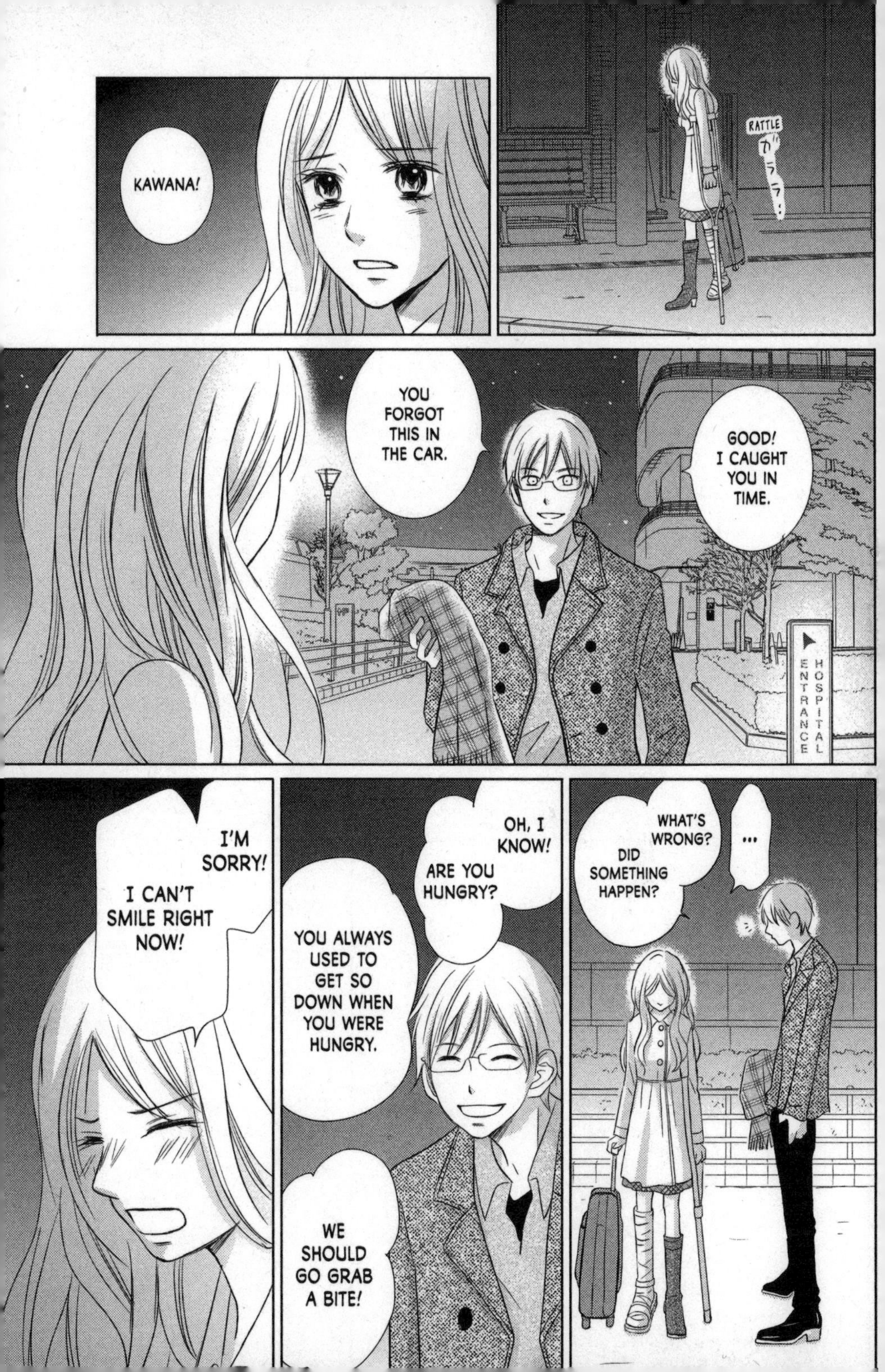
RATTLE
KAWANA!
GOOD! I CAUGHT YOU IN TIME.
YOU FORGOT THIS IN THE CAR.
HOSPITAL ENTRANCE
WHAT'S WRONG? DID SOMETHING HAPPEN?
...
OH, I KNOW! ARE YOU HUNGRY?
YOU ALWAYS USED TO GET SO DOWN WHEN YOU WERE HUNGRY.
WE SHOULD GO GRAB A BITE!
I'M SORRY! I CAN'T SMILE RIGHT NOW!

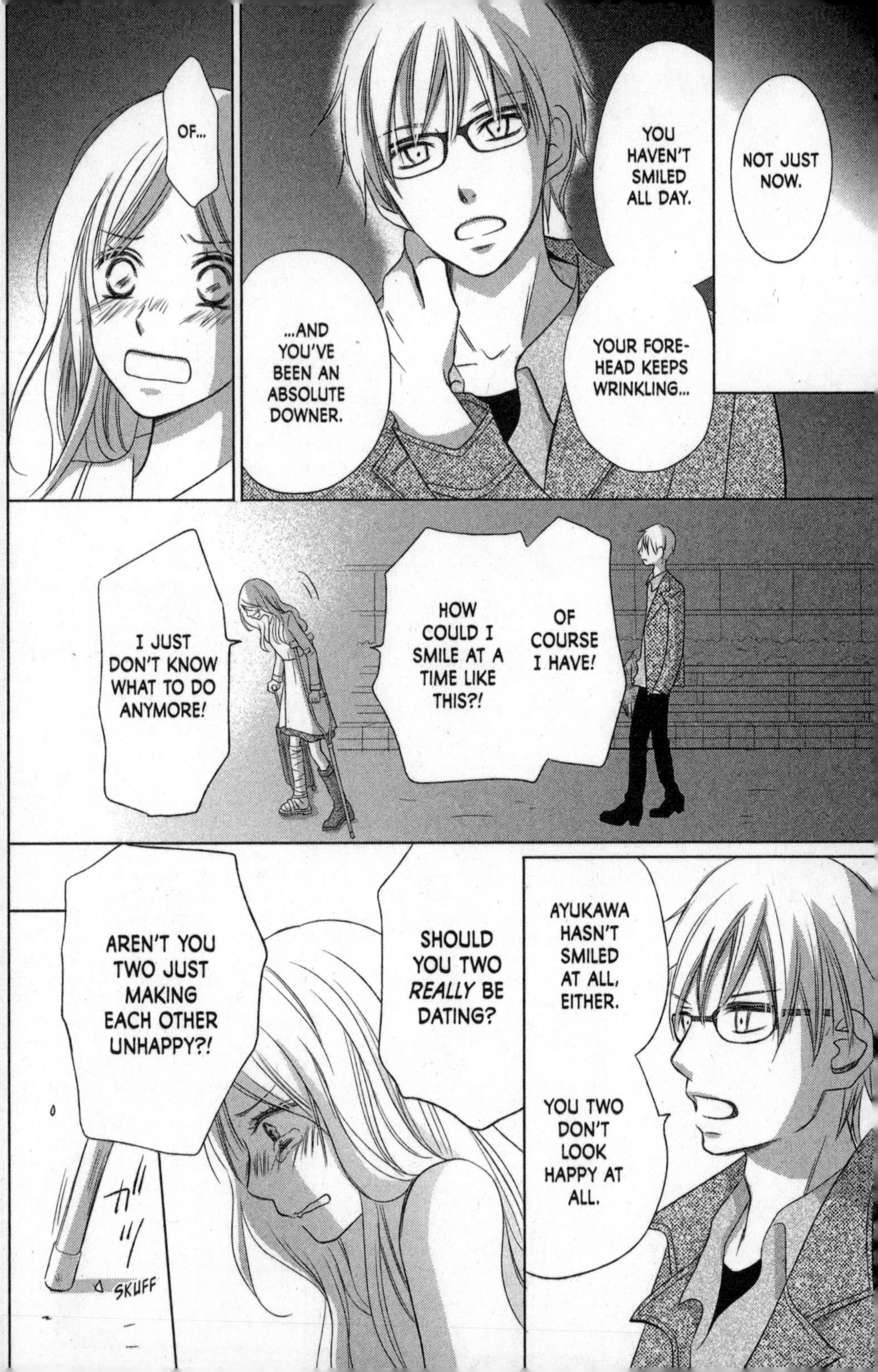
NOT JUST NOW.
YOU HAVEN'T SMILED ALL DAY.
YOUR FORE-HEAD KEEPS WRINKLING...
...AND YOU'VE BEEN AN ABSOLUTE DOWNER.
OF...
OF COURSE I HAVE!
HOW COULD I SMILE AT A TIME LIKE THIS?!
I JUST DON'T KNOW WHAT TO DO ANYMORE!
AYUKAWA HASN'T SMILED AT ALL, EITHER.
YOU TWO DON'T LOOK HAPPY AT ALL.
SHOULD YOU TWO *REALLY* BE DATING?
AREN'T YOU TWO JUST MAKING EACH OTHER UNHAPPY?!
SKUFF

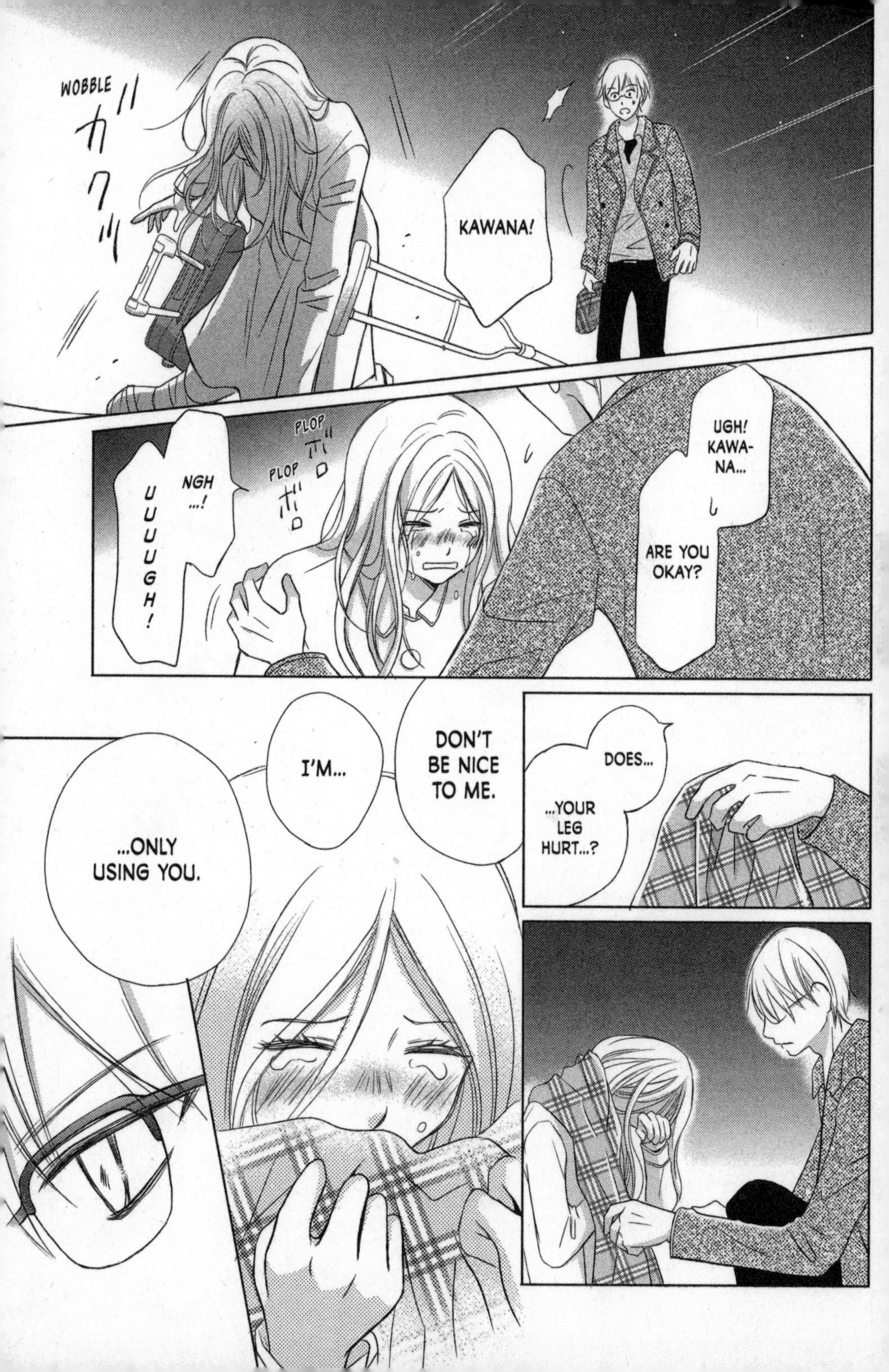
WOBBLE
KAWANA!
UGH! KAWANA...
ARE YOU OKAY?
PLOP
PLOP
NGH...!
UUUUGH!
DOES...
...YOUR LEG HURT...?
DON'T BE NICE TO ME.
I'M...
...ONLY USING YOU.

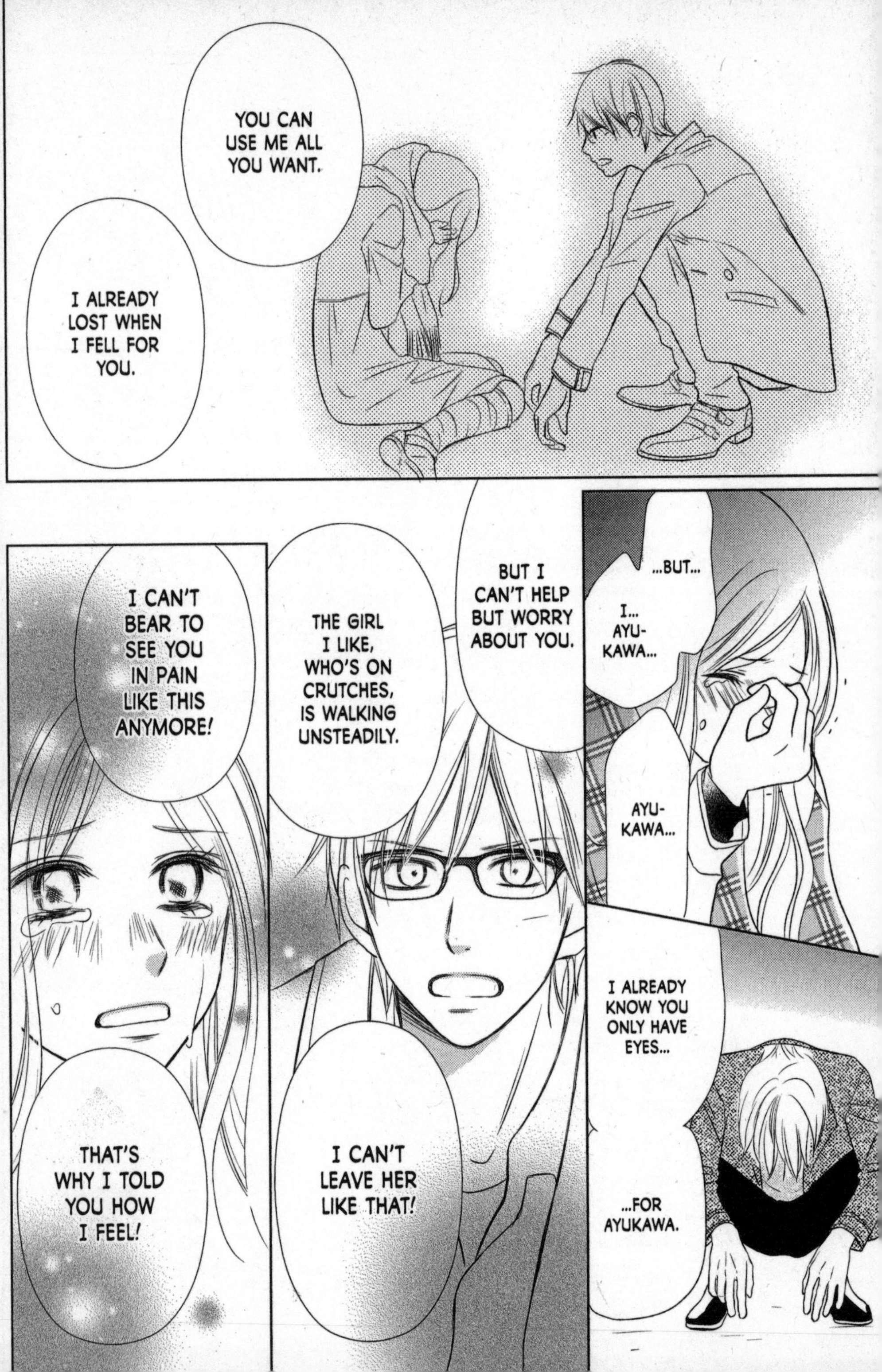
YOU CAN USE ME ALL YOU WANT.
I ALREADY LOST WHEN I FELL FOR YOU.
...BUT...
I... AYUKAWA...
AYUKAWA...
I ALREADY KNOW YOU ONLY HAVE EYES...
...FOR AYUKAWA.
BUT I CAN'T HELP BUT WORRY ABOUT YOU.
THE GIRL I LIKE, WHO'S ON CRUTCHES, IS WALKING UNSTEADILY.
I CAN'T LEAVE HER LIKE THAT!
I CAN'T BEAR TO SEE YOU IN PAIN LIKE THIS ANYMORE!
THAT'S WHY I TOLD YOU HOW I FEEL!

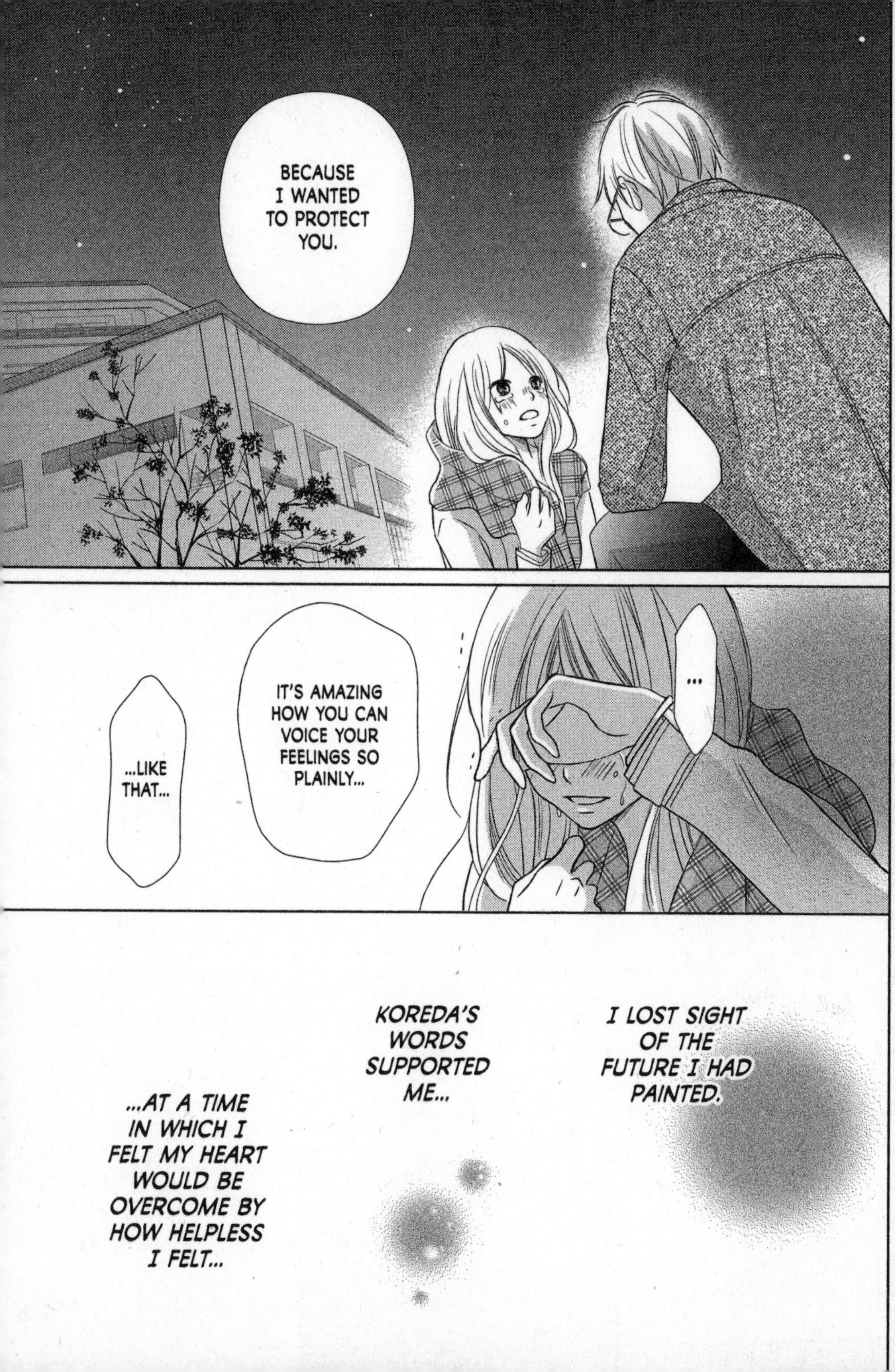
BECAUSE I WANTED TO PROTECT YOU.
...
IT'S AMAZING HOW YOU CAN VOICE YOUR FEELINGS SO PLAINLY...
...LIKE THAT...
I LOST SIGHT OF THE FUTURE I HAD PAINTED.
KOREDA'S WORDS SUPPORTED ME...
...AT A TIME IN WHICH I FELT MY HEART WOULD BE OVERCOME BY HOW HELPLESS I FELT...

PERFECT WORLD

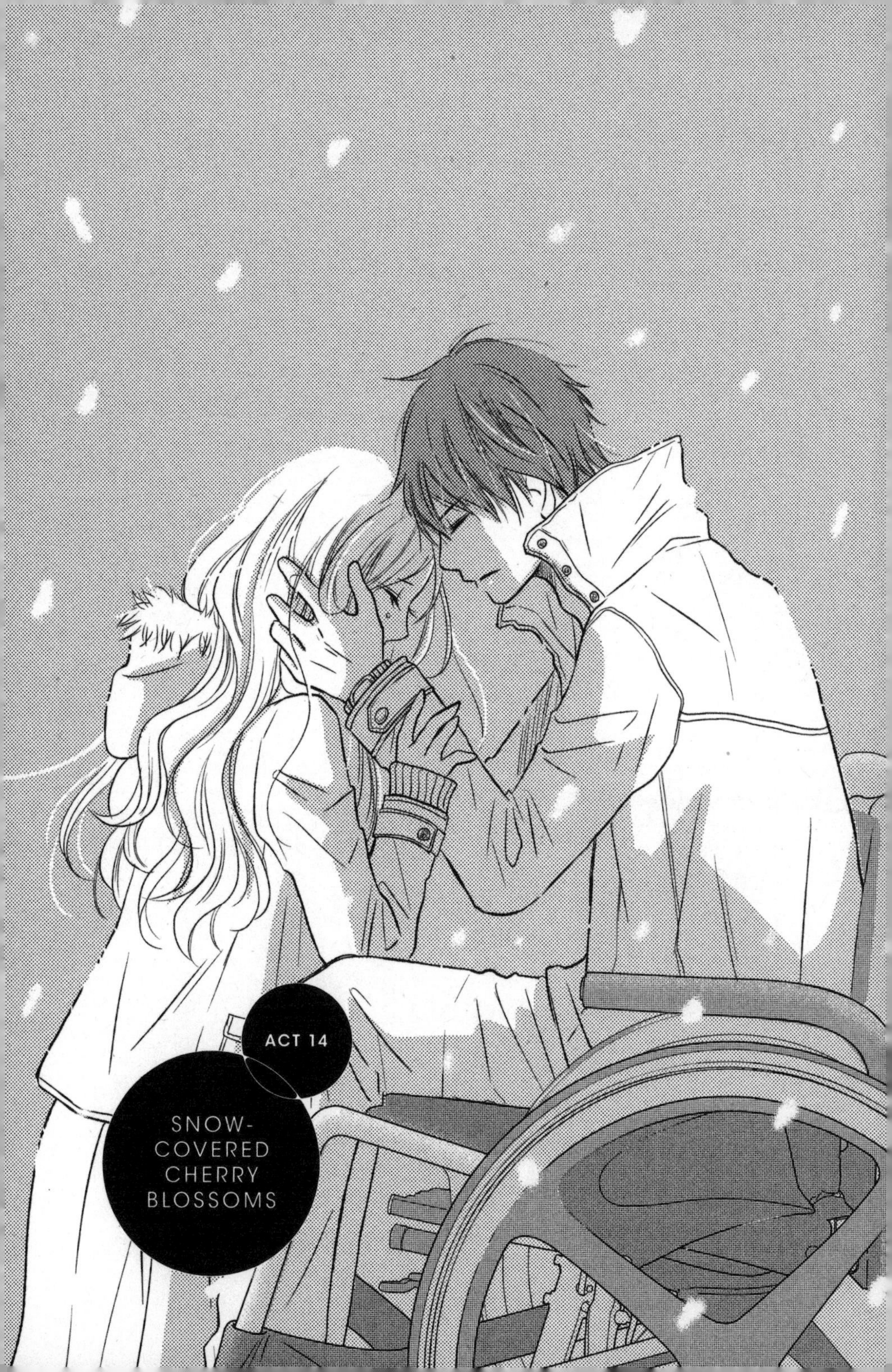
ACT 14
SNOW-
COVERED
CHERRY
BLOSSOMS

KOREDA'S WORDS SUPPORTED ME...

...AT A TIME IN WHICH I FELT MY HEART WOULD BE OVERCOME BY HOW HELPLESS I FELT...

I LOST SIGHT OF THE FUTURE I HAD PAINTED.

WHAT SHOULD I DO...?

BUT...

I DON'T WANT TO BREAK UP WITH AYUKAWA.

...

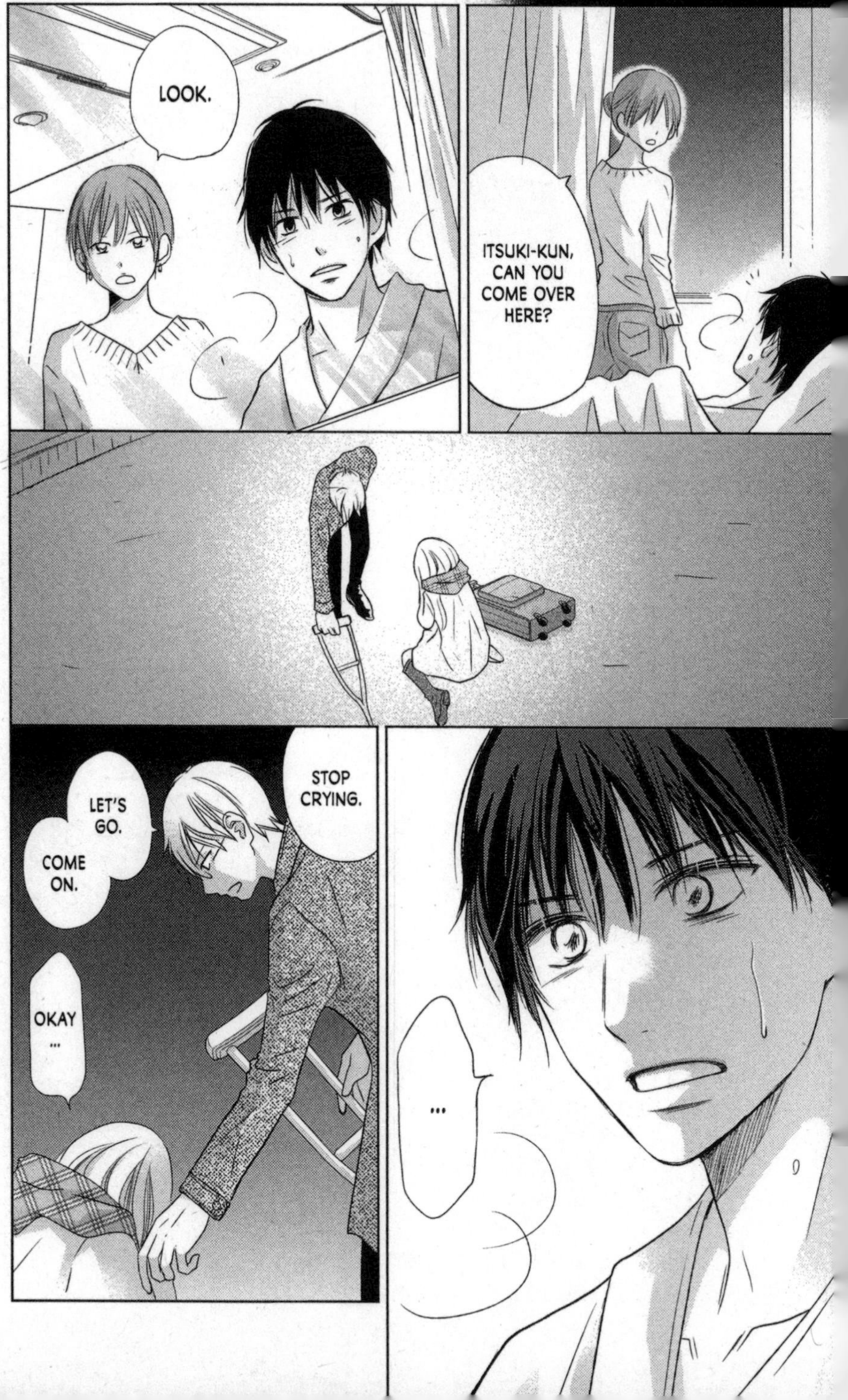
ITSUKI-KUN, CAN YOU COME OVER HERE?
LOOK.
...
STOP CRYING.
LET'S GO.
COME ON.
OKAY ...

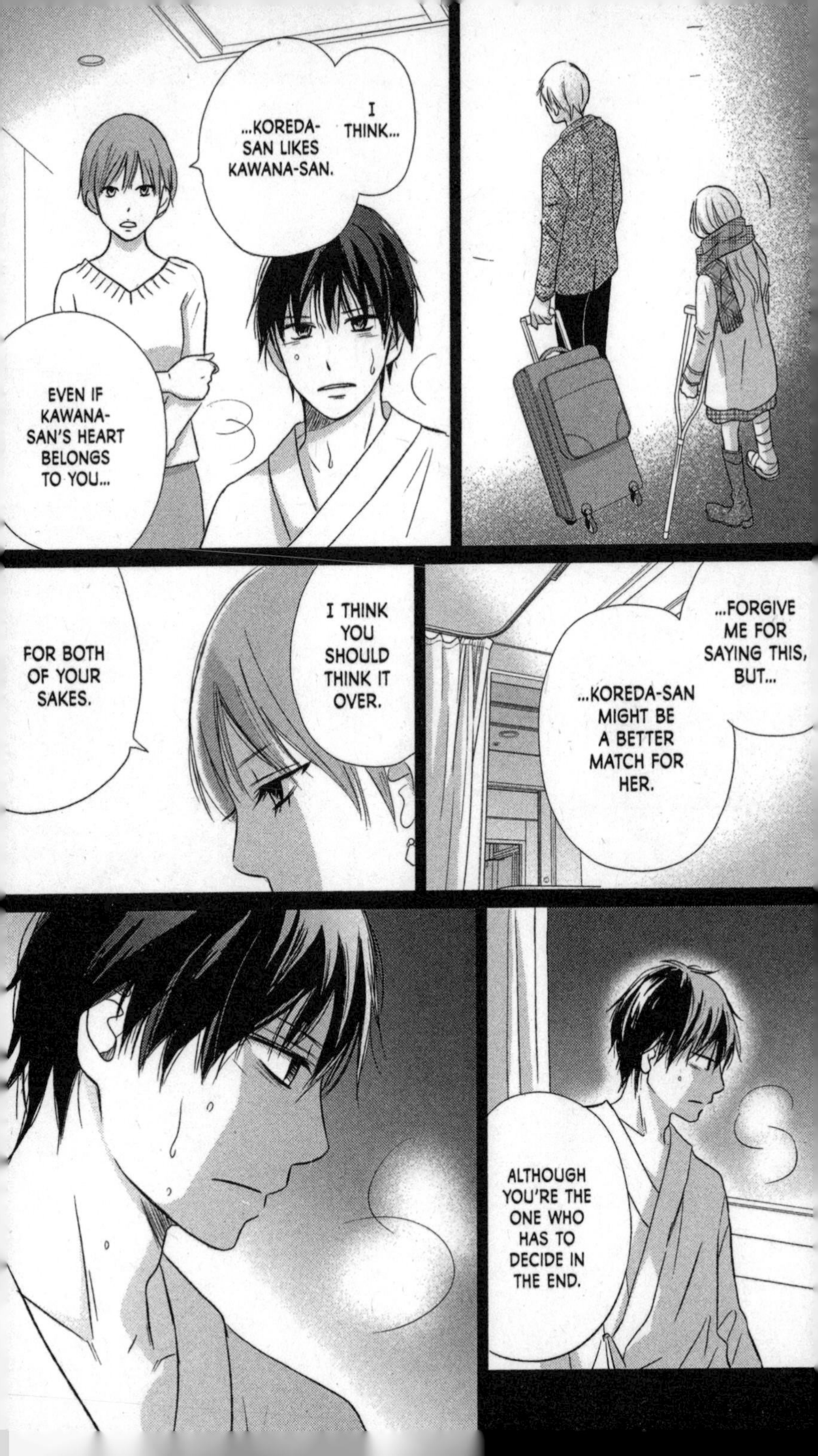
I THINK...
...KOREDA-SAN LIKES KAWANA-SAN.
EVEN IF KAWANA-SAN'S HEART BELONGS TO YOU...
...FORGIVE ME FOR SAYING THIS, BUT...
...KOREDA-SAN MIGHT BE A BETTER MATCH FOR HER.
I THINK YOU SHOULD THINK IT OVER.
FOR BOTH OF YOUR SAKES.
ALTHOUGH YOU'RE THE ONE WHO HAS TO DECIDE IN THE END.

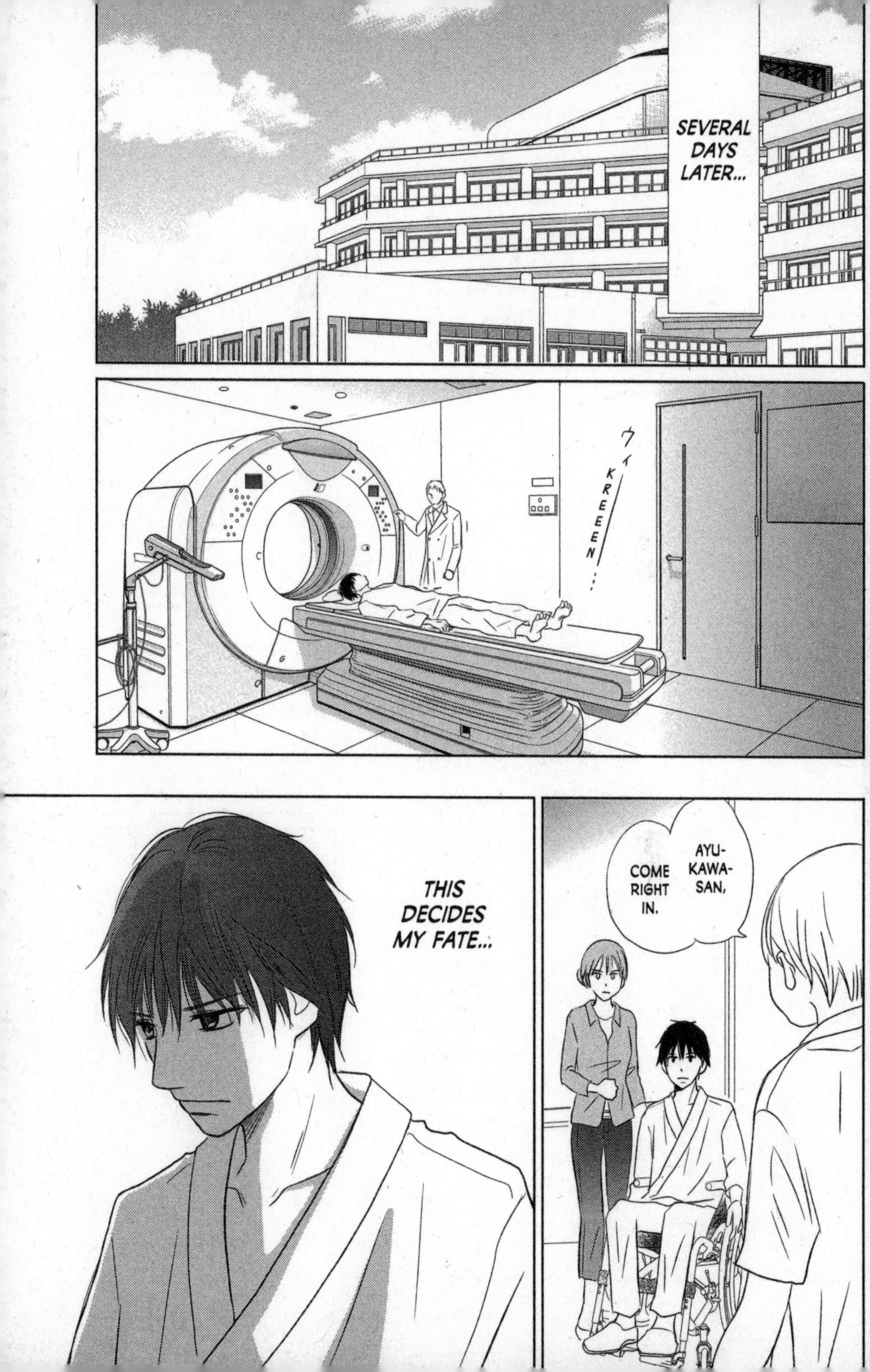
SEVERAL DAYS LATER...
ウィ
KREEEEN...
AYU-KAWA-SAN,
COME RIGHT IN.
THIS DECIDES MY FATE...

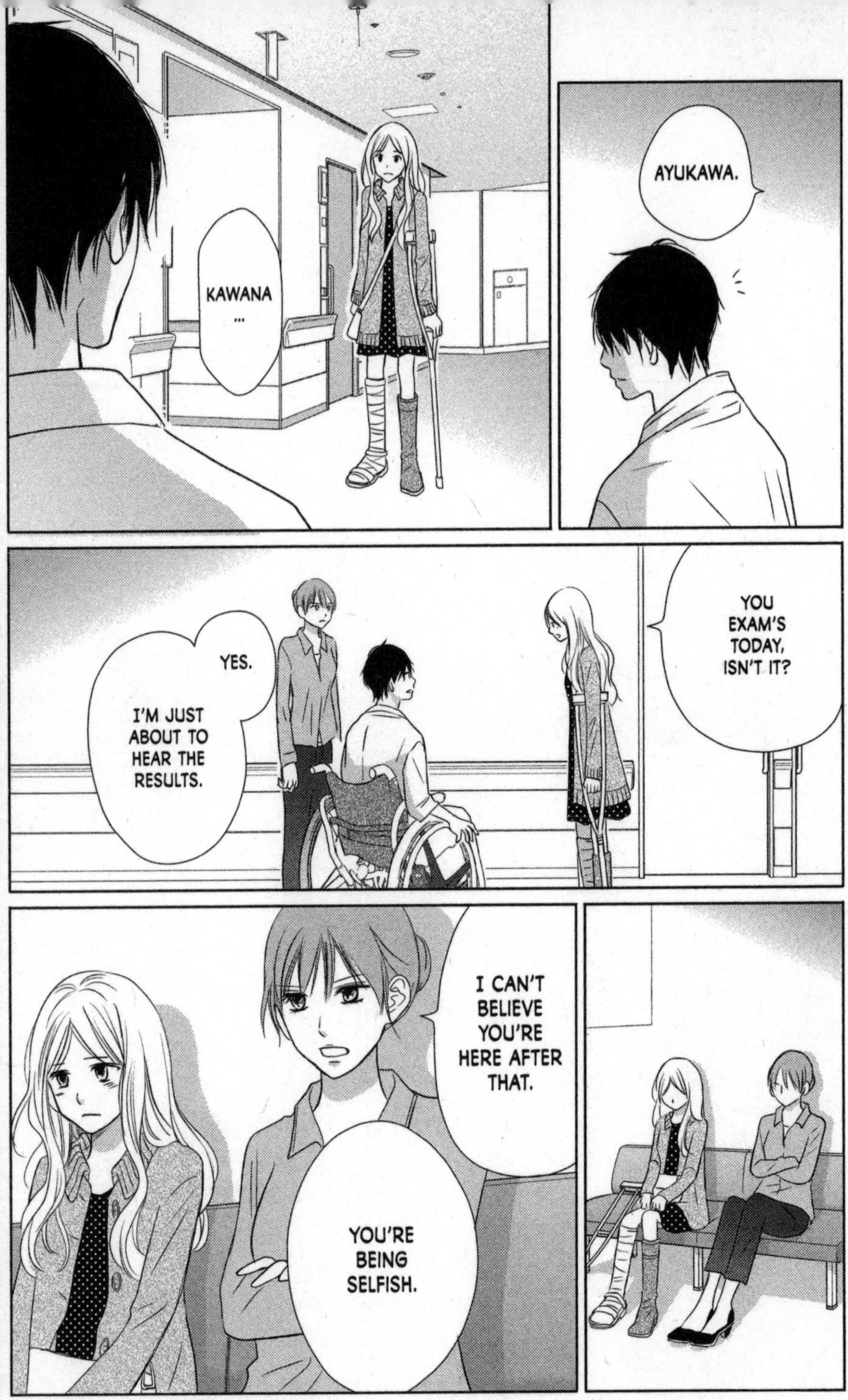
AYUKAWA.
KAWANA ...
YOU EXAM'S TODAY, ISN'T IT?
YES.
I'M JUST ABOUT TO HEAR THE RESULTS.
I CAN'T BELIEVE YOU'RE HERE AFTER THAT.
YOU'RE BEING SELFISH.

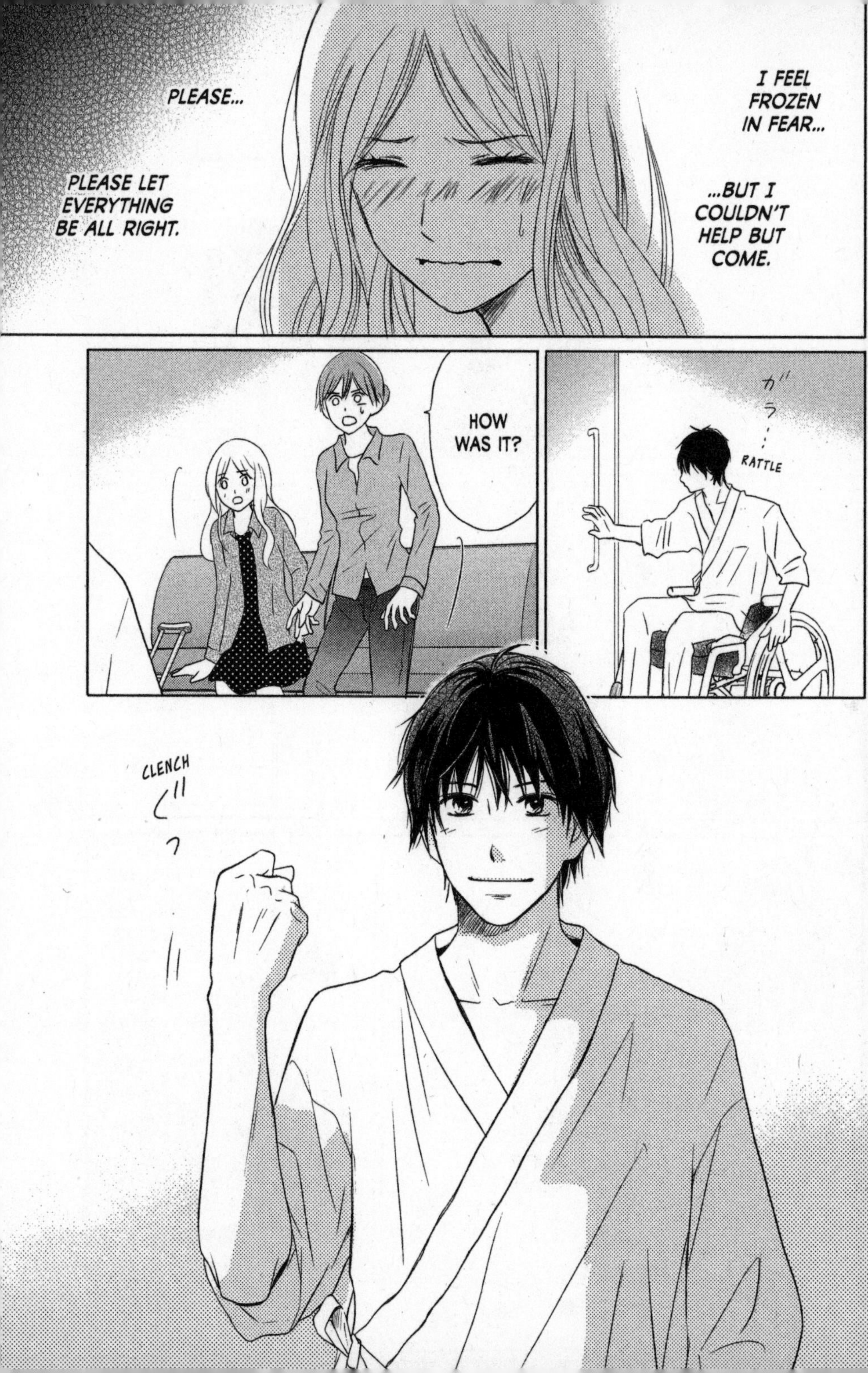
I FEEL FROZEN IN FEAR...
...BUT I COULDN'T HELP BUT COME.
PLEASE...
PLEASE LET EVERYTHING BE ALL RIGHT.
ガラ
RATTLE
HOW WAS IT?
CLENCH
ぐっ

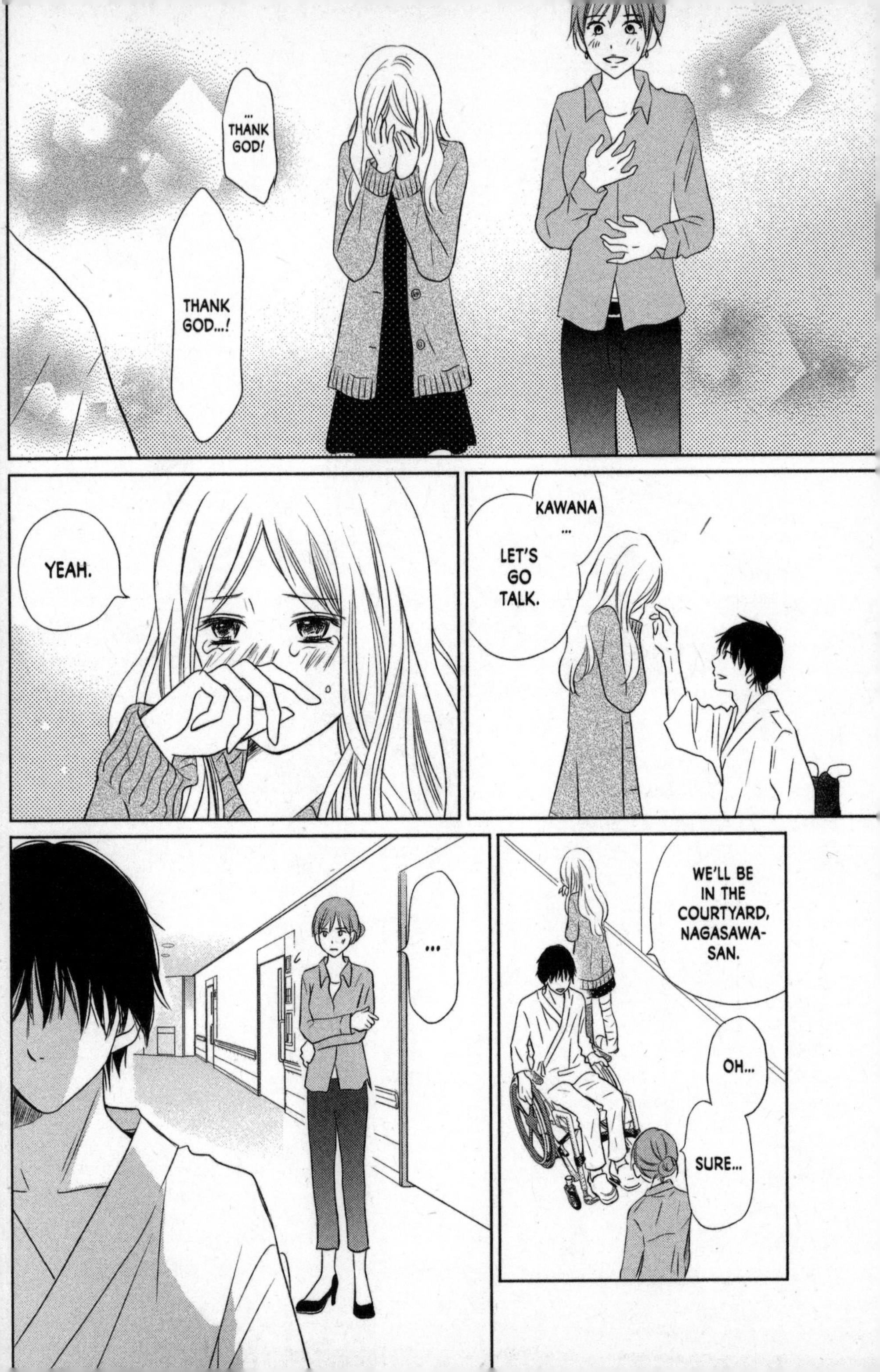
...THANK GOD!
THANK GOD...!
KAWANA... LET'S GO TALK.
YEAH.
WE'LL BE IN THE COURTYARD, NAGASAWA-SAN.
OH...
SURE...
...

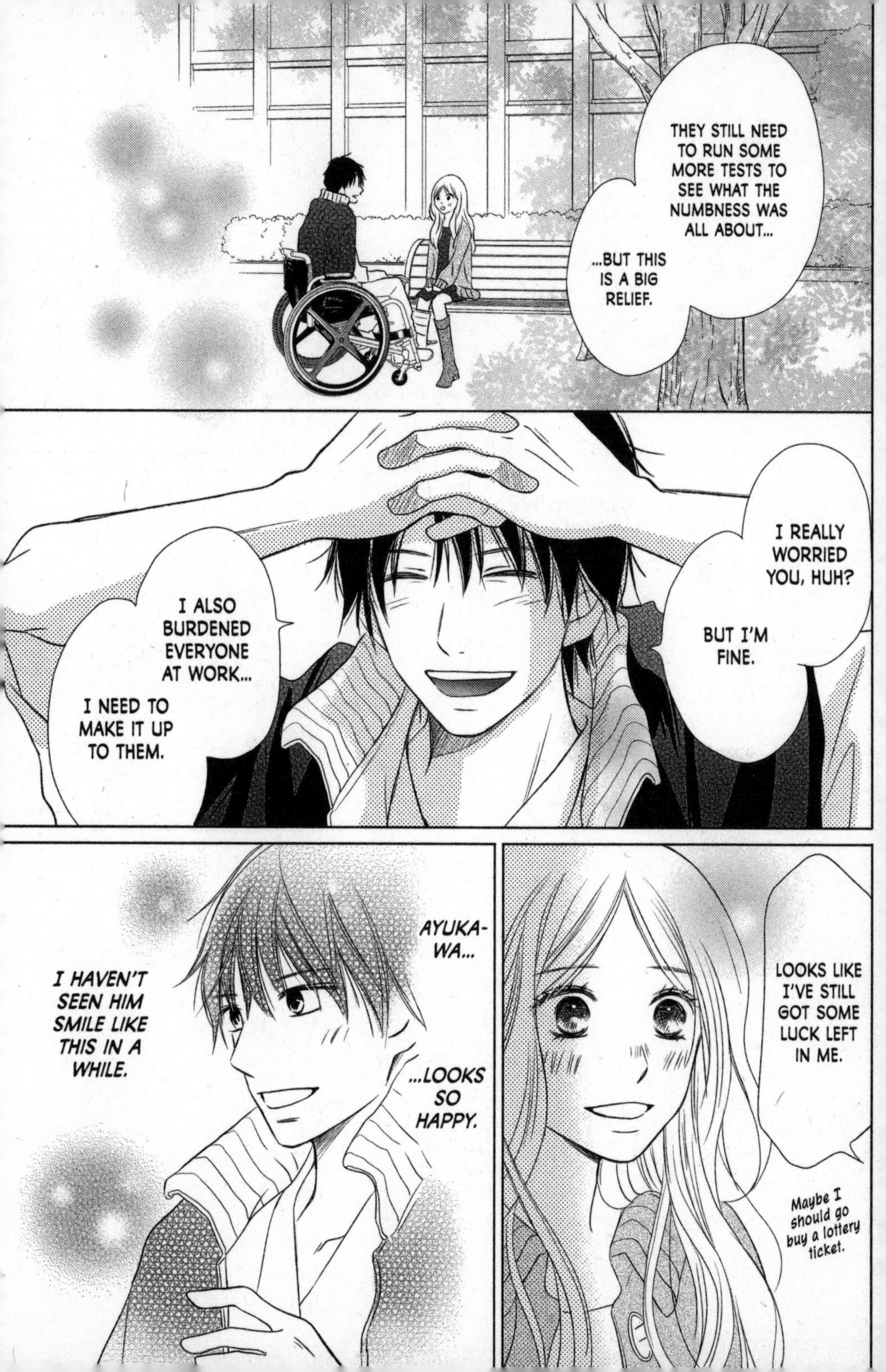
THEY STILL NEED TO RUN SOME MORE TESTS TO SEE WHAT THE NUMBNESS WAS ALL ABOUT...
...BUT THIS IS A BIG RELIEF.
I REALLY WORRIED YOU, HUH?
BUT I'M FINE.
I ALSO BURDENED EVERYONE AT WORK...
I NEED TO MAKE IT UP TO THEM.
LOOKS LIKE I'VE STILL GOT SOME LUCK LEFT IN ME.
Maybe I should go buy a lottery ticket.
AYUKA-WA...
...LOOKS SO HAPPY.
I HAVEN'T SEEN HIM SMILE LIKE THIS IN A WHILE.

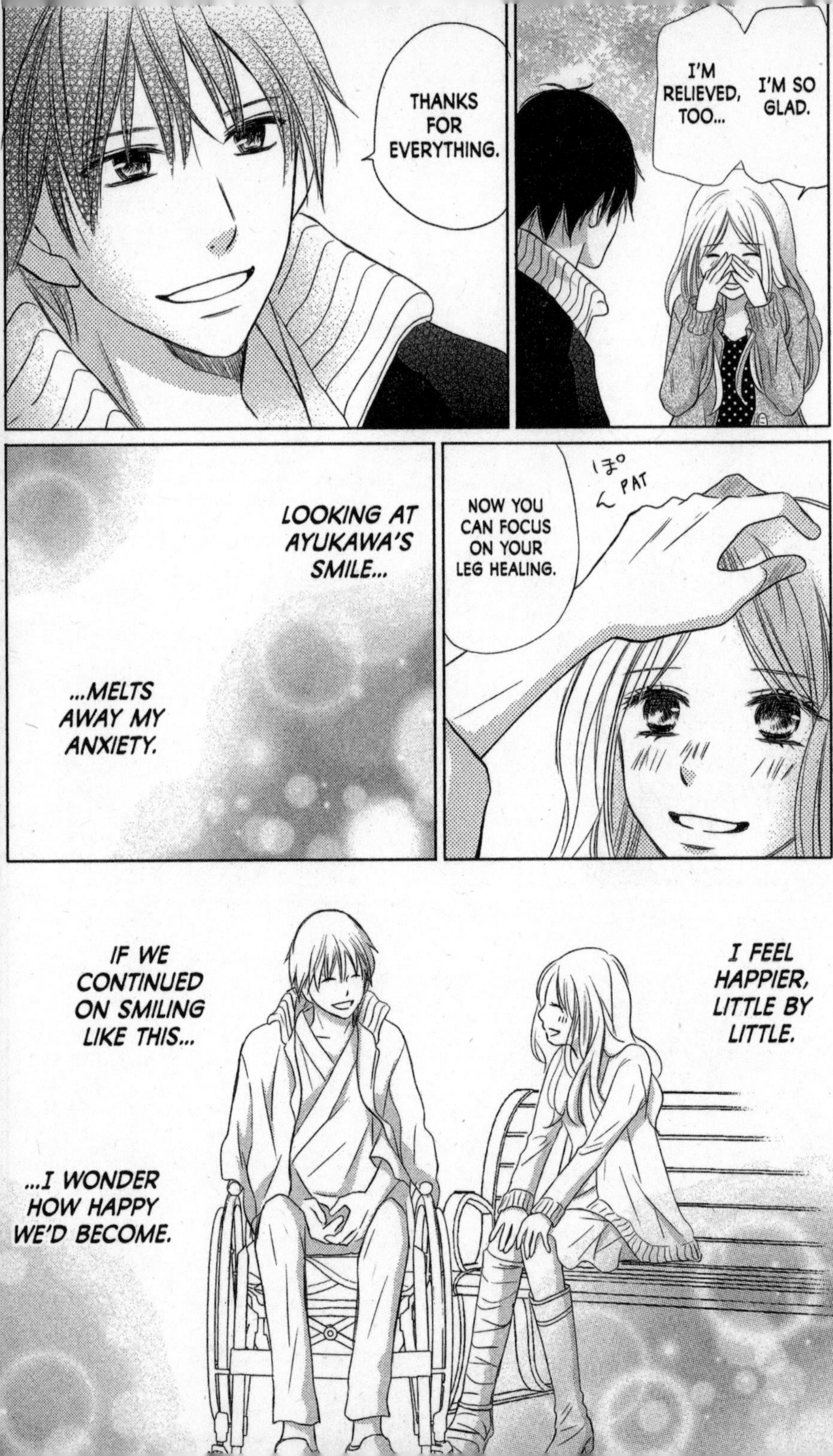
I'M SO GLAD.
I'M RELIEVED, TOO...
THANKS FOR EVERYTHING.
ぽん PAT
NOW YOU CAN FOCUS ON YOUR LEG HEALING.
LOOKING AT AYUKAWA'S SMILE...
...MELTS AWAY MY ANXIETY.
I FEEL HAPPIER, LITTLE BY LITTLE.
IF WE CONTINUED ON SMILING LIKE THIS...
...I WONDER HOW HAPPY WE'D BECOME.

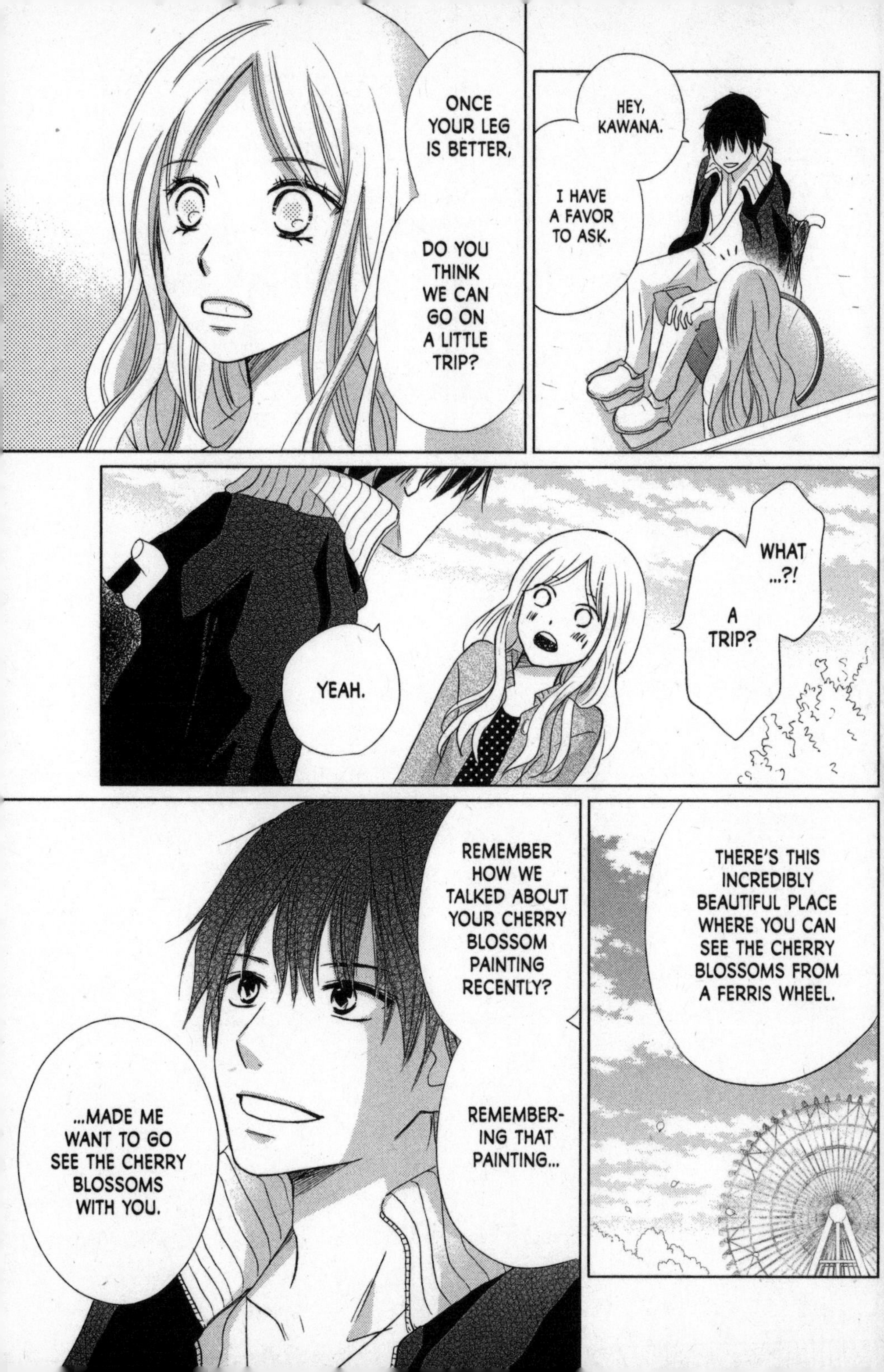
HEY, KAWANA.
I HAVE A FAVOR TO ASK.
ONCE YOUR LEG IS BETTER,
DO YOU THINK WE CAN GO ON A LITTLE TRIP?
WHAT ...?!
A TRIP?
YEAH.
THERE'S THIS INCREDIBLY BEAUTIFUL PLACE WHERE YOU CAN SEE THE CHERRY BLOSSOMS FROM A FERRIS WHEEL.
REMEMBER HOW WE TALKED ABOUT YOUR CHERRY BLOSSOM PAINTING RECENTLY?
REMEMBER-ING THAT PAINTING...
...MADE ME WANT TO GO SEE THE CHERRY BLOSSOMS WITH YOU.

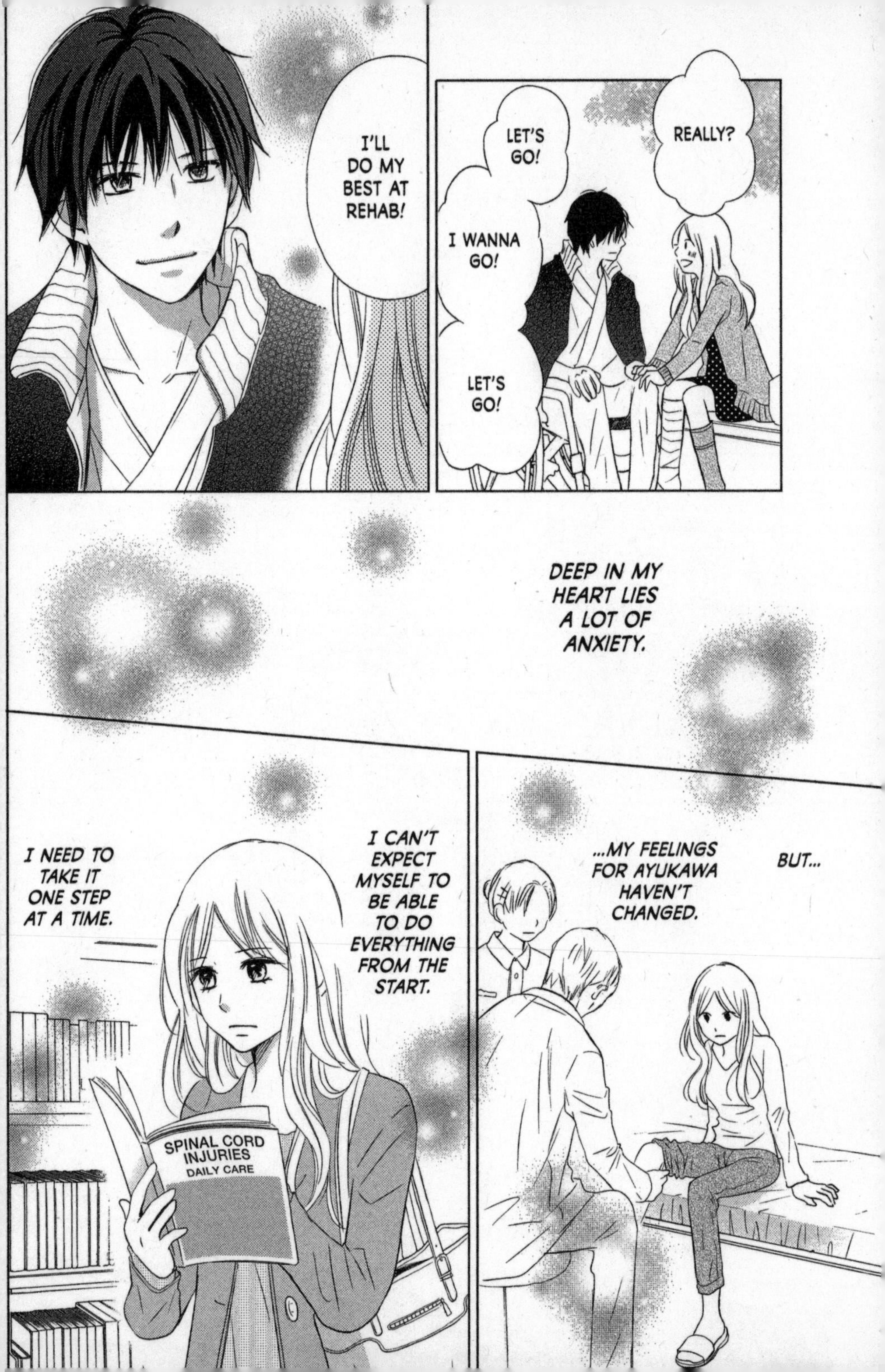
REALLY?
LET'S GO!
I WANNA GO!
LET'S GO!
I'LL DO MY BEST AT REHAB!
DEEP IN MY HEART LIES A LOT OF ANXIETY.
BUT...
...MY FEELINGS FOR AYUKAWA HAVEN'T CHANGED.
I CAN'T EXPECT MYSELF TO BE ABLE TO DO EVERYTHING FROM THE START.
I NEED TO TAKE IT ONE STEP AT A TIME.
SPINAL CORD INJURIES
DAILY CARE

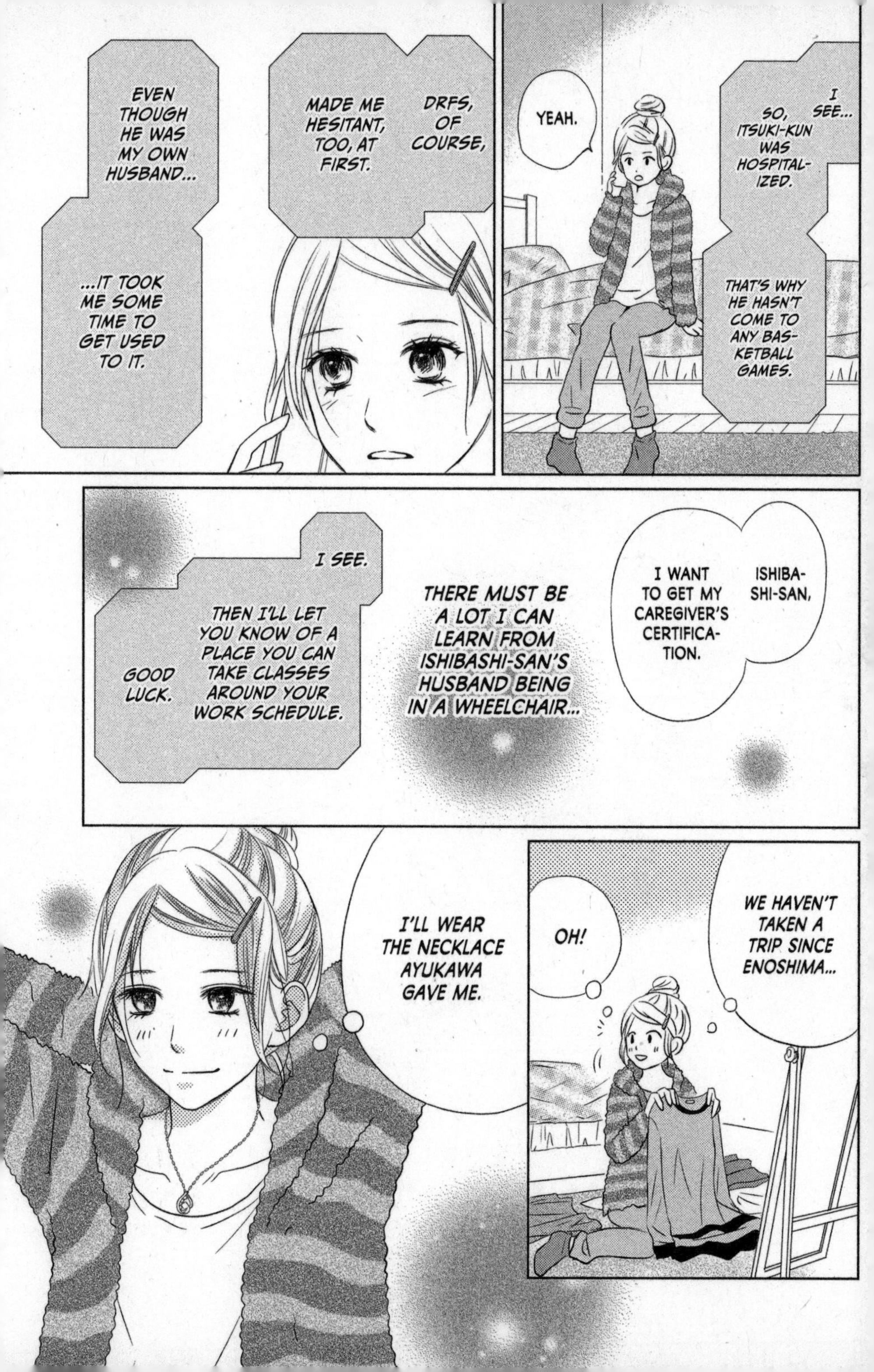
I SEE...
SO, ITSUKI-KUN WAS HOSPITALIZED.
YEAH.
THAT'S WHY HE HASN'T COME TO ANY BASKETBALL GAMES.
DRFS, OF COURSE,
MADE ME HESITANT, TOO, AT FIRST.
EVEN THOUGH HE WAS MY OWN HUSBAND...
...IT TOOK ME SOME TIME TO GET USED TO IT.
ISHIBASHI-SAN,
I WANT TO GET MY CAREGIVER'S CERTIFICATION.
THERE MUST BE A LOT I CAN LEARN FROM ISHIBASHI-SAN'S HUSBAND BEING IN A WHEELCHAIR...
I SEE.
THEN I'LL LET YOU KNOW OF A PLACE YOU CAN TAKE CLASSES AROUND YOUR WORK SCHEDULE.
GOOD LUCK.
WE HAVEN'T TAKEN A TRIP SINCE ENOSHIMA...
OH!
I'LL WEAR THE NECKLACE AYUKAWA GAVE ME.

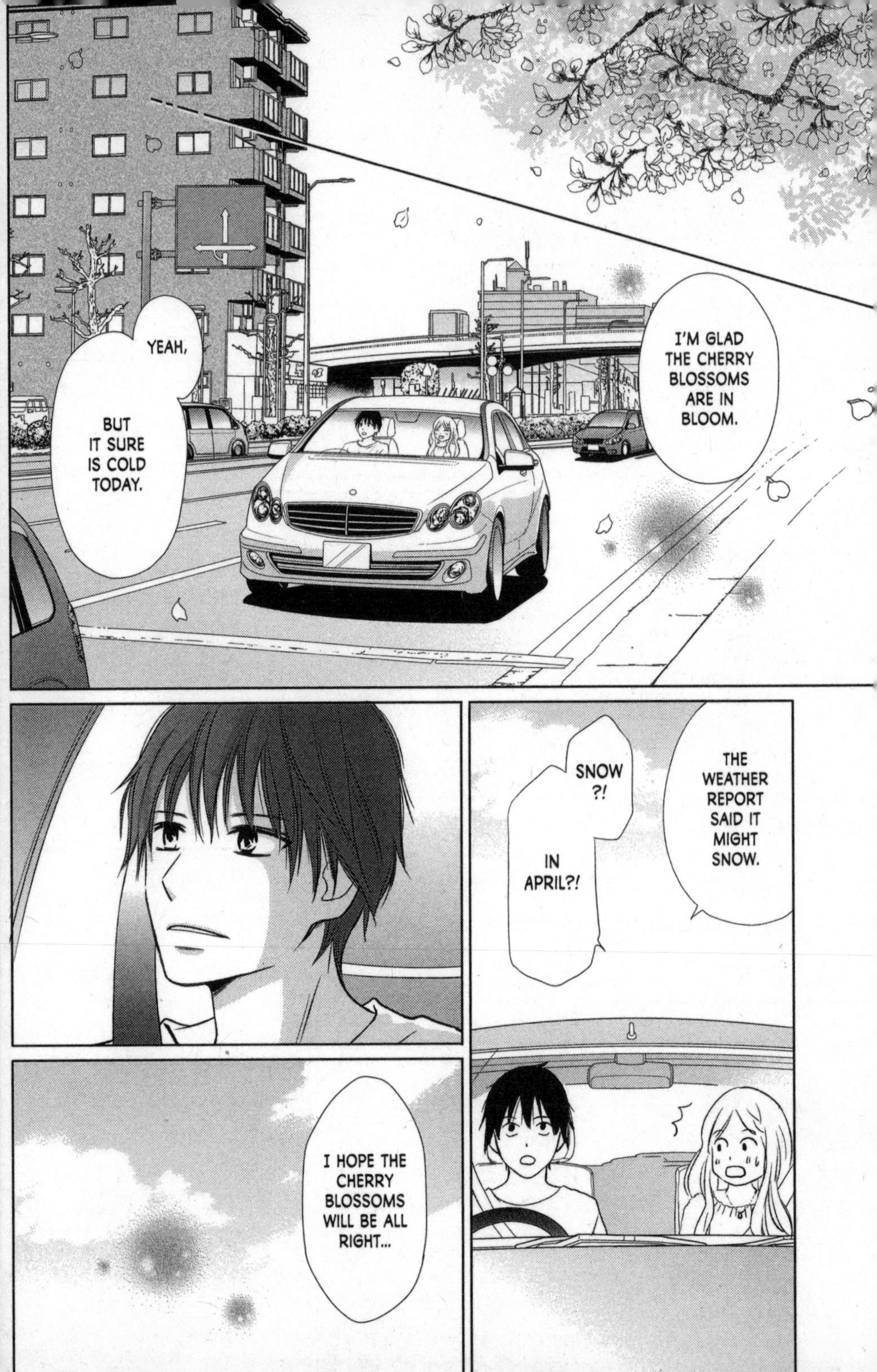
I'M GLAD THE CHERRY BLOSSOMS ARE IN BLOOM.
YEAH,
BUT IT SURE IS COLD TODAY.
THE WEATHER REPORT SAID IT MIGHT SNOW.
SNOW?!
IN APRIL?!
I HOPE THE CHERRY BLOSSOMS WILL BE ALL RIGHT...

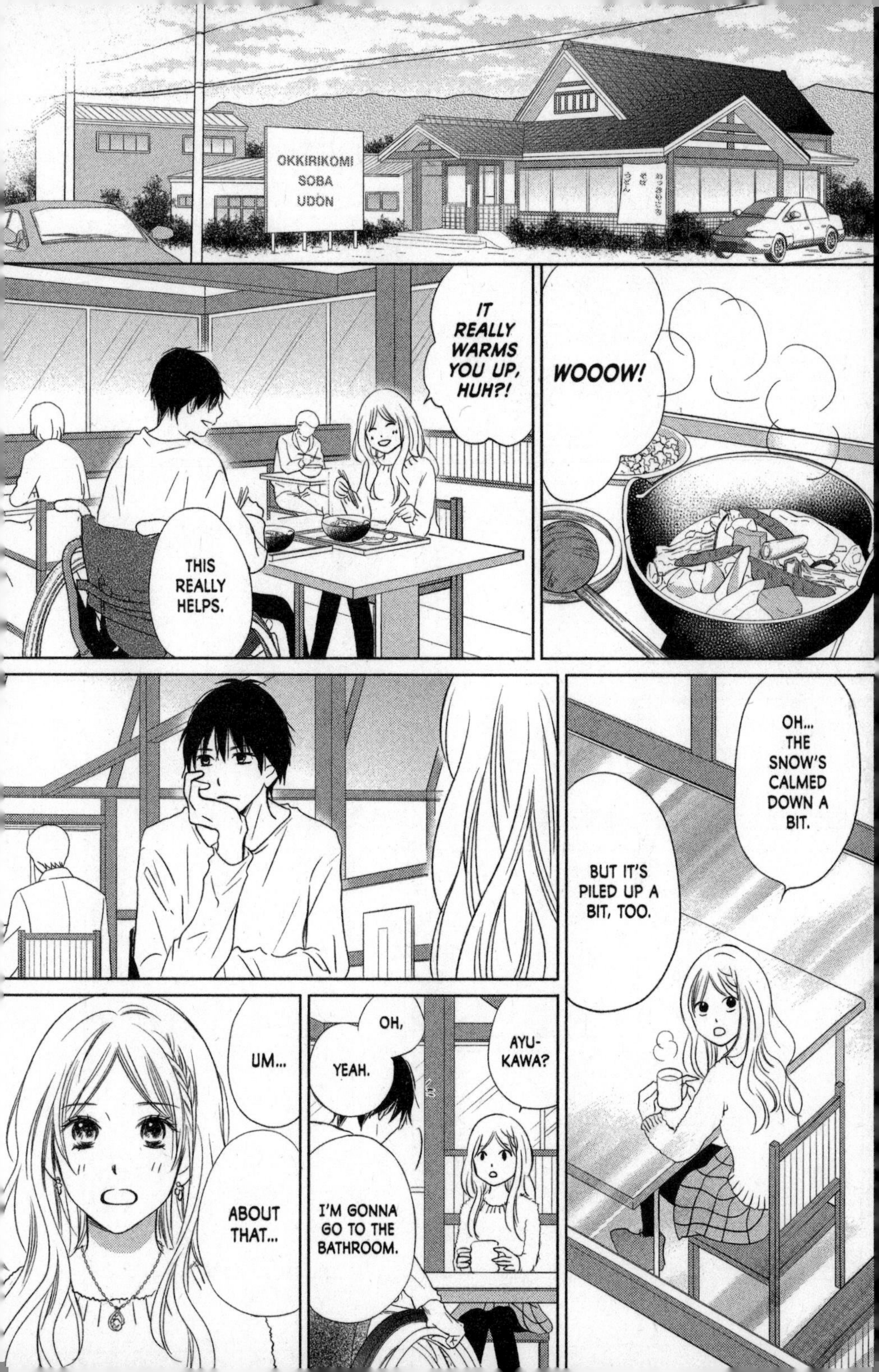
OKKIRIKOMI
SOBA
UDON
WOOOW!
IT REALLY WARMS YOU UP, HUH?!
THIS REALLY HELPS.
OH... THE SNOW'S CALMED DOWN A BIT.
BUT IT'S PILED UP A BIT, TOO.
AYU-KAWA?
OH,
YEAH.
I'M GONNA GO TO THE BATHROOM.
UM...
ABOUT THAT...

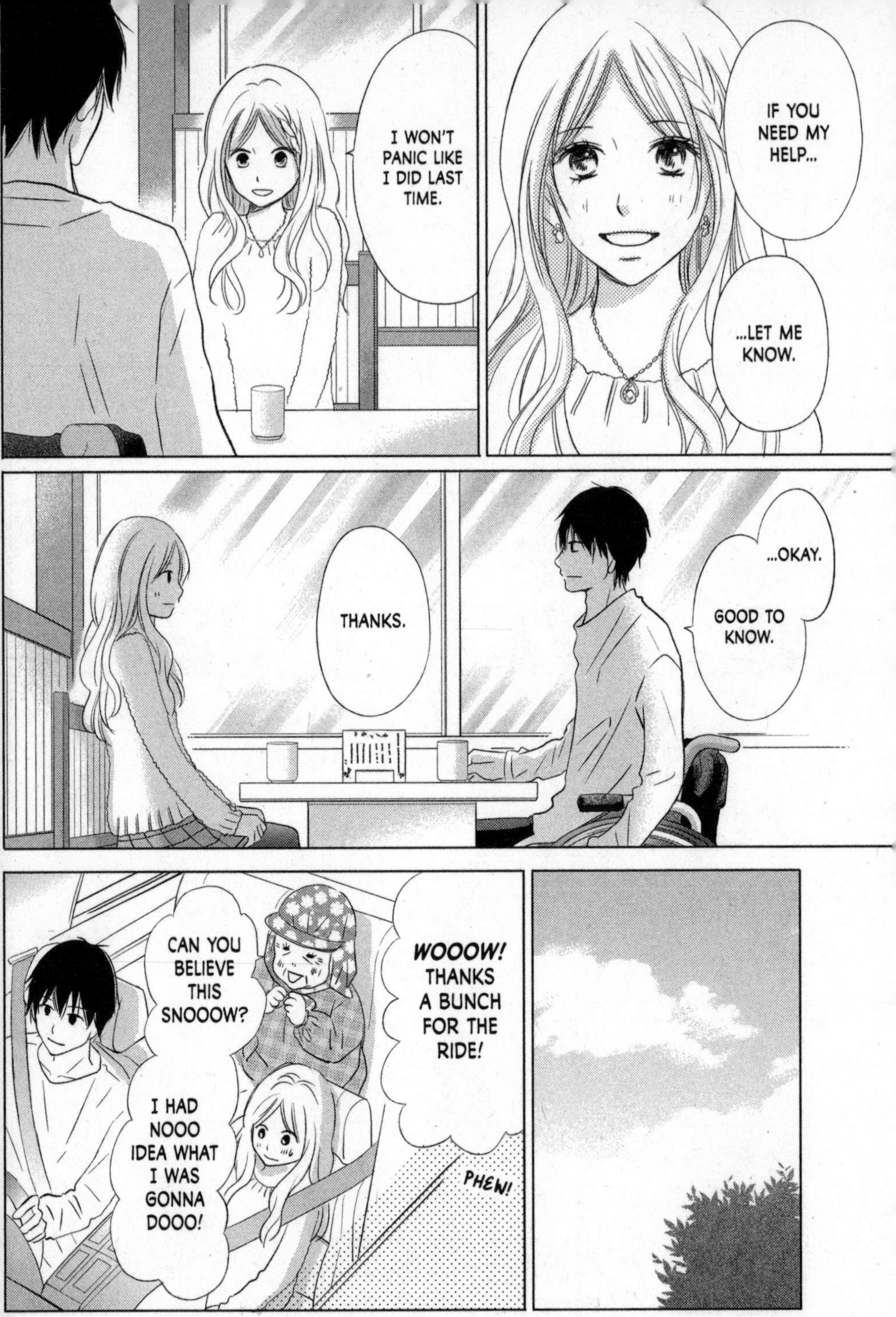
IF YOU NEED MY HELP...
...LET ME KNOW.
I WON'T PANIC LIKE I DID LAST TIME.
...OKAY.
GOOD TO KNOW.
THANKS.
WOOOW! THANKS A BUNCH FOR THE RIDE!
CAN YOU BELIEVE THIS SNOOOW?
I HAD NOOO IDEA WHAT I WAS GONNA DOOO!
PHEW!

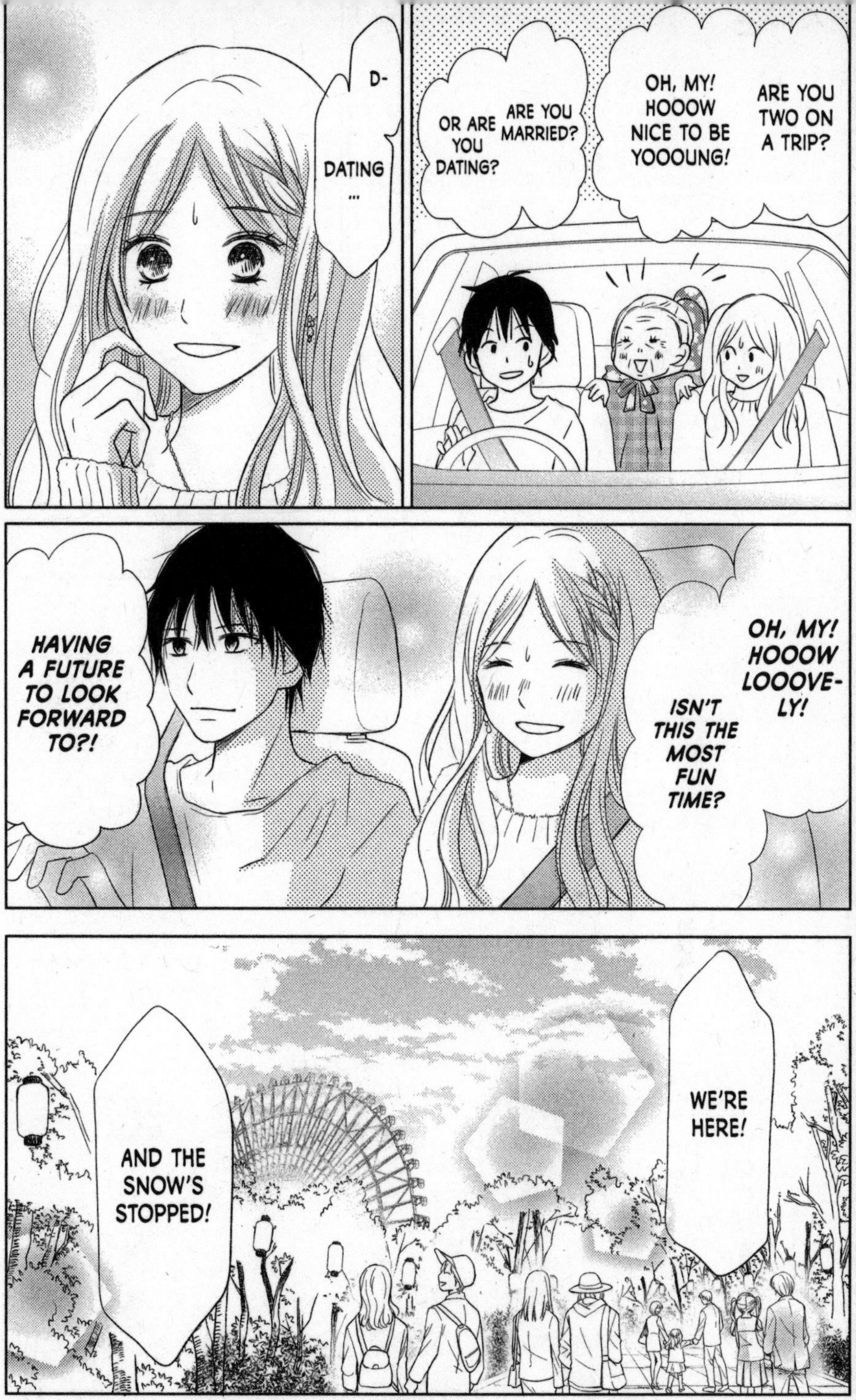

ARE YOU TWO ON A TRIP?
OH, MY! HOOOW NICE TO BE YOOOUNG!
ARE YOU MARRIED?
OR ARE YOU DATING?
D-
DATING …
OH, MY! HOOOW LOOOVE-LY!
ISN'T THIS THE MOST FUN TIME?
HAVING A FUTURE TO LOOK FORWARD TO?!
WE'RE HERE!
AND THE SNOW'S STOPPED!

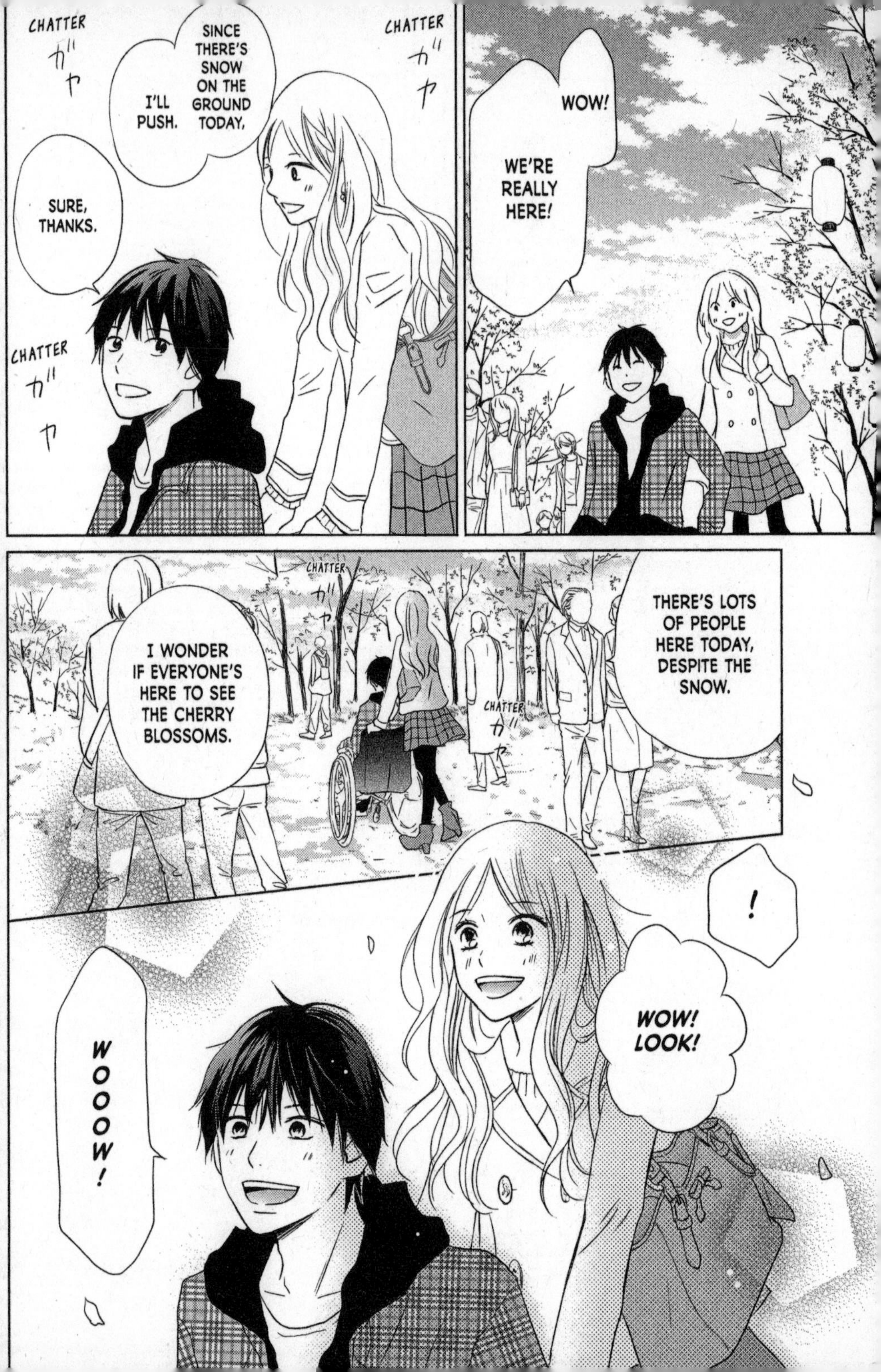
WOW!
WE'RE REALLY HERE!
CHATTER ガヤ
SINCE THERE'S SNOW ON THE GROUND TODAY, I'LL PUSH.
SURE, THANKS.
CHATTER ガヤ
CHATTER ガヤ
THERE'S LOTS OF PEOPLE HERE TODAY, DESPITE THE SNOW.
CHATTER ガヤ
CHATTER ガヤ
I WONDER IF EVERYONE'S HERE TO SEE THE CHERRY BLOSSOMS.
!
WOW! LOOK!
WOOOW!

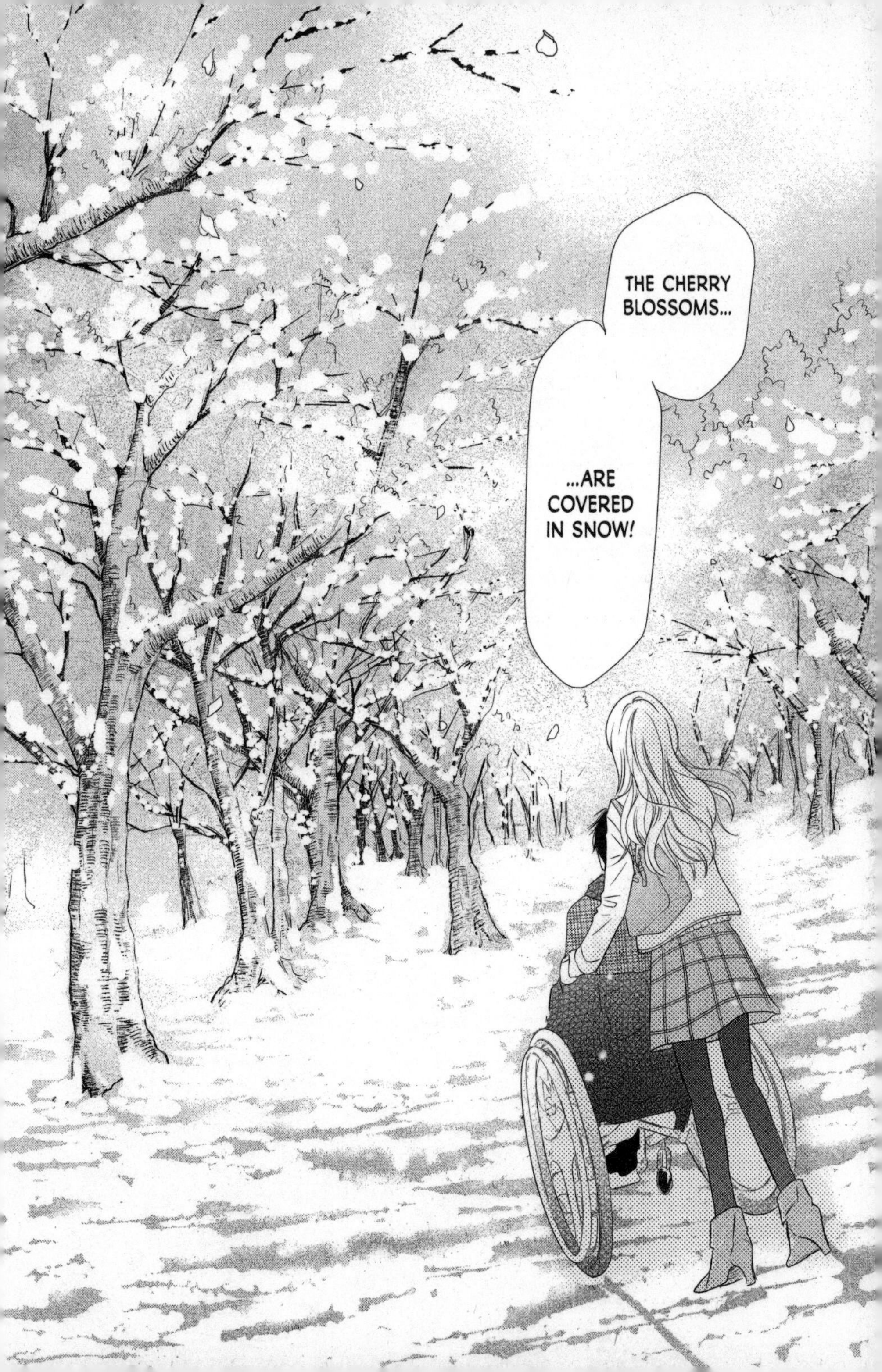
THE CHERRY BLOSSOMS...
...ARE COVERED IN SNOW!

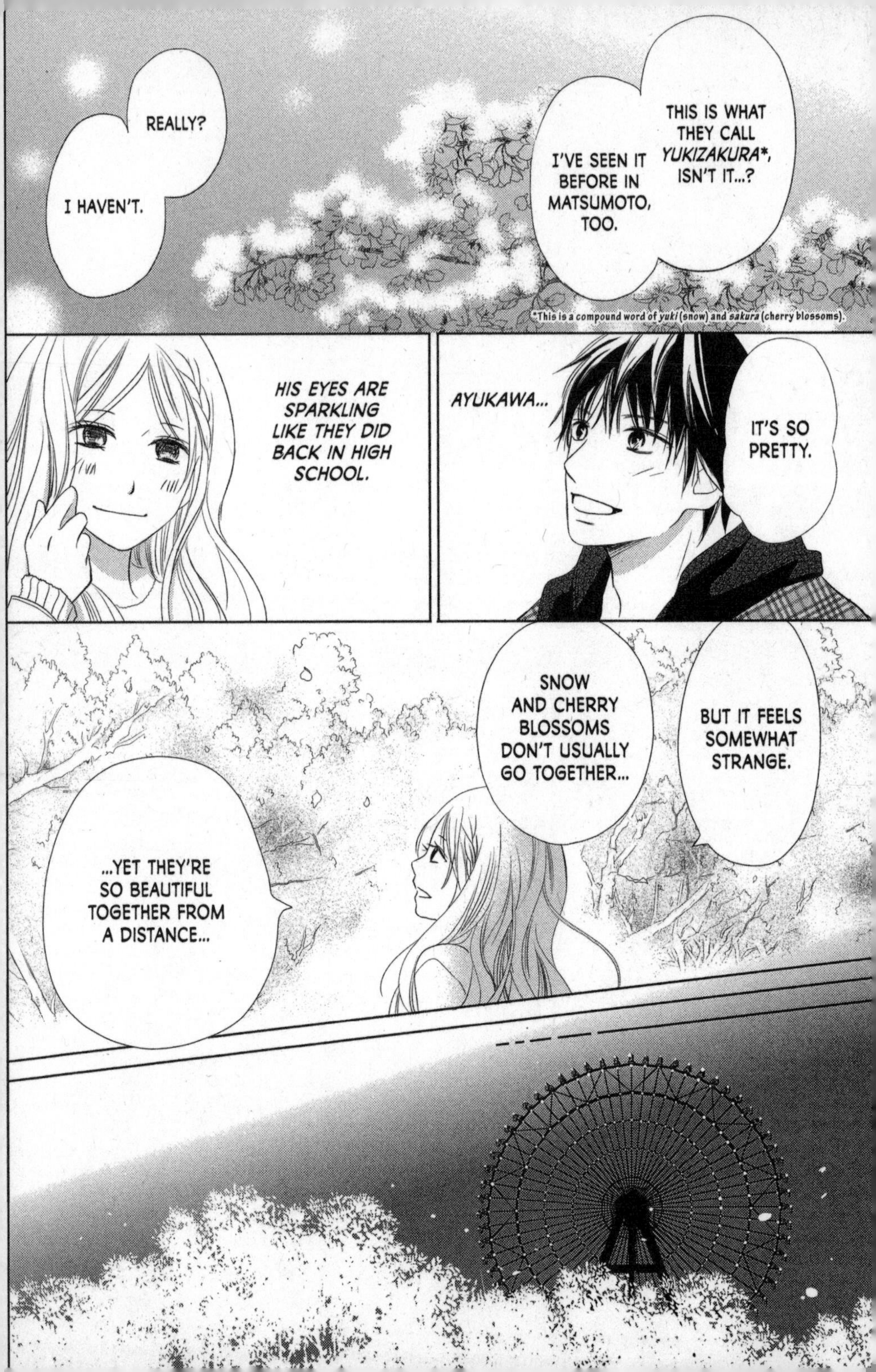
THIS IS WHAT THEY CALL *YUKIZAKURA**, ISN'T IT...?
I'VE SEEN IT BEFORE IN MATSUMOTO, TOO.
REALLY?
I HAVEN'T.
IT'S SO PRETTY.
AYUKAWA...
HIS EYES ARE SPARKLING LIKE THEY DID BACK IN HIGH SCHOOL.
BUT IT FEELS SOMEWHAT STRANGE.
SNOW AND CHERRY BLOSSOMS DON'T USUALLY GO TOGETHER...
...YET THEY'RE SO BEAUTIFUL TOGETHER FROM A DISTANCE...

*This is a compound word of *yuki* (snow) and *sakura* (cherry blossoms).

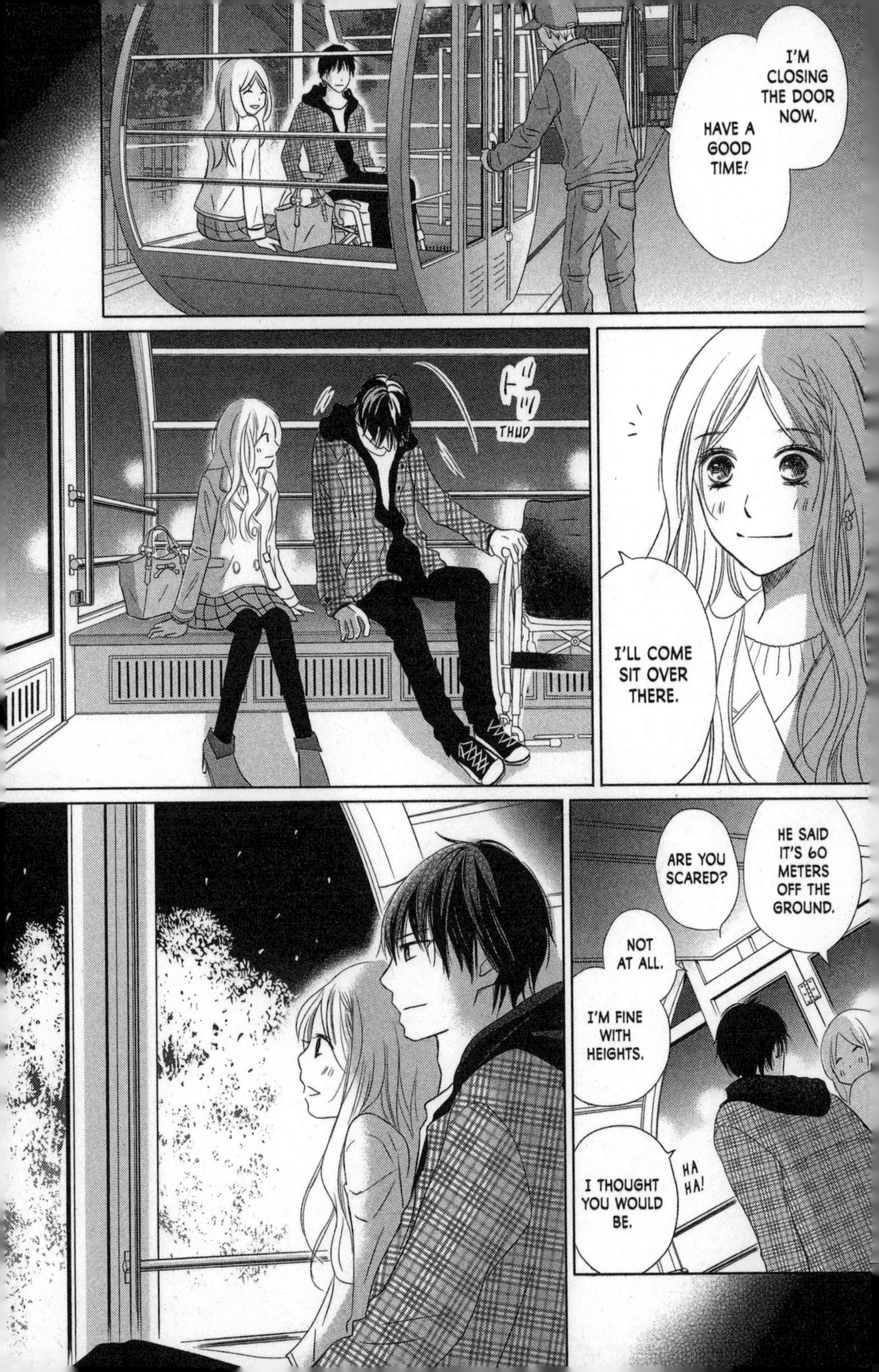
I'M CLOSING THE DOOR NOW.
HAVE A GOOD TIME!
I'LL COME SIT OVER THERE.
THUD
HE SAID IT'S 60 METERS OFF THE GROUND.
ARE YOU SCARED?
NOT AT ALL.
I'M FINE WITH HEIGHTS.
HA HA!
I THOUGHT YOU WOULD BE.

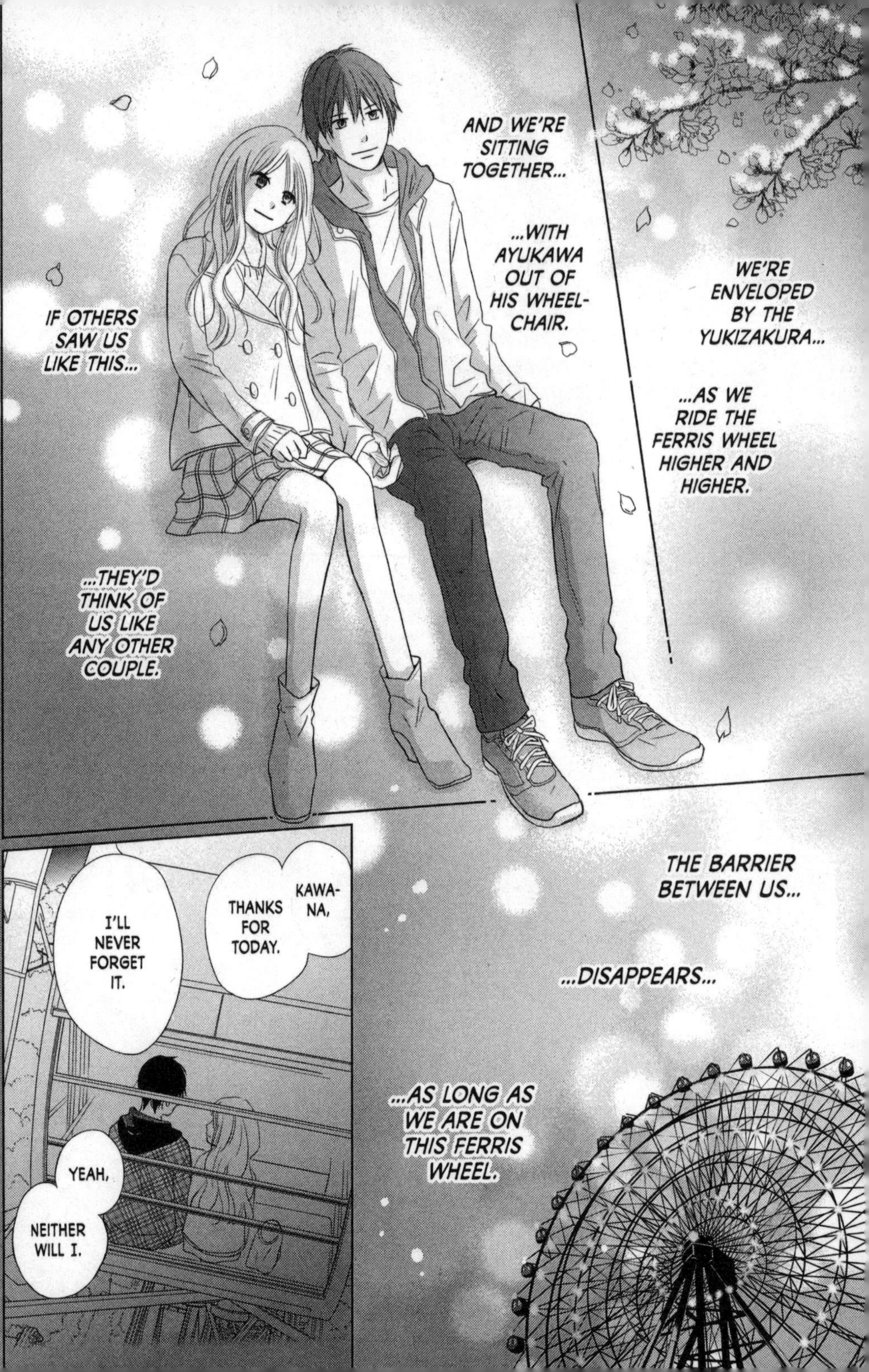
WE'RE ENVELOPED BY THE YUKIZAKURA...
...AS WE RIDE THE FERRIS WHEEL HIGHER AND HIGHER.
AND WE'RE SITTING TOGETHER...
...WITH AYUKAWA OUT OF HIS WHEEL-CHAIR.
IF OTHERS SAW US LIKE THIS...
...THEY'D THINK OF US LIKE ANY OTHER COUPLE.
THE BARRIER BETWEEN US...
...DISAPPEARS...
...AS LONG AS WE ARE ON THIS FERRIS WHEEL.
KAWA-NA,
THANKS FOR TODAY.
I'LL NEVER FORGET IT.
YEAH,
NEITHER WILL I.

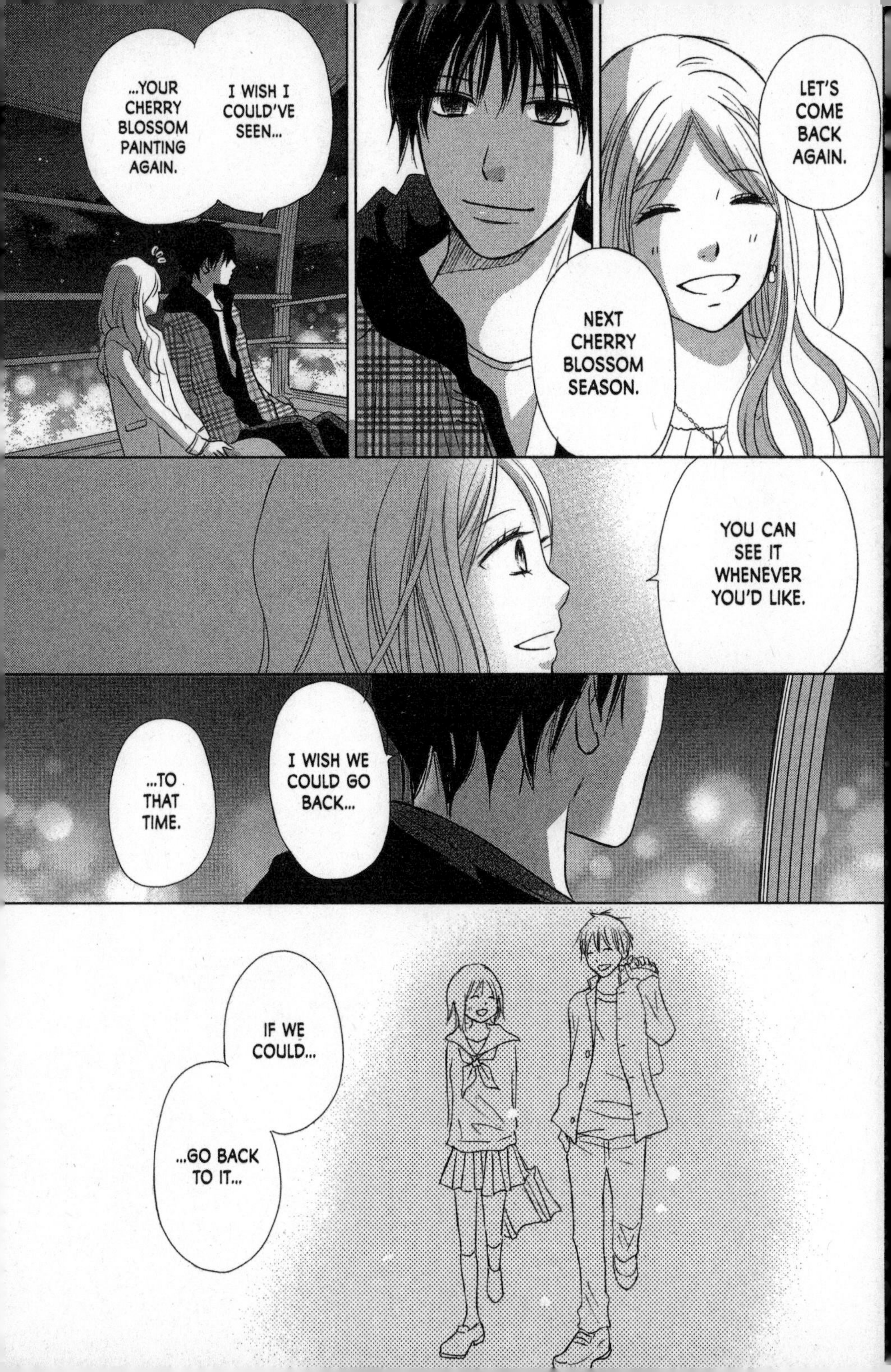
LET'S COME BACK AGAIN.
NEXT CHERRY BLOSSOM SEASON.
I WISH I COULD'VE SEEN...
...YOUR CHERRY BLOSSOM PAINTING AGAIN.
YOU CAN SEE IT WHENEVER YOU'D LIKE.
I WISH WE COULD GO BACK...
...TO THAT TIME.
IF WE COULD...
...GO BACK TO IT...

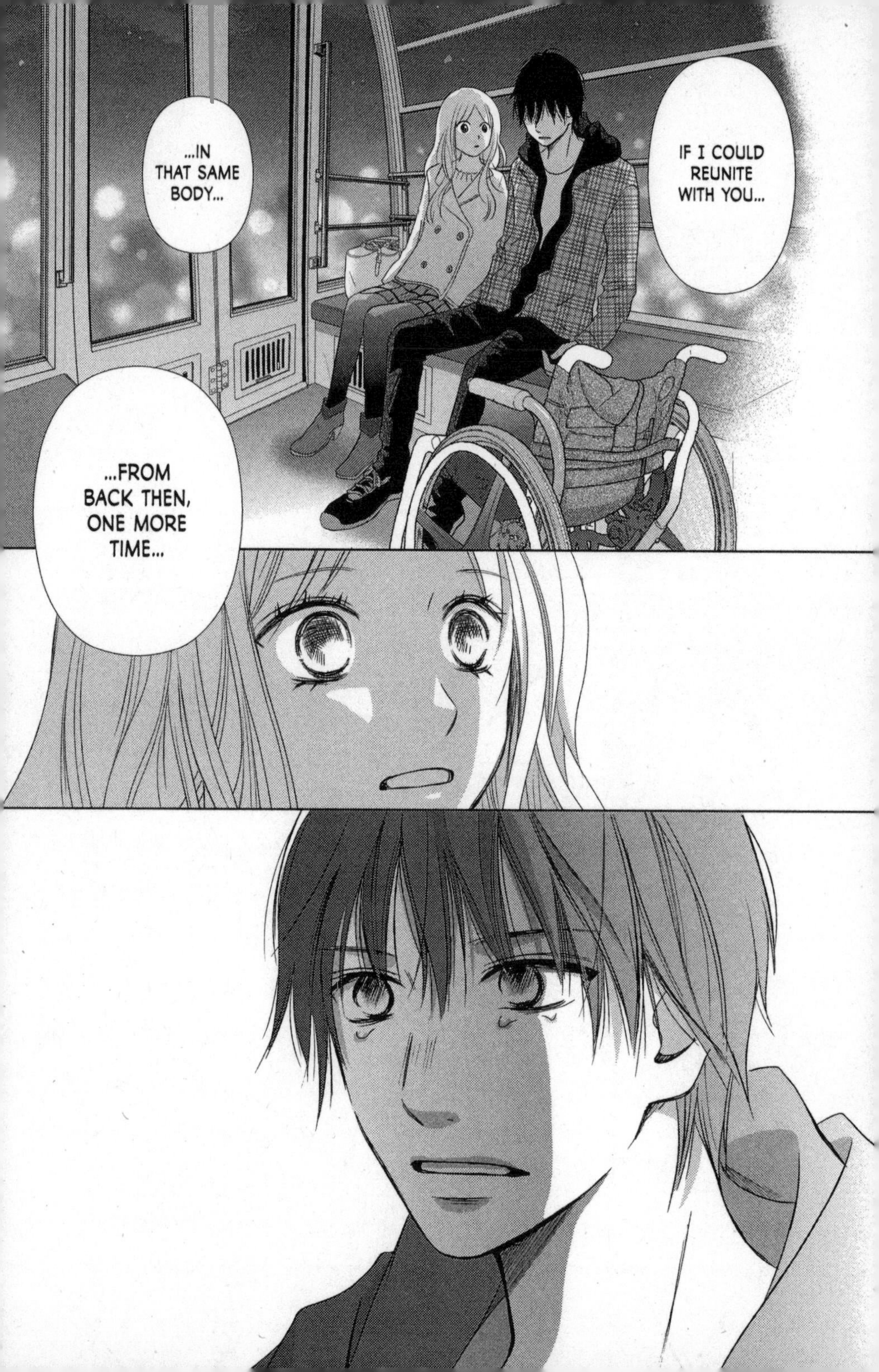
IF I COULD REUNITE WITH YOU...
...IN THAT SAME BODY...
...FROM BACK THEN, ONE MORE TIME...

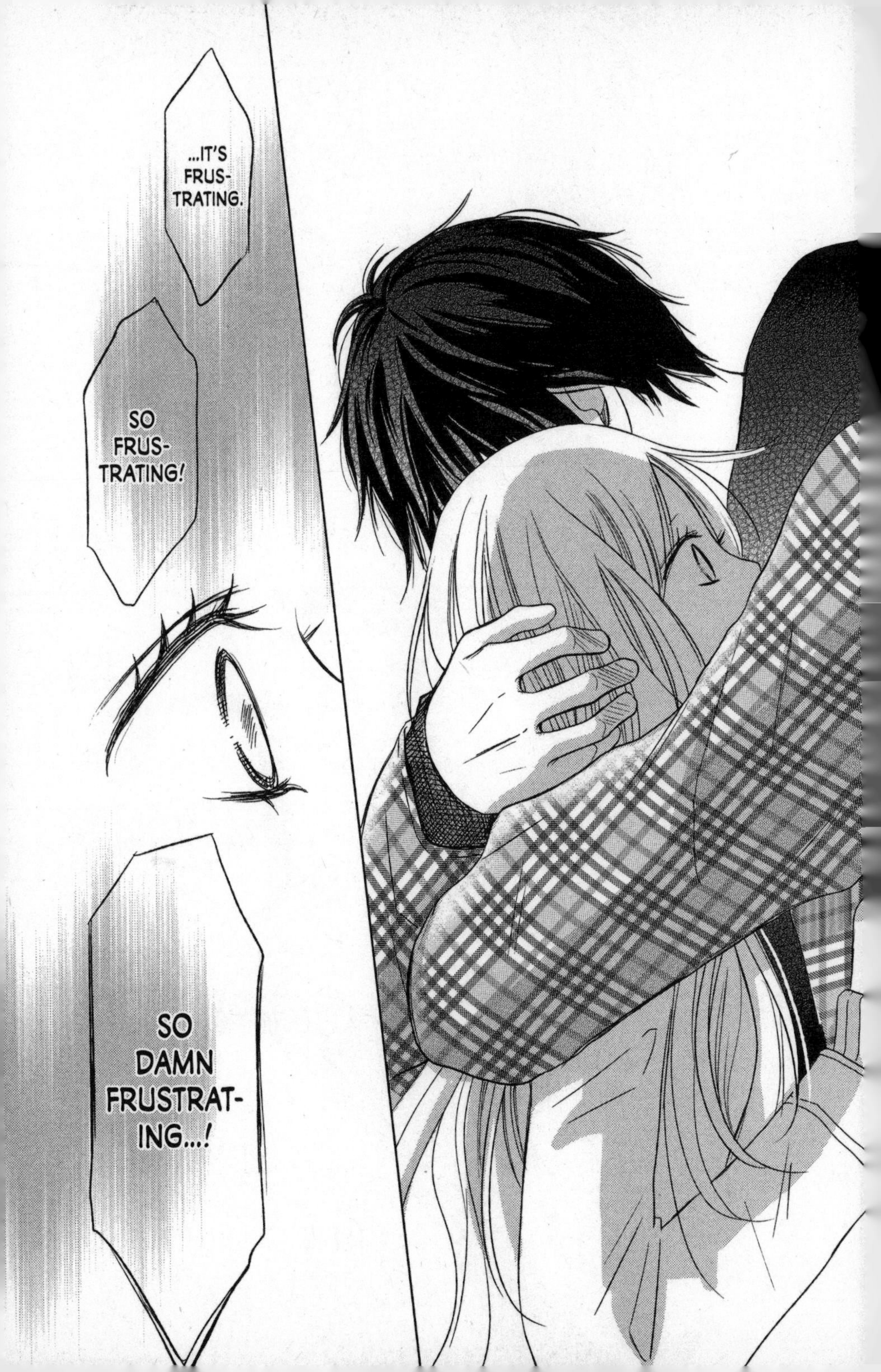
...IT'S FRUS-TRATING.
SO FRUS-TRATING!
SO DAMN FRUSTRAT-ING...!

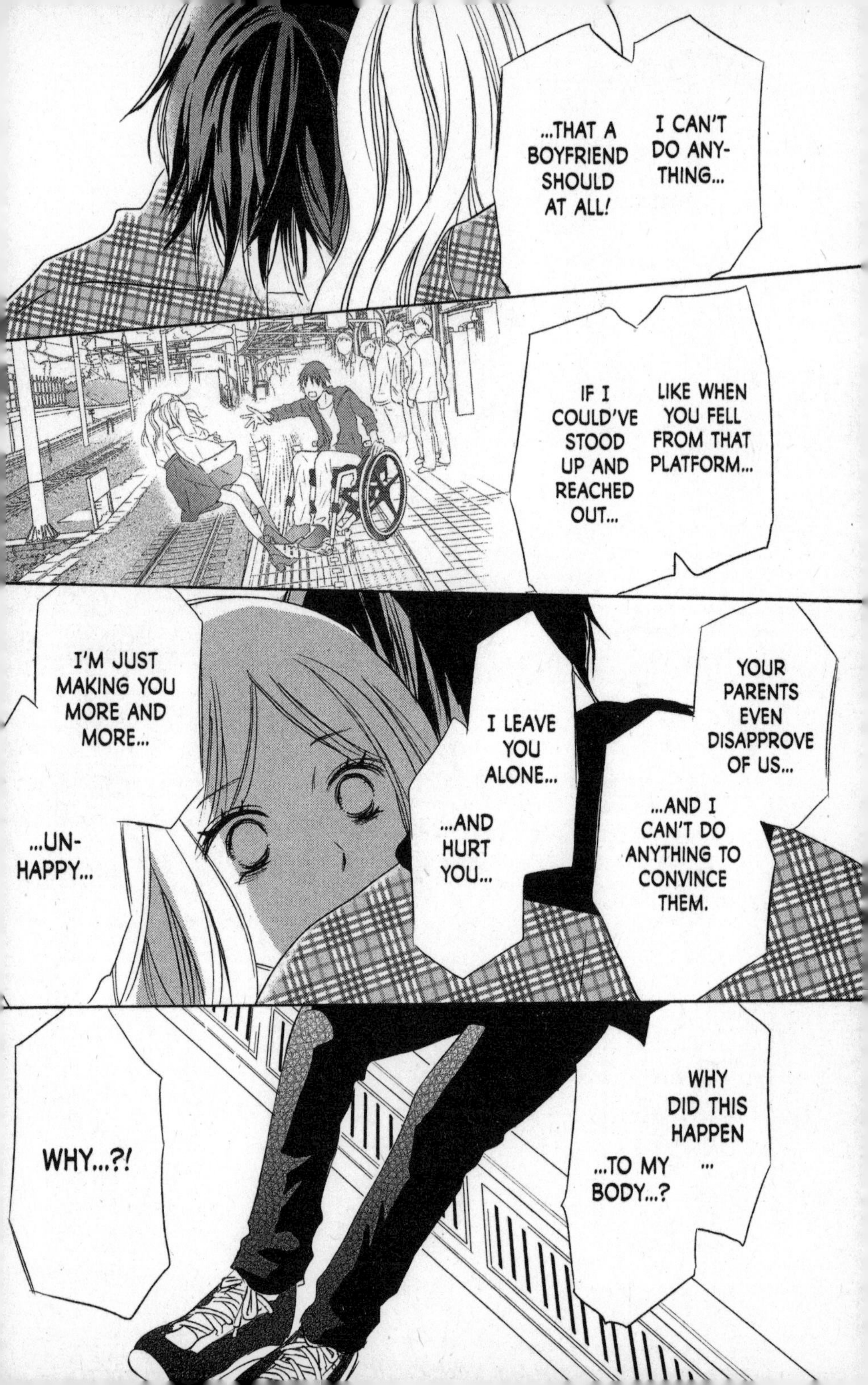
I CAN'T DO ANY-THING...
...THAT A BOYFRIEND SHOULD AT ALL!
LIKE WHEN YOU FELL FROM THAT PLATFORM...
IF I COULD'VE STOOD UP AND REACHED OUT...
YOUR PARENTS EVEN DISAPPROVE OF US...
...AND I CAN'T DO ANYTHING TO CONVINCE THEM.
I LEAVE YOU ALONE...
...AND HURT YOU...
I'M JUST MAKING YOU MORE AND MORE...
...UN-HAPPY...
WHY DID THIS HAPPEN ...
...TO MY BODY...?
WHY...?!

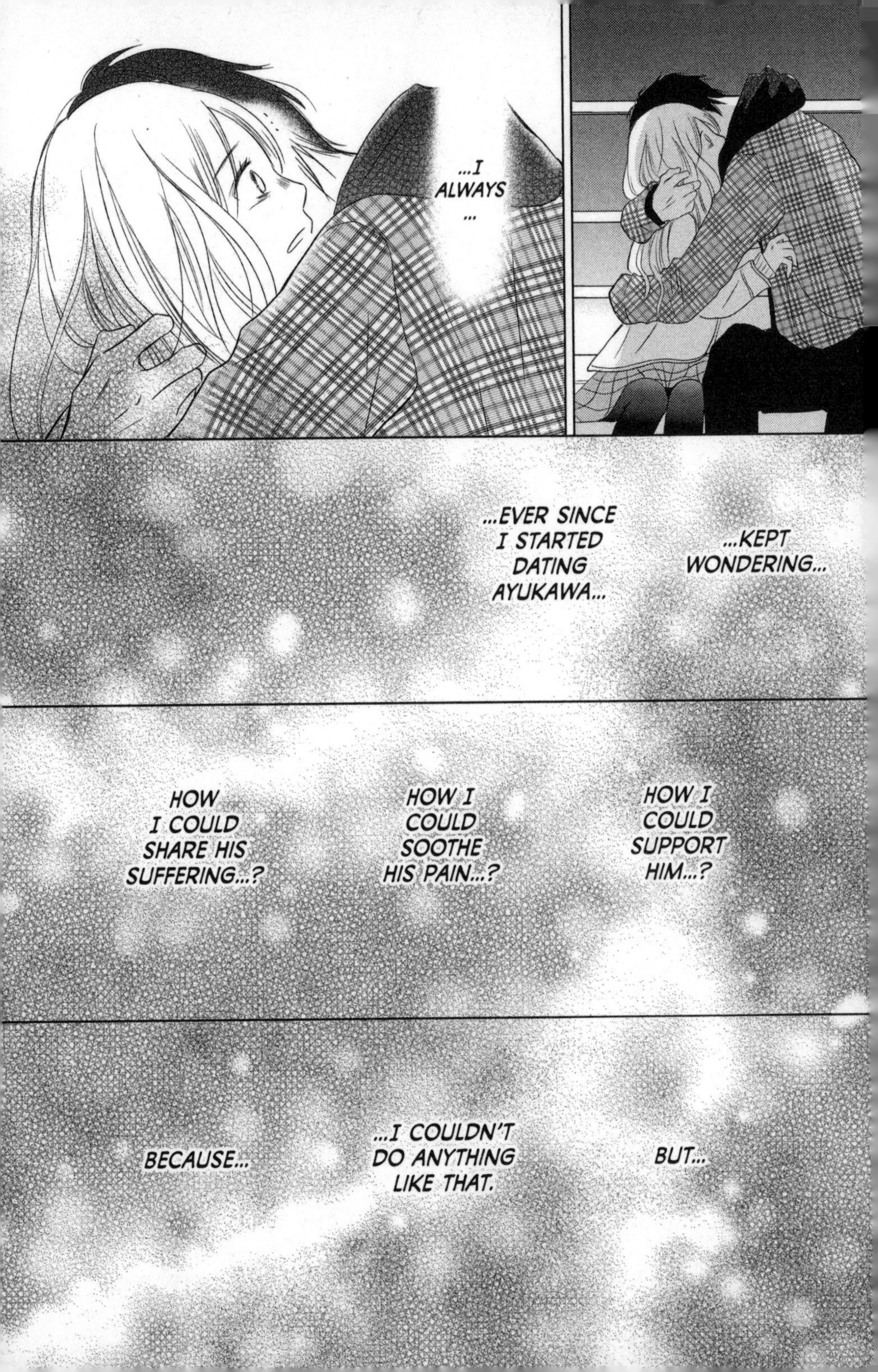
...I ALWAYS ...
...KEPT WONDERING...
...EVER SINCE I STARTED DATING AYUKAWA...
HOW I COULD SUPPORT HIM...?
HOW I COULD SOOTHE HIS PAIN...?
HOW I COULD SHARE HIS SUFFERING...?
BUT...
...I COULDN'T DO ANYTHING LIKE THAT.
BECAUSE...

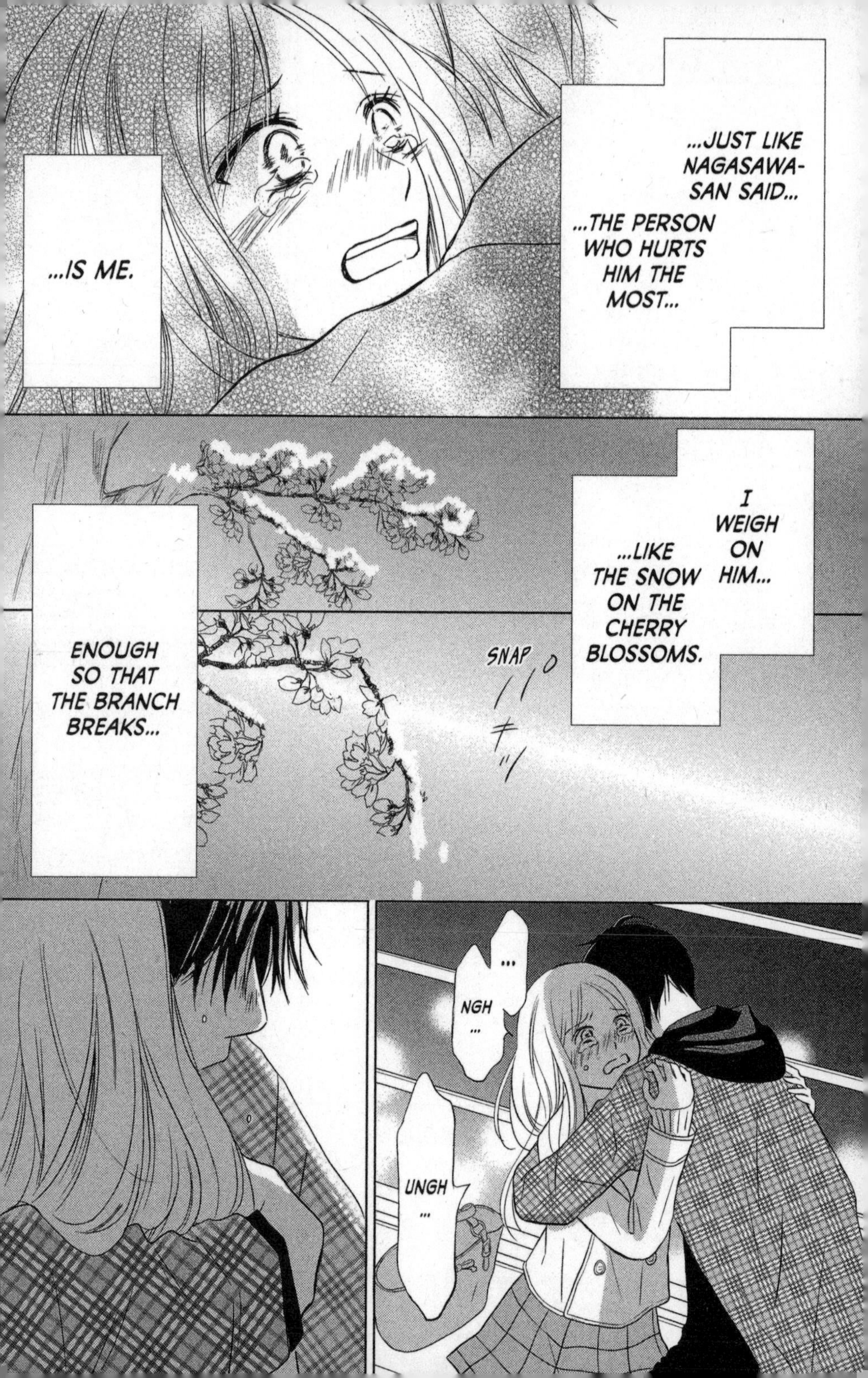
...JUST LIKE NAGASAWA-SAN SAID...
...THE PERSON WHO HURTS HIM THE MOST...
...IS ME.
I WEIGH ON HIM...
...LIKE THE SNOW ON THE CHERRY BLOSSOMS.
SNAP
ENOUGH SO THAT THE BRANCH BREAKS...
...
NGH ...
UNGH ...

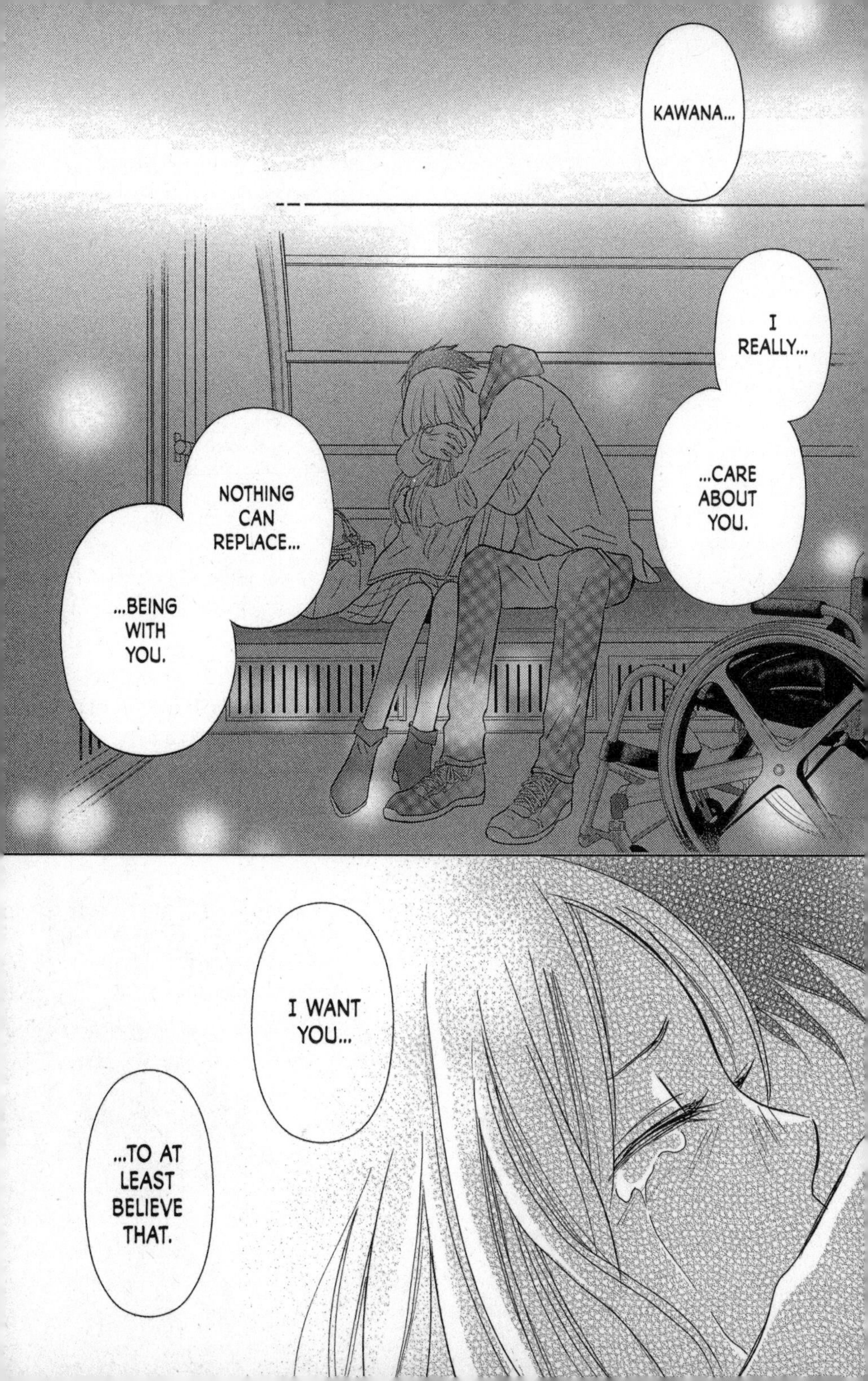
KAWANA...
I REALLY...
...CARE ABOUT YOU.
NOTHING CAN REPLACE...
...BEING WITH YOU.
I WANT YOU...
...TO AT LEAST BELIEVE THAT.

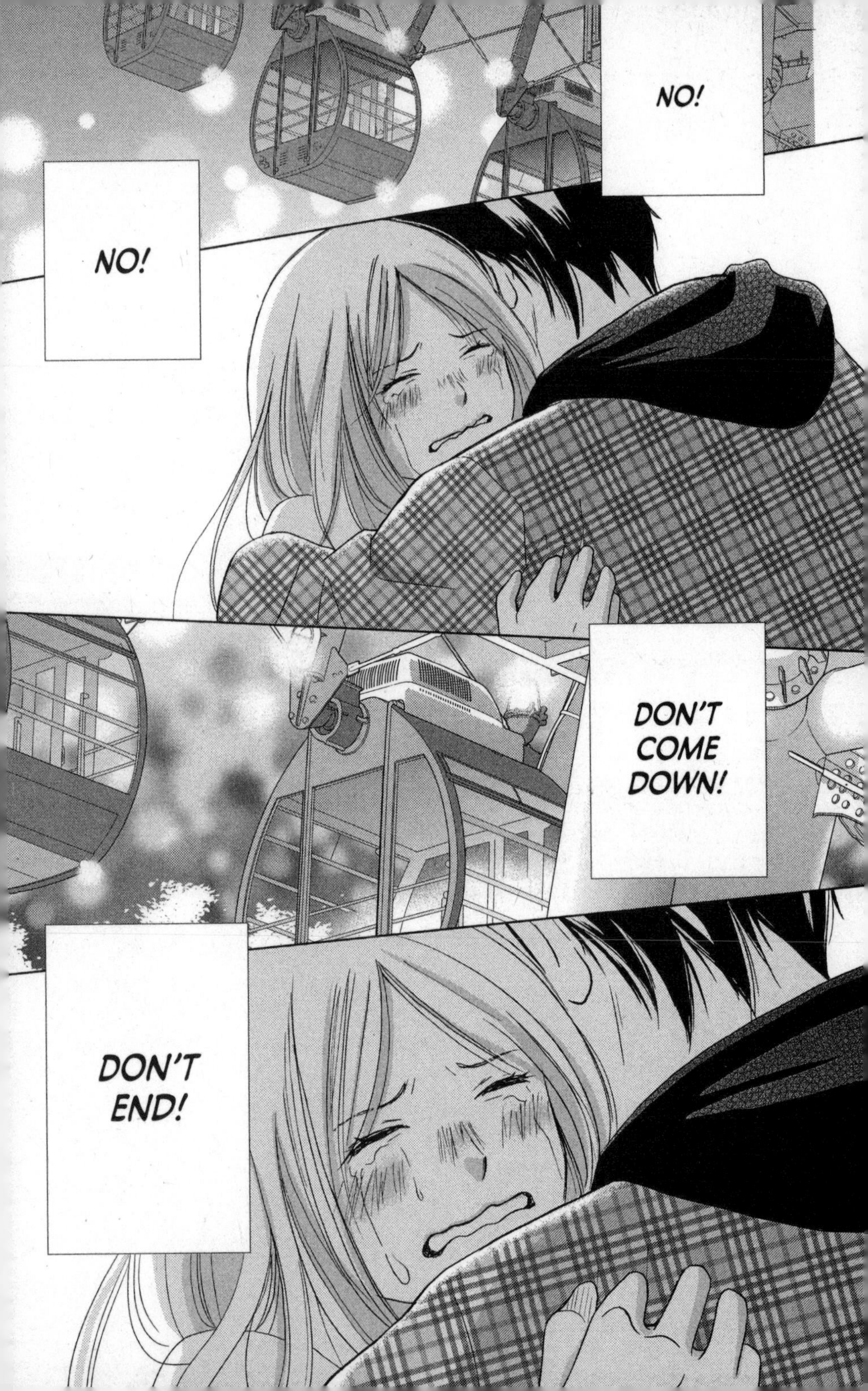
NO!
NO!
DON'T COME DOWN!
DON'T END!

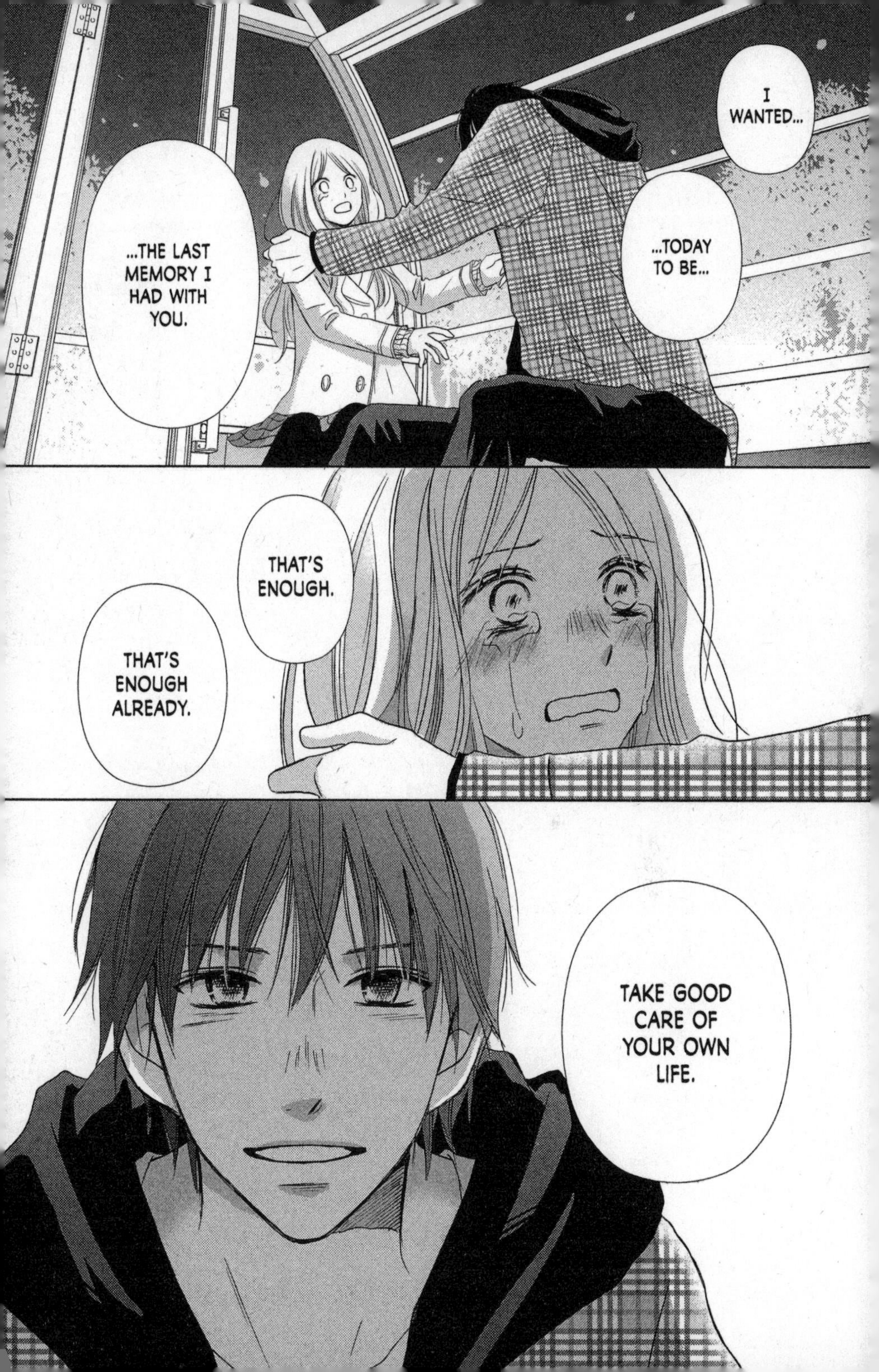
I WANTED...
...TODAY TO BE...
...THE LAST MEMORY I HAD WITH YOU.
THAT'S ENOUGH.
THAT'S ENOUGH ALREADY.
TAKE GOOD CARE OF YOUR OWN LIFE.

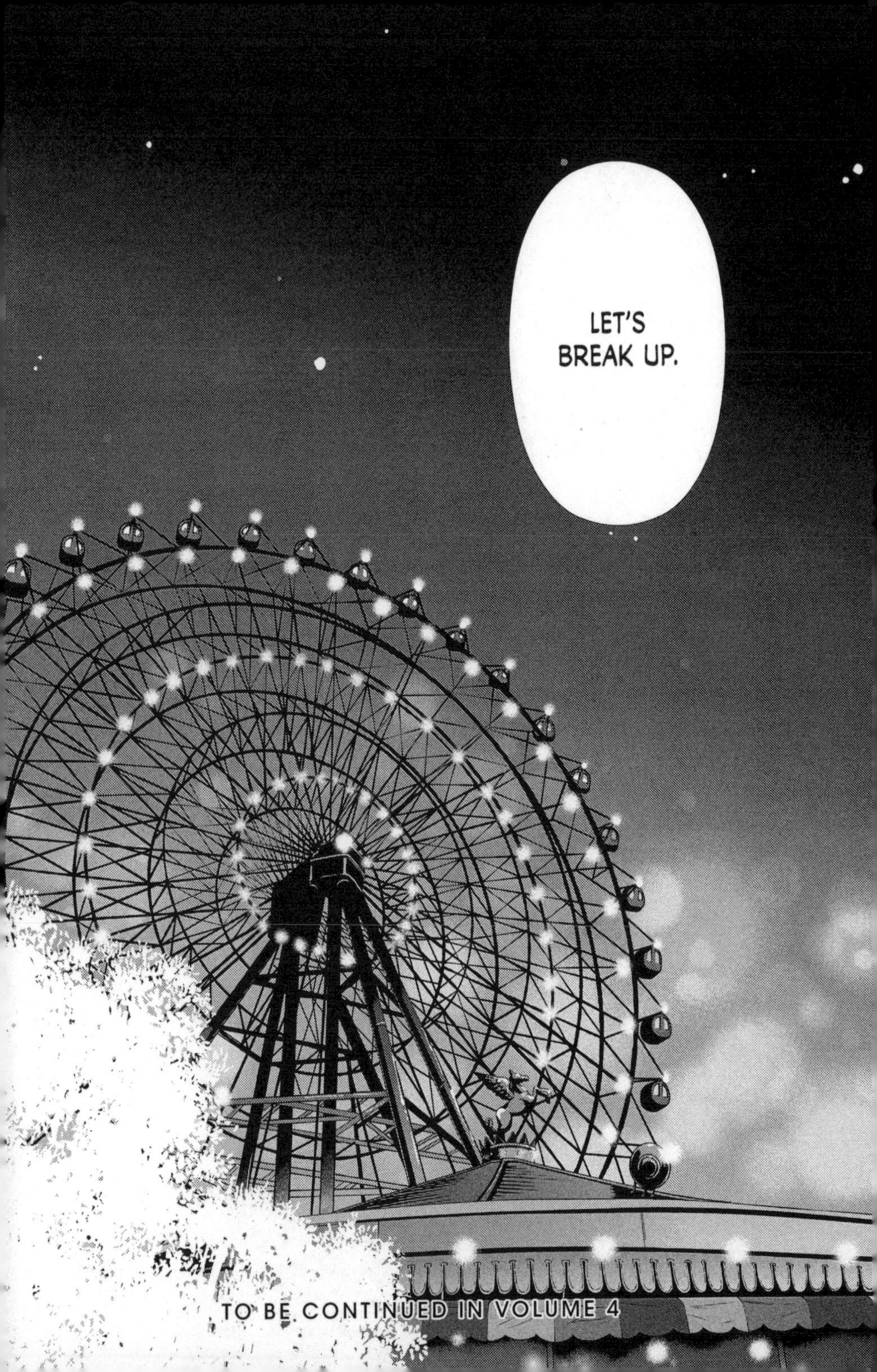
LET'S BREAK UP.
TO BE CONTINUED IN VOLUME 4

Thank you for reading *Perfect World* volume 3!

All of the feedback I've gotten through Twitter, my blog, and letters has been a great encouragement. I've been taking particularly good care of the letters. They're a treasure!
I'm sorry I haven't been able to respond much.
Some people have written, "I'm not sure if you'll read this, being so busy..." but that's not the case at all! I'm reading them all because they're so special to me!
Please continue to write to me.

I feel like we've arrived at a new point in *Perfect World*'s story.
I'll work hard so that you can continue reading the story next volume.

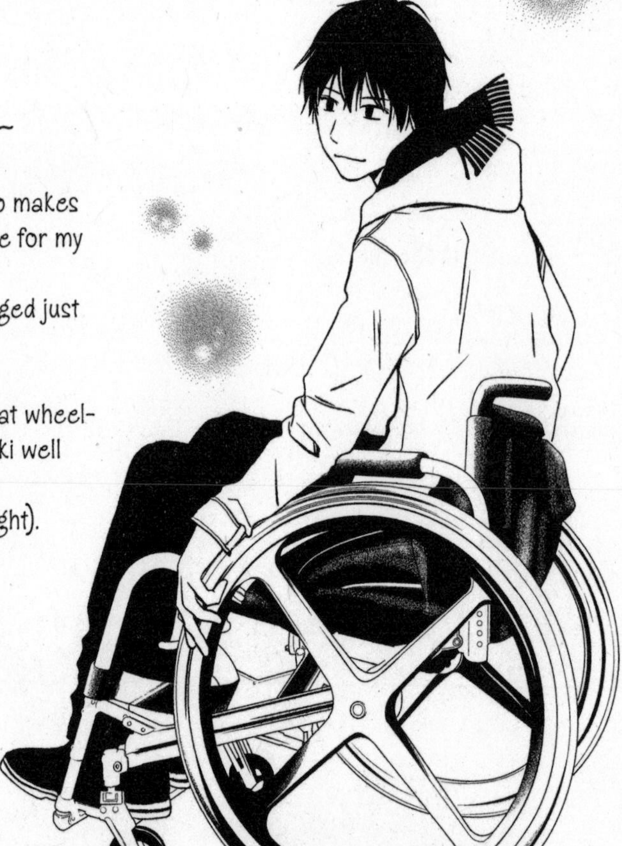

~About the wheelchair.~

I used OX Engineering, who makes wheelchairs, as a reference for my drawings.
(The design has been changed just a bit.)

They helped me decide what wheelchair model would suit Itsuki well according to his needs
(like disability level and height).
I'm thankful for their help!

A wheel with spokes would've been very cool, but unfortunately they're hard to draw, so I gave up.

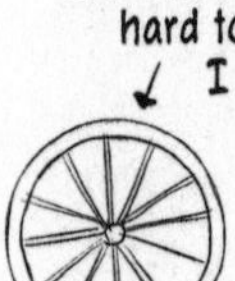

Like this.

– From the bottom of my heart, thank you to all of those who helped me. –

* Kazuo Abe-sama from Abe Kensetsu Inc.
* Ouchi-sama
* Yaguchi-sama
* Tomomi-sama
* Those at OX Kanto ViVit
* Those at Minato Rehabilitation Hospital in Chiba

* My editor, Ito-sama
* Everyone from the editorial department at *Kiss*
* The designer, Kusume-sama
* My assistants, T-sama, K-sama, and TN-sama

* Those who I met on Twitter who are in the medical/nursing field
* Everyone involved in getting this sold

My family, friends,
and also my readers.

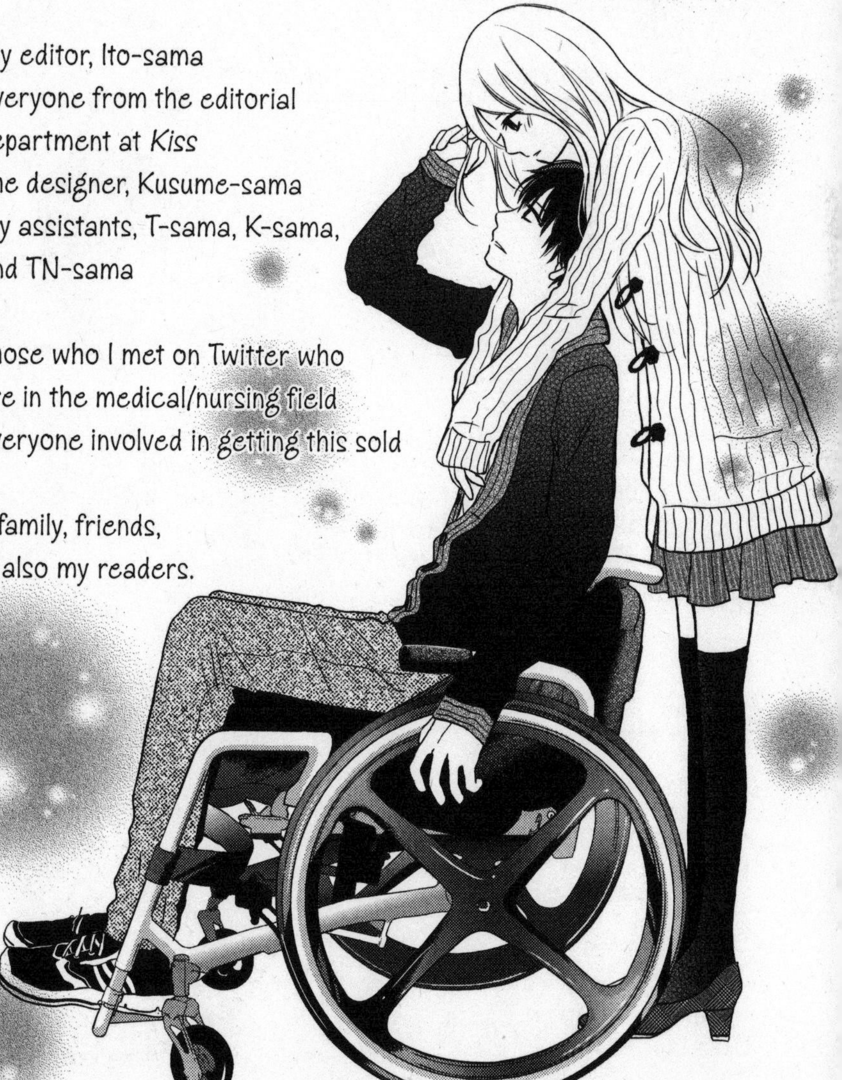

A SMART, NEW ROMANTIC COMEDY FOR FANS OF *SHORTCAKE CAKE* AND *TERRACE HOUSE!*

A romance manga starring high school girl Meeko, who learns to live on her own in a boarding house whose living room is home to the odd (but handsome) Matsunaga-san. She begins to adjust to her new life away from her parents, but Meeko soon learns that no matter how far away from home she is, she's still a young girl at heart — especially when she finds herself falling for Matsunaga-san.

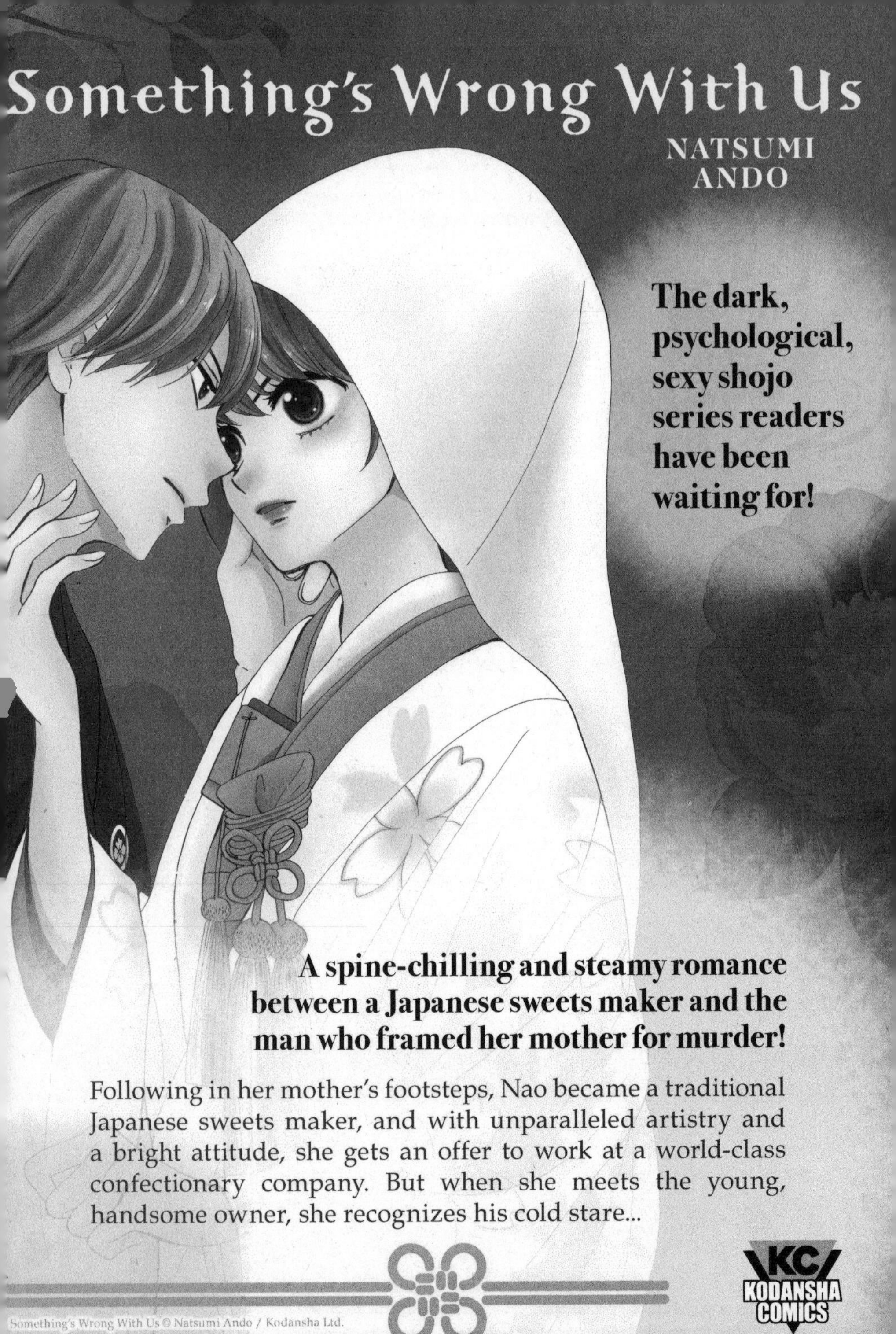

THE SWEET SCENT OF LOVE IS IN THE AIR! FOR FANS OF OFFBEAT ROMANCES LIKE *WOTAKOI*

Sweat and Soap © Kintetsu Yamada / Kodansha Ltd.

In an office romance, there's a fine line between sexy and awkward... and that line is where Asako — a woman who sweats copiously — meets Koutarou — a perfume developer who can't get enough of Asako's, er, scent. Don't miss a romcom manga like no other!

One of CLAMP's biggest hits returns in this definitive, premium, hardcover 20th anniversary collector's edition!

CLAMP

Chobits 1

20TH ANNIVERSARY EDITION

"A wonderfully entertaining story that would be a great installment in anybody's manga collection."
— Anime News Network

"CLAMP is an all-female manga-creating team whose feminine touch shows in this entertaining, sci-fi soap opera."
— Publishers Weekly

Poor college student Hideki is down on his luck. All he wants is a good job, a girlfriend, and his very own "persocom"—the latest and greatest in humanoid computer technology. Hideki's luck changes one night when he finds Chi—a persocom thrown out in a pile of trash. But Hideki soon discovers that there's much more to his cute new persocom than meets the eye.

KC
KODANSHA COMICS

THE MAGICAL GIRL CLASSIC THAT BROUGHT A GENERATION OF READERS TO MANGA, NOW BACK IN A DEFINITIVE, HARDCOVER COLLECTOR'S EDITION!

CARDCAPTOR SAKURA
COLLECTOR'S EDITION
C L A M P

Ten-year-old Sakura Kinomoto lives a pretty normal life with her older brother, Tōya, and widowed father, Fujitaka—until the day she discovers a strange book in her father's library, and her life takes a magical turn...

- A deluxe large-format hardcover edition of CLAMP's shojo manga classic
- All-new foil-stamped cover art on each volume
- Comes with exclusive collectible art card

KC
KODANSHA COMICS

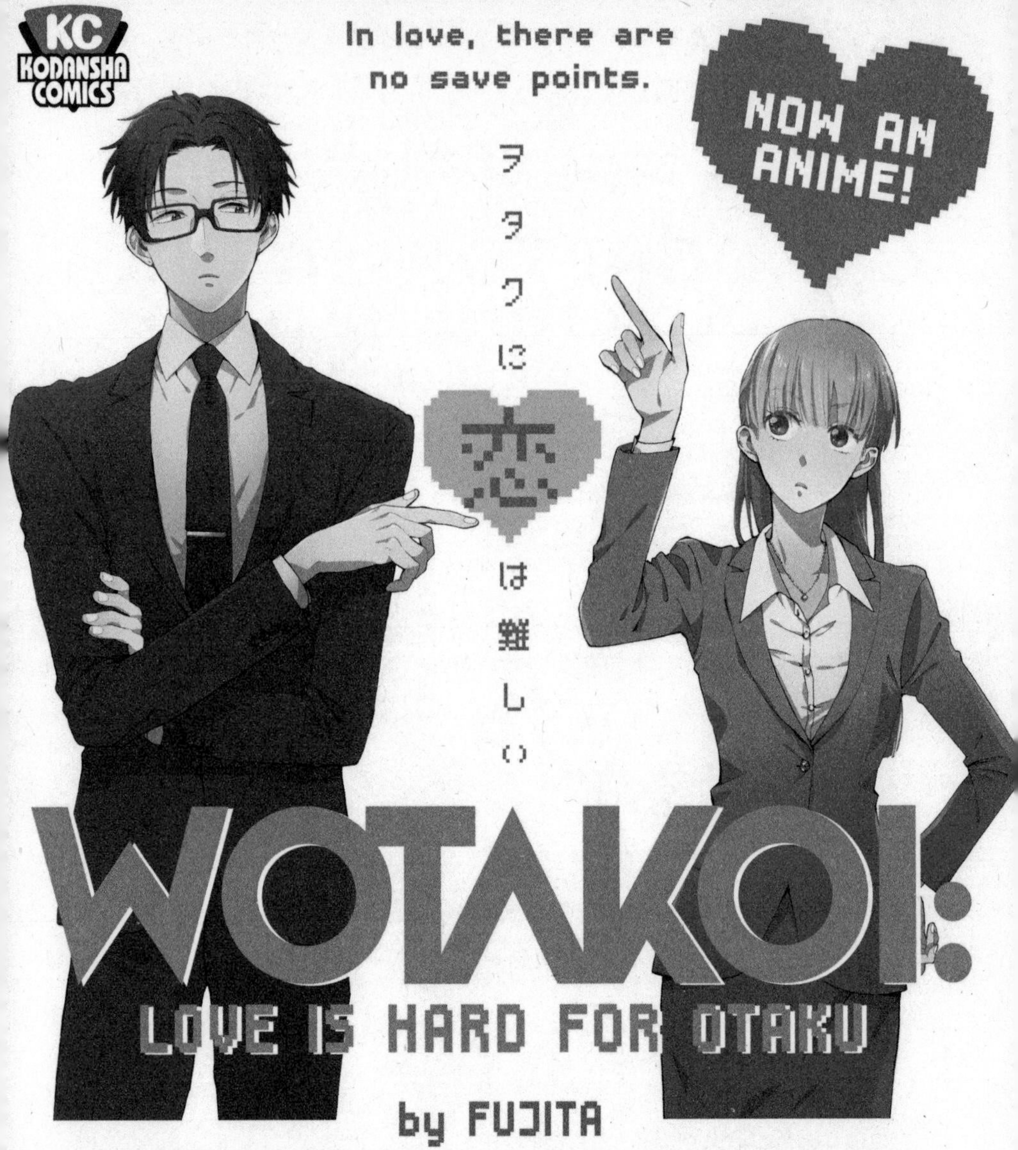

KC
KODANSHA COMICS
In love, there are no save points.
NOW AN ANIME!
ヲタクに恋は難しい
WOTAKOI:
LOVE IS HARD FOR OTAKU
by FUJITA

Narumi has had it rough: Every boyfriend she's had dumped her once they found out she was an otaku, so she's gone to great lengths to hide it. At her new job, she bumps into Hirotaka, her childhood friend and fellow otaku. When Hirotaka almost gets her secret outed at work, she comes up with a plan to keep him quiet. But he comes up with a counter-proposal: Why doesn't she just date him instead?

A Kodansha Comics Trade Paperback Original
Perfect World 3 copyright © 2016 Rie Aruga
English translation copyright © 2020 Rie Aruga

All rights reserved.

Published in the United States by Kodansha Comics, an imprint of Kodansha USA Publishing, LLC, New York.

Publication rights for this English edition arranged through Kodansha Ltd., Tokyo.

First published in Japan in 2016 by Kodansha Ltd., Tokyo as *Perfect World*, volume 3.

ISBN 978-1-63236-995-6

Original cover design by Tomohiro Kusume and Maiko Mori (arcoinc)

Printed in the United States of America.

www.kodanshacomics.com

9 8 7 6 5 4 3 2 1
Translation: Rachel Murakawa
Lettering: Thea Willis
Additional lettering: Sara Linsley
Editing: Jesika Brooks and Tiff Ferentini
Kodansha Comics edition cover design by Phil Balsman

Publisher: Kiichiro Sugawara

Director of publishing services: Ben Applegate
Associate director of operations: Stephen Pakula
Publishing services managing editor: Noelle Webster
Assistant production manager: Emi Lotto, Angela Zurlo